THE CURBCHEK COLLECTION

A TRILOGY OF TRUE CRIME

ZACH FORTIER

steeleshark press

Cover design, interior book design, and eBook design
by Blue Harvest Creative
www.blueharvestcreative.com

THE CURBCHECK COLLECTION: A TRILOGY OF TRUE CRIME

Copyright © 2014 Zach Fortier

All rights reserved. Except as permitted under the U.S. Copyright Act of 1976, no part of this publication may be reproduced, distributed, or transmitted in any form or by any means, or stored in a database or retrieval system, without prior written permission of the publisher.

Published by
SteeleShark Press

ISBN-13: 978-0615966830
ISBN-10: 0-615-96683-7

Visit the author at:
Website: *www.zachfortier.com*
Blog: *www.authorzachfortier.blogspot.com*
Facebook: *www.facebook.com/authorzach.fortier*
Twitter: *www.twitter.com/zachfortier1*
Goodreads: *www.goodreads.com/author/show/5164780.Zach_Fortier*

PRAISE FOR
CurbChek

"If you are reading this as a Police Officer, you will find your head nodding along in agreement with the thoughts and place yourself in each situation, as you have been there yourself."
• *Justin, Website Administrator of www.officerresource.com & Police Officer* •

"A gritty, fascinating read, and I recommend it to anyone."
• *www.katesreads.com* •

"Exciting, scary, sad, and sometimes darn right funny."
• *www.allbooksreviewint.com* •

"Truly loved this book very much. Well done!"
• *Janine (goodreads.com)* •

"At times laughing out loud, other times holding back my tears."
• *Lisa Meiners (goodreads.com)* •

"This book is amazing; I mean really amazing."
• *Aimeekay (goodreads.com)* •

"*CurbChek* is a realistic, no bullshit portrayal. A fast and entertaining read; not for the faint of heart."
• *National Police Wives Association/facebook* •

"The writing is gritty, realistic, and readable. A well-written book with brutal scenes."
• *www.bookstackreviews.com* •

PRAISE FOR
STREET CREDS

"...a GREAT read for anybody who wants to get a taste of real police work! Every rookie cop should read thisbook...oh hell, everyone should read this book!"
• *Chad Ledford, Police Officer* •

"A roller coaster ride. This book will grab you from the first paragraph and you won't want to put it down until your done."
• *Jennifer Zuna, www.momzunas.blogspot.com* •

"I highly recommend *Street Creds* for an in-depth look at how gangs operate and the law officers deal with them. It's a gritty world."
• *Esmoewl12, www.readerjots.wordpress.com* •

"Awesome read! Zach does a great job at sharing with readers the true moments of law enforcement with the good and the bad."
• *Day, Police Officer*
Support K-9 page/Facebook.com Administrator •

"Once I started reading *Street Creds* I couldn't stop. The book is brutally honest and gives the average person a peek into the world of gang culture."
• *Linda, Administrator National police wives association page/facebook.com* •

"Kudos to Mr. Fortier who opens up without qualms and shows the world the good, the bad, the funny, and the ugly of police work."
• *Shannon Gambino, www.hodgepodgegalore.wordpress.com* •

"Incredible. I think what the author went through was amazing. Thank you Zach, for an intro into the life of a gang police officer I would absolutely love to read anything else you write!"
• *Stephani, www.stephs-books-reviews.blogspot.com* •

PRAISE FOR
CURBCHEK
RELOAD

"If you like no nonsense, cut to the chase monologs, this is for you. I couldn't help but flash back to the old 1960s TV show as I read this book. Anyone who enjoys their police stories to be hard hitting and factual will really enjoy this."
• *Jeannie Walker—Award Winning Author of "Fighting the Devil"* •

"Following the already dark and gritty 2011 release of *CurbChek*, *CurbChek Reload* ramps everything up a level, the cops, the criminals, the anger and frustration…everything that made the first book interesting, albeit disturbing and heartbreaking, is back but with a vengeance!"
• *Nylon Admiral* •

"This is a really good book, which tells how things are out there at night in the ghettos of America, where hope has left the building. I say buy this book. It is a page turner—no kidding. This guy can write."
• *Rip Kitty* •

"You haven't seen anything until you have read *CurbChek Reload*. Fortier takes you on a ride with him at many of his most difficult, violent, heart wrenching, and disturbing calls. Do I want to go on a ride-along? Not a chance…and especially not with Zach. This was a great read!"
• *J. Pearson* •

"These are gritty, honest, no-holds-barred glimpses into the life of a street cop. Told in the language we (cops and ex cops) use—no BS, no sugar coating, no avoiding the hard topics, and always with a dose of very dark humor for the most inappropriate things. Highly recommended!"
• *Holly Cochran* •

ALSO BY ZACH FORTIER

CurbChek

Street Creds

CurbChek Reload

Hero to Zero

Landed on Black
Available 2014

THE COLLECTION

11
CurbChek

173
Street Creds

365
CurbChek Reload

BOOK ONE
CURBCHEK

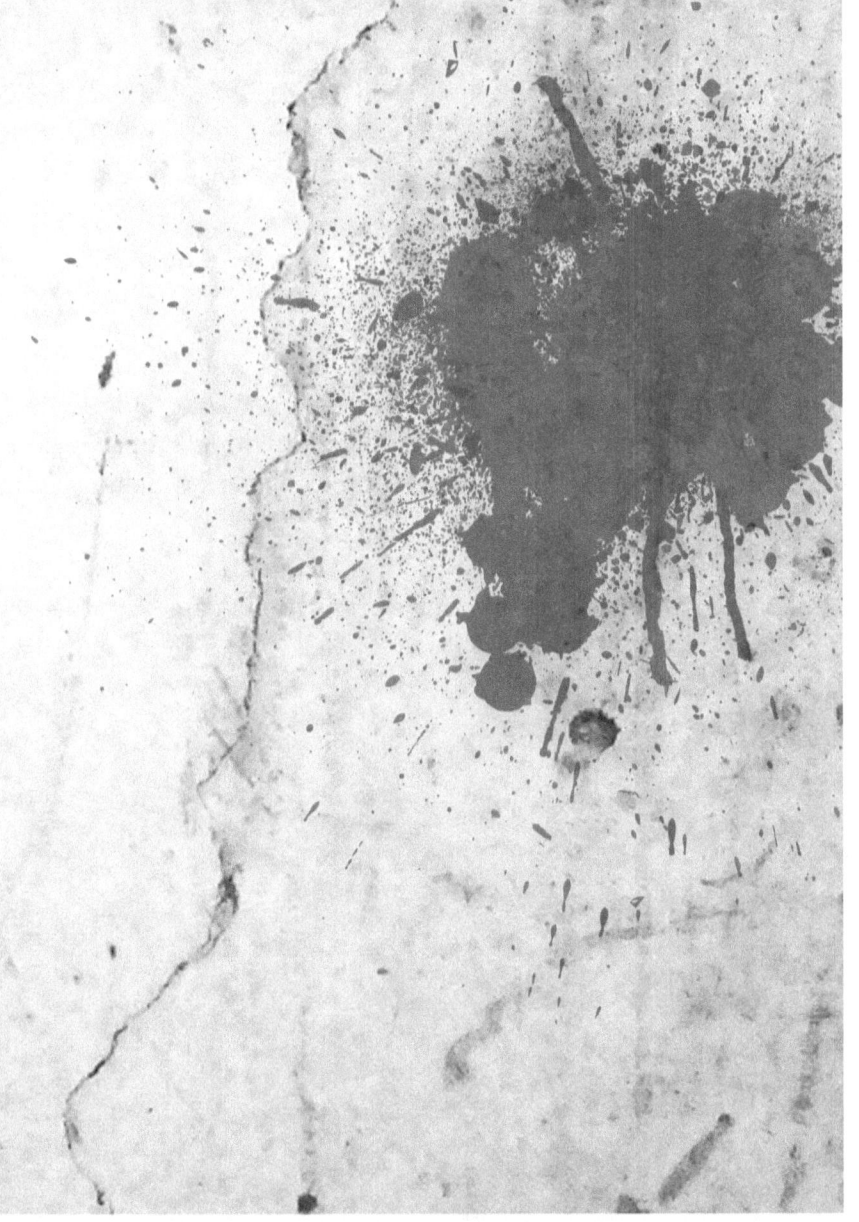

CurbChek

"Placing an unconscious or immobile individual's head against a curb with their mouth open, then stomping on or kicking them in the head."

"When a driver inadvertently hits or runs into a curb."

ONE
IS THERE A PROBLEM OFFICER?

THE POPULATION IS UP TO three-quarter million, but it's still a place where it's fairly easy to spot something out of place.

I was the south car that night, having returned to my old hometown—where I never intended to return.

I wonder how the taxpayers might feel if they knew that only three cars patrolled the entire unincorporated area of the county, all that space between the city and towns, the wide open patches between the islands of civilization. That's three cars and a sergeant, and maybe a K-9 unit—if we're lucky.

I was conducting extra patrols that homeowners or businesses had requested.

Most guys pencil-whipped this shit, but I was a little more obsessive about it. Seemed like we should check them; if there ever were a problem, I would've regretted not checking.

I checked this shopping unit complex every day I worked the south side. It was a photo supply business near the mouth of the canyon, and it was reporting break-ins. Nothing had ever been there before—but then one night I found a truck parked back behind the complex.

It was hidden, so the driver had to be trying to shield it from anyone's view on the street.

Tucked back in behind the building and in some trees, it gave me the creeps.

I backed out and re-approached, checking the area for snipers; there were none, of course. (I'd just come from a military background, and that was still fresh in my mind.)

I ran the license plates and checked them against the VIN; it all matched. I ran the car through NCIC, and it wasn't stolen. I checked the entire complex, and none of the businesses had been broken into.

This was weird shit.

The vehicle was parked that way for a reason; I just couldn't figure out why.

I had dispatch print the plate and cross-reference the registered owner with warrants, NCIC, and driver's license; nothing came up. I asked them to print it all out. I kept records of my own at the time to learn from, go back over, and see what I'd missed.

This was the part of police work that I'd always love: the small window of independence.

The military was good for training in tactics, firearms, marksmanship, and the extreme fitness that I still maintain today; however, there was no room for independent thinking or questioning anything. You did what you were told—always. You were never in charge; instead, you always waited for some rear echelon motherfucker—we called them REMFs'—to make a decision.

Move before you were told and you paid dearly.

Rank structure was severely ingrained in me.

Anyone who outranked you was in charge—which was just the opposite of real police work; on the street, the call was yours and yours alone.

At first, that was hard for me to get used to. A sergeant would show up, and the military training would kick in and I'd subordinate immediately.

Once I realized I could take the call and run with it, that it wasn't a test to see if I were insubordinate—I was all over it. I loved taking the call.

I respected no one's position in life based on his or her job or money, and I wasn't intimidated by much, so I'd listen to both sides and make my decisions.

Anyway, that night I was puzzled. What in the hell was going on?

I went to dispatch to pick up the printouts, and as I was leaving one of the dispatchers said she just got a call from a lady who wanted a friend of hers checked on.

She said the woman claimed that her friend's ex-husband had been calling her from Wyoming and making threats. The ex was a paranoid schizophrenic, and he sounded like he was off his meds. Her friend had called, and when she answered the phone it was dead. When she called back, there was no answer.

The last name matched the owner of the truck I'd just checked on—and the truck was from Wyoming.

I felt like an ass.

There I was, sitting there fumbling around with this truck; meanwhile, this guy was out there.

I hauled ass down to this missing woman's mobile home, which was near the mouth of the canyon where I'd come upon the parked truck that was so carefully hidden.

The door of the mobile home had been kicked in, so I called for backup and went in, clearing room-by-room, my gun out, searching.

I checked the entire trailer—which smelled like a damn litter box—and in the only bedroom I found an unmade bed covered in blood.

There was no one in the house.

I called for techs to process the scene and put out an attempt-to-locate on the woman's car; it was gone—and she with it.

I was pissed off.

I drove around the immediate area, looking for her car; then, call it intuition or whatever, I decided to park back up on a hill and blacked out (turned out my headlights).

I just sat, waiting.

I know this sounds weird, but I knew something was going to happen. Call it luck or gut instinct—whatever you want to call it to feel comfortable—but I knew I had to park and wait...something was coming.

Fifteen minutes later, her car came down the dugway.

I had one light out on my patrol car—which, as it turns out, was excellent strategy and perhaps should be taught at the academy.

I called in the car and began to follow until backup arrived. When backup showed up, I pulled the car over.

We lit it up big time and exited fast with two spotlights, both high beams, and take down lights pointed at the car.

I could see that there were two people, a male driving and a female passenger in the front seat—covered in blood.

She kept looking back, scared and bleeding; she looked like hell, but she was alive.

I walked to the driver, my gun out and pointed right at his head.

He said to me, "Is there a problem, officer?"

No shit, fuckhead. The woman bleeding next to you is not normal.

Thinking that this fucker was going to blow her brains out before I got there and get her away from him, I was wound-up, nervous, and edgy.

I told him, "Look at the barrel of my gun."

He did.

I said, "If you take your eyes off of it, move even a little bit, I will blow your fucking brains out. Do you understand?"

He said, "Yes, sir—but what's the problem?"

Seriously, he actually said it again.

Phil, my backup, had walked up to the other side of the car.

He asked, "Have you got him?"

I said, "Ya."

He said, "I'm gonna get her out of there. Be careful; shoot him if he moves."

We got her out, and I arrested the guy.

I was scared shitless, afraid I'd make a mistake and he'd get over on me and kill her before we could get her out.

I had been on the department about a year then, and I had very little experience with this kind of thing.

She said he'd told her that he was taking her out to kill her. He'd driven past the mobile home while we were processing the scene and was afraid because we were on to him so fast. When I dropped down the hill behind him with one light out, he relaxed.

She said she remembered his comment: "Cops never have a headlight out."

So he kept driving, calmly looking for a place to pull over somewhere near his truck and kill her, then walk back to his truck.

He'd broken into her home, pistol-whipped her, and dragged her by her hair out to her car to kill her.

I later found out that she was a teacher at one of the elementary schools nearby. She also knew my mother-in-law at the time… weird to see how she lived, and then taught kids? It blew my mind there was cat shit and garbage everywhere inside the trailer, and the filth was incredible.

This was my first real hard ass case; not the usual bullshit domestics, not running radar—but what I thought was real police work.

It was also what I saw as my first failure.

I felt that way because I was new and stupid, she'd nearly been killed.

I was very idealistic then, feeling I could make a difference—which, as it turns out, is a very stupid idea.

Anyway, after all that, a judge gave him probation because he'd gone off his meds and was mentally ill.

His breaking into her home, beating her up, and then taking her out to kill her in his state of mind supposedly didn't establish any intent to kill.

He was sent back to Wyoming and asked not to return. The judge made him promise to stay on his meds, and he was free to go. I was amazed that he wasn't forced into a grueling "pinky swear" marathon.

The next day at work, I found out that in police work if you do something well, the reaction from co-workers can be bizarre; some people hate you, and others envy you.

The sergeants I worked for were suddenly jealous of me, threatened by me—making me feel like I was isolated.

Other cops asked the lamest, most ass-backward questions.

"What was that like, kind of a rush?"

For me to get my thrills, I'd prefer that a woman isn't getting her head smashed in and living or dying based on my gut feelings.

I was at a loss; I had no idea what to think.

Later, when I went to the city force, I found out that prosecutors and the city cops all felt that the sheriff's office was a joke.

I could relate with that; I really didn't fit in there.

I felt like I needed to develop my skills, and if you worked at the county, the frequency of contact with real hardcore criminals was infrequent.

So, after a while I started to look seriously at the city police force; I felt it would be a better fit, giving me what I felt I was missing—but I was wrong...

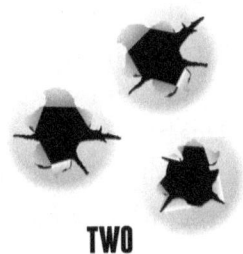

TWO
INSIDE AND OUTSIDE REALITY

TWO WEEKS AFTER THE MARINE Barracks bombing in Lebanon in 1983, I was sent to Saudi Arabia as part of the military response deployed to stabilize the region.

You'd think that military training would translate into police work, just as I mistakenly thought when I found myself returning to my hometown years later; my best laid plans, though, quickly turned to shit.

Even back then, I was a cop, military police.

I knew that with my personality and various triggers, it was better for everyone concerned that I be something of an authority figure rather than be subject to authority figures without recourse.

In 1983, we waited in bunkers for suicide bombers from Iran to try to take out the AWACS stationed in Riyadh.

It was the easiest duty I ever had in the military; basically, I was there to keep the AWACS safe while the war was in session.

I'd dropped into a war zone from our Strategic Air Command (SAC) post. Coming from a base with nuclear capacity aircraft, I found Saudi a welcome relief.

We were given intelligence that said that small planes loaded with explosives flying under the radar were coming from Iran and to be prepared.

This was eighteen years before the 9/11 attacks on the World Trade Center and the Pentagon in 2001.

As soon as I got off the plane, the cops were separated from the rest of the military personnel. This was becoming a pattern: cops set apart from the rest of the population.

The hotel I was housed in was trenched, and cement barriers were in place all around it. There were machine gunners on the roof, but it was actually a break from SAC.

I slept like a baby, sat in bunkers all day in the heat, and drank a ton of water.

I watched the local vehicle traffic for any false moves, as well as constantly checking the skies for the prophesied Jihadist's small planes trying to kamikaze the AWACS; they never came.

I became friends with the Arab guards and learned some Arabic, broke bread, and ate lamb and rice.

I got along better with them than with some of the MPs who called them "sand niggers" and told me I was shit for befriending them. Fuck that!

I learned that they hated guys like Saddam and loved Jimmy Carter. They also thought that we Americans were arrogant pieces of shit.

After a while there, I couldn't help noticing some validity to their argument.

I agreed that you could pick out the Americans in a crowd, all loud, obnoxious, and foulmouthed; it was usually groups of kids one to three years out of high school, showing the world what America was all about.

Needless to say, there were times when I was embarrassed by the way my own people acted.

I had only one real brush with hostility while I was there.

One day, I went through the wrong gate and had an Arab guard hold a gun to my head.

He asked me if I was Islamic.

I said no.

He said I would die if I didn't swear to follow Allah.

I wasn't about to show any fear; I was—as I am now—stubborn (stupidly stubborn), so I refused and eventually told him to either get on with it and blow my brains out or let me through.

I warned him, though, that if he did shoot me he'd better start praying to Allah—because my MP brothers would torture him before they killed him.

We stared hard at each other, and he eventually decided to let me through.

Being stubborn—and a complete dumb ass—I couldn't let it end there, so I went back to my bunker and grabbed two cold drinks.

Then I drove back as fast as possible.

I was reckless—but obviously U.S. military with subdued decals on the vehicle.

I skidded to a halt, got out with M-16 in hand, and walked towards him with a purpose.

I stared at him hard for a second, then offered him one of the drinks as I cracked a smile.

He was shaking and scared, but he accepted my hospitality; he couldn't be sure I wasn't crazy.

Hardcore psychological warfare!

He'd been "Sacumsized!" a term we often used to describe the painful process of learning to survive in the command.

I was young and stupid, but he never messed with me again.

After that, I made a point out of going through his gate regularly; we even became friendly and on a first-name basis.

After about three months there, coming back to America was tough; having to go back to the grind of training, training, training—and then, just for a change, more training.

In the military, they try to break you with training.

We trained nonstop for a Russian nuclear attack, performing constant drills and training.

The planes would mock launch and roll down the runway, then stop and idle for a while, waiting for orders either to launch or return; eventually, they'd get their orders and turn around.

We trained for various scenarios, usually suicide attacks. We had a timed response to every possible penetration called a "15 in 5": we had to have a minimum of fifteen troops deployed in a minimum five minutes, ready and able to return fire at anything and everything.

Guarding the nukes, 15 in 5s, exercise after exercise, low-crawling in the dirt and then inspection the next day in the same boots, spit and polished—and they'd better be perfect.

After a few years, I worked my way into a Command and Control Center and watched one of these exercises from an observation tower.

One day while I was watching, it hit me: we were a suicide squad as well; constant drills lowered our ability to think about it, and our response was an immediate conditioned response, Pavlov dog style.

We trained to scan fields and buildings and watch traffic flows for anything out of the ordinary.

Seeing suspicious activity in nothing at all, paranoia became the norm, and having no real world threat or anything to gauge our imaginations against made us extremely neurotic.

Several guys had nervous breakdowns, and some would end up drinking heavily, fighting, and doing all kinds of stupid shit.

Looking back on it now, it was scary how an apparently normal guy could fall apart in a few short months under the stress. Some attempted suicide, and a few even succeeded. A lot went AWOL, showing up later in the correctional facility on base and doing hard labor.

We were the grunts of the Air Force; trained in army tactics, honed, and expected to be spit-polished, yet able to get down and dirty at the drop of a hat.

Some of us got good at it.

I buried myself in the combat competitions hosted by the SAC command. Doing this probably saved my bent head for a time.

Every SAC base sent a team to compete, and I was selected for our base's team and trained in combat tactics.

We practiced fighting teams of MPs in the field, studying and working out everyday.

The competition was away from the meat grinder of the nukes and the 15 in 5s; it was hard work, but a welcome break from the Nukes.

We won the Air Force obstacle course tournament as a team, and I set a course record my first year.

Suddenly, I was a celebrity—and I quickly learned that it wasn't a good thing and that people hated me for winning.

I ate dinner with generals, colonels, and the wing commander loved me and knew me by my first name. My uncle was a major and a B-52 pilot. The wing commander hated him, which made my uncle even more hostile toward me at my already fucked up family gatherings.

The police competition team of six cops from each base competed worldwide.

We were small tactical units defending nuclear weapons, aircraft, and the air bases. We practiced firearms training and overcoming larger groups of enemy teams with fields of fire and suppressive fire techniques.

It required extreme physical fitness and expert marksmanship and was considered a very elite competition, and our success got me the Saudi deployment.

We worked tactically, moving through fields and urban areas, looking for snipers, and conducting surveillance of areas you're assigned to protect.

SWAT training, building entry, aircraft and large vehicle recovery, becoming familiar—and even comfortable—with entering into dangerous situations, thinking and reacting based on training; essentially, what you'd learned and how you prepared mattered.

It required constant preparation, and after a while you could see the results. Those who didn't prepare or take it seriously were soon to fail—and fail hard; that, too, was a lesson.

Cops always have to be training and learning new things.

Being an MP in SAC also taught us to be respectful while remaining authoritative. It wasn't an easy task to respect a captain or a major who had violated some minor nuclear safety rule; to point the M-16 at their heads made it clear to them that you were respectful of their rank—but if they fucked up you'd most definitely kill them, or at the very least kick their ass.

Prima donna bitches that they were, the pilots hated this; they were coddled by everyone else but us, the MPs.

It was the recurring theme in my life: I was different even from the rest of the people who wore the uniform.

We were tasked with enforcing and protecting the nuclear arsenal from everyone, including the pilots who flew the planes loaded with the nukes themselves.

Set apart from the world, it was a familiar place to be, and it would continue to be throughout my career.

That was our mandate, our mission: to protect the nukes from everyone and anyone who might try to diminish the mission.

Everyone was suspect; no one was above the regulations.

Being an MP lacked opportunities for real experiences—besides training and drilling—that could transfer to civilian police work.

Independent thinking wasn't encouraged, and you were never in charge. Someone higher up always had to make the key decisions, and it seemed like there was no end to higher-ups. Rank was everything; on the "outside" (our term for the civilian world), the call is yours.

When I came in to police work on the outside, my military training was seen as a negative thing.

Cop tactics weren't military tactics; it was the late 80s, and the military was seen in a less than favorable light.

Tactics were seen as foolish and pointless, but as time passed they were seen as increasingly useful.

Moving as a small unit against an opponent requires fields of fire and trust in the guy next to you and behind you; you trust that they'll do their job, and you must do yours.

It teaches you to scan your surrounding environment, constantly searching for anything hostile. Just because you checked it once doesn't mean you shouldn't check it again—and then again.

You learned to handle your weapon in the dark, reloading, unloading, fixing failures by feel, not by sight, and we learned to shoot effectively at night before the invention of night sights.

Night shooting requires you to look off-center; the optical nerve is positioned in such a way that looking straight on at night makes it hard to see, and looking off-center enables you to see using your peripheral vision. I used that a lot in the inner city at night, walking in dark alleys in the never-sleeping city.

When I landed in the civilian cop world, the current idea on lighting when you entered a room or building was to flash the room and see what you could in a brief moment; the idea being that you didn't announce and excessively illuminate yourself, thereby making easy targets of yourself and others.

This was the cop theory at the time.

The reality, though, is that once you flash the room you've announced yourself quite well, and in the process destroyed your visual purple for at least another thirty minutes.

("Purple" being the moniker for the chemical that enables you to see at night.)

My thinking was to keep the light off until you needed it.

Once you turn it on, leave it on; you have at least 50-50 odds this way, and no one has the advantage—instead of being at a disadvantage, blind in the dark while your opponent can turn on his light to disorient you.

I was told, though, that this was a very stupid idea, and I was even ridiculed by my supervisors for arguing it.

I was being reckless and foolish with light according to the FBI, which is the cop source of validation in tactics and procedure.

Later—much later—the FBI came out and changed its opinion: keep the lights on.

I was no longer a reckless idiot, and the new theory was followed as mindlessly as the old one.

THREE
HOMELESS, NOT HARMLESS

THE DARKER SIDE OF THE population, what lurks beneath, always fascinated me; like something reptilian and hungry that roils around in all of us, probing for openings and looking for a way out.

This was the layer under the day-to-day people (we called them "Daywalkers") who go to work, then go home and get to bed early enough to wake up in time to go to work again.

I'd begun stopping transients in the rail yards that bisected the county. With plenty of "No Trespassing" signs, I had immediate probable cause. I would FI (field interview) and check them for warrants. If they had none, they went on their way…have a nice day.

If they had warrants, I arrested them and booked them into jail.

I found an amazing number of people on the run. It could be some really scary shit. Most of them have some serious mental illness; some are just trying to stay away from society.

Almost all of them, though, are armed—and some of them, I learned the hard way, are truly damn dangerous.

Transients hide troll-like under bridges and in every other place imaginable, pretty much anywhere there's heat or shelter or near the free medical or food services offered in every city.

They also campout, and there's a pecking order—with those who panhandle outside of liquor stores at the top.

Some put together fairly serious shelters, with even the occasional gas generator or corrugated metal sheets they scrounged for roofing. Some even take legit jobs at times.

I developed a series of locations that I'd hit and check for transients and their temporary camps. They really liked this old abandoned boxcar at the west end of the rail yards. It was parked near one of the free food kitchens, and the door opened away from the constant winds.

The railway workers never liked to mess with transients; they were too afraid of them. One of the bolder workers who confronted a transient who had crawled into an engine cabin had been stabbed.

One day I was looking in on that boxcar, and there were several guys inside of it, six or seven grown men. I checked them all and got to the last guy named Dan Campbell.

He was a big guy, about 6-foot-5, maybe 270 pounds—of which I am neither; he had me by at least 6 inches and 100 pounds.

He was talking shit to me, but he showed me his ID.

I ran him, and he was clean, no warrants.

I saw, though, that he had all these other IDs under different names and dates of birth, so I confronted him about it and asked him why he had so many—even though I already knew they used them to get food stamps in different states. They liked to trade the food stamps for cash, getting about fifty cents on the dollar, with which they could then buy booze.

Dan said just that, that he went from state to state and made more on food stamps than I made as "a Barney Fife here in this shit hole town."

I said, "Not anymore. Which one are you, really?"

He growled, "I'm all of them, but here I go by 'Dan Campbell.'"

"Well, Dan Campbell, here's your ID," I said. "I'm keeping the rest since they're all illegal IDs."

Pissed off now, he said, "You will give them back, or I'll kill you right here."

The fight was on.

He came at me, and I drew my nightstick and hit him in the chest, driving the point of the stick into him as hard I could; it didn't even slow him down.

I took two "home run" swings at his right knee, a knockout blow baton instructors promised would end any attack because the bad guy's knee would collapse; Dan's knee did *not*.

I threw the nightstick as far as I could so he couldn't use it against me, then I started to fight him hand-to-hand.

The guys he was with were cheering and rooting for him, yelling at him to kill me and talking shit to me about how they were going to take my gun and badge after he did.

I somehow managed to call for backup as we were wrestling, but no one knew how to get to where I was.

While we battled, police cars rolled back and forth and lights and sirens were going off.

There were city and county cars and lots of lights and noise—but not a lot of brains; no one could seem to find us.

After I pushed him against my car, I finally got one handcuff on his left wrist. I then kept him against the car, kidney punching him and trying to get his left arm back behind him.

When the sirens started getting closer, his supporters ran back to the boxcar as a group.

I thought they were getting the hell out of there, hoping not to get caught...I was wrong.

They went back to Dan's pack and got out a .22 caliber handgun that he kept there and loaded it. Then they looked out.

I was slowly wearing Campbell down; he was getting tired.

Suddenly, though, he reached back with his right hand and grabbed my holstered gun. I tried to break his grip but couldn't; he had it solid.

Two weeks before, I'd purchased a Safariland Level 2 retention holster from one of my few friends at the sheriff's office. He was a dealer in that kind of equipment, and I felt it would be a wise investment with all the interviews I was doing in the rail yards. This turned out to be a really good idea.

Campbell was aware that he had a hold of my gun and that I couldn't break his grip. He was too damn strong and big, so my only remaining advantage was endurance.

He pulled hard, trying to get my gun out of the holster and lifting me off the ground in the process, leaving both my feet dangling like a little kid. Fortunately, though, the holster held. Then, I got a burst of adrenaline, broke free, and started punching his kidneys as fast as I could, using both hands as I let his cuffed hand go. It was a gamble, but it worked.

He was really hurt at that point, so I pulled him to the ground by the hair and finally cuffed him.

Meanwhile, the group had started to depart the boxcar with the loaded gun and walked toward us, so I knelt on Dan's back, drew my gun, and faced his friends as they started towards me; they all stopped.

I heard one say, "Holy shit, he got the best of Dan!"

I started talking shit back to them.

"So which one of you transient fucks was gonna take my badge?"

They threw something in the boxcar, then ran off in different directions.

I was breathing hard, so I tried to rest up.

I radioed the patrol cars still driving around with lights and sirens going and directed them to the boxcar. I then arrested Campbell and recovered his gun—which was what his friends had thrown back into the boxcar—then booked him into jail.

Sometime during this period, I started to figure out that it wasn't "us against them" as I'd been led to believe.

When you're in the academy and new on the street, you're taught either directly or indirectly that it's us (cops) versus them (everyone who isn't a cop).

Campbell would be the first of many experiences that led me to realize that that mindset was wrong.

An hour after I booked his giant ass into jail, I was called back to do a medical transport. Guess who?

Campbell was complaining of chest pain from where I drove the stick into his chest, and his knee had swollen up huge.

He was blind drunk when we went toes and had felt nothing—but now I had to take this bruised shit bag to the hospital to be treated?

I was annoyed, but I had to do it; I was the south car, and that was one of my responsibilities.

On the way, he tried to apologize to me, saying he'd been drinking whiskey all night and that it made him crazy. He said that he meant no harm. His apology, taking him to the hospital, and dealing with the damage I'd inflicted during our battle made him seem human to me, and not just an enemy.

Having to see that he was beat to hell really hurt me, and sorrow truly struck me.

Of course, I never acknowledged that to him—or anyone else—but it bothered me that I believed him. I realized that we're all in this together.

People make huge mistakes in their lives. They have poor coping skills, act on impulse, and later regret what they've done. They get waking-up-on-the-lawn drunk and do things they'd normally never even consider. Their judgment goes out the window—and their lives with it.

Basically, the reality is as hard to handle as it is to accept: given the right set of circumstances, anyone is capable of anything.

So, from that point on, this incident with the homicidally-drunk and later apologetically-sober hulking rail rider changed how I talked to people, as well as how I treated them.

He was truly sorry—but that didn't change the fact he wanted me dead and had seriously tried to kill me.

He was later convicted and did a few months in jail. I never saw him again.

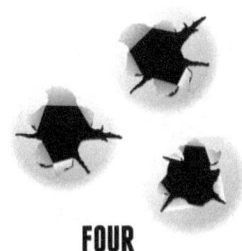

FOUR
HUFFING TO DEATH

ONE DAY, I WAS DISPATCHED to a report by frantic parents and neighbors for a kid who had passed out in a garage on the north side. They had no idea what was wrong. He started screaming horribly after he regained consciousness.

He was only about ten or eleven years old and was told by a friend that sniffing starter fluid would make him really high.

He'd skipped school, and after his parents left for work he'd gone back into the garage and started to huff starter fluid.

Apparently, he'd done this enough times before that he needed to increase the amount in order to get the same effects.

This time he'd passed out, falling on the can—and landing on it in such a way that it continued to spray onto his face until it had emptied.

He awoke a while later and was immediately in considerable pain, at first uncomfortable but it quickly became unbearable.

He began to scream, and the neighbors heard him and called us.

I'd arrived before medical and backup, but none of us were able to help; no one had ever heard of something like this before.

When we arrived, his face had begun to swell; the starter fluid had caused a cold burn, damaging his facial tissue by freezing it, and as the flesh warmed up it began to swell.

He continued to scream loudly, but there wasn't much we could do except to try to calm a tortured and terrified little boy.

Emergency medical arrived and immediately called for a "life flight" helicopter to take him to a hospital burn unit that might have some experience with what we were watching.

His face continued to swell to the point where his eyelids squeezed shut, and his tongue and lips also swelled until they were rock hard. It got so bad, one eye orbit popped the gel inside—and the eyeball drained down his face. He just continued screaming in agony.

The helicopter landed, and the paramedics immediately loaded him up and flew off. He never made it to the hospital; he died en route, his lungs filling with fluid—which caused him to drown.

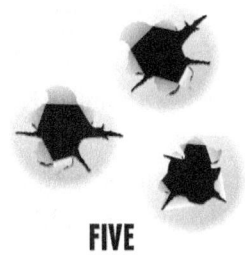

FIVE
MOVE ALONG, CITIZEN

ANOTHER NIGHT WHILE PATROLLING, I came across a vehicle parked in the canyon.

I'd been checking the area thoroughly since residents had been calling in about a transient who'd made his way from the rail yards to the canyon and was living in the woods above their houses.

I stopped and got out to check on the small pickup truck. Maybe it was some drunk or possibly someone kicked out of his house by his wife, left with no choice but to sleep in the truck; instead, I found a guy who had on a satin blouse, bra, mini-skirt, and high heels.

As I approached, I saw that he wore makeup, had on earrings, and had pulled up the mini-skirt and pulled down his panties and pantyhose—and was masturbating to several magazines featuring naked men that were spread out around the inside of the truck.

I asked him, "What do you think you're doing?"

He jumped.

He hadn't heard me walk up; he was so engrossed, he had no idea I was there.

"Nothing," he said as he pulled up his underwear and readjusted his skirt.

I asked him for his license and registration, then checked him for warrants; he had none. His record may have been clean, but I still had questions.

I went back and talked to him, explaining that he had no warrants but that he wasn't free to go until we discussed what the hell he was doing in his truck alone in the dark, dressed up like a woman. I had to get a sense as to whether or not he was any kind of threat to the residents nearby.

He told me that he frequently dressed up and pretended to be female, and he said that he often came up into the canyon "to get in touch with his feminine side."

He said that he was married and that his wife didn't know about this behavior—and that he'd appreciate it if she didn't find out. I said that she wouldn't.

He wasn't gay, he said, just interested in cross-dressing because he felt that there was a woman inside him that occasionally needed to escape.

I said, "OK, but in the future let her escape somewhere else. I don't want to see you up here again—or your wife *will* find out. Deal?"

He agreed and left.

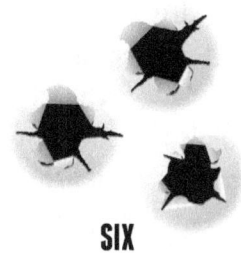

SIX
LEARNING THE HARD WAY

STILL VERY GREEN AND OUT to help the public, I was on patrol one night and spotted a driver going the wrong way on a one-way street at two in the morning. Foolishly, I thought he had to be lost, so I pulled the car over.

I was still developing my personal technique for traffic stops—and this one was about to change it drastically.

Immediately after I turned on the overheads, the driver pulled over and exited the vehicle. His passenger also got out.

The two men were both walking back to my patrol car with a purpose, almost running. They even made eye contact with me. They weren't acting like anyone I had ever pulled over before.

It was then that I realized that I'd made a huge mistake. Mentally, I was in the wrong place.

Intent on helping the poor citizen obviously lost and going the wrong way, I'd prematurely made up my mind about what was going on and how the stop would unfold—instead of just letting the situation define itself and being ready for whatever that would be.

In seconds, I was in real shit—and sorely unprepared: I was wearing a seat belt, the car door was closed, and I hadn't even come to a full stop yet.

I had to get the belt off, the door open, and get the car stopped immediately—or they'd be on me.

I barely accomplished all this in time to draw my weapon, yelling at the driver to get back to his car with my gun in his face.

In hindsight, that, too, was stupid. The gun was too close to him; he could have grabbed it—and then I would've been completely screwed.

I also hadn't kept an eye on his partner. Fortunately for me, though, they barely knew each other.

Somehow, I got out of my car in time to stand behind my car door, and I aimed my gun at the driver, yelling at him to get back into his vehicle. He decided to do what I told him, and so did the passenger.

I then called for backup, and fortunately my sergeant was only a few blocks away. When he rolled up, I started to dig into what the hell was going on.

It turned out that the driver was fresh out of prison; he'd been released for less than twenty-four hours, and he'd stolen the car and met the passenger in a bar. He wanted to buy some cocaine, and the passenger knew where he could get some. They were on their way to the dealer when I stopped them.

The passenger said that when I pulled them over, the guy told him he wasn't going back to prison and that he intended to get to my car and kill me before I could get out.

The passenger was afraid of him, so he went along with the plan out of fear.

I was lucky there was no real alliance, agreement, or understanding between them. The passenger was done with the plan the moment my gun came out, and he saw that any fight would be deadly for both of them. I really didn't have anything on the passenger, so I let him go and booked the driver into jail.

He was, of course, very pissed off, and he started talking shit and threatened that once he got out of prison he'd kill my entire family, torture my children, rape my wife, my dog, the neighbor's cat, blah, blah. All of it was added to the paperwork for his parole officer.

I never saw him again, but I also never wore my seatbelt again—even though it was required by department policy.

From then on, I always started my traffic stops from a greater distance, and I made sure that the car door was slightly ajar.

The thought of assisting the needy, harmless public was gone; in my mind, any stop that I made was for that same guy—with his same intent to kill me. This strategy would save my ass over and over again.

I'm aware of the fact that helping the wayward public is a nice idea, but the fact is, that's rarely the reality. Cops aren't firemen; we have to battle with people who don't want us to do the job that we're hired to do.

Another incident that made me stop and think was a call from a couple who answered a knock at their door to find a woman they didn't know. She just walked into their home, acting strangely, then locked herself into their bathroom and refused to come out.

I was patrolling a foothill part of the city at the south end of the county when the call came over that the woman had finally come out of the bathroom and left, taking the keys to the couple's truck.

The chase led all over the suburbs just to the south, and it soon came toward me. She was running stop signs and somehow hadn't hit anything.

I started out last in the long line of several cars chasing her. The acceleration contest then led up to the area known as "The Dugway," four lanes cut into the hillside for about five miles with a long drop over the south side if a motorist got through the guard rail.

She weaved across the oncoming lanes of traffic once or twice, almost touching the guardrail, and we thought she was going to launch.

Driving at speeds of over 100 mph, by the time she led us over the Dugway she was headed to the start of the main drag that spanned about fifteen miles northbound and led to the heart of the county—which was filled with some 180,000 people who were mostly sound asleep and had no idea that we were coming; all they heard were sirens in the night.

Eventually, I'd somehow become first in line and was rolling behind her at 120 miles an hour, running red lights as fast as my Crown Vic could go.

When I pulled up slightly behind her and to her right, she tried to hit me a few times. Gradually, I pulled up alongside her, and we made eye contact—and she promptly smiled, then tried to ram me again.

I pulled a little ahead of her and rolled down my window, then threw a large soft drink at her windshield, which caused a big spray of water.

The guys behind her yelled to each other over the radio that it wouldn't be long now; they thought she'd just blown a radiator hose. I threw the drink because I was pissed off that she'd tried to hit me; this was getting personal.

By then, other units had been able to form a safe corridor, blocking all the intersections ahead; so, we kept going.

We'd covered some ten miles in about four minutes when she suddenly cut east to turn onto the state highway that led up a canyon.

Not really a highway, it's just a road cut out between a river and a mountainside with no shoulders most of the way; just a single narrow lane in each direction.

She had an amazing control of the vehicle while she flew up the canyon at about sixty-five miles per hour, doubling the posted speed limit.

I was having trouble keeping up; she was somehow able to hold that speed, but I couldn't. I had to slow down while she power slid through the sharp corners into oncoming traffic lanes, somehow free from oncoming cars. All the way up the canyon we went, about nine miles total.

We drove past the dam at the top of the canyon, then started running alongside its reservoir.

At that point, another patrol car joined me, and we tried to box her in three times—but she'd always accelerate or weave at the right time.

Finally, though, she accelerated too much and rolled over, tumbling down into the reservoir.

We stopped and left our cars, running down through the brush to where the truck had gone into the water. We stopped at the water's edge, and I was thinking that I'd have to dive in and get her out when I suddenly heard splashing and coughing farther out in the water.

She'd been thrown clear of the now destroyed, totaled truck and was swimming back to shore—and she'd somehow come out of this rollover and 125 mile-an-hour chase with nothing more than minor scratches.

Later, we found out that she was so high on cocaine that she had no idea what she was doing.

Riverview PD had to clean up the mess because it was technically their case; we just wrote reports.

I couldn't help wondering *What the hell? Flying across the county through the city and up the canyon at these speeds because some woman was coked up?*

It seriously made me rethink chases, and I realized that I had to calm down and not get so drawn into the moment, instead looking at the bigger picture.

High-speed chases are always debated and probably always will be. You either endanger the citizens while chasing criminals or endanger the people if the criminals know you won't chase.

If either choice allows a suspect to hurt someone down the road, the department gets sued and attorneys pull your GPS to track every inch of every move you either made or chose not to make. Classic "Damned if you do, damned if you don't."

On-the-job training isn't just about the crazed ones who come right at you; it's also about those who look away.

I'd answered a call from a woman whose house was broken into in a town called Wolfstone. The burglar made himself at home, taking the time to eat and rifling through her underwear drawer.

It made for an unusual crime scene; it would've been more typical if a stereo or at least some silverware had been taken.

What the burglar had done had an intimate feel to it; he'd made a point to get as close to her sexually as he could. She no longer felt safe in her own home.

When I asked who she thought might have done this, she hesitated at first, then finally said her paperboy, a 14- or 15-year-old kid.

He gave her the creeps with the way he looked at her, and he was always hanging around. She thought she'd seen him outside one of her windows late at night, but he'd vanished when she got up to look.

I had her walk me through what had been taken or tampered with. The kid drank a two-liter bottle of Mountain Dew, ate some cookies, then opened her drawers and had gone through her underwear. She said that panties were missing and she described them, then she gave me his name and address.

I went to talk to the family, speaking to the parents and explaining what had happened and that the boy was a suspect.

I asked for permission to talk to him, and they agreed.

After about an hour in my car with me, the boy admitted to going into the home and drinking the soda and eating the cookies—but he wouldn't admit to taking the panties.

I then sat him down and talked to him and his parents together.

Crying and screaming, he denied it—but in the end it was obvious that he'd been in the house and through her drawers.

He left the room, and I talked to the parents, asking them to get him some help. This was a burglary; by definition it was a felony, but the complainant didn't want to press charges. She just wanted him to stop and get help.

I explained this to them, letting them know that if he didn't get help it was very possible that he'd escalate his behavior and move on to larger, worse crimes.

The parents exchanged a strange glance, then stared hard at each other for a few minutes.

The father then began to cry, and the mother said something about thinking that they were protected from this sort of thing.

She said, "We're Christians, devout churchgoers living the life the gospel requires. This isn't supposed to happen to us."

Their home was filled with paintings of Jesus and other religious imagery amid the sparse furniture. The father just sat there and cried quietly for a while, then they said that they'd get some help for their son and thanked me.

Something about that long stare that they shared bothered me; it seemed that there was a lot of nonverbal communication passing between them, so I started to dig.

I had a hard time getting any information at first, but eventually I found out that the dad had a record. He'd gone through the expungement process, though, and there wasn't much left. One department had a picture of him in an old file—but it was just a picture, nothing else.

Then I found out that the couple's other two sons had been arrested as juveniles for sexually abusing the neighborhood kids, raping and sodomizing the littlest ones.

Something about the dad still bothered me, though, but all I had was the picture, so I went around with it from police department to police department—then finally a veteran cop recognized him immediately.

He said the father had been a serial rapist from the late 60s and early 70s.

He'd raped several women on the east side of the city and was finally caught when he raped a little girl.

The old-timer said he was brutal and had made the comment that if he'd killed the little girl when he had the chance he never would've been caught; she was the only victim who could positively identify him.

I kept checking and found out that the guy had taught school after he'd been released from prison.

His record had been expunged after he'd been let go for molesting little kids in elementary schools. He hadn't been charged; just fired. I learned about this from talking to teachers and janitors at the schools; one story led to another, and then another.

I also found out that he'd met his wife through church.

She honestly believed that if they lived the life the church required, his evil ass nature would be cured. She also thought that as long as they paid their tithing, attended church regularly, said their prayers, and lived by the scriptures, everything would be fine.

She'd married a serial rapist, knowing exactly what he was; she was aware that he'd continued on to sexually abuse children as a teacher.

I'd guess he abused his own children as well. The statute of limitations had passed, but it was an eye-opener for me to see just how criminals hide out in plain sight.

Years later, I'd meet the kids.

When I spoke with them, it seriously freaked them out that I knew who they were. They were paranoid, openly upset, and they wanted to know how I knew them.

I just told them that I knew them from Wolfstone; there wasn't much to talk about after that. I was no longer a cop by then, but what I learned while I was talking to their parents that day made me much more aware of the nonverbal cues that people give out.

It's important to listen to what's not being said; usually, it's much more important than what *is* being said.

Another hard lesson learned came when I was still with the county but in one of the bigger cities.

There was a large auditorium in one of the civic centers and the managers were trying to it make profitable by renting it out. Normally, this wouldn't be our problem; we were county cops, and this was in the city. One night, however, one of our guys had been poaching in the city, trying to get drunken driving arrests.

He came upon a large riot in progress at the civic center as a large wedding in the auditorium had ended, spilling out onto the grounds. When he called for help, I responded.

The scene was a chaotic mess with people running everywhere, swinging bats, sticks, and chains, and one group was beating the hell out of a guy on the ground.

That's where the other deputy was when I arrived; he was trying to break up the group kicking the hell out of the guy.

I pulled up fast, high beams and overheads on, and hit the siren.

The group scattered, then the other deputy yelled at me to chase a specific guy—as he had a knife and had been stabbing the victim.

I was out of the car and running after him. He took off behind the building, and I was right behind him; once again, like a dumbass I was caught up in the chase.

The area was all rail yards and gravel, and we ran all across tracks and around boxcars. Finally he gave out, and I landed on top of him, cuffed him, and then caught my breath. I never found the knife.

For a few minutes, we just lay there, both of us breathing hard—then we heard his friends; the same ones who had been kicking the shit out of the guy on the ground were now looking for us. We were in the pitch dark, and they were trying to find him.

They were all around us, calling out to him. He yelled back once, then they started running around, frantically trying to locate where the sound came from.

"Let us know where you're at, Holmes," they said, "and we'll get you out of here!" I heard one guy say, "We'll fuck that cop up! He's alone…we'll get you out of here. Where are you?"

Then I heard, "Here piggy, piggy, piggy. We're gonna fuck you up, bitch!"

I grabbed my suspect by the throat and clamped down until he started to gag.

I then said to him in as violent a whisper as I could, "One fucking word, and I will crush your fucking throat. You will have an accident: you got hurt when you fell down. Understand, motherfucker?"

He managed to gasp, "Ya."

We lay there for a while, listening to his friends running around in the gravel, trying desperately to find him while calling to each other and making threats to me.

Finally, some city cops showed up and shined flashlights into the rail yards, looking for us; this scared off his friends.

When it was safe, we got up and walked back the deputy who'd sent me off on this little chase.

I was pretty proud of myself; I'd caught the guy and got off with no injuries. I walked over to the deputy and tried to give the bad guy over to him, as this was part of his case. He refused to take him, though.

I was confused. "What's up, man? You told me to chase him. He was supposed to have a knife, remember? You said he stabbed your guy?"

He looked me straight in the eye and said, "Well, I never saw any of that. I didn't think you'd be able to catch him, and I can't identify him from the group. Besides, I don't want to write a report on this. Just book him for intoxication, and let's go."

I couldn't believe this shit!

I was hot—*really* fucking hot. I checked, and the guy did have warrants, so I booked him on the warrants as well. The city cops wouldn't even look at him as a suspect. Their exact words were, "One

Mexican stabbed another Mexican. Happens all the time! We don't fucking care. He's yours."

I did some more checking, and I found out that he was a gang member out of California hanging out with a local gang family in the city.

The whole night had been surreal. I'd done it again: got caught up in someone else's call, caught up in the moment and the emotion, and put myself in danger again for nothing.

My fellow deputy and I were no longer on speaking terms after that. He had the balls to tell everyone that I'd gone after the guy for no reason and didn't let anyone know where I was going. He also told them that I was careless and unsafe and to be careful around me.

I was learning.

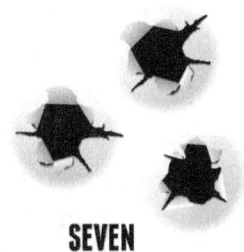

SEVEN
SWAT—SOMETIMES IT'S PERSONAL

YOU MAY BE SURPRISED TO hear that SWAT calls can actually be a time for thoughtful introspection, a time to think about things as we're getting paid to put on the gear, arm up, then park our asses and wait on an outcome.

After getting the call, we'd hustle in from whatever detail we were on. We tried to get to the scene fast enough to gear up while team commanders measured the actions required to end whatever cluster the patrol division had already cordoned off.

This gathering of pent-up officers, though, soon fell abruptly at ease for hours, which would give us down time for things to gel in our heads.

Often, I'd think about things like how damn strange it was coming back to my hometown as a police officer.

I never had any intention of coming back to this place; the site of my massively dysfunctional childhood was no place to reminisce.

I came back for my second wife—huge mistake.

We'd known each other in high school (not as well as I thought, it turned out) and kept in touch. When we got married, the real nightmare began.

My marriages tend to work out only when I pull night shifts, giving me more time with the kids while avoiding the wife...well, at least my first three marriages did.

Cops never seem to marry well, though, so at least we all had that in common to chat about.

"Love" isn't enough; there's something about the lurid demands of a job you can never explain to a spouse who just doesn't want to hear about it anyway.

"How was your day?"

"Shit up to my knees, and you?"

Then my first child was born, and there was no going back; making the city a better place suddenly became very important to me.

I also still had this feeling that I could make a difference with my military experience, having grown up in the city as well. I never really mentioned that to anyone until now, but it was always there in the back of my mind.

During the waiting time, the lulls on SWAT calls, I also had the chance to become amazed at my fellow officers' lack of any real connection with the people whose circumstances we'd surrounded; of course, most of them weren't deploying in their old childhood stomping grounds like I was every time we set up in the inner city. My fellow "ninja turtles" were often learning that fact about me for the first time.

I'd already kicked ass enough times, though, that I guess they knew it wouldn't be an issue. Nobody ever said anything about my roots. Of course, I never gave up much about my childhood. I didn't see it as much to tell.

To this day, I think I'm still owed a childhood and have got one coming, as mine wasn't childlike at all; it was more like a fifteen-round title bout. I'm much more edgy than most people—even more than most cops.

I think it was something that I developed even before I became a cop, likely from an upbringing of battling nonstop and having nowhere to turn to escape, no time to be a kid and just grow up naturally.

I went from a hostile home environment to a hostile school environment, and on the way to and from there were battles every day. Most kids might get into a fight once in a while, but not me.

My mother was quite literally a crazy woman; she pitted my brother and me against each other from the time we could walk.

We hated each other, a relationship that still grows richer in its span of distance to this day. He'd pick fights for me with the older kids, loving to antagonize them against me.

I'd be walking home, and they'd be waiting, older, bigger, and stronger. As a result, I learned how to handle myself—and fuck people up severely if I had to.

Most days, we'd pass the old Clark Market. It was where my brother liked to wait for me.

One day, I was in a fight again—and I was losing—hating, as I always did, the way I felt fighting.

I was still confused as to why I had to fight more than anyone else I knew—then survival kicked in, and I got out from under the older kid and really hurt him.

There was lots of blood in the snow around us, his and mine; I'd gone crazy.

Old man Clark came out and pulled me off—then I hit him, too, launching F-bombs everywhere as he threw me down and called me an animal.

I was the animal?

He said that I should leave the older kid—the bigger kid—alone; I was in the first grade, and he was in the fifth—and twice my size.

I jumped back on him, not wanting him to be able to fight me another time, then Old man Clark went after me again.

That was how I grew up. My parents either didn't care or were unaware of it—and looking back, I wonder why they had us at all.

So, I had this weird craving for peace, and at the same time I never wanted to be the subject of some cheese dick's authority over me.

Police work somehow made sense.

Standing around on SWAT calls led me too often to these thoughts and others. Often, more important for me was bracing for the occasion when I'd have to draw down on some fucked up bastard I'd known for years; the possibility was much more likely on SWAT calls.

SWAT comes in after the fact; there was no chance for me to be among the first on the scene, where I could talk to people and probe for some kind of connection, like an uncle or a cousin of the suspect's that I might know. When SWAT was called out, that point was long past for the most part.

So when I put on the camo, the helmet, the body armor, and took up the assault rifle, that was when I had to wonder if I might have to shoot someone that I'd sat next to in the third grade, or whose father I went to high school with, or maybe I dated his daughter or fought his brother in a schoolyard fight...the possible combinations were mind-numbing, and it was difficult to put them out of my head.

One day, a SWAT call became more personal for my teammates.

Finally, all at once, all my fellow officers would know what it was like to go out on a messy human entanglement where they had a personal, visceral connection; I'd get to stop wondering how these chumps couldn't see what it could do to your insides to roll up on someone you knew.

It was the first time that I saw on their faces some kind of an emotional reaction to a call.

Suzanne Wilson was a dispatcher whom I'd known since I started working in law enforcement. She worked nights, as I did, and I became friends with her and others. We'd often talk about calls because dispatchers hardly ever hear about the outcomes after they send patrol cars and ambulances out cruising around the county.

They had all kinds of information at their fingertips, though, with access to multiple massive databases. So we'd talk about the job, kids, spouses, or whatever came up.

This SWAT page came for a little town on the west side of the county. While composed mainly of city officers, it was multi-jurisdictional, so we could end up anywhere.

This was a hostage situation; the caller had asked for help after her husband had gone ballistic, and several shots had been fired.

We were staging in the basement of a home down the street.

The entire team showed up, about sixteen guys total, but the situation dragged on for a while. Snipers were out on the perimeter, and it was a brutally cold night.

Negotiators were working with the guy inside the house, trying to keep a conversation going. Initially, he wouldn't say what had happened; just that he wanted out of the relationship with his wife.

She and her oldest daughter had confronted him, accusing him of having an affair. They all got into an argument, and when he felt that his wife was trying to destroy his life, he just lost it.

As it turned out, this was Suzanne's husband.

It took a while for us to put together the fact that this was the same Suzanne Wilson, emergency dispatcher.

Suddenly, it was all very personal.

This wasn't some random family of strangers nobody knew; I'd talked to her for hours, shared our personal lives, and laughed over the same things.

Suzanne was in the house, and we didn't know if she was dead or alive; all we knew for sure was that we had contact with her husband and he wouldn't let the women come to the phone.

We waited while the negotiators did their thing, ready to go into the house at a moment's notice.

Eventually, they got Mr. Wilson talking, and he opened up and admitted to shooting Suzanne and her daughter. He didn't know if they were dead or not. He came out peaceably and surrendered to us, then we went in and cleared the house.

Suzanne and her daughter were both dead and had been for hours. It was a hollow feeling, alternately filled with pangs of helplessness, then rage.

It would turn out that the folks of any substance I knew before had gotten out of the inner city, and the time would come when I'd put a bullet in someone I knew—blowing holes in my childhood.

EIGHT
DAS BOOT

ALZHEIMER'S AND THE DEVIL MAKE for one terrified old woman, I'd discover one night as I was dispatched to an unknown call, a possible burglary in progress.

An elderly lady had reported someone prowling around outside of her house. She said that she was alone and afraid, and could we please hurry.

When I arrived and got out of the car, I heard this incredible screaming—but it wasn't just any screaming; it was unlike anything I've heard before…an agonizing, blood-curdling, continuous cry of pure anguish like someone was getting viciously tortured inside the house.

There was no time to wait for backup; just time enough to describe the situation to dispatch and tell them that I was going in. I asked them to start medical rolling.

I stood at the door, gun drawn, and yelled, "Police! Open the door!"

More horrific screams came, then an eerie silence as I heard footsteps approaching the door from the other side.

A deep, guttural male voice said, "Go away," then I heard more footsteps away from the door—and the screams started again.

I leaned back and kicked the door in, and it slammed against something small and white, sending it skidding under a table.

I cleared the house, going from room to room and yelling, "Police! Show me your hands!" looking for the suspect in what I was sure would be a horrific scene.

No one was there, though, so I continued to yell out, "Let me see your hands!"

It was a bluff; I couldn't find anyone.

Then I heard something behind me; a rustling of some kind back in the living room where I entered the home.

Completely mystified, I entered the room and noticed movement under the table. I decided to challenge whoever was underneath. "Come out, hands first! Slowly..."

Two small, frail, aged and bloodied hands came shaking out from under the table, skin torn on the forearms; it was a small, terrified elderly woman, shaking and timid. I helped her up and asked what happened.

To make a long story short, she had both Alzheimer's and a devout religious faith. She was the only one in the house and had called because she was frightened; she was sure the devil was prowling outside, trying to get in to take her away—and I'd unwittingly fulfilled that prophecy with my pounding at her door.

She said she came to the door and made her voice as deep and menacing as possible, hoping to scare me—"the devil"—away.

Then, when I kicked the door in, she was still behind it—and was knocked across the room and under the table, scraping the skin on her arms. Other than that, she wasn't injured.

Embarrassed beyond belief, I canceled back up and waited.

Dee, the dispatcher on the call whom I knew really well, kept checking on me and couldn't understand what had happened—and I wasn't about to tell her. She had a wicked sense of humor, and I wasn't ready to be humiliated. I still had a small glimmer of hope that I could find a way out of this with minimal embarrassment.

For the moment, the woman was mentally clear, and as she recalled her story for me she turned and asked, "Dear, I don't mean to be rude, but is someone coming that's *actually* going to help me?"

Man, I felt like shit.

Medical finally arrived, and I had to explain the lady's injuries; they could barely contain their laughter. This was getting worse, a lot worse.

The neighbors then came over, and again I had to recount what had happened.

Eventually, the people who watched over her showed up. They'd gone to a movie and thought that they could leave her alone for a short while.

I explained the door, as well as the screams and the injuries.

They didn't see any humor in the situation and explained to me that the woman was deathly afraid that Satan was coming to take her any moment now.

I left and wrote it up, hoping it would just go away...it didn't.

Dee got the medical team to tell her all about it, and she'd never let me forget it.

She gave me the nickname "Boot."

NINE
BORN THAT WAY

ONE NIGHT I WAS PATROLLING as the upper valley car, checking the canyon housing and surroundings in search of a mystery vehicle.

Residents had been reporting it as just parked in some remote area, usually at night, sometimes on private property, sometimes on federal forestland. So far, nobody had recognized it as being from the area.

Then one night, I finally came across the car hidden well back in the woods.

The windows were steamed up, and the occupants had no idea I was there.

I knocked on the window, and they rolled it down while frantically trying to get dressed—it was two men who I'd just seen locked in the 69 position in the back seat.

While they got dressed, I asked for their identification. At first, they didn't want to provide it, but they eventually did.

I didn't know the pair, both Hispanic males from the city.

I checked them for warrants, and they had none, so I filled out FI cards and told them that they were free to go—but not before advising them not to come back because the residents had spotted their car and complained.

About a year later, after I'd transferred to the city, I was dispatched to a gang fight.

Two rival sets were brawling, and we were called to clean it up and disperse the combatants. I went to deal with one group of gangbangers that was walking away from the scene but moving slower than we liked, and still talking shit to the gang that they'd been fighting with.

I recognized one of them from that night in the canyon; he was one of the occupants who had been steaming up the windows in the vehicle.

At first, I thought no biggie—but then when I went to help disperse the other group, there was the other guy from that night.

I was thinking, *how the hell did that happen?*

The two groups hated each other; it was multi-generational, and their gangs were at war every single night. How did these two gay guys from different gangs who wanted each other dead actually hook up? I couldn't even begin to imagine that conversation!

A few years later, I had the opportunity to ask one of them about it.

He said that they'd known each other in school before they'd cliqued up, each joining their respective gang. They'd admitted to each other that they were gay and mutually attracted to one another. They'd kept the secret hidden from everyone—including their fellow gangbangers, who they backed-up each night; they were linked by gang loyalties, which were often more important than family ties, and they ran with homies who would have beaten them to death if they knew the truth.

So, when they met on the street, they'd talk a lot of trash and maybe fight but never seriously harm each other. They'd been lovers for years.

He said that was why they drove off to the canyon out in the county to meet; it was because "Nobody in the woods knew us."

He asked that I keep the secret since it would be doubly fatal for each of them: not only would they draw a beating from their homies for being gay. They'd also get it for being with a rival gang member.

I never told anyone, and I never used it against them to extract information; I figured they had more than enough to deal with.

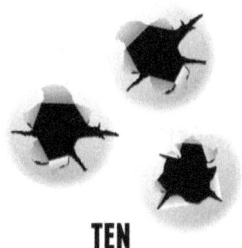

TEN
OUTLIVING CHILDREN

ADULT VICTIMS CAN SOMETIMES BE hard to sympathize with; some make choices that put them in a place where they knowingly become victims.

Not children; they're born helpless and grow up dependent, trusting, carefree, walking wide-eyed, innocent, and joyous through a world that will prey upon them once exposed. If they're left alone, unguided, or overlooked even for a second—it's over.

I wouldn't wish the painful aftermath from a child's death on my worst enemy.

That being said, not everyone should be allowed to have children. That becomes obvious on this job; so unavoidably, some children are born into lives where they just never have a chance.

Cammi Paulson was a 4-year-old girl who had been playing with friends at her grandfather's house and disappeared.

A 15-year-old boy, Daniel Wilkerson, claimed to have seen her picked up by some people in a car. He even helped out in the search for her.

This being one of my first cases as a city patrol officer, I was in field training with John Garcia. He was my mentor for years, and we called him "Father Time" for his calm, steady demeanor.

We went door-to-door, looking for the girl, literally going from room to room in every house and apartment in the central city. We searched for her all shift long for what I remember as several days; I'm pretty sure, though, that I'm blocking a lot of it out.

During the search, we fielded plenty of false reports from people who claimed to have seen her playing with their neighbors or walking past their house.

The last of the searching I remember was looking in garbage cans. We never said that we'd given up hope, but there was this unspoken feeling that it was time to search in garbage cans, in holes under houses, and anywhere a small body could be stuffed and hidden because we weren't going to find her alive.

This was before cell phones were everywhere, and I remember trying to control my panic and anxiety.

I felt somehow that my own baby girl was in danger, and I needed to call—but I couldn't; I had to keep on searching.

The search was methodical, systematic, and impressive; each city block was checked off when it was covered. I was actually very impressed by the organizational skills of the incident commanders. The communication actually went up and down the chain of command efficiently, unlike the cluster fuck I'd experienced at county. It felt like teamwork for once...figures that it would take something sick and twisted to bring a department together.

Eventually, Garcia came to me and said that the search had been called off.

The Wilkerson boy had confessed to killing and raping the little girl. He'd hidden her body in a plastic garbage bag and put her in the shed behind his house.

At the time, I didn't let on that I was really affected by this—but I struggled with my emotions, furious and stricken at the thought of what was done to this child.

I'd later read the entire report and talk to the veteran detective who got the confession so that I might learn everything I could from him. I wanted to be the guy who brought cases like this one to a close with a solid arrest.

He told me, like he later testified in court, that it was routine to question Wilkerson when it became apparent that he might have been the last person to see Cammi alive.

During the questioning, the kid's body language changed at one point; he suddenly stopped making eye contact and became distracted, acting like someone who was about to reveal something embarrassing about himself—not necessarily criminal.

The detective had seen this very thing happen many times before—a vulnerable moment—so he took a shot:

"Daniel, where's Cammi?"

He wasn't ready for the answer, and it shocked him when Wilkerson lost it and said that she was in the shed behind his house. Everything just emptied out of the kid after that.

I remember watching Wilkerson when they walked him through the station house, thinking that he wasn't noteworthy or unique; he was just a kid, like any other 15-year-old—except this one had raped and murdered a little girl.

I expected him to be so obviously a monster and a killer that I'd see it immediately, whatever "It" was…but there was nothing telling or unusual about him.

We went to a 7-11 afterward and got a drink, just sitting and slowly drinking in silence. No one said a word; we all just stared, thinking our own private thoughts.

People would come in and ask us how the search was going, asking if we'd found her yet. This was horrible. All I wanted to do was go be alone and deal with the mix of emotions and rage. We couldn't tell them she'd been found dead; they were controlling that through the press release.

We left the 7-11 and drove around for a while, just wanting it to be quiet and to get away from the public.

The prosecutors wanted to execute Wilkerson, but when they checked with the state Supreme Court they found out he was too young; he had to be sixteen to qualify for the death penalty.

His mother was a drunk and an addict, and his father was some brutal dickhead constantly in and out of prison, who beat and raped her regularly. That was about all we learned about the kid's home life. We were dealing with district court, not the behavioral research institute—and courts just establish blame.

I remember the kid's public defender making some whacked argument that he shouldn't be charged with rape; instead, he should be charged with desecration of a corpse since she was dead by then...just one of those glittering moments to remind him why he went to law school, I suppose.

These kinds of cases are the ones that really haunt you; as hard as you try to forget, it's always with you.

On another night, I was called to an address in the inner city. It was a basement apartment in the bottom of a fourplex, one of those old dilapidated places that no one cares enough about to keep up.

The occupant was a woman who had asked her new boyfriend to watch her infant son; she had to go to work and had no sitter. She'd dated the boyfriend for about six weeks and felt she could trust him with her son, plus she was in a bind. The boyfriend agreed, and she left.

What she didn't know, though, was that her boyfriend had a very low threshold for stress. She'd never seen him alone with the baby; she was always around and had no idea he couldn't care for the child alone.

According to the boyfriend, the baby started to cry and he couldn't comfort it or get it to stop crying. Eventually, frustration led to anger, and he reached a point where he couldn't stand it any longer—and he blew up.

At first, he said he started to punch the child—which only made the crying louder—so he threw the infant around the apartment and against the walls, and at one point he even dropkicked the baby to the ceiling like a football.

When he was finished, he just sat on the couch, staring at all the blood splatters and the pieces of the dead baby left everywhere; I tried my best to get him to do something, anything, to make any move that I could use as an excuse to seriously beat his fucking ass. But, he did nothing; with a flat affect, he just stared straight ahead and cooperated fully, and during the interview he started to talk about his own childhood and the abuse that he'd survived.

He said his mother whipped him with a coat hanger repeatedly and stubbed out cigarettes on his chest and back.

I didn't believe him until he lifted his shirt and showed me the worst scarring I'd ever seen; after that, I was quiet and in shock.

This wasn't what I wanted to see or believe. He had been tortured physically and emotionally and was a ticking time bomb that had finally gone off.

I pulled up his name on the computer and realized that I'd dealt with him before when he was a young boy. He'd been a runaway for several months, and I'd found him living on the streets, so I turned him over to juvenile court officials. At the time he was only ten years old, and he said he'd been living on the street for about five weeks.

A few years later, I ran into him again at a party, the people there wanting him removed; they were uncomfortable with how he was acting, bizarre and threatening. I checked, and he had a warrant for the sexual abuse of a child, so I took him to juvenile detention.

I asked him what had happened since I'd seen him last. He said he'd been in state care, bouncing from foster home to foster home, which he said he didn't like but that it was better than living with his mom.

I didn't see him again until the murder of the baby.

I didn't recognize him that night; life had hardened him and made him barely resemble the child I once knew.

He was booked on the murder of the baby and pled to the charges. His confession had sealed the case.

ELEVEN
DEVIL FAMILY

WORKING SWAT, OF COURSE, IS a glory gig that some cops aspire to; it certainly shines up the resume.

But it's also a job like any other, with petty in-house jealousies, grudges, cliques, and office politics—only magnified somewhat since everybody's armed to the teeth.

Like any job, some of my co-workers could be the subject matter of a behavioral pathology thesis—what with most of them being flat out nut jobs and eligible for any local psyche ward.

Henry Blair lived on the north end of the city in one of the newer but barely middle class areas lacking enough in destitution to be linked to the inner city.

One day, Henry had a small meltdown: his son came over to the house, and Henry came out and shot him with a rifle; he just shot his own son for no apparent reason and went back into the house.

A patrolman responding to the first call dragged the son to safety while Henry barricaded himself inside, and SWAT staged from a house nearby.

This call, however, was a really sweet set-up.

The staging house was really nice; we had full run of the place, with access to everything from the TV to the couches. Plus, we slept on carpeted floors and in chairs while we waited for Henry to be negotiated out of the house.

The snipers were out on rotating shifts while we on the entry teams were inside eating pizza, watching a big screen TV, and playing cards. I would say sleeping, too, but that's not really what it was.

When you're on that kind of call, you don't really sleep; you might catnap, but you can't really sleep. Henry had already shot one person, and we had to presume that he was ready to do it again—to one of us.

Usually, the situation is really tense, and the waiting can make you crazy if you don't have some way to release the tension.

I remember talking with one of the squad members, laughing about the mental image of sneaking over to the house, surprising Henry, and dragging him out of the house.

We envisioned tying him to a fence, bending him over, and yanking his crazy old man trousers down—then engaging him in candid anal rape while explaining the rules of "Team Bruised Anus."

We had to have a code word for our squad to identify itself to other teams as friendly if it ever came to the so-called thick of battle. Ours was "Black Angus," and that easily morphed into "Bruised Anus" for the purposes of payback on Henry; after all, it was his fault that we had to sit around in this house away from our families, forced to listen to the brass pontificate.

This career highlight of a SWAT assignment also included getting to know the brass in these calm times of waiting—and we always regretted it. We were surprisingly united on this point.

In police work, we have a saying: "Shit floats."

It means the good cops never rise through the ranks to float, so to speak, in the upper echelons. There's a reason that the saying continues to this day: shit continues to float.

As we sat laughing about Henry, the SWAT commander and the sergeant, the number two guy, came over and asked our opinion.

"I'm tired of waiting and talking the suspect out. I want some action," said top dog. "I want to go in and kick that old man's ass," added the sergeant.

At first, I thought they were joking—but they weren't.

I said I thought it would be best if we let the negotiators do their jobs. If we went in too early, the press might get wind of it—then all hell would break loose. They sort of nodded and walked away.

"What the fuck was that about?" I asked Jimmy, my fellow squad member.

He shrugged and said, "I don't know. They're bored. You know they're not right mentally anyway; no one wants to get into a fight like those two do. Why do you think they're nicknamed 'The Mini-Commandos?'"

"Christ, is *anyone* on this team normal?" I said, tired and a bit stunned. "Our squad leader reads Soldier of Fortune like it's a comic book, the commander is a fucking nut, the sergeant is an idiot douche, and here we are joking about sodomizing an old man bent over a fence," I said.

We started laughing again, mumbling, "Bruised anus...bruised anus."

Eventually, Henry was talked out of the house and arrested.

He'd fortified the place and tied the doors shut, and he'd made entry into the home possible through only one way so he could ambush whoever came in while he was behind cover; if we had stormed the house the way leadership wanted, we all would have been slaughtered.

This was a SWAT team that had what I considered an enviable record these days. Having never shot a suspect in twenty-five years of existence, we were the only SWAT team in the state left without a shooting.

You had to wonder, though, if that chapped the ass of the SWAT leadership. One more call would just about do it for me with this crazy ass bunch; this kind of "glory" wasn't what it was cracked up to be.

TWELVE

DEMON FAMILY

MAX ORTIZ LIVED ON THE west side of the city in an apartment on the end of a dead end street; "Over the viaduct," as they say, a rundown part of town that was seriously gang-infested.

He was supposed to be dealing cocaine out of the apartment.

Our briefing was that he was dangerous, armed, and that his whole family was armed as well. Max was a big dude back then and very intimidating, and the family name was well known on the streets. He had multiple weapons in the house—and even the elementary school-age kids were to be considered dangerous.

So, when we got ready to enter the apartment, the entire team was really jacked up.

I didn't know the kids, but later every one of the Ortiz girls would become informants for me—even against their own family.

We stacked up on the front door, prepared to do a no-knock search warrant and arrest everyone. I was third in line, and when we hit the door the front guy got hung up. So, the next guy opened the door per protocol, which made me the first through the door.

I went in and down the stairs as planned, running in to one of the girls and putting her on the floor, then handcuffing her.

The entry wasn't what we expected.

We were told that the entire family was streetwise and combative and that they'd be carrying weapons and were ready to fight; instead, there I was handcuffing a scared little girl who was crying, sobbing, and screaming for her life.

They had no idea what was happening, and I felt like an asshole.

I looked around and saw the rest of the team fucking this family up; they were afraid of going to battle with this "demon family" that didn't exist.

True, Max was a bad ass and his wife a prostitute rumored to carry a knife—but the girls were just little girls, and Max, Jr., was just a little boy.

After calming my suspect down by telling her that I wouldn't let her be harmed, I looked around the room.

One of our guys had his submachine gun to the head of one of the girls—and she was already cuffed.

The "battle" was over, the house secured, and all the suspects in cuffs. We were done with the entire operation in less than five seconds—yet he had his gun inches from her head, finger on the trigger, gun set on full auto, calling her a "fucking bitch" and screaming shit like "Who's the bad ass now?"

She was terrified, so I grabbed his weapon and yanked it away from her head—and instantly he was on me. "What the fuck are you doing?" he yelled.

As calmly as I could, I said that she was cuffed and not resisting. I then told him that he had his finger on the trigger and the gun pointed at her head—and that the gun was set to fire—cautioning him that he didn't want to have an accidental shooting of a cuffed suspect.

He just raged, "Never touch my weapon! NEVER!"

"Fuck you," I replied. "You're out of control. She's a little girl; grow the fuck up."

I got her up, and we left him glaring at me, speechless.

As we walked out, I watched him in case there was more.

He started to stare at the little girl, and his demeanor changed; suddenly, he decompressed like he was coming up from a deep-sea dive and finally saw that she was, indeed, just a helpless little girl.

In the SWAT vehicle on the way back to the station house, he stared at me a while, then finally said, "OK, you were right."

After that, we became friends briefly before he, too, left SWAT.

Years later, the Ortiz family moved into my patrol area, and I somewhat became friends with them—that is, as much as that was possible.

Max had beaten them often, and they were relieved whenever he was sent off to prison. The kids would mention that SWAT raid at times, the emotional scars obvious.

At first they'd laugh as they talked about how terrified they were, but the tears would always come—and I never told them that I was there.

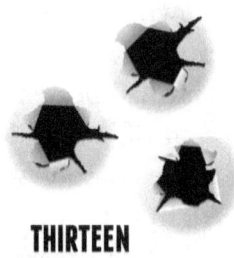

THIRTEEN
WORKING THE CROWD

ONE NIGHT, I WAS CALLED to the scene where someone had been shot and robbed in the central city.

The usual stuff, it gets routine after a while: looking for anyone who will admit to having seen or heard anything.

You have to understand that retaliation is a very real fear for the impoverished dwellers of our decaying urban cores.

After I spent some time interviewing witnesses who worked hard to elaborate on all the details they *didn't* know concerning what had just happened, I finally found a guy who would at least talk to me.

He said loudly that he'd never talk, no matter what—but his eye contact and facial expression said otherwise. He wanted me to act like I was arresting him, so I applied the cuffs and hauled him off.

Once we were outside visual range of his friends and neighbors, he told me what had happened, who the robber was, and even where the suspect lived. He even went so far as to sign an official statement at the police station. Ultimately, we located the suspect and arrested him, and I released the witness, thanked him, and went on to the next call.

After about a week went by, I was dispatched to a house to meet with a woman who'd been raped at knifepoint. She'd met the assailant at a house a few blocks away, and he'd walked her home, offering to keep her safe. She'd then invited him in for a drink.

When it came time for him to leave, though, he picked up a knife and told her that she was going to repay him for his kindness one way or another.

She had kids in the house and didn't want them to see or hear what was about to happen, so she convinced him to take her to her car, which was parked in the driveway.

It was inoperable, and she hoped that once they got there she might be able to talk him out of doing anything; unfortunately, when they got into the car he raped her anyway and left.

She told me she knew his name and where he lived—and guess who? It was Mr. Helpful from the armed robbery a week earlier.

I went to his place, and we talked amiably.

I thanked him for his help on the earlier robbery, then asked him to come down to the station to clarify some of the points in his statement.

Of course, this was all a ruse; once we were out of the neighborhood, I drove him past the rape victim's house and watched for his reaction.

He became upset and wanted to know where we were going. I told him that I just wanted to check on a friend who had called; I'd promised her that I'd drive by her house every once in a while.

Noticeably nervous, he was quite relieved when we got to the station. He was hoping to start talking about the robbery case, but that never happened.

I asked him if he knew the woman at the address that we'd just driven by, and he said that he'd never been there. I told him I had witnesses indicating otherwise, witnesses who had seen him walk her home—and that I knew he had, in fact, been there.

He agreed, trying to keep his cool. He said he misunderstood me; he'd been there, but just to walk her home.

I told him that I knew from his helping out on the robbery case that he was a good guy and that this woman was a little bit crazy.

He laughed and said, "She sure is. You don't know the half of it."

I asked him to explain that remark.

He said that after he walked her home, she wanted to have sex with him in her car and that she'd forced herself on him. Initially he refused, he said; it just didn't seem right. She was so insistent, though, and it seemed important to her, so he eventually gave in and they had sex. He did her a favor.

"That was it?" I asked.

He said yes and that he'd then left and gone home.

"What about the knife?" I inquired. "She said you had a knife."

He denied this, so I ran it all past him again, about what a good guy he was, taking a risk to help us out on the robbery, and would he consider helping us again to clear up this delusional woman's crazy story? I told him she had a cut from the knife and that she said he had a knife, so how did this happen?

He replied that she "liked it rough" and convinced him to hold a knife to her throat during his sloppy fucking. Her wish was his command. He said he must have slipped and accidentally nicked her.

I had him write down his admission to this "rough sex," then arrested him and booked him into jail on suspicion of aggravated rape.

Then, while at the booking center in front of other prisoners in the holding cell area, I thanked him for helping us with the earlier robbery case before I left—making sure they heard me, which was sure to make his time behind bars memorable; snitches are highly frowned upon in jail.

I suppose he thought he'd earned himself one free aggravated rape for helping solve a prior aggravated felony.

He pleaded guilty to the rape, and surprisingly we still got the conviction on the robbery; luckily, raping someone at knifepoint doesn't make you a liar in the eyes of the court.

FOURTEEN
DAYWALKERS

THERE ARE DAY PEOPLE, AND there are night people—and there's a huge difference.

The city, any city, transforms at night.

The world is quieter and still, in anticipation. It smells different and feels different, and your senses are heightened; you feel less numb and more aware.

There's a reason that predators in the wild choose the night, and human predators are the same, being naturally drawn to the cover of darkness with fewer eyes to see them.

That was my element, where we worked. We understood that even the day cops were different. They weren't as feral or aware; they didn't fit at night.

Night enhanced the battleground.

It was Us vs. Them, squaring off in the most rundown parts of the city, where economic pressures contort the already dysfunctional.

The 95% of the population that lived in the "Daywalker" world were gone; the killers and the people who took them on were out, holding ground until the sun started back around and the birds awoke, bringing the Daywalkers back out of their beds.

As the sky slowly brightened behind the mountains, the predators would retreat, and we'd go home as well.

One night, I was with Tim, a fairly new guy, working the graveyard. It was around Christmas, and we were hanging out on a break in a convenience store parking lot when we got a report from a passerby hearing moaning coming from a backyard, an inner city alleyway area.

We laughed at first ("moaning?!"), thinking we were going to a call from some voyeurs who wanted us to witness them having sex.

It happens often enough: people make an anonymous call about something happening at their house—then get busy, screwing with their drapes or blinds open so we'll see them going at it when we roll up.

When we responded, we parked a couple houses down and walked to the address. It was an apartment complex.

We knocked, and no one answered.

We weren't even a little bit on edge; we were joking and laughing and talking quietly while we hung at the door.

We knocked again, and still no answer.

We checked back with dispatch, and they had no further information, so we were about to clear the call as unfounded. Before we did, though, we decided to go around to the back of the house—where we came across the body of a female, Aubrey Snyder.

She was lying face up, her blouse and bra pulled up to expose her breasts. One leg was folded under her body, and her bowels had evacuated, as they will in a sudden, violent death. Her head was covered in blood, and she wasn't moving.

I checked her pulse, and as I expected, she had none. I checked her eyes, and the pupils were blown. She was dead.

Staring, Tim had turned to stone. I don't know for sure, but I think it was his first dead body.

I started to talk him through it, explaining the scene and what we had to do, helping him to process the shock of what he was seeing.

This was an attack from someone very angry, a revenge killing—and it was a blitz attack on top of that. The killer knew her and was an organized offender, as they say in the reading material on homicide crime scenes; he exposed her chest in some kind of an attempt at misdirection because there was no sexual assault.

We called out what we had, letting the rest of the units on that night know what had happened.

The back door of the house was open, but there was nobody inside, and a search revealed nothing. The place wasn't ransacked, nothing was broken nor opened nor missing. The murder weapon had been removed from the scene, where a lot of leaves were covered with blood, and there was some splatter on the bricks of the house.

Later, investigators would learn that her estranged husband had killed her with the claw end of a hammer; he learned that she'd been having an affair with a cop from a smaller jurisdiction outside the city.

We protected the scene until detectives and CSI showed up. By then, our shift was over.

The case was really hard to make fit with the "real world" that we returned to; while Tim and I had talked and joked at the 7-11, Aubrey Snyder was getting her head caved in a couple blocks away.

This was the city, and after a while you just accepted the fact that violence was going to happen. We knew that, but leaving that scene left us with such a bleak feeling, like being short of oxygen or getting too much, unable to touch down again.

The kids were awake when I got home, and the wife was mad; I hadn't got home soon enough after working graves to help her with them in the morning.

We had a very large extended family, so the kids were still excited about Christmas. It took several days to visit everyone, so it was like Christmas week for the kids.

I was quiet, thinking about this woman who'd been beaten to death and trying to make that scene mesh with this one. That they were both in the same world on the same day, within an hour of each other, didn't work for me: a blood-soaked, shit-stained woman, beaten to death—and happy children, full of energy, laughing, giggling, and excited for more Christmas.

My wife at the time didn't want to hear about it, about why I needed a moment.

"Keep that horrible work stuff at work; don't bring it here to our home."

So, I just had to carry Aubrey around in silence.

Daywalkers rarely see mutual combat, and it can take the edge off in dealing with some victims, especially when they won't cooperate with police after a wicked bar fight.

One in particular was at a bar known for a lot of bar fights. More than the usual crowd had gathered for this contest, drawing numerous calls to dispatch since the bar was also on the main drag downtown.

I happened to be closest and rolled up first on the scene. The crowd was huge and there was much milling about, and when I pulled in most of them started to run.

A small group at the front waved me over.

A guy had a bar towel wrapped around his face and in a weird shape above his left eye. I asked what had happened, and the owner told me that the guy with the bar towel and another man had been in a fight earlier in the evening, with bar towel guy winning and the loser departing.

At closing time, the guy came back and wanted a rematch, but bar towel guy triumphed again even faster the second time around.

As he turned to walk away, one of the loser's friends jumped him from behind and stabbed him in the head with a "knife sharpener."

All the patrons were Hispanics, and their English wasn't perfect, so I wasn't exactly sure what they meant by "knife sharpener," even after asking several times.

So the guy with the bar towel unwrapped his head.

It turned out that it was actually one of those full-size knife sharpeners; the kind that looks like a metal rod that comes to a point that you run knife blades back and forth across—and it was jammed all the way up to the handle and downward into his left eye socket. The other end was sticking out below his jaw, near his throat.

Medical took him to the hospital, where he lost the eye, but surgery was able to repair the broken left side of his face. Even after all that, he refused to cooperate with our investigation, not giving us anything to go on; however, with so many witnesses, we were able to find out that the altercation was due to a dispute that originated in Mexico.

The two combatants were from rival states which had been in a feud with each other for years, a historical urban warfare. They'd been fighting and killing each other for some perceived slight of honor that had occurred decades ago.

God only knows what was coming next, as the witnesses assured us that the sharpener to the eye socket wasn't the end of it…more continued conflict was yet to come.

FIFTEEN
SKIDMARK

"SKIDMARK" WAS HIS NICKNAME; HIS real name was Skidlaski. That was what we called him when we thought about him—which wasn't much.

It wasn't because he smelled bad (which he did); we just had to consider him because he made our jobs more difficult.

He had zero common sense and no feel for the street.

He was one of those guys who thought he knew more than everyone else and wouldn't listen to anyone.

My first memory of him is of him pulling over a vehicle in a grocery store parking lot so that lots of people could see him. He'd been assigned to my area, so I had to take some calls with him.

It was Christmas Eve, and it's an unwritten rule between us cops that Christmas is hands-off; no bullshit tickets, no arrests unless it's absolutely necessary—and only when there's no other choice. We'd talk about it in briefing with no objections from the sergeants.

So Skidmark pulled over this vehicle and started running the occupants; son-of-a-bitch was digging for warrants—and he'd already violated the rule by stopping them.

I drove past to see that he had this station wagon full of wrapped presents and three scared little kids in the back; as I drove off, Skidmark waved at me as I passed as if he was thanking me for checking on him.

I left this bullshit scene and listened for the outcome of the stop on the radio: the plates on the station wagon had expired, and the mother was driving on an expired license.

Skidmark called for a wrecker and impounded the car with the gifts inside; he actually put the kids and the mom on the street on Christmas Eve. He did at least call someone to come pick them up after giving her a ticket…a regular St. Dick he was.

From that point on, I was done with him.

I cancelled him on every call; I wouldn't work with him.

He had a really fucked up way of seeing the world, which I couldn't understand and didn't want to. I became one of his most outspoken opponents in the department and on the street.

I started to hear from people in the area where we worked about how poorly he treated everyone and how they really didn't like him and couldn't talk to him, which was pretty much unraveling everything the rest of us had worked so damn hard to establish; it was blowing relationships and eroding all the trust that we were trying to build. He was constantly making our jobs harder by being such a horse's ass. He was a real cheese dick.

One night, Skidmark had arrested a guy for drinking beer in one of the city parks. He felt like he was cleaning up the area by arresting everyone for anything he could think of anytime they moved; like I said, he had no feel for the street.

We overlooked a lot of smaller crimes because we needed the cooperation of the residents of the city to land the bigger fish. Maybe you mention the statute of limitations, that we could get the charges filed anytime in the next two or four years, whatever it was; maybe you don't mention it at all if you don't need to.

Inner city dwellers knew about how the criminal justice system worked as well as we did.

Skidmark couldn't grasp this concept, though, and he arrested everyone for even the slightest of violations in order to pump up his stats.

In some misguided attempt to break up cliques in the department, management had come up with a shift bid system where the highest performers on each squad could pick their shift the following year.

They called it the golden squad; we called it the golden shower squad. It didn't work, but it lasted for a long, long time.

New guys like Skidmark saw this as a way to get better shifts without having to pay their dues on the street like all the rest of us had.

He wanted to get off the graveyard shift as soon as possible; I, on the other hand, loved graves, particularly since my latest marriage was coming undone. It allowed me to avoid the wife and spend time with my kids.

On this particular day, Skidmark had arrested this guy for drinking in the park; it was under an obscure ordinance meant to help us keep the parks clear of drunks, not common citizens sharing a few beers while barbecuing.

The guy Skidmark arrested was pissed off, and Skidmark was talking shit to him as he was taking him to his car, telling him what a waste of a human being he was, a pain in Skidmark's fat ass.

He handcuffed him, put him in the car, seat belted him in, and locked the door. He then left to go back to the park to arrest a couple more guys he saw drinking there.

This was really stupid, not to mention a safety problem—a real potential for a cluster; any cop that's worked the streets will tell you that. You don't load up your car with drunks to take to jail just so you can get stats.

Skidmark arrested another guy and brought him back to his car—only to find it empty with the passenger door wide open; the first guy had unlocked the car and run off with his handcuffs.

The cuffs were your personal property back then. We had to buy them, and of course Skidmark always carried a lot of them.

He jumped on the radio, screaming for backup because he had an escaped prisoner. I didn't move; I just listened to the shit storm unfold and shook my head.

Several units looked for the guy for hours but couldn't find him. How impressive is that: shaking people down for details on the guy who stole an officer's cuffs?

I just stayed out of it. I didn't want anyone on the street to see me with this dickhead or associate me with helping him.

He finally gave up and took the rest of his catch to jail, then bitched for days about "that piece of shit who stole my cuffs" and how he'd get even. Gave his pitiful little life direction, I guess.

About a week went by, and I got a call to meet a woman I knew at her home.

When I showed up, she was sitting on the front porch with her son and daughter. She said that she wanted me to hear what her son had to say.

He was just a kid, maybe nineteen or twenty.

I listened, and he told me about how he was arrested and escaped with the officer's handcuffs. It was Skidmark's escaped bad guy!

My reaction wasn't what he expected.

The kid was all tense and edgy, and I think he expected to get hit or take a beating; instead, I started to laugh—and laugh hard!

"Really? That was you?" I asked.

He said that it was, and he recounted how Skidmark—he didn't know it was Skidmark, he called him "Officer Cheesedick" (quite funny, really)—made him angry talking down to him, so after he was left in the car he felt it was his duty to try to escape.

He also described how Skidmark had a distinctive odor and was fat and wheezed.

The kid said, "I felt like a bitch going down without fighting this guy."

I was laughing really hard by now at his descriptions, amazed that it was almost exactly how most of Skidmark's fellow officers felt about him.

However, his mother wasn't happy and didn't see the humor in it; she didn't want her son to feel that this was acceptable behavior. To hell with that.

I explained that "Skidmark" was his nickname and that he was exactly what her son had described—and although I didn't endorse his escape, I did understand it.

She asked, "What are you going to do now?"

I looked at the son and said, "Well, that's up to you. I don't wanna lose my cuffs. If you're gonna run, have at it, man. Go!"

He didn't move.

I told him that if he went with me, he'd go willingly, then gave him my cuffs and told him to put them on. His jaw dropped. He asked if I was serious.

"Yeah, man," I said. "You put them on, then you can show me how you got out of Skidmark's car."

He liked that idea. He was proud of the fact that he'd escaped. He even put them on behind his back.

I took him to the car, buckled him in, locked the door, and said, "Go!"

He was out in fifteen seconds.

I was seriously impressed with his method—which, for obvious reasons, will not be revealed.

I sat there with him and, with his help, figured out a way to defeat his escape. We then laughed and joked, talking and exchanging ideas.

Then I let him tell his mom goodbye, took him to jail, and booked him on the warrant of the escape charge against him. I told him that Skidmark was on duty that night. "He's gonna want to come talk shit to you. The cuffs you took were his favorite set," I said.

The kid said he thought maybe that explained why they smelled kind of odd.

"You don't still have them, do you?" I asked.

He said no, that he'd cut them off and thrown them away.

I called Skidmark on the radio and told him that his escapee had been booked into jail.

He replied that he was on his way to the jail; for him, this was personal. I warned the kid about him being on his way, then left.

Nothing ever came of it. Skidmark continued doing his thing; I just made a point of not working with him.

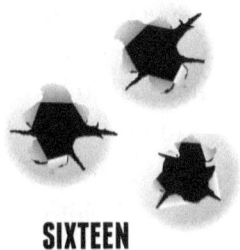

SIXTEEN
TULIPS BY ANY OTHER NAME STILL SMELLED LIKE SHIT

THREE IN THE MORNING IS like some dead zone on patrol.

The bars have emptied out for the most part, and chasing drunk drivers home is pretty much over. The last of the debris from party time in private homes is still stumbling around, hoping not to get caught.

I first ran into this guy during that time.

Someone had walked through the park and thought he was dead, but he wasn't; he was just really drunk. I don't remember his first name, but his last name is Tulips. Seriously! He had the identification to prove it.

I woke him up and ran his identification, which I had to take from his wallet. He was too drunk to answer questions or even talk or get up on his feet; he just sat there mumbling while I ran the identification.

I learned that Mr. Tulips had an outstanding warrant, so I pulled him to his feet and walked him to the jail, which was nearby.

I made a tactical decision that I didn't want to put him in my car; he had an incredible stench of shit, urine, and some foul ass smell I couldn't recognize.

As we searched him at the jail, it turned out he had a colostomy bag. It hadn't leaked or spilled, but he wasn't very careful when he emptied it, and some of the contents had ended up on his clothing; thankfully, this time I was spared the "full blast of the bag." I booked him and left.

The correctional officers, on the other hand, were *not* happy.

They'd dealt with Mr. Tulips before, and they hated handling this guy because of the smell and the fact that he'd lay on the bag when he passed out—causing it to burst.

They also told me, for future reference, that it wasn't wise to call him "Tulips"; he could fly into a rage at hearing the name pronounced as it was written. He preferred a French-sounding pronunciation, and he found "Twallup" more aristocratic. (Never mind that he smelled like shit; in his mind, he was French.)

About three months later, I was called to the downtown park near the jail again.

It was 3 a.m. again, and there was another report of a man possibly dead. The caller said the man looked beat up; he was bleeding from a small head wound and lying in an awkward position, and the caller couldn't tell if he was breathing.

I arrived and found that it was the French Mr. Tulips again. He'd been robbed, his few possessions stolen, and this time his colostomy bag had ruptured. He was covered in shit from head to toe, and in his drunken stupor he'd rolled around in it; it was all pretty disgusting.

I requested medical and advised dispatch of Mr. Tulip's condition—and medical wasn't happy when they arrived; gagging and dry heaving, they treated his injuries while I watched, then they released him back to me.

I walked him to the jail again; he had another warrant for missing the court appearances from his last arrest. He'd also been given community service and hadn't completed it.

The correctional officer was the same guy as the last time, and he also wasn't happy. He put Tulips in a holding cell and hosed him off—literally.

I left, feeling bad for the correctional officer. The French man reeked like no other that night, but he was aware enough for me to test the "Tulips" pronunciation warning.

I pronounced his name as "Tulips" (like the flowers) when I addressed him, and he stopped and looked at me—glaring real rage in his eyes, his shit-soaked hair hanging in his face.

"Don't ever refer to me by that name again," he said.

He was ready to fight, but my curiosity was satisfied, so I backed off immediately and apologized profusely—not wanting to battle a shit-soaked man.

In my mind, a shit-covered man had a lot of liberties. He could say almost anything he wanted, and I'd agree with him; I didn't want to have to touch him—much less fight him. I never saw him again after that.

I did, though, hear Skidmark sign out on him one night.

Tulips was drunk in the park, and Skidmark was hunting his stats again. He was describing the guy being covered in shit and having a colostomy bag.

I came over the radio and told Skidmark that the guy's name was Tulips. I said that he liked to be referred to as "Mr. Tulips" and that if he didn't want the remaining contents of the bag to get all over him, he'd be wise to refer to him as such.

A few moments later, Skidmark was screaming for back up; Tulips was fighting him, and Skidmark was all covered in shit.

I was laughing so hard, I had to pull over.

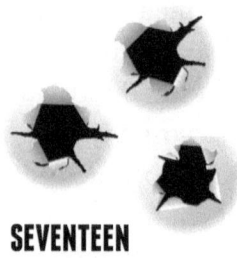

SEVENTEEN
IT CAN MAKE YOU CRAZY

ONE NIGHT, WE WERE SEARCHING for a guy after a domestic was reported.

The caller said a man had beaten a woman, threatened her with a gun, then left.

We caught him running around an industrial area, and the veteran sergeant on duty was summoned since he was known for handling difficult suspects.

They called in Sgt. Kenny Duke (nicknamed the "Mad Monk" for his monk-like appearance) because the suspect was being a complete ass, a real fuck stick.

I then heard him calling for an additional unit, which caught my attention.

The Mad Monk never called for more back up than he needed; he was one of my mentors, and he was great at talking down suspects and rarely involved in scuffles, even though he could take on anyone if he needed to.

Being a power lifter and runner, he was very fit; I once saw him pick up a 185-pound man with one arm and shake him.

Duke was fifty-eight at the time, having turned down a lieutenant's promotion to stay on patrol on graveyards with us.

When I rolled up, they had the ass clown surrounded, and they were trying to talk him into revealing where the gun was.

He was arrested, but no gun had been recovered, and our fear was that he'd dropped it or stashed it somewhere along the way as he fled. There was a reason for our anxiety.

Earlier that summer, some kids had found a gun which had been used by gang members in a drive-by. The gang bangers threw it out of the car after the shooting, and responding units were unable to locate it.

A couple days later, some neighborhood kids found it and thought it was a toy. One of the children had been accidentally shot in the head and killed.

At the moment, this was the biggest concern that the entire shift had. We didn't want kids finding another discarded handgun.

Sgt. Duke gave up trying to talk to the guy; he had this incredibly aggravating demeanor, which immediately set everyone on edge.

Duke waved me over and said, "Slick, can you talk to this guy? You're the calmest of us right now. He's really worked the squad up, and we can't be civil with him. You try to find out where the gun is, and we'll walk away and leave you two alone."

I agreed to try.

The guy was extremely combative, but I eventually calmed him down and tried to get the location of the gun out of him.

He was over-the-top irritating and foul-mouthed. It wasn't his swearing so much as the way he did it; he truly meant it when he said, "Fuck you"—conveying real hatred and animosity.

I thought I would explain why we were so concerned about the gun, thinking it would change his mind; it would have little effect on his prosecution, though, since we had multiple witnesses who would testify to seeing the gun anyway. I explained about the kids and our little guy who'd been accidentally shot in the head and killed.

This cocky ass looked me straight in the eye and said, "I don't give a fuck if some little Spic kid shoots himself in the head. Why the fuck would I care?"

I don't remember much after that—but I do remember seeing red in my vision, like the red filter effect on a camera.

Duke said that I slammed his head hard onto the trunk of the car and broke his nose. He said I slammed it so fast, he could hardly see the guy; he was just a blur. Duke came running, as did the other guys.

I rarely lost it, ever. I was one of the calmest guys on the department; I talked a lot more than most, and if I did fight, it was fast, over quickly, and always started by the other guy.

This guy, though, had gotten to me instantly.

I had him by the hair, ready for face slam number three, and I do remember violently whispering to him to tell me where the gun was or I'd kill his ass.

It was surreal, like I was watching a movie of someone else slamming this guy into the trunk of the patrol car. I was in a rage. Blood was everywhere, and Duke told me to leave.

He then had another guy take the car and wash it while yet another guy took face plant to the hospital to be treated. I never heard a word about this from anyone.

It was funny, though; people treated me differently after this. I was given a lot of room from the people I worked with.

They were just different and seemed almost afraid of me—except for the Mad Monk. He just laughed when he said to me later, "I thought I was just having a bad day—but shit, he got under your skin, too, and fast. I've never seen you mad like that."

Mad not so often, but annoyed plenty of times.

Eventually, I moved over to detectives and another patrolman took over my old area. The guy was something of a rival; I'll call him "Divot" since "Gash" could be misunderstood.

Divot said he'd take over my "shit hole" of an area and "turn it around." This made me laugh; I couldn't wait to see him try.

I was out in my unmarked car one of those very first nights on my new assignment, learning the ropes, when a call came over of shots fired in my old area.

Divot took the call and said he was en route, but he was slow, and as usual I arrived first.

I found a guy lying face down in the driveway of a home with a huge bullet hole in his back, and it was a through-and-through.

He'd also been run over several times and left in the driveway of the home next to a small market. Someone really wanted to make sure he was dead.

I was alone there for some time before I finally called Divot on the radio and asked his location. He replied that he was still at the police station; he was probably "polishing the brass" but would be en route as soon as he could.

I replied that I'd just wait and secure the scene of his homicide for him while he finished his real work at the station house. He finally got off his fat ass and actually showed up.

We exchanged a few words about his ability to turn this shit hole area around with his amazing work ethic, and finally someone separated us.

The victim had been shot with a .44 caliber handgun during an argument with his ex brother-in-law. The ex brother-in-law then backed his car over him in the driveway, stopped and pulled forward, drove over him again, then backed up to run over him one more time before leaving the area.

Patrol units saturated the area looking for witnesses, eventually turning up two people who said that they witnessed the entire thing.

After they watched this guy get blown away right in front of them, then repeatedly run over by a car—they just stepped over the body and went into the nearby store to buy cigarettes. After they bought their smokes, they returned again—stepping over the body on their way home.

They were completely unmoved by the experience of witnessing the murder—and this is the reality of the central city; the people there are harsh and survival-oriented, with violence being a daily event.

Divot cleaned up the scene, and I assisted the homicide detectives assigned to the case.

The owner of the little store came out and demanded that we get the investigation off his property; his parking lot was part of the crime scene, and he felt strongly that we were slowing his business down by being there. It took a threat of going to jail for criminal interference with a public servant to shut him up.

The shooter left the state, and after eventually getting arrested in New Mexico for intoxication and mistakenly released, he entered Mexico. As far as I know, he was never caught.

Your mentality as a cop seriously becomes a lot like combat, like going to war with the walking shit bags that prowl the streets at night, gang rapists, drug dealers, and killers. You learn to own the shit that happens, and you want to make them pay for what they've done; it's yours to own and take responsibility for.

Daywalkers don't realize that.

They see it as a job—but it isn't a job; it's personal.

It's a chess game with these colossal fuckers, and the rules are stacked against you. Things go down right in front of you, and you take out those responsible, taking them right off the street—then they make bail and wave "Hello" the next day. Then it's three months, six months—even years—as their case winds through a courthouse.

Building up like a bomb ready to explode inside of you is the feeling that the courts are against you, the laws are against you—and yet somehow you're supposed to bring the wolves to justice and protect the sheep.

EIGHTEEN
LET'S GO FOR A RIDE

I HAVE MY DARK SIDE, my evil side. We all do; it's just a matter of what will bring it out in us—and watching helpless people being beaten brings it out in me.

I had a recurring domestic in an apartment building in one of the dilapidated parts of town no one cares about. A middle-aged woman named Mary lived in the basement on the right hand side with her boyfriend.

The boyfriend's name escapes me, but what I do remember was that he was a mean drunk.

They both liked to drink, and I think Mary was on Social Security for some type of disability. Basically, he was living off her—so he was impressive almost immediately.

The guy was constantly beating the hell out of Mary, and I'd take him to jail—only for him to get out, come back, and convince her to take him back.

The "Honeymoon" period is a classic pattern. Some try to tell you it's the thin line between love and hate crossing back and forth, and all that passion—but it's bullshit.

It apparently has something to do with testosterone: battered women shelters tend to fill up after the opening weekend of the deer hunt, the day after Super Bowl Sunday, and just after Christmas for good measure.

Some women will take it as long as they can (in some sick way, some honestly like the abuse), especially if the dickhead is the father of her children. He's so good during the honeymoon stretch; the man who beat her self-esteem into splintered bones is the one who then lifts her back up. It's a cycle regular as clockwork.

Mary's guy would be good for about six weeks, and then beat her ass again.

I'm surprised I can't remember his name; we spent so much quality time together. I used to check in on Mary to see how she was, which only angered the shit bag more. He'd get all pissed off and accuse me of getting blowjobs from her when he wasn't around. He was an evil fuck.

After getting a call from her one night, I went by.

Once I arrived, I entered the apartment at her request.

He was drunk and had broken every one of the fingers on her right hand. He did it one at a time, apparently concerned that someone might mistake him for a human being.

"Show him your fucking hand, you bitch!" he yelled at Mary; told you: supreme dickhead, this guy.

She was in tears, wailing kind of quietly, her fingers sticking out in all directions. Even Stephen King didn't think of this for one of his horror movies.

He was strutting around the apartment, acting defiant, talking all kinds of shit, chain smoking, and throwing things around—and I was starting to get crazy angry.

"What happened to her hand?" I asked, thinking about my next move.

He said that she was getting mouthy and that he started "breaking fingers to shut the fucking bitch up." He said it as an answer to me, but he yelled it at her.

I'd had enough.

I cuffed him and started to haul him out of the apartment.

He said, "This again, Slick? ("Slick" is one of my nicknames.) You know that this is a waste of time. I'll do what the fuck I want. That bitch loves me. She can't do without my cock. Trust me, she loves my shit."

I opened the door to my patrol car and slammed his head hard against the doorpost twice as he got in; needless to say, he was stunned.

"Bitch, I will have your fucking job! You're gonna be begging for fucking food when I'm done with you!"

I seat-belted him in the car, then pulled up to the door and told Mary that we were going to jail and that she needed to get her hand looked at. She didn't want me to call for medical because an ambulance ride was too expensive. She said she'd get it looked at as soon as possible and thanked me.

The entire way to jail, he was still talking shit.

I knew I had to find a way to reach this shit bag, or he'd end up killing Mary. The system wasn't working, and he feared nothing...it was time to change that.

I drove past the jail, heading west out of town.

"Hey, fuckface," he said, "you missed the jail; it's back there."

I stared straight ahead and didn't comment for a while until he ran out of steam, making him wonder what the fuck was going on.

Calmly and quietly, I said, "You're right. You *WILL* go back and hurt her again. So, I'm taking you out west. I'm gonna blow your fucking brains out, bitch. Then I'm gonna dig the bullet out of your skull, cut your fucking hands and feet off, and leave you there to fucking rot. I'm taking you to the animal dump to die like the shit bag you are."

Far out on the west side of the county, there was an animal dump where farmers and ranchers disposed of their dead livestock, like cattle, horses, and pigs.

I could tell that he was scared now, but he was trying to stay calm; by the time we got to the dump, though, he was crying, sobbing hysterically.

It was pitch dark, and there were no headlights to tell him that someone would come save him.

When I got him out of the car, I dropped him face down next to a rancid, bloated, rotting cow carcass that had been dumped—and he started sobbing even more hysterically, spitting out the dirt and pieces of decomposing flesh that he'd inhaled when he hit the ground.

Screaming that he was sorry, he promised he'd never do it again and that if I let him live he'd move out and swore I'd never see him again.

I let him beg and plead, smelling the shit and the dead animals rotting around him; I liked seeing him in fear for once.

I got out a sharp knife that I kept in my trunk and made sure that he saw it, then laid out a tarp and gloves next to him.

I also had some duct tape and needle-nose pliers; I really had no use for the tape, but the effect was brutal cool. I kept at my preparations quietly, and by that time he was making little whimpering sounds while saying "please...please," sort of gurgling over and over.

"See...you can be polite," I said.

I put on the gloves, picked up the knife, and stood in front of him for a minute; he actually started shaking.

"Well, that should about do it. Say goodbye, fuckhead," I said, then put my gun to the back of his head.

He was kneeling and kept repeating, "Please give me another chance" and "I'll never bother her again" over and over.

"Why should I believe your punk ass, bitch?"

"Because I mean it this time," he answered. "I mean it. I see that you're serious. I won't go back and touch her—I swear."

"Pinky swear?" I said, smirking.

Crazy? Maybe.

With that, he toppled over sideways, sobbing and shaking like he was having a seizure; he was almost epileptic, thrashing in the mud and shit and rotting entrails.

I picked him up, slammed him against my car, and grabbed him by the throat. "If I let you live, I'll never see you again, right? Because if I do—it's on, motherfucker. No one will ever find you...*ever*. You don't have to do anything to her; all you have to do is show up and let me see you—and I will fucking *end* you. Do you get that?"

He said that he did.

Suddenly falling quiet, his eyes started blinking wildly, darting about in shock; he thought I was going to kill him and that his life had ended.

After cleaning him up a bit, I put him in my car, then drove him to the jail and booked him. I never saw him again.

For some time after that, I checked on Mary almost daily.

One day, she said that he came back and got his stuff from the apartment. He told her he was sorry, really sorry, and that he was leaving. He was wrong for hurting her, and maybe he wasn't the right guy for her. He said that he had to leave and that he couldn't stay. She said he was acting really terrified, jumpy as hell and looking out the windows, and that he left right away.

She smiled at me and said she didn't know what I'd done, but he couldn't get out of there fast enough. She moved out of my area a short time later.

I kept in touch with her enough to know that she was living a much happier life after this guy had his epiphany...being a brutal, psychotic bastard works sometimes.

NINETEEN
SOME NIGHTS WERE DIFFERENT

WHO SAYS COPS DON'T HAVE any fun?

One night, I arrested a guy for public intoxication. I'd been dealing with him on a regular basis: he would pass out on people's porches and in their front yards, then I'd get a call from freaked out homeowners about the drunken stranger on the porch or in their lawn chair, and I'd take him to jail to sober up.

However, this particular night I thought I'd have some fun tormenting him in his inebriated state: he was falling down drunk, so I put him in my car, then proceeded to drive backwards to the jail.

It was one of those late nights/early mornings when the only people on the streets were newspaper carriers and cops.

At first, he didn't pick up on it; then he realized something was very wrong but that it was probably in his own head.

I continued to play it off like we were going forward, talking to him like nothing was wrong.

I drove with my mirrors and kept looking forward as much as possible—and the illusion worked.

"I really got to quit drinking," he kept saying.

After about a mile, he closed his eyes and told me, "Officer, I know that you said we're going forward, but I swear to you it looks like we're going backward."

It was probably one of the few times someone was glad to arrive at the county jail.

Later that night, my sergeant asked me quite calmly why I was driving backwards through the central city.

"Man, I'm glad you never picked me up drunk," he said.

I never saw my serial drunk again. I don't know if he quit drinking, but I like to think that maybe he did.

Some officers are just lightning rods for cops' twisted sense of humor, and Sgt. Gus was one of those targets.

We'd just finished a big case, an ambush just outside the mall downtown. One gang had crept up on another and emptied a handgun into their car while they were trapped in traffic, waiting for a stoplight; two in the car were wounded.

The attack happened in broad daylight, so we had to solve it fast. In less than twenty-four hours, the suspects were in custody, locked up with enough evidence that we didn't even need to try for confessions.

Gus was debriefing us, making sure he had all the details of the shoot and the arrests before he called the duty lieutenant whose shift had just ended a little earlier.

The duty lieutenant, or watch commander, had to be brought up to speed in case the media called, as lieutenants are the only officers authorized to give public statements.

Gus thought of himself as an efficiency expert.

He had all kinds of phone lists miniaturized and laminated in his wallet, and he'd pull one out and show it to us, making sure we saw how efficient he was. (He wrote with excellent grammar and lovely penmanship.)

We rolled our eyes and waited for him to finish showing off his little wallet cards. In light of all this, we figured he could make the call, using the numbers on his little lists.

This is where he really blew it badly.

Gus and the Chief were always at odds—and definitely not friends.

Gus had applied for the Chief's position when it had opened up some eight months earlier, competing with the man who was now his boss. On top of all that, they'd already been adversaries in the department for years.

Gus thought of himself as an intellectual cop, while the Chief saw himself as a military man by way of his Army reserve experience. They couldn't have been more opposite in their outlook and approach to police work, as well as life in general.

The Chief hated Gus, who was overweight and a prankster, never serious, and always joking. He even moonlighted as a comedian at a local comedy club. The Chief, however, almost never laughed—ever.

So Gus calls who he thinks is the duty lieutenant (who has the same first name as the chief) and starts his usual joking and talking shit.

He starts saying he's surprised that James is asleep already, then goes on about how James is no doubt tired from banging his new girlfriend, asking if she's as hot as she appears to be. He then makes comments about how he imagines she performs in the sack; she was a dispatcher who we all knew to be a bit wild.

So he continued to ramp it up, still not realizing that it was Chief James he was talking to.

He even told him, "At least you're not at home with a ball gag in your mouth, taking it up the ass like the chief...his wife runs him *and* their house."

Gus actually started picking up speed then, noting, "Mrs. Chief probably keeps a strap-on in the drawer by the bed, and no lubricant—just like the chief likes it."

He started laughing his ass off at the picture he was painting for Lieutenant James, believing it all quite funny—when all of a sudden he stopped and his demeanor suddenly changed.

He instantly sat up straight as a rail and said, "Yes, Sir," then "Yes, Sir" again, giving a quick brief of the shoot and apologizing profusely "for any inconvenience."

Gus then hung up (looking like he was about to hurl), put his head down on the desk, and said, "Oh shit...I am so fucked...oh God...I am so fucked."

He was always pulling pranks, so we just thought he was messing with us. We weren't buying his act, so he stood up and screamed at us, saying, "This isn't fucking funny! I'm serious."

Still not believing him, we asked what had happened.

He slowly, painfully said that he'd mistakenly called Chief James instead of Lieutenant James.

We all looked at each other in shock, thinking about what he'd said in that conversation—then we all burst out laughing. We laughed so hard, some of us grabbed trashcans while others dry heaved, coughing, choking, and trying to breathe.

Gus stormed out of the office, leaving us there with tears streaming down our faces. He and the Chief had many fun times together, but none of them quite got Gus fired.

Six months later, for instance, Gus and the Chief had another warm exchange.

Gus was having an affair. He'd been married for some time and loved his wife, but he had this low self-esteem to deal with.

He had a part-time job at a local department store, working as their security chief. One of the girls there liked his sense of humor and was going through a divorce, and she made it clear to him that she was up for whatever he had in mind. This was a first for Gus; he was really overweight and dumpy looking, so he ran with it.

One day he took her to a city park, a popular one with a large pond that drew in lots of geese and ducks, as well as a large parking lot that drew in a lot of thieves.

Gus didn't know that the major crimes division had staked out the parking lot for a series of car burglaries and that they were currently running surveillance with cameras.

So here came Gus, skipping and jumping over rocks in full frolic while carrying the picnic basket he'd packed for his lady love on the down low.

The major crimes detectives were working hard, catching every moment, kiss, butt fondle, and tit grab, and when they finished they packed up and left—but not before dropping a note on Gus' car (unsigned, of course) about the fine pictures they had of him and the girl...cop humor is brutal.

Gus was beside himself. He didn't know what to do or who had taken the questionable pictures.

The state police academy had been known to pull an officer's certification over extramarital affairs; it was an urge that came and went arbitrarily based on politics, so you never knew what could happen.

Gus fell back on the engrained experience of confessing and explaining his actions—but who was he to confess to?

He decided that he should confess to Chief James since he believed the Chief had the department detectives conduct surveillance of him for his illicit affair, and he did just that, requesting a meeting with the chief and the assistant chiefs (his need for penance was just that strong).

He went into great detail, telling them everything—including every time he met with the girl and everything they did—confessing that he knew how wrong it was but that he couldn't help himself.

I heard that the chief was in shock and asked Gus why he was telling them all this, to which Gus replied by outlining the picnic and the note left on his car; he felt sure that the chief had ordered the surveillance, and he wanted to come clean about everything.

The chief called him a fool, saying he couldn't care less about his affair. He then told him that he knew nothing about it until Gus turned himself in, then ordered him the hell out of his office.

I was walking past as Gus departed the chief's presence; he had the same "I am so fucked" look on his face as he had the night that he made the accidental phone call to the chief.

I later found out why and made sure that all the guys in the unit heard about it, after which we left him little picnic baskets with notes attached on his desk every now and then. He didn't think it was funny—but we did.

A few months later, Gus got me back in short order.

He'd fallen down a rickety flight of stairs during a bust of a dope house, and he needed a little patching up at the hospital.

In his report on his injuries for the case file, he wrote only one sentence: "Officer Fortier pushed me down the stairs."

I had some awkward moments detailing that one for the lieutenants, trying to prove a negative before Gus updated his report a few days later. I didn't think it was funny—but he did.

Sgt. Kenny Duke was the master of the deadpan delivery.

He was nicknamed "The Mad Monk" for his appearance and quiet demeanor—that is, until you pissed him off...then, "The Mad Monk" came out.

One night in midnight briefing, Kenny said that for years when the phone would ring and his wife answered, he'd break out in a sweat, wondering if it was a girlfriend calling who had somehow obtained his home number. He'd wait, listening to the tone of her voice, awaiting any clue that he might have to leave or prepare to defend himself in case she came for him.

His wife was a volatile woman, prone to scream and rant—but that was part of what he liked about her. That really hit me: stone-cold Kenny Duke sweating at the sound of a phone ringing.

He said one night he came home and had no early warning.

After thinking that he was out all night "womanizing," his wife was waiting for him with his service revolver. She shot at him six times, emptying the gun; she tried to kill him.

In that straight-faced delivery of his, Kenny said it instantly occurred to him that he was really glad he hadn't taught her how to shoot.

It also occurred to him that he might want to move out or at least store his gun where she couldn't get at it.

He said he wasn't entirely sure that she hadn't hit him, so he checked his chest and legs, feeling for blood. All six shots came in a small room at point blank range, but somehow she'd missed. He said he took her a little more seriously after that.

It was all in his delivery.

We couldn't help laughing, imagining Sgt. Duke dodging bullets while trying to reason with a crazed wife.

That story really struck a nerve with us, probably because we'd all been there at some point—and most of us were still living that nightmare to one degree or another.

TWENTY
OUTRANKED

SGT. LEEDS WAS ALWAYS TALKING about his quest for a spirit animal guide.

While waiting for the owner of a building we'd cleared to show up and turn off the alarm, Leeds started telling us this story.

He'd been reading Indian lore on how to go about getting a spirit animal guide; he wanted to commune with the spirit world to get out there and mingle with the dead.

As he spoke, emotion made his voice crack a little.

He said he needed guidance from something "appropriately carnivorous"; after all, he was a warrior. He was also concerned that it was taking so long for this spirit animal to reveal itself to him.

Setting up his primitive camp alone, he'd actually sit in the mountains east of where we were for days at a time, squatting out in the elements, dressed in his buckskins and moccasins with warrior paint on his face, fasting, chanting, and beating on a drum.

He told his wife he was off camping so she'd think he just needed to get away; little did she know, he was a crazed, drooling, wannabe shaman.

So far, there was nothing. No sign; not even a curious coyote offering a fish or the wind in his hair, whispering ancient messages. Hell, even a tap on the shoulder would've been nice.

His Irish-Catholic roots hadn't done it for him: there was no animal soul included in that particular map to spiritual fulfillment.

He really worried about his spirit guide not being an "appropriate" animal; he thought himself too manly to accept a docile animal, such as a ground squirrel.

Just then, the owner of the building showed up.

It turned out to be just a routine false alarm; we'd checked the building, and the alarm had proven unfounded.

"Who wants the wisdom of a ground squirrel?" said the sergeant as he got back into his car, leaving us to clear the call. "I'm hoping for a bear or a wolf, maybe an eagle."

We just stared as he drove off; shit-faced drunks we caught pissing in the park didn't talk this crazy shit.

He was bat shit crazy, like the night he matched testosterone levels with a group of "pee wee" gang bangers just getting into the life.

He and some of the patrolmen (his "followers," as we called them) had a group of the youngsters cornered in an elementary school parking lot. I'd heard them all sign out at the same time, so I knew something was up.

When I got there, Leeds was standing in the middle of the group of 11- and 12-year-olds.

It was late at night, and he'd thrown down his spare nightstick and dared each member of the group to pick it up and fight him.

The kids on the street aren't that naïve; you don't survive on the street being that stupid.

The reality was, Leeds was a nightstick instructor and also trained in martial arts, so any fight with an adult would've been no contest—let alone a kid. None of the bangers went for it, so Leeds called them cowards and "limp dicks," then stomped off.

It was a set-up: not only would they have gotten their asses kicked, but he'd also have cause to arrest them since threatening someone with a weapon is actually something we arrest people for all the time.

I'd asked around about Leeds and found out that he was connected at the hip with one of the assistant chiefs. They were allies who worked together to further their careers at the expense of others, partnering in many internal investigations and manipulating the facts in ways to target officers they just didn't like who didn't have the sense to play along with the prevailing winds.

Most people were reluctant to talk about him, but I did hear from one lieutenant who'd been on an awards evaluation committee.

In a situation with a man with a gun, the guy had drawn down on Leeds, catching him off guard. The suspect pulled the trigger, but it hadn't gone off. Leeds thumped the hell out of him, and submitted himself for a Medal of Valor.

The first go-round, the medal was refused.

The awards committee felt that he shouldn't be awarded for making a mistake that almost got him shot: Leeds had bullied the guy—as was his style—instead of using accepted arrest control techniques.

After Leeds went to the Chief and complained that he'd actually been quite heroic and deserved some recognition, the Chief asked the committee to find some way of recognizing him.

Eventually, the committee ended up giving Leeds the lesser Medal of Merit.

The officer who told me about it resigned from the committee; he felt it was a slap in the face of the officers who'd actually earned their medals. This kind of shit went on in the department all the time.

In another incident, two young kids were walking down the street at 2 a.m., carrying stereo speakers. It was only late spring, and gang activity had started up early with car prowls, thefts, fights, and shootings. With tension already up, the department was bracing for a long summer, so we checked it out.

I arrived at the same time that Leeds rolled up and I started talking to one of the kids while he had the other.

Then Leeds said to me, "I'm tired of this fucking shit. These little fucking Mexicans are gonna learn a lesson tonight."

"What the hell are you talking about?" I said. "They're walking with stereo speakers. You don't know if these are stolen—and if they are, from where."

"Fuck that. I'm tired of this shit. These spics are controlling the streets, and it's time we did something about it."

He took his kid behind his patrol car and cuffed him, then started kicking the hell out of him. I could hear the kid crying, obviously getting hurt, so I cuffed my guy, put him in my car, and told him not to try to get out—no matter what.

I then locked the car as Leeds started coming for him.

"Get that spic out of your car," he barked.

I said "No, it's not gonna happen; he stays where he is."

Leeds started pounding on my car, pulling on the door handles and screaming at me to open it up.

I responded by saying, "That was pretty impressive how you kicked that little kid's ass after you handcuffed him. I didn't realize you were so afraid of Mexicans."

Leeds whirled around, his attention on me now, and we shared a few quiet moments as other cars (not necessarily his followers) were rolling up on the scene.

I was able to explain clearly that he shouldn't do anything like that in front of me again.

I said, "I'm not to be trusted if you and your redneck fuck friends are gonna fuck up little Mexican kids. Are there any questions? Make sure the word gets out, dickhead." Then I left.

Leeds got his guy charged with resisting arrest.

I took mine to his home and dropped him off, bearing new tales of some white cops that are crazy—but maybe not all of them.

I'd heard that he'd done that a lot, earning a reputation on the street for bullying Hispanics. He hated Mexicans, even if they were Nicaraguan, Cuban, Dominican, or Guatemalan—it didn't fucking matter to him.

The reality was, if too many witnesses were around, he'd just yell; if no witnesses were around, he'd slap them around, then take out the stick and beat on them.

Another night, Leeds was screaming on the radio for back up; his tendency toward beating Mexicans was coming back around to bite him in the ass.

He'd gone in on a bar check alone, which was unheard of. On top of that, it was a Hispanic bar where his reputation for racism had preceded him.

Now was the time for payback, and they were kicking the hell out of him.

They'd locked the doors of the bar, and he was on the radio saying that the whole bar was against him and that he was fighting his way to the door.

I was a little surprised at the lack of responses from officers saying that they were en route—including me; maybe I wasn't the only one tired of his stupid shit.

When I did get there, he came flying out the door, his hair messed up and shirt torn; the dickweed had survived somehow, and he started trying to get back inside once he saw that other cars had finally rolled up...too bad the bar occupants had locked the door.

Leeds then put on the radio that he wanted officers to go to the back door to keep them all inside the bar.

With their revenge taken, the bar patrons wisely knew they had to depart since they'd just gone the rounds with a uniformed sergeant—and they all somehow made it out that back door.

Leeds came around back, and he was pissed that we hadn't "kept all those greasy fucking spics in the bar so I could kick every one of their asses."

I asked him how come the whole bar had decided to kick his ass? I knew why, but I just wanted to hear what he had to say.

He said that when he went in, some guy was staring at him. No one would speak English, so he just knew they were planning something. He walked up to a guy staring at him and asked what his problem was.

The guy said, "No hablo ingles," then Leeds called him a spic and flipped the cowboy hat off his head. (Seriously, this was the stupid kind of shit he did.) The guy got pissed off, and the fight was on with the whole bar.

Leeds was a high maintenance sergeant; he needed constant and immediate attention.

Another night, he was again screaming for back up on the radio, again surrounded by Mexicans—this time in cars and trucks.

He demanded that every single unit drop what they were doing and come to his aid, so we hauled ass, what with it sounding like real danger.

Instead of finding him circled by gang bangers in some kind of combat formation, though, we found this: he'd pulled over a CB radio fan, part of a club of CBrs. Mostly misfits and bored white guys, they drove around all night and talked on their CBs to each other, playing a game they called "skunk."

Basically, it's Hide N' Seek in the city with cars, trucks, and CB radios: you describe where you are, and the rest of the group tries to find you.

Leeds had pulled over the Mexican-looking lead car that was hiding from the rest, then slowly, one-by-one, the other vehicles in the game had showed up at the scene with their engines idling and headlights on until about a dozen of them had Leeds surrounded and terrified.

We laughed—and hard—before getting around to explaining it to him.

He then said, "Fuck you" and drove off.

Who could believe that Leeds, a sergeant, didn't know about these guys?

I actually reported a lot of Leeds' little tics to prosecutors, then left it in their hands; I told them I couldn't be expected to testify, then work on the street with Leeds and his minions.

They said it was all kept confidential and that they'd go after him—but they never did.

A few days later, Leeds confronted me all by himself—and threatened to beat the shit out of me; he said he knew that I'd been to the prosecutors. He said that the "muscle stuff" with the Mexicans was to prove a point, to take a stand, and that if I didn't understand that then maybe I shouldn't be a cop.

Bullshit.

I told him he was out of control and had lost his perspective, which made it harder for the rest of us to do our jobs.

He disagreed and threatened again to beat hell out of me. I told him to bring it but that we both knew he was wrong. It was pretty heated.

Ultimately, he called me a pussy and stormed off, saying I should take a closer look at where I was headed.

What I learned from that little episode was that I couldn't trust the prosecutors. I was starting to feel really alone.

At one point a year or so later, Leeds actually stood up in front of briefing and apologized to the whole shift for the way he'd been acting the past few years, saying, "For a time, I lost my mind." He said he was better now and that he hoped we could all move on and work together.

This was a rare moment—but it only lasted for about a day; after that, Leeds found his mind again, so it didn't make that much of a difference in his behavior. It was most likely just a moment of supposed leadership, something the brass could check off.

I never taught at the police academy; I didn't think I'd be one of the guys they'd want the new recruits to meet. I was damaged and edgy, really fucked up, and I don't think they'd want the new people to see what the potential was in this job for totally messing with your head.

Leeds, however, would teach at the police academy.

Years later, when I was finally out of law enforcement, a young co-worker who was trying to get into police work excitedly began telling me about his academy classes when he found out I was an ex-cop.

He told me about one instructor whom I immediately recognized as Leeds. When I told him I knew Leeds, he began talking about the cases that Leeds would talk about, cases he handled both on patrol and as a detective, and how he learned over the years to talk to people to earn their trust.

I couldn't believe it; the bitch was recounting *my* cases as his cases. I guess night-sticking Mexicans didn't make it in to the curriculum.

I never did take the sergeant's exam.

I saw what they could become. There was something about getting anointed as an uber-cop and put in charge of others; maybe the extra spotlight, I don't know.

They start jostling for position to take the next step up, the next step away from being a real cop: making lieutenant.

Almost always, guys like Leeds got promoted to lieutenant. Don't even worry about it: placed in charge of an entire shift of officers—four, five, and six squads, plus sergeants—evaluating everyone's performance...I didn't want to be associated with those guys.

TWENTY-ONE
NOT KNOWING YOUR PLACE MEANS LIFE OR DEATH

ONE NIGHT, FOUR SEASONED GANGBANGERS were patrolling the main boulevard that marked the unofficial edge of wealthy suburbia. They were calm, looking for innocents to fuck with.

They were also too far above the part of town where gang members could walk at 2 a.m. without suspicion.

They'd hooted, luridly hissed, and made sexual remarks at a group of girls coming out of a convenience store. The girls then ran to their boyfriends and reported what had happened, and the boyfriends immediately went driving off in search of the bangers.

When they approached them, the gangbangers were still walking confidently along the boulevard.

Whatever the overconfident college boys said, it wasn't enough to intimidate the high school aged bangers, who startled them with their reaction: veterans of many gang fights, they spread out laterally as if they'd drilled for it, then approached in step—still calm—across the boulevard toward the college guys.

The largest of the four pulled out a knife; they were all gangbangers and young teens, but they were still gangsters, already veterans of the street, living up to an unwritten code.

It was the four suburban boyfriends in their early twenties who fled, piling back into their Volkswagen.

The large banger with the knife approached the driver's side window and flashed his knife inside, sinking it deep into the driver's chest.

The Volkswagen pulled forward, slowly at first, then lurched and bucked as the dying driver lost his life.

No one could remember a murder above the upscale foothill boulevard; "Probably never" was the general consensus.

Suddenly, though, the clean-living and wealthy were set upon by no doubt drug-addicted gang bangers who'd forgotten their place.

The incident got a lot of attention, and as Lead Detective, Skidmark had actually hustled his worthless ass and picked up three of the four assailants fairly quickly.

A couple months had passed, and Lt. Leeds was in his office, yelling at Skidmark. Both sworn enemies of mine, they were talking anxiously about Skidmark's idea for nabbing the fourth guy, the big guy who had the knife.

Leeds, Skidmark, and I had clashed regularly back when we were all in patrol.

Leeds had since been promoted from a sergeant to the lieutenant's spot and assigned to the Major Crimes Unit, which solved murders, and Skidmark was now one of his lead detectives.

I had been in the gang unit for a while, but even though this was a gang-involved crime, Major Crimes claimed it.

Skidmark's idea was actually a good one.

It was logical, it made sense, and it was painfully obvious: given the unit's expertise and regular dealings with these guys, he suggested coordinating with one of the gang detectives—in particular, he suggested me.

The gang unit had been a joke when it first formed up, not acting much differently than any other patrol squad.

A few of us, though, had transformed it with a different approach: instead of trying to beat hell out of every gangbanger we identified, we built a database, organized the names by groups, and got to know them by developing intelligence files.

We were exploring new ground by utilizing the tendency of rival gangs to quietly rat each other out to police when motivated and given the opportunity.

No one was supposed to talk to us, but they all did, and we'd collected thousands of names.

Skidmark told Leeds that he'd talked to everyone he knew, asking them all for help.

He'd also interrogated the hell out of every gangster in the city, but he couldn't find the last guy involved in the murder, the one who was the actual killer and had the most to lose. He'd gone deep.

I'd just dropped by the detective division to talk to the few people I still got along with and was just leaving as I passed Leeds' door and caught wind of what the two of them were talking about.

"You know I don't want to ask him for help, but if we're gonna get this last guy, we have to try."

"I don't fucking like this; you know what I think of that guy," Leeds growled. "He's not a team player. He's not...well, you know how he is. You of all people know. He's not one of us; not one of us at all. If you get any information from him, you keep it quiet. We can solve our own cases. This is bullshit. He won't find him anyway, and if he does you don't tell anyone he helped you. Do you understand me?"

He was yelling at that point, telling Skidmark to go ahead with his idea.

Leaning against the wall a few feet down the hall from Leeds' office, I was smiling when Skidmark came out; when he saw me, his shoulders dropped.

With all that I'd just heard, I couldn't help thinking of that line from an old zombie horror movie. I forget the name, but the zombies were prone to chanting in unison, "One of us...one of us..."

Skidmark called me at home that night.

He said he knew I'd overheard the conversation in Leeds' office, and he needed my help.

He then told me what he knew about the fourth man, specifically which gang he belonged to and the guy's nickname, "Joker."

"Do you know him?" he asked.

"Of course, I fucking know him," I said. *Don't insult me; I've already reached my limit with you.*

Then he asked me to give him information on my informants.

I laughed. There was no way that was going to happen.

It didn't immediately occur to me that I might have to explain the whole concept of confidentiality to Skidmark; nevertheless, I said I had an understanding with my informants and that I never disclosed who gave me information—no matter what.

A gangster's own homeboys would beat his ass if they knew he even *looked* at a police officer—so if the rival gang got wind of him providing intelligence, he was dead.

I made it clear that no one—not Skidmark, Leeds, the Chief—no one would ever get that information, *ever*.

After a long pause, he said, "OK."

I told him if he wanted my help, I'd ask around, and if I got any information on Joker I'd call him. For his part, he had to guarantee that no matter what time of day or night I called, he would come; if he couldn't make that promise, then I wouldn't help him. He agreed.

He then said that he could pay my informants if they produced. I told him they all worked for free, but if he wanted to give me money to pass along I'd do it after the fact. He wasn't comfortable with this, but he agreed. He wanted control; too fucking bad.

I called an informant who I knew would know about Joker's gang and asked where he'd been and if he was still in the city. The guy asked why I wanted to know.

He hadn't heard, so I filled him in on the details of the murder—quick to add that the police department's finest couldn't locate Joker anywhere and "needed the help of two fucked up, wannabe thugs like us to get this dude." I knew he'd like that. He laughed, and we exchanged insults on which of us really was the wannabe.

I knew he'd ask around and see what he could find out. He loved this shit, acting like an undercover cop; he was thrilled by the chance to make a difference in his town and outperform some of the more abusive cops when it came to hunting down bad guys.

He didn't like Leeds or Skidmark, and he knew Joker had fucked up.

I told him to call anytime, day or night (our standard practice). He knew I'd never give him up; when I asked for a favor, it was always big.

Two days later, at 10:30 p.m., I got the call.

Joker was at an apartment building in the inner city just a block up from Main Street, one of those apartments clustered for partying and affordable housing for parolees, gangbangers, and shitbags of the night. I got the address and called Skidmark.

He was reluctant. It was late, and he was tired.

I unloaded. "Look, motherfucker, if you want this dude, he's there now. I'm on my way, and this isn't even my fucking case. Get off your fucking ass and get in here, or I'll arrest him myself and let Leeds know you had a shot and didn't take it."

After hearing that, Skidmark said he was on his way.

When he arrived, we coordinated deployment.

He wanted the front, and I was supposed to go around to the back.

In typical Skidmark standard operating procedure, he was trying to bully his way in the front door with a patrol unit behind him.

We were working without warrants, and he needed to apply some finesse—but he didn't have any.

I was in the back, listening to his bullshit game and thinking to myself that some people will never learn.

Suddenly, the back door opened—and there was Joker.

He stepped out of the apartment and slowly walked down the stairs, all stealth and silent. Hidden in the shadows with my gun pointed at his head, I spoke up.

"'Sup, Joker."

He turned to me and said, "'Sup Pacman."

Another one of my nicknames.

"Not a thing," I said. "Just out to get some air."

"Ya, it's nice out tonight."

"So, what's it gonna be? You tired of running? We gonna fight, or do we do this like men?"

"Ya, I'm tired of running."

I had him turn around, then I cuffed him.

No disrespect; it was over.

I told him, "Skidmark is up front, and you gave him a run for his money. In the end, the motherfucker had to come to me to find you, so you keep your head up. You didn't go down like a bitch, alright?"

"Thanks, man," he said.

We went to the front of the apartment where Skidmark was still trying to bully his way in, and I handed Joker over to him.

He said thanks to me, then immediately started in on Joker about what a piece of shit he was.

I went home and called my informant. He had a perfect record for finds and information, and I gave him the play-by-play on what had happened. I also mentioned that he might get some money this time and asked if he was interested. He said that he was, so I passed a couple hundred bucks along to him.

For some time after that, I thought I might have to testify. To make matters worse, Leeds and Skidmark wouldn't even look at me if we passed in the hallway.

Joker's family hired a lawyer who played the media like a flute, promising to bring Joker's twisted background out at trial. He was underprivileged, unemployed, and even likely had brain damage from early drug use and unhealthy gang influences…Christ, he was only seventeen.

When the family ran out of money, the attorney just pled him in. Didn't even bring any of that stupid shit up at sentencing; just pled him in. Just the lawyer's standard "I'll submit it, Your Honor" when the judge asked if the defense had any statement to assist the court.

The fact that I was the officer who found and arrested Joker for murder was never made public.

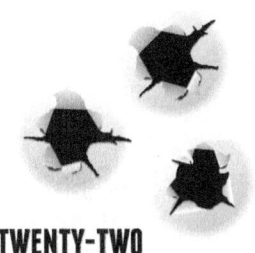

TWENTY-TWO

LISTENING...A LOST ART

WORKING THE WORST AREA OF the largest city has had effects on me that I'm still just finding out about.

One day I was on the street, talking with a woman from central city, the oldest part of town with the lowest rents and highest number of parolees, ex-cons, and mental subjects.

She said that the residents saw us as too afraid to get out of our patrol cars, afraid to get out and face what the city had become. We didn't walk it, live it, and breathe it like they did.

I thought she was joking, messing with me maybe.

I left the call I was on and thought about it as I drove around in the car and listened to the radio.

I watched the people as I passed by, hearing dispatch describe the usual horrific details of life in the boiled-down, foreign language of the 10-code.

I stopped and talked to an older guy I knew who'd lived in the area a long time, asking him what he thought. Did people see us as afraid?

"Yep," he said. "You guys do seem afraid, driving around, never getting out of your cars, never talking to folks, yep, it does look that way."

I made up my mind then and there that I'd get out and walk as much as I could. Never again would I leave a call to do paperwork and not return.

I made it a point to write my paperwork at the scene and get out of the car on slow nights or early in the morning and walk, look around, and listen.

The world was different on foot; screams, gunshots, and blood trails appeared out of nowhere on the sidewalk, then disappeared just as well. The whole feel of the city was different on foot.

As a field-training officer, I made my trainees get out as well.

There was one guy that I really liked; we hit it off immediately. He was quiet, thoughtful, and listened to people—and yet he could be hard and tough as nails; one didn't cancel out the other.

Working the central city one quiet Friday morning, maybe 3 a.m., I pulled over and told him to get out and walk.

At first, he looked at me like I was crazy and just shook his head no. Then I shut off the engine and got out, and he followed.

I said, "I mean it; we're gonna walk."

He rolled his eyes but walked beside me.

I told him the story of the woman and what she'd said to me, as well as the old man's comments. I then told him that I never felt afraid but that if people thought we were afraid, we'd lost their respect.

The further away from the car we walked, the more jumpy he became, looking behind us as we walked. Every scream and gunshot made him hop, but I just kept walking and talking to him.

When we were several blocks from the car, I stopped and turned to him and said, "You're afraid, aren't you?"

He said he felt vulnerable; he was away from the car, which was his security with its mobility and communication. He felt safer by the car.

"Look at it from their point of view, the people we work for, the people who live here," I said. "You've got forty-five rounds of ammo, a bulletproof vest, a night stick, pepper spray, and training. You get on the radio, and you have back up in seconds. Is that right?"

"Sure," he said.

I continued, "What do they have? The women, kids, and old people who live in this area? They have nothing like that. They have you and me. They depend on us to be there for them."

He got a strange look on his face; I could see that I'd reached him.

"You may be afraid, but you have to walk this area, any area you get. You can't let your fear make *them* live in fear. Get out and walk and listen to your area. Listen for how it's supposed to sound, and when it doesn't, talk to people. See what's going on in the neighborhoods you patrol."

I can get preachy like that, rambling sometimes, so just to lighten the message I added, "Don't feel like you have to put your ear to the sidewalk. Listening is just a big part of this job; it can make it much easier."

We started to walk again. Still visibly nervous, he was much more relaxed at that point, understanding that he was setting an example.

A block later, we came across a huge pool of blood.

It was relatively fresh on the sidewalk, and a trail led away from it. It didn't really go anywhere, eventually disappearing in the grass of a vacant lot.

"You see, this is what the people on the street see, what they live in. We never would have found this if we hadn't gotten out and walked."

We never did find out what the pool of blood was about or who its owner was.

I checked the area, then the local hospitals, but no one had come in either injured, stabbed, or shot. Whoever it was had lost a lot of blood; nevertheless, I'd impacted my trainee.

After he was out on his own, complete with a patrol car and bloody streets to monitor, I heard him frequently sign out in his area and go it on foot. I don't know if anyone else thought it mattered or not, but it did to me.

You can't expect people to walk the streets if armed Cops won't.

Later, while working in central city again (as was usual those days), I had another trainee with me.

His name was Jeff McKell, and he was actually a reservist, not yet a certified peace officer hired and sworn. He asked to ride with me, and after a few hours he said to me, "You don't work like anyone else I've ridden with."

We heard a call come over about a large male breaking into an apartment a few blocks away. He'd beaten the occupants pretty badly, then left on foot, running.

Manu Rio had been active in the street gangs there, but he'd left town a few years earlier when his gang had fallen apart, taken over by a rival gang. Rio had a girl in the city and had missed her a lot.

Finally, he had enough and came back to visit, riding the bus from several states over.

When he got there, there she was in her apartment—having sex with some other dude.

He was devastated.

He kicked the guy's ass and beat her up pretty badly, and we came across him on foot some four blocks west of the chaos he'd just left behind.

Manu was a huge man, maybe 6-foot-4, and he was built like a linebacker and mean as hell. He had a reputation on the street as a brawler, particularly a guy who liked to fight cops.

I got out and approached him—and he squared off with me right away, assuming a fighting stance; he was covered with sweat, all warmed up and ready to go.

I could see that he was exhausted and visibly devastated, so I started to try to talk him down; it was obvious that he didn't want to fight if he didn't have to.

I started to talk to him quietly, then just listened to get him talking.

He told me about his girl and the long drive he'd just made, thinking about how much he missed her. They had a baby together, and he wanted to be a man and be the baby's father. He went on and on, getting everything off his chest.

He was emotionally wounded and upset, so I just listened to him and let him vent.

When he looked like he was about done, I let the other cars know that I had him and gave them our location.

They lit up lights and sirens, and we could hear them coming.

I told Manu that he had a choice to make, that I wanted to help him and understood what he was going through, but I also needed him to trust me.

Naturally, he was suspicious; he's a banger, and I'm a cop. I told him, though, that with all the other units coming I had a minimal amount of time to get him safely into my car; I didn't want to see him hurt, but the reality was that we had a lot of new guys who were hotheaded and looking to make a name for themselves.

On top of that, they'd heard of him and his attitude toward cops. So, I asked him again to trust me and let me take him into custody before the other guys showed up.

As the sirens closed in, he stood his ground and said, "Fuck it. I wanna fight them bitches."

"Look man," I said, "Let's resolve this like men. You don't have to prove shit to anyone. I'll even give you the cuffs, and you can put them on and get into my car."

As I handed him my cuffs, McKell's eyes were huge and his mouth dropped open. I had nothing to lose. If he listened and cuffed himself, I didn't have to fight him and he'd be in my car when the backup arrived; if he didn't, we'd be fighting—but I'd have a lot of help in the next few moments.

He stared at me for a few seconds, holding the cuffs and listening to the sirens getting closer. Finally, he said "OK" and cuffed himself. I opened the door, and he got into the car. Then I seat-belted him in and closed the door as the first unit arrived, officers jumping from the car with their nightsticks out. They wanted to know where Manu was. Did he already run off?

I said, "No, he's here," and explained that I'd asked him politely to cuff himself and get into my car—and he had. As proof, I pointed to him sitting in my patrol car.

"Bullshit!" they exclaimed. "You did *not* get Manu Rio in your car without a fight."

I said, "OK, if you say so," then got in the car as more units arrived.

While I spoke to Manu, taking down his information for my report, they all stood outside the car, nightsticks quivering, glaring like I was the high school principal who'd canceled the rumble after a big game.

They asked McKell if what I said had actually happened.

"Ya, I wouldn't have believed it if I hadn't seen it," he said.

I was pretty proud of that moment.

I thought of it as an accomplishment—and I'd certainly disappointed a lot of my co-workers.

Listening wasn't rocket science; it was just common sense.

TWENTY-THREE
BAD STOP BEN

ONCE I HAD A NEW guy, Ben, develop a really interesting habit of stopping cars.

He had no legal reason to stop and search them with no probable cause, which was the lowest legal standard of evidence on which we were allowed to act.

It's a fairly simple concept, really: "probable" as in it probably could be suspicious to a reasonable person.

He made a lot of arrests with this "style" of his, but they wouldn't stick; prosecutors wouldn't file charges on them, and any defense attorney worth his pay could get them thrown out.

One night, I was called to back up Ben, "back" as we called it; it happened a lot that he always needed a back.

He was at the south end on one of the main streets of the city, which wasn't a cop-friendly area. He'd stopped a truck that had left a suspected drug house. We'd do it if we could—but we can't, so we don't.

Pulling over everyone who departs a suspicious house not only wastes a lot of time, but it can get a department sued more than it needs to be. Besides, "suspected drug house" just isn't enough to go on.

Probable cause is also the standard for a warrant to shut down a drug house, and if we had it we'd close the place.

Anyway, Ben had the suspected drug house customers pulled over and asked me to standby while he talked to the three people in the truck.

He asked the driver if he could search the truck; the driver consented. Ben searched the truck and found nothing.

He then searched the passengers, and one had a purse with drugs inside. He arrested all the occupants and impounded the truck.

I knew the search was bad and that the arrests wouldn't hold up, and I tried to explain it to Ben—but he wouldn't listen.

Trying for common sense, I told him to take the drugs, flush them somewhere, and send them on their way. Ben wouldn't budge.

About a week later, he got a letter from the prosecutors telling him that the search was illegal and that the arrests had been thrown out and squashed.

This went on for months: Ben stopping people, illegal searches, arrests being tossed.

Another night, he pulled over a car because "it was a car full of Mexicans driving around at four in the morning."

I couldn't believe he said it out loud. He had all the occupants out sitting on the curb in handcuffs.

Several other cars had rolled up, as well as a Sergeant, and Ben started to search the car when he got permission from the non-English speaking driver who agreed with whatever Ben said to him.

The trunk was full of used car stereos, and Ben and the Sergeant decided that the property was obviously stolen, so they arrested everybody. We, the rest of the squad, about shit ourselves at this brilliance.

The stop was bad—which made the search illegal—and the property hadn't been proven to be stolen. The people hadn't even been checked for warrants yet, but they were checked later—and they would all have none.

We all left, driving off and refusing to come back.

Ben and the Sergeant dealt with all the paperwork: the impounding of the illegally stopped vehicle, property forms for the illegally seized stereos, and booking of the illegally arrested Mexicans.

The next day, we had a heated debate with the Sergeant in shift briefing.

He said he never wanted to see that lack of teamwork again, but we pushed back, bringing the Constitution into the discussion, as well as the Fourth Amendment, search and seizure rights, oaths, and our assertion that this stop was bad from jump.

Regardless, this went on and on.

The Chief and Assistant Chiefs came in one day and awarded Ben "Officer of the Year" for all of his felony arrests, then sat in the shift briefing and told each of us that we needed to learn from his example. He had twice as many arrests and seized more property than any of us "and he's new."

You could almost hear our respect for the brass evaporate from the room.

Ben lost almost every case he made an arrest on, but the department didn't track convictions. This got to be a joke on patrol: just go out and be an idiot, and management will reward you.

It didn't really stop until Ben caught his wife with another man and planned to kill her—but passed out drunk in the midst of the attempt. He'd left a murder/suicide note, and she found it and called the police.

Ben was arrested and ultimately lost his police certification over it. Years later, he and I became friends; he was a good guy when he was sober and not asked to be a cop.

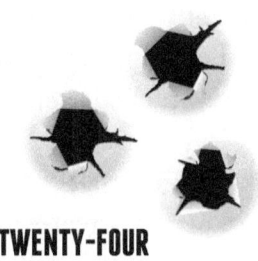

TWENTY-FOUR
GRECKO WRESTLING

ROBERT ALLEN WAS A MEAN schizophrenic, and he could have easily taken on both Manu and Doobie.

He lived in some mid-block apartment in the central city and suddenly got very loud and violent for no apparent reason but his illness. I got a call to his apartment from his neighbors.

He was enormous, almost 6-and-a-half feet tall and 300 pounds or more, depending on his condition at the time. His weight could vary a lot.

When I got the call, dispatch told me that Allen's address had been flagged as the occupant being very dangerous and prone to fighting cops in the nude for fun.

They sent me a back-up as well; the back that night was Skidmark—and with no **Street Creds** or common sense, he'd get both our asses kicked by Allen, so I canceled his ass and went in alone.

I knocked on the door for several minutes, listening to Allen yelling inside as he carried on a conversation with—it later turned out—himself.

He finally answered the door, totally naked, yelling and screaming at me, "What the fuck do you want? What son of a bitch has called you to my house?"

Dispatch then informed me that Allen did have a warrant, and that made the call a lot more interesting; now, I was required to arrest him since I'd found him there at the house.

I talked to Allen for some time, with dispatch checking on me frequently; they were nervous.

The last group of cops who had come there had battled with Allen, and he'd fucked them up pretty bad. Dispatch had pulled the case and read it: the cops had been some guys considered heavyweights in the department, guys who were known for being able to handle themselves on the street—and Allen had beaten the hell out of them.

So, Allen was well known to the force.

He had a habit of talking to you one minute—then in the next, in mid-sentence, changing his manner and growling or barking or charging at you, trying to start a fight.

I didn't respond to his aggression; instead, I just kept talking to him.

He finally asked me, "What are you planning on doing, officer? Are you gonna arrest me or what?"

I told him that I was going to arrest him and that he had a choice as to how that was going to happen.

I told him that he had quite a reputation for fighting and that he'd harmed some of the officers who arrested him the last time.

I said that I could tell he wasn't the kind of guy that he acted like he was and that I was going to give him the chance to prove it. I'd come alone, and we could either walk out like men or fight; the choice was his.

Just then, Chad Stiver showed up. He was a guy I trusted. He wasn't well liked in the department either, but we'd clicked.

He sat back and listened to me deal with Allen. Dispatch had called him, worried about Allen going off. He knew about Allen and his history, but he didn't interfere with how I was handling him.

When Allen saw Stiver, he did go off, flying into a rage. I calmed him back down, though, after he charged me multiple times, still naked and mad as hell.

I explained that Stiver was there because of the previous time that we'd shown up and he'd beaten up a couple cops. He wasn't there to fight; instead, he'd shown up to see if Allen was going to go willingly this time, not fighting like a crazy man.

He got angry about this, yelling, "I *am* fucking crazy! I *am* fucking crazy, and you know that!"

I had to think quickly; he was escalating, breathing hard and sweating, getting amped up for a fight.

So, talking more and more quietly as he became increasingly angry, I said, "You may be crazy, Robert; I don't know. I don't care about that. I've been honest with you and told you that I have to arrest you. I've treated you with respect, and I hope that I've earned your respect. Now get your clothes on, and let's go to the jail. I'll walk you out so that all your neighbors can see that you aren't a bad man and they shouldn't be afraid of you."

He watched me for a few minutes, panting and glaring; I stared back, not saying a word.

Then, in a split second he said, "OK I'll go if you promise not to beat me up like last time."

I did promise, and so did Stiver.

Allen got dressed and allowed me to handcuff him. I then walked him to my car, and we laughed and joked along the way, his neighbors watching our every move; they were terrified of him.

He was booked into jail without incident.

The next day in the shift briefing, Stiver told everyone that he saw something last night that he'd never seen before. "Slick talked Robert Allen into walking to his car without a fight. Allen is one of the most dangerous people in the whole fucking city, and he had him eating out of his hand."

He looked at the sergeant and said, "This is the kind of shit we should be recognizing instead of bullshit bad arrests and ass kissers."

They glared at each other for a while, and the room was quiet. Stiver had a way of making friends with the brass like I did.

I had a lot of experience with mentally ill people. Central city is stuffed full of them. Halfway houses, people living on Social Security for mental problems, lesbians, gays—not saying they're mental, but the ones who end up in central city have a lot of issues, such as sexual abuse, poor coping skills, and the inability to attach in a healthy relationship.

Seriously, we used to refer to central city as the dumping ground of the broken and damaged.

I learned a lot from working the area day after day.

Allen could have ripped me apart if he wanted, but I sensed something in him "like a dog that barks too much." The real killers are quiet and might growl before they strike. They don't bark to warn you; he did.

All of this made me suspect with the rest of the force. I was criticized for going in to too many calls without back. I did that, though, so I'd have a chance to talk and listen.

There were too many guys who would cowboy in and make the situation worse with the tough guy bullshit; I'd cancel back-up once I heard who the officer would be, not because of the call.

Fighting wasn't a victory for me.

I don't like how it makes me feel; I feel like a failure when I fight because it means that I misjudged the situation. I believe I should be able to think my way out of anything, and most times I did.

Most cops see things from the perspective of being in control; I don't see that at all. As cops, I never think that we're in control of anything, so I don't try to be. It's a fallacy.

I let the scene unfold, the interviews unfold, the cases unfold. I don't force it.

I was never afraid of not rising to the occasion. My fear was that when it was over, I'd have reacted too quickly, too harshly, and not be able to live with it.

TWENTY-FIVE
GIVING VICTIMS A BAD NAME

ONE NIGHT, I WAS DISPATCHED to this formerly very exclusive club in town; it was one of those places that for so long had been a men-only club, then a membership joint for the high rollers who could afford it.

It was old school and old money but was so far out of step with reality that it finally closed altogether and is now either a wedding reception parlor or a bingo club. I forget which.

This night, one of the waitresses was missing; the manager said that the girl had just disappeared in the middle of her shift, and he was worried that she'd been abducted—or worse. The waitress was extremely dependable, so he was convinced that something bad had happened.

I called in other units, and we checked the club and the parking lot for any signs of the young missing waitress. She'd left her purse behind, but nothing else.

Apparently, no one had seen her leave. The people at the tables she'd been serving said that one minute she was there, and the next she was gone.

The bar patrons were a surprisingly uncooperative bunch. We were rarely summoned there.

When I was in vice, I heard rumors of college girls making large sums of money for having sex with businessmen there; however, I could never prove it.

I did interview one girl who told me about dating "Q-tips"; that was her term for older gray or white-haired men. She said that the Q-tips would have a lot of money and were more mature than younger men. She felt that they'd have better places to take a girl who was willing to be entertained. She denied having sex with any of the Q-tips for money, but she said that if they left her a gift after sex, she wouldn't refuse it. She was only twenty years old.

Anyway, we searched for signs of the missing waitress with only the abandoned purse to go on. I put out a BOLO ("Be On the Look Out") for her and cleared the club.

Checking her apartment turned up nothing. I stopped to write up the case, and when I was almost done a call came in reporting a woman who had turned up at some guy's door, claiming to have been raped. It was the missing waitress.

Our victim said she'd been abducted from the club by a group of men, then driven around the city in a car while they took turns raping her. When they were done, she said they dumped her off and she went to the nearest house for help.

I interviewed her as she was attended to by medical, then followed as she was transported to the hospital, speaking to her in the Emergency Room.

She claimed that she'd been serving a table of professional men at the club who had been making suggestive remarks to her all night; she hadn't responded to them, instead remaining polite in her refusals.

Finally, they'd left, and she went on break for a minute, when she saw one of them in the parking lot alone; she said that he "looked sad," so she went over to see what was wrong.

She said he then hit her on the head and knocked her out.

When she came to, she was in the back of a vehicle with many men in the car who took turns raping her, cheering each other on.

I did see that her clothes were torn and that she had some mud on her arms and face. Her hair was also messy, but something about her demeanor wasn't right.

Her blouse had all the buttons, and her socks were clean—as were her shoes—and she showed no signs of physical violence; she just looked disheveled. Her eye contact was really good as well.

She was sitting on a gurney in her black and white waitress outfit while we talked.

Her manner and behavior changed as I questioned her: she started biting her lip, and she made suggestive eye contact as she started flirting with me. I was surprised, but I didn't respond; instead, I waited to see how this would unfold.

Finally, she ran her hand up the inside of her legs and slowly opened them while looking away; she was making sure that I looked at her crotch, her legs spread there on the gurney in the ER as we discussed her gang rape; I did look, and I noticed that she still had her panties on. They were white cotton panties with no blood, no dirt—and they weren't even semen-stained.

As we kept talking, I noticed that her eyes were more dilated than they should have been in the well-lit room. So, I asked her if she'd been drinking, and she said that she hadn't and that it wasn't allowed on the job.

She sat for the Perk kit test, as they call it, to check for fluids in her vaginal tract.

The doctor later said that there was no evidence collected; there was nothing there, no semen, no hair, and no sign that she'd had sex recently.

Checking with the ER nurse, I was told that every patient who gets a blood draw has an alcohol screen done as well. Her blood alcohol level was at .17—more than twice the legal limit.

I told the victim that I was going to go out and look for the men who had raped her; instead, I went back to the club.

I kept asking around until I finally found a waitress who would talk to me. She said that the victim had been flirting with a table of guys and that she'd observed her sneaking a drink with them as the night progressed. The guys had asked her to leave with them, and she told the other waitress that she was leaving with them and to "fuck this shitty job" as she was "going to party."

I wrote up my report and forwarded it to detectives.

I then went to our victim's apartment to tell her that the detectives would contact her in the morning. I found her there, drinking beer with a group of guys and listening to music—and she was the only woman in the apartment.

She claimed that I didn't care about her and said that all cops were worthless and that I could just go to hell! She then went back to partying.

The detective did contact her, and she eventually admitted that she hadn't been raped and had made up the whole story to try to keep her job; she said that she'd gotten drunk at work and left and that this was all she could think of to avoid getting fired.

We made sure that this was unofficially relayed to the club—and she was then fired.

TWENTY-SIX
BLOODBATH

I WAS PARKED IN THE early morning hours, talking to dispatch on a pay phone in a downtown parking lot.

It was located near an old medical building, one of those pay phones you could pull up to and drive right alongside and dial without leaving your car.

I used it as often as possible because drug dealers also liked it; it makes them pissed to see a fully equipped, decked-out police cruiser with all the decals and electronics parked at their work phone.

I can't go up to a drug dealer and tell him to get off the phone—not legally, at least—but I can totally fuck up his day using that same phone myself, answering it when it rings and wrecking his **Street Creds.**

"Police department, can I help you?" The line goes dead; another satisfied customer. The little things make me smile.

That night, I was getting the details on a case that I was working, when around the corner of the building about thirty yards away came a woman stumbling across the parking lot.

It was dark, and there were no lights, so she looked to me like a transient, a drunk one.

Her hair was a mess, and I could see that her clothes were filthy as well. I thought she was probably going to stumble up to me to try to ask for money or a ride somewhere, and I didn't want to be bothered with some nasty ass, panhandling, alcohol—soaked transient needing a favor.

I couldn't tell if she'd seen me yet, as I was parked in the dark, talking on the phone, so I waited for her to get closer; sure enough, I could see that she truly was a mess, hair all screwed up like her clothes—and in the early morning light it looked like she'd pissed her pants.

I hung up the phone, cursing, and turned on my headlights and spotlight at the same time to encourage her, hopefully, just to go away.

The picture in my mind of what this woman would look like—leaves in her hair, missing teeth, urine-stained clothes, and more than likely vomit on her shirt and pants—was instantly transformed. She was lit up, night became day, and it took a moment for the real image to sink in.

She was a 16-year-old girl, stumbling across the parking lot. She was in shock—not drunk—and she was covered in blood from head to toe.

The hair that I assumed would be filled with leaves and lice was instead caked in blood clots; it stuck out in different directions, stiffened from dried blood. Her face was streaked with blood, and her clothes torn and covered in blood.

What I assumed would be urine stains on her pants was actually blood shining in the light, dark red and fresh. She looked like she'd just walked out of a horror movie; picture the original "Carrie" by Stephen King with Sissy Spacek in the prom bloodbath, and you get the idea.

I'd never seen anyone alive and covered in this much blood—much less walking.

She didn't react to my spotlight or headlights and just kept walking towards me, eyes staring straight ahead.

I drove toward her and got out of the car. I was sure that she'd been in a bad car accident and had somehow walked this far; there was just too much blood for it to be anything else.

I asked her what happened, and she stared at me, registering for the first time that she was somewhere else. She blinked, mouth open, eyes blank, and mouthing words—but no sound came out. She finally said, "My boyfriend raped me."

At first, I didn't believe her. There was way too much blood to be from one person, much less from a rape. She started to faint, and I grabbed her.

She told me, "I want to see my mommy."

"Mommy…" Just like that…said it like the child she used to be.

I told her I had to call the paramedics and that we'd see her mom as soon as we could, but the paramedics had to come first.

She started getting hysterical, crying that she "wanted her mommy."

I finally had to say, "OK, OK. We'll do that right now. You'll have to get into my car, and we'll go find her. Can you remember where you live?"

She said yes.

I got an old army blanket for her from the trunk of my car, helped her get in, then seat-belted her. She stared out the window, just blank, oblivious…no emotion.

I asked her who her boyfriend was, and she calmly gave me a name: Robert Harris, Jr. She said that they'd agreed to meet that night at his house to have sex. They'd been dating only a short while and hadn't had sex yet, so tonight was going to be the first time.

When she got to his place, things immediately went to shit.

First, he demanded a blowjob—and when she refused, it got ugly. He pulled out a knife and began cutting her repeatedly, she said, anally and vaginally. Then he smeared the blood on her face and hair. It all happened in his room in the basement of the house.

I asked her to show me where he lived, which was only a block from where we'd run into each other.

She said she'd waited a very long time for him to fall asleep, then fled.

We pulled up in front of the house, and I stopped.

Was he alone in the house? She thought so.

I sat there, thinking. I wanted to go in and put a bullet in his head, seriously mulling this over. I imagined walking in to his room, with him asleep on a bloodstained bed—and I'd add his brains to the mess.

I gripped the steering wheel tighter and started breathing hard. In the straining silence, the girl finally spoke again, asking, "You're not gonna go in there, are you?"

I told her I was thinking about it, that he deserved to die. Then I asked her, "What do you want me to do?"

"Mommy," she replied.

Suddenly, I was struck by how stupid I was handling this.

I had to take care of her first; that was the main priority. I wanted him dead—no doubt—but I didn't have that luxury now. I had to get her to her mother without her going into shock, then to the nearest hospital.

I was shaking with rage—actually seeing red like I was looking through a camera lens with a red filter—but I drove away on to her mother's house; necessity had just saved Robert, Jr.'s life.

I told the girl to stay in the car while I went to the front door for her mom.

After several knocks, she finally answered, and I informed her that I needed her to come with her daughter and me to the hospital right away.

She started yelling and screaming, "I'm sick of that fucking kid. All she ever does is cause problems. You can take her to jail and throw away the keys. I don't fucking care."

Then she started down the front porch steps to go chew her daughter out, the "no good piece of shit."

I grabbed her by the shirt and slammed her against the post of the porch. Then, talking quietly right in her face, I said, "Listen, you stupid bitch. Your daughter is seriously fucking hurt, bleeding, and in shock. I need to get her to the hospital, but she demanded that I bring her to you first. She said that she wanted 'her mommy.'

"You are going to get in the car and for once in your fucked up life be a parent. You say one word, anything that's less than kind, and I will personally beat your fucking ass."

I was in no mood for this dysfunctional shit.

I asked her, "You got that?" Startled at that point, and a bit frightened, she said that she did.

I walked her to the car and put her in the back seat, then told the girl her mom was there and that we were going to the hospital. She reached over to the back seat for her mother, who held her hand, then closed her eyes and was much calmer, her breathing beginning to slow down. Her mom looked at me with real fear. I don't know if she was afraid of me or afraid for her daughter, but she was very quiet in the back seat, staring at me.

Meanwhile, we were on our way to the closest hospital. I called ahead and said that we were en route to the ER and that I needed them to have a wheelchair ready and waiting outside the door.

I was in the ER often because of the area I worked (the inner city), so they knew me. The nurse I spoke to was a friend and asked what I was bringing them. As code, I told her that she'd need a PERK kit; that's the medical kit they use to do a rape exam in order to collect semen or other evidence.

She said, "OK. Is it bad?"

I said "Yes, very."

We pulled into the ER parking lot, and they had the chair waiting. When they saw the girl, they had the same reaction that I did: total shock.

They carefully helped her out of the car and immediately took her to a room.

While they did the exam, I called for a detective. One showed up a short time later, coming in with the typical casual attitude.

He said, "So is this the usual 'I got caught by my parents having sex and now it's rape?'"

I said no, then explained the case, emphasizing how bad it was—and his demeanor changed instantly.

"Let's go talk to her," he said.

We looked into the room she was in, and CSI was taking pictures of the bloody handprints on her back, chest, and legs. She was sitting on a gurney, still bleeding on the white sheets, and she turned to us and looked at the detective, her hair still matted with blood.

She turned away, ashamed, and a doctor told us to leave, which we did.

The detective was visibly shaken, even with his seventeen years or so of experience on the force.

"Is all that blood hers?"

I said that it was. I told him what had happened and told him about Robert, Jr. He said he would take care of it.

I finished my report at the hospital and left the case for him to finish.

The doctor told me it was the worst case of rape that he'd seen in over twenty-five years as an ER doctor. They had her into surgery for all the internal damage, and he didn't know if she'd be able to have children. He was pretty angry when we spoke.

"I hope you find this piece of shit and give him some of that street justice you guys talk about."

I was really surprised by this. Usually, doctors weren't real fond of our stories of scuffles and battles; since they had to clean up our mess, they weren't happy about it.

The girl eventually recovered, and Robert, Jr. was caught.

He fled the state first, though, and the FBI eventually picked him up after his family, mother, and sister turned him in for the reward money.

When we went to court, his attorney was one of the veterans; gruff, overbearing, and skilled at intimidating cops into making mistakes on the stand.

At the preliminary hearing, a mini-trial meant to get a judge's blessing that at least enough evidence existed to advance a case to trial, he asked to speak to me before the hearing.

The victim couldn't remember much of what had happened, and he wanted to know what I would testify to about the "alleged rape." He framed it that way: "alleged."

I noted what his "alleged client" had done and what the girl had looked like stumbling up to me, blood-soaked, in the parking lot. "Please do take this to a jury," I said. "I would love to explain this to them."

He looked me in the eye as I spoke, measuring how I'd come across on the stand, then said, "OK, we're through" and walked away to meet with his client in another room.

After a while, he came out and in open court told the judge that Robert, Jr., was going to plead guilty straight up to all four counts of aggravated sexual assault against him, five-to-life coming with each one.

He claimed that he was on meth that night and didn't remember much; at least that was his story. He remembered enough to run to California for six months before his own family turned him in.

I would love to be able to erase that night with her in the parking lot.

Years later, during my divorce, my ex-wife would run into the mom who I'd threatened that night. She asked my ex if she was married to the cop she knew who did so much for her daughter. She told her story about that night and asked her to thank me for what I'd done.

The ex—one of many—called me and told me of the encounter. "Why didn't you ever tell me this story?"

I answered that she never wanted to talk about my work and wouldn't have listened.

"Well, I guess you finally did at least one thing that was good," she said.

There was a reason we were getting a divorce.

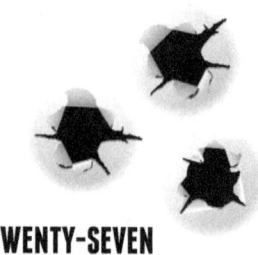

TWENTY-SEVEN
STUPID IS AS STUPID DOES

I GUESS IT'S OBVIOUS BY now that I don't often see people at their best on this job. It makes cops suspicious, wary of pretty much everybody—all of you, even your beliefs.

The notion of a God, a higher power, even the idea that some kind of order exists in the universe, is victimized on a regular basis on police calls.

We've got to cope somehow, and sometimes it's in a sick way. It's just comical, and the laughs can come perfectly timed to ease the load of pondering all the serious dysfunction we have to walk through.

One night, I was dispatched to the parking lot of the ER at a hospital.

A night clerk had gone out to her car and unlocked the doors. She had a lot of personal items to load into the back seat, and she set her keys on the hood of the car while she did so. Then, she got into the car and locked the doors because she was afraid of getting car-jacked or attacked.

She looked all over the car for her keys, going through her pockets, her purse, and all the stuff on the back seat, but she couldn't find them.

She sat there a while, trying to remember where they were. Then it finally came to her: they were on the hood of the car right in front of her. Panicked, she started to cry, then called 911.

She told the dispatcher what had happened, the nature of her plight, and that she was locked in her car. Dispatch had sent me to make sure that this wasn't some kind of distress code; they wanted me to ensure that nothing else was wrong because it was simply unbelievable that someone could be this dumb.

I could picture the scene in dispatch, with the other dispatchers gathering around to listen to this drama unfolding.

Since all 911 calls are recorded, their professionalism this time came down to keeping a straight face.

Many questions would have to remain unanswered: how did this woman ever score a driver license? Is she allowed to vote? Are there children involved? Has she reproduced? They couldn't believe she was for real, as several minutes were needed to calm her down.

"Push the unlock button on the driver's side door," the dispatcher instructed calmly.

The woman did this, and magically the car unlocked.

She was so relieved, no longer imprisoned and needing someone or a locksmith to get the keys off the hood to open the door, or maybe the fire department to extricate her. Her prayers had been answered.

Other times, the concept of God, a higher power or order in the universe, takes a beating from one of its own anointed representatives—which can also be hilarious.

I think it was Albert Einstein who said that the idea of God was just too specific for the human mind. Whatever that means, I'm sure I don't know; maybe it's an idea that can only exist in some kind of isolation, where stained glass windows color the only light that gets in. You probably don't want to ask cops about God.

Dispatched to a health food store downtown on a Sunday night, I was about to talk with one of the deity's local representatives.

It was almost midnight, and the owner was claiming that he'd just been robbed. I arrived to find an older white male, about sixty-five, wearing what appeared to be clothing that you'd wear to church: slacks, a white shirt, tie, and dress shoes.

He came to me and reached out to shake my hand. I didn't extend mine; by now, such pleasantries had become suspicious, this one being a common ploy to get the officer to extend his gun hand—and once in a handshake, he's unable to access his sidearm.

He said to me, "Thank you for coming brother."

I looked at him and said, "You assume a lot. Why did you call me here?"

He was annoying me very quickly with his alleged offer of friendship, and now he was calling me his brother? Obviously, this approach had worked for him before.

I asked him for identification, and he took a "temple recommend," as they're called, indicating certified worthiness for entry into his religion's temple, from his shirt pocket and handed it to me. This was only getting more aggravating.

"Do you have any legitimate ID? This is meaningless."

Maybe I shouldn't have said it quite that way, but it later became clear that I was right.

He proceeded to try to tell me that this piece of identification spoke more to his character than any driver's license.

I asked him to please save the shit for someone else. I was well aware of what the document was for, and if he didn't start talking fast, I was leaving.

Frustrated, he paused and just looked at me, glaring. Then he started to tell me what had happened.

He'd come down to the store to do his weekly run to a cheese factory a couple counties over, as he did every Sunday after church services to stock his health food store.

He said that this night he'd come back to the store to unload the cheese, and when he finished he came out to his car and was robbed by a strange female. He said that she took his wallet and wouldn't give it back and that she was in a car right now, parked in front of the store.

This was making no sense.

He says he was robbed after a midnight cheese run by a woman that stayed at the scene? I went to the car and spoke to the woman—and instantly, it all became clear.

She was a prostitute; we'd run into each other many times on the street. Sometimes she gave me information. She'd never lied to me, so I asked her what had happened.

She said that the old man was one of her regular clients and that he liked to have her meet him on Sundays late in the evening after he came back from his cheese runs for his store. This was how he kept their arrangement hidden from his wife; they'd meet at the store, and he'd pay her for whatever sexual act he wanted her to perform that week.

She said that after she was done with him that night, he wouldn't pay her, so she took his wallet. He threatened to call the police, and she told him to go right ahead; she'd wait right there.

I asked her what she wanted done, and she said that all she wanted was the money that he owed her, the money that he'd promised. She hadn't taken anything from his wallet.

I asked her for the wallet, and she gave it to me. I then told her that I'd do what I could but that I couldn't promise anything.

I went back to the old man with his wallet and let him see it.

He reached for it, but I refused to return it until we cleared a few things up.

I asked him why he kept the temple recommend in his shirt pocket and not in his wallet. He said he liked to keep it "closer to his heart."

"Uh huh...is that right?" I replied.

I asked him how the girl had enforced the robbery. "Did she have a weapon? Did she make threats?"

He said that she asked to use his phone inside the business, and as a servant of the Lord he felt it was his duty to help those less fortunate than he, so he let her use it. While he was opening the door to his store, she'd forced him against the door and took the wallet from his pants pocket.

I stared at him for a long while, not saying a word.

Finally, he said, "Are you going to take the word of a prostitute over me?"

I smiled. "How did you know she was a prostitute?"

I'd never mentioned it.

"Look," I said. "I'm gonna make this really clear for you. She's a prostitute. I know her, and so do you. She says that she's been seeing you for some time after your little midnight cheese runs. She also says that you refused to pay her for what she did tonight, and that was why she took your wallet. She didn't take one dime from it and freely gave it back to me."

He interrupted me to say that he was "a high ranking official in his church" and that she was a common whore. Who was I going to believe?

"The common whore," I calmly replied. "You know there's a Supreme Court case that says just because someone's a thief or a whore, whatever, it can't be assumed that they're also a liar...you're probably not interested. Anyway, she's never lied to me, and you haven't told me one word of truth here tonight."

He tried to grab his wallet from me again, stating that he'd had enough and was going home.

"Not yet, you're not. You have some choices to make. First, keeping ID in a shirt pocket is common practice for people who see hookers. See, while she's giving you a blowjob and your pants are down, she has access to your wallet—and most men who frequent hookers know this. After losing their wallet a time or two, they put the important ID in their shirt pocket, where it wouldn't be stolen. Funny how you did just that...keeping it closer to your heart."

He was silent.

"She only wants to be paid," I continued. "If she doesn't get paid, I'm gonna arrest you both. She's been arrested many times, so it will mean nothing to her; you, however, will be front page news."

After growing even quieter, he said, "What do I have to do to keep that from happening, sir?"

"Pay her, which is all she wants—and an apology would be nice. Then I'll clear this call as 'unfounded.' No report will be written, and there won't be any record of all this. The choice is yours."

"I'll pay and apologize," he said. Which he did.

The expression on her face was priceless. Smiling, she went on her way and he went back to his life, temple recommend close to his heart, façade intact.

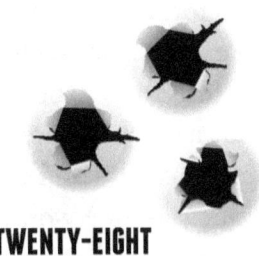

TWENTY-EIGHT
OFFICER-ASSISTED SUICIDE

IT'S A WORTHY GOAL, AN inspirational one, not to get shot, right up there with not having to shoot anyone. One night, I had the chance to work on those career goals.

Working the central city, it was a little slow, and dispatch asked me to take a call on the west side.

The area car, Officer Divot, was busy at the station—most likely getting bodily fluids all over the shoes of management.

It was a car burglary.

Dale Dirk had his car broken into and reported it, and he called back to ask when a cop would be en route; he wanted to get the paperwork done so he could go to bed.

So I headed west, and on the way I asked the dispatcher to call back and find out the apartment number. The address was a little motel just over a bridge, and I knew it fairly well. I didn't usually ask this particular question. If it wasn't a hot call, I liked to walk around first and scout the area to see what was going on, then go to the call; for some reason, though, this time I asked about the apartment.

I was annoyed at the officer who was assigned to the area for not being there, and I also had newly promoted Sgt. Peabody to deal with. He was an ass beyond belief, and we didn't connect—and never would. I was a little irritated and hurried.

As a field-training officer, Peabody had just been an ass; as a sergeant, though, he was an unbearable dickhead. He was controlling and nitpicky and would make huge mistakes that he'd then put on others for not keeping him informed enough to make better decisions.

Peabody had made a career out of blaming his errors on the lack of good info from others; he was quite skilled at it, actually.

I was just turning into the driveway when Barb, the dispatcher, asked where I was. I told her I was just arriving.

She said one word, "Stop," as calm as could be—but in a way that made me jam the brake pedal to the floor.

Barb was probably one of the better dispatchers we had; incredibly competent, knew her shit, and never got ruffled or stressed on the radio. She'd warned me with the mere inflection in her voice.

Barb told me that when she called Dale Dirk, our car burg victim, his father answered the phone. There was no car burglary.

The father stated that his son had been drinking after breaking up with his girlfriend and at that moment was outside with a gun, hiding behind a car and waiting for the cop he called to show up.

He intended to ambush the cop, said his father, trying to provoke a shooting to get himself killed in a suicide-by-cop. This happens often enough, unfortunately.

I looked down the driveway to Dirk's apartment and saw no one; he was still hiding. I put the car in reverse and backed the hell out of there as fast as I could go. I was smoking the tires, hoping not to get shot as I backed up almost an entire city block.

Dirk was waiting with a .357 Magnum handgun, and when he saw me back out he went inside and got on the phone with dispatch, wanting to know where the hell I was going.

While he was on the phone, his Dad fled the apartment.

Dispatch told Dirk what his dad had said, that there was no car burglary, and that he'd told them he just wanted to shoot a cop.

He said, "So?" He wanted to die, and he said he would find a way, then hung up.

Meanwhile, Peabody "super-hero sergeant" was on his way to the scene...praise the Lord, save us all.

He ordered a perimeter set up—which was good—and while he was doing that I was on my cell phone with Dirk, talking to him to try to establish a rapport of some kind.

This pissed Peabody off to no end. He wanted to be in control of the scene and wanted to do the talking himself, so he demanded that I hang up and allow him to talk to Dirk.

I ignored him; I was reaching Dirk, and I wasn't about to turn him over to Peabody.

Peabody then started calling me on the radio, ordering me to hang up so that he could talk to Dirk—and being quite a dick about it.

I had to shut the radio off so I could continue with Dirk, and eventually I did negotiate him out. He came out with his hands up and surrendered.

Instead of being happy about the successful conclusion to the call, though, Peabody went off. He was screaming at me as I was putting Dirk in my car, red face twisted and spitting all over the place.

He felt that I'd undermined his authority—never mind the fact that I'd narrowly missed an ambush, then negotiated the suspect out of the house without a shot being fired and no SWAT call out; I hadn't jumped when "Peabody The Amazing" had said jump.

In the car on the way to jail, I talked with Dirk for some time about his little girl and family. I also showed him pictures of my kids. I wanted him to realize that I had a life as well and that he could have ended that life in addition to his own with stupid shit like this.

He cried in the car and apologized.

Peabody tried to write me up for insubordination; just part of being the department's up-and-coming jackass at the time.

Someone higher up, though, squashed the paperwork.

I never found out who it was, but whoever did it apparently had my back and didn't want me to know about it.

TWENTY-NINE
SMARTER THAN A SERGEANT

YOU MIGHT BE AMAZED (I know we were) at how often some of the shit bags we chased fell for something known as "Knock and Talk."

It's just like it sounds: officers simply knock on the door of a known criminal's address and try to talk their way in without a warrant.

It never ceased to amaze me how often guys with warrants—who consider themselves career streetwise thugs who never held jobs and were proud of it—would invite police officers inside to talk.

It was a psych game, and it was most effective on drug houses where the suspects have lost any common sense with their prolonged drug abuse.

It was worth a try on just about any place we thought some kind of illegal activity was going on. There was no bluff about having a warrant, just a simple ."..would like to ask you a few questions...need your help on something...where'd you get those shoes?"

The cheese dick suspect who opened the door would always worry that not letting the officer in would draw suspicion—even though things were well past suspicious, just not enough to get a judge to sign a warrant.

Of course, it doesn't work on the real bad asses who know the game—and even the law—and just slam the door.

Once inside, the officer is looking for anything that can lend itself to a warrant under the "plain view" doctrine.

One day, one of our guys pulled the knock and talk on a hotel room downtown where we'd heard drugs were being sold. He got in the door and saw the dope, just lying there on a table, distribution quantity.

That was enough for a warrant.

The officer had legally gained entry and now had to prevent the destruction of evidence, so he called it in and asked for back-up as well.

The dumb ass who opened the door was arrested immediately, but his partner—much wiser and more determined to escape—went out a bathroom window measuring 1 foot by 1 foot.

But he left some ID in the room, and we found he had outstanding warrants, even an NCIC hit, which are felonies only. He had warrants for drug possession and aggravated assault, so it was on.

It was a late Saturday afternoon and things were a little slow, so a lot of units got involved. We were searching everywhere and couldn't find this guy. He was all over the radio, K-9 was out running the dogs, and uniforms were on foot going from house to house, checking sheds and garages and any conceivable hiding place.

No one found anything; it was like this guy just disappeared.

I was on the west end, listening over the radio, and I thought, *What would I do to disappear in the middle of a city? Find the nearest phone and call a cab?*

I suggested this to the sergeant handling the search—Peabody again, an arrogant prick who rode everybody under him hard while ass-kissing everyone above him; you couldn't get his nose out of the chief's ass with a crowbar.

Sergeant Peabody said point blank that the idea was ridiculous.

"Young pup," he told me, "you have a lot to learn about drug dealers and crime in general. Sit back and watch what experience can teach you."

Thrilled at such an opportunity, I walked away, got on my cell phone, and called dispatch on the side. I asked them to check the cab companies (there were only a few) and told them to keep it quiet; I told them what Peabody said and that I didn't want him in my ass for checking this out in spite of his ridicule.

They were more than happy to assist with my hunch, Peabody having made no friends at dispatch either.

They called cabbies and simply asked if a man had been picked up in the vicinity of the hotel in the past twenty minutes—and guess what? They'd picked up a sweaty guy who "just wanted to get out of the area as soon as possible."

Dispatch asked the cabbie where he was and if he could stay on the line with the dispatcher until we could get close. He said he would.

Dispatch was loving this, and when I got in the vicinity of the cab they made sure it went out on the air what we'd done and that I was a block from the suspect—just to rub it in Peabody's face.

I asked for back, and three patrol cars showed up within moments. We picked up the lucky suspect, the one who almost got away, and paid the cabbie for driving slow and working with us.

He'd been alarmed to learn that he had danger in the back seat, and he was glad to join in the capture of the guy.

I was also pretty jacked up.

For a "young pup who had a lot to learn about drug dealers," I was quite happy to be the stupid guy who got it right.

THIRTY
LEFT HOOK/RIGHT GUARD

GIVEN THE RIGHT CIRCUMSTANCE AND opportunity, anything can be used as a weapon.

I was called to a family fight, but when I arrived it was already over. At the scene, I found a small, compact woman who claimed her husband had been out with another woman. She also claimed that he'd attacked her when she confronted him about the affair, saying that he threw her around the room and left.

Surprisingly, she seemed unhurt with only a few minor abrasions showing.

As I started to take the information from her about what had happened and what his name was, he walked in.

More than a foot taller than his wife, he was a mess, covered in blood.

When I asked him what had happened, he described coming home from a friend's house to have his wife accuse him of being with another woman. He told her that was ridiculous—then she attacked him, a barely five-foot package of woman, enraged.

He said she hit him in the head over and over again with a metal spray can. She chased him all through the house until he was able to lock himself in the bathroom. She then grabbed a knife and drove it through the wooden bathroom door several times, trying to get at him.

Growing impatient with that approach, she brought out a bag of charcoal and a can of lighter fluid, then poured it all out around the base of the door and tried to light it while screaming, "I'm gonna fucking KILL your white ass! Nobody fucks around on me!"

When he smelled the lighter fluid and saw smoke, he said he panicked. He knew if she got her planned barbecue going, he'd be trapped with no escape, so he opened the door and blew past her. Running as fast as he could, he knocked her down as he fled out the front door.

Deep semi-circular cuts were easily visible all over his head, some right down to the bone and still bleeding.

I called for medical and checked the bathroom; charcoal was all around the base of the doorway, wet with liquid that smelled like charcoal lighter.

I went back to the woman, now sitting quietly on the couch. I tried to get her explanation for the charcoal and the cuts on her husband's head, but she refused to talk.

I reached to grab her arm to get her attention as she sat catatonic on the couch—and the touch caused her to turn into a screaming crazy woman, jumping and flailing, scratching and biting.

I was able to get her to the floor and handcuff her.

I checked the couch and found the metal aerosol can: a "Right Guard" brand spray can. It had strands of hair and blood on the bottom edges.

I arrested her for aggravated assault and attempted arson, then booked her into jail.

A week later, they were back together again, walking down the street.

When I saw them, I called the prosecutors, who told me that the charges had been dropped; he'd refused to testify against her... imagine that.

THIRTY-ONE
TRIANGULATED

ONE NIGHT, I WAS GETTING in some overtime "cleaning up the board," as the sergeants called it, meaning I'd take all the non-priority calls running all over the city to get them off the dispatch logs as soon as possible.

It made our stats look good, and it got me out of my assigned area for a while. For us, it's a chance for some freelancing, cruising around putting out minor fires, nothing too serious; but this night, that didn't last long.

A call came in from a gas station near the eastern foothills that promised some guy looking for a confrontation, preferably with the cops.

The caller dialed 911 to say that he was "Wyatt Earp" and that we'd better get up there fast. He said he had a knife, and then he hung up and waited.

I was on the west side, listening; it sounded like trouble, so I started towards the location.

I was about halfway there when officers on the scene radioed, yelling for help; meanwhile, Mr. Earp's girlfriend had called dispatch to say that he was suicidal and wanted to provoke the police into shooting him.

I was next to arrive and found a patrolman and a sergeant backing away from Earp, who was walking around with a huge fucking blade, a big Bowie knife. The scent of pepper spray was in the air; it was already tried on Earp with no effect.

He kept advancing on the two officers, ignoring any attempts to talk him down. I yelled to get his attention, and he started towards me.

I had a car between us, and we actually ran around it a few times—him chasing me and me pepper-spraying him. The spray continued to have no effect; he just wiped it off and kept coming, closing in on me. (This was a few years before Tasers.)

I backed away from the car and pulled out my Glock, trying to talk him down, but he wouldn't respond; he just kept coming at me with that huge knife, head down, eyes locked on mine.

It was easy to see him gutting me with no regrets, so I settled into a firing stance.

Just then, the other two officers fell in behind him. We were all in each other's field of fire; triangulated, but a flat triangle.

So, I holstered up and got ready to fight, go toe to toe—"going toes" as we called it. He kept closing in, still quiet and determined.

It was terrifying.

The sound of your blood rushing in your ears isn't fiction; there's a background buzz, a hazy noise as your metabolism launches with adrenaline, preparing you for battle.

This guy wasn't swinging the knife where I could grab for his arm and hold on; instead, he held it close to his body, which would make it very hard to fight him and come out of this without my guts dumped all over the pavement.

Realizing I was about to get seriously fucked up, my pulse elevated; I was getting angry, getting ready to rip this guy apart.

Rage and fear are powerful emotions, and even more volatile when mixed. I wasn't going to die. Not in my mind. I envisioned crushing his throat and ripping out his eyes; losing this battle was *not* an option.

Then out of nowhere, Bobby Grimes drove his patrol car between me and Earp, hitting Earp with a glancing blow from the car—which probably saved my life. I couldn't believe it.

Earp was furious, and he viciously attacked the car, striking the driver's window over and over.

Sparks flew from the metal frame around the door glass, and then the door, as he tried to smash his way through to get at Grimes. With Bobby behind the determined attacker, I still didn't have a shot.

Earp eventually tired of trying to kill Grimes in the car, and turned back towards the other two officers. Grimes was then able to get out of the car, and we both approached Earp.

Fortunately, Grimes had a shot and took it.

He double-tapped Earp, hitting him twice in the torso, which immediately dropped him to the ground.

I holstered and started first aid, calling dispatch to send medical. Earp, his real name Darin Eest, was gasping doing what was called agonal breathing, the last gasps.

He died at the scene, and the press crucified Grimes because some eyewitness who was an ex-con claimed that Eest had no knife; he said that the one we reported had been planted.

The guys in the department talked a lot of shit about Grimes as well; after an incident like this, you find out really quickly that you have very few friends in police work.

The Internal Affairs investigation was grueling.

The IA investigator asked me why I hadn't shot Eest.

I explained that I couldn't because of the background; in the rush of events, we were in each other's way and our triangulation stressed.

Every time I had a shot, an officer would turn up behind Eest.

"So you're trying to tell me that every time you had a shot, another officer stepped behind the suspect and put himself in jeopardy, seeing that your gun was out and pointed in his direction?" he asked.

"I can't tell you what he saw," I answered. "You know, Eest never did stop to ask us where we wanted him to stand. It was a fluid situation."

The department seemed to be looking for a way to rule it as a bad shoot, but eventually Grimes was cleared and he came back to work.

I always had a hard time around Bobby after that. He saved my life, and I could never repay him.

The department and the media treated him poorly. He suffered. He cried over killing that kid; Bobby was as solid as they come, brave as hell, tough, smart—but he cried over this guy.

I even heard that his wife was spat on in a grocery store by a group of people who called Bobby a killer. I was enraged by what he was going through.

It turned out that the department hadn't even read my report on the shooting; I had to go in and explain it to one of the lieutenants, telling him about how he'd saved my life.

I put him in for a Medal of Valor, but it was repeatedly denied.

I raised hell with anyone who'd listen, but the bottom line was that the brass didn't like Bobby. I was almost fired for insubordination, having pushed against the sergeant on the scene at the time of the incident and then the duty lieutenant who worked that night.

I wouldn't let it go; they had to make this right.

They finally did, but I had to go over some heads to an assistant chief to get heard, further cementing my lack of popularity.

I'd never had anyone step up during a life-threatening situation and help me like Bobby had.

THIRTY-TWO
SOMETHING FOR THE TROPHY CASE

STARTING OUT ON A SLOW night that was about to heat up, I was babysitting a bank parking lot. As you might imagine, when bankers complain, the department responds.

The financial hub was just off Main Street, which the kids like to traverse, "Cruising The Boulevard," as it's called.

Cruising involves various collection points where the kids can pull off and gather, and well-kept parking lots such as a bank's are very popular. The bank was having a lot of problems with the kids partying there, leaving a lot of trash and usually causing some property damage.

So often, this is a simple matter to solve; just park a patrol car there. This also worked in moving the hookers around.

When an establishment complains that too many of the working girls are hanging out, just have a uniformed officer park in the area; instantly, they relocate. These are just nuisance calls.

Same with boulevard cruisers who congregate in parking lots to talk and compare cars. If they're trashing the place, just having a patrol car take up residency solves what's largely a litter problem and moves them along. We're not garbage men.

I was camped out in the bank parking lot this night when I saw a trooper in a chase with Jack Converse; they went flying past me, westbound across Main.

I knew Jack, a troubled kid. I grew up with his dad, an abusive alcoholic providing nothing but a volatile home life for Jack. I saw Jack as a nice kid who had little chance at any kind of normal life; this night, he gave up.

The troopers didn't have access to our radio frequencies back then, and we weren't able to hear theirs; so, I called in the chase with dispatch and tried to parallel them, attempting to catch up.

They zigzagged back and forth in the area, and I couldn't find them. Then they turned east, crossing Main again, going up four blocks and back into the inner city again before I finally caught up with them.

As I rounded the corner, I saw that both Jack and the trooper were out of their vehicles, facing each other with guns drawn.

The trooper backed off some, waiting for backup and moving closer to his cruiser, leaving Jack standing out in the middle of the street, defiant and emboldened.

I got out and challenged him from about sixty feet away.

He started to move toward the sidewalk, and I moved to cut him off.

Another patrol car arrived, and with the trooper we had him cornered. Jack wouldn't back down, though, instead ignoring commands and waving his gun around.

I had no idea why he ran on the trooper, but this was now something else. Why wouldn't he just put his gun down and surrender? This was a little more obvious; it appeared that he wanted to die...he knew what he was setting himself up for.

He pointed the gun first at the trooper, then at the other patrolman. Finally, he settled on me.

We'd spoken just a few weeks earlier, friendly talking about the trouble he was drifting into. I don't know if it was his interest in gangs or drugs that was driving him, or more likely that he just didn't like going home before his virulent, alcoholic father passed out for the night.

He was barely eighteen, but I think somehow in this fucked up world he found himself in, he wanted to die.

He was no longer just pointing the gun, but decidedly aiming at me.

I fired four times, the other officers firing almost simultaneously.

The shooting was strangely quiet for me; I only heard my gun go off. The patrol cars all had their sirens on, but I never heard any of that.

I never heard the other guys' guns go off, either.

All I had in focus was Jack aiming at me, and that was what I concentrated on.

He dropped to the ground, and I started First Aid.

The shoot bothered me only in that I knew where Jack was coming from and what his life was like. It still left me numb.

Jack was looking for his way out—through me. I had no desire to kill or hurt him; I just wanted to live myself.

What was also burned into my consciousness from that night was my sergeant, Leeds again. He turned on me, fearing I had a leg up on him as he'd never had what he saw as the "macho romance" of a shootout.

From that point on, he actively went after me every chance he got.

He was one sick fuck, angry that his career ended years later without ever shooting anyone, leaving his trophy case apparently empty.

Jack lived.

On the way home that night, I called the hospital and checked on him. Two of his fingers had been shot off, one round went into his chest, and another blew his dick off. At the hospital, they laughed that they'd roughly cleaned up the injured gangster without an anesthetic.

I hung up, no longer sure what planet I was on.

Once healed, Jack was sent to prison.

A little later, one of the patrolmen contacted me to say that they were removing a bullet from an inmate I shot and wanted to know if I needed it as a memento. It wasn't mine, and why would I want it if it were?

THIRTY-THREE
THE CHIEF AND PARKING

ONE DAY I CAME TO work and, sitting in the afternoon briefing, heard this: we were told that under no circumstances would we be parking against traffic in the city from that day forward.

We all looked at each other, puzzled at such a ridiculous statement.

We asked why this was being brought up. There had to be a reason to contradict the state law that said we could violate any traffic law necessary to effect an arrest or come to the aid of a citizen or another officer—so what was up?

It turned out that the Chief had been chewed out by the city council for someone parking against traffic. He felt threatened by it and felt that his job was in jeopardy.

We were told that his exact words were that he "would not go down for this alone." If anyone was caught parking against traffic, they'd be given days off without pay and lose the privilege of the take-home patrol car.

We were getting used to this from the Chief; everything that happened was about him, how it related to him, and how he was perceived in the press and by the city council.

He didn't look out for the best interests of the department; he just looked out for his own best interests.

He'd been self-centered as a sergeant and a lieutenant, and now as a Chief he was unbearable.

So we left the briefing, and right out of the office I got a call; it was a woman and a man in a dispute over property in one of the poorer parts of the city.

I headed out east bound, then arrived and saw a woman pushing a shopping cart full of her possessions. She was almost to the intersection of a main street, only one or two houses west of it, and she was in a heated argument with a large white male. He was extremely animated and shoved her a couple times, slamming her into her cart.

I caught a break in traffic, then cut across, parked against the traffic, got out, and interrupted the fight, stopping it before it really got out of hand.

There was a crowd gathering to watch the possible fight, and I dispersed them.

I was busy dealing with the two people.

The woman had called and wanted her things from the guy, who happened to be her landlord; it was a civil case, which is always a pain in the ass.

She was basically going to be homeless because the landlord wanted his rent money and had legally evicted her.

I was there as a mediator, trying to get the two upset adults back into "adult mode" thinking, back into reality, and I was just about finished when Sgt. Gus walked up.

Looking upset, he said to me, "Are you almost done?"

I said that I was. He said good and told me to meet him in the station when I was done. I had no idea why, but I could tell it wasn't good.

Turned out, the Chief drove past the call while I was parked against traffic—and he was furious.

He sent out orders to have both me and my Sgt. relieved of duty for not obeying his "order" about parking against traffic.

I spent the rest of the shift writing and explaining to Sgt. Gus and the Duty Lieutenant why I did what I did.

I didn't do it to challenge the Chief; I did it to protect the woman from getting her ass kicked.

I made sure that I quoted state law and explained what I did with the public's well-being in mind.

When I left that day, I was relieved of duty, as was Sgt. Gus. The Sergeant and the Duty Lieutenant both said, though, that they thought that I'd acted correctly and that the Chief was really out of line.

By the next afternoon, I was back on duty and all punishment had been dropped for both Sgt. Gus and me.

Apparently, the senior staff had confronted the Chief and told him that they wouldn't support his action.

They also told him that he'd have a revolt from within the department if he continued to punish us for taking the correct action in protecting the public and doing our duty.

I heard that the final deciding factor for the Chief was that, if it got out to the press, it would be really hard to explain that one of the officers had put himself in danger to protect a citizen, driving against and parking against traffic due to the emergent nature of the situation and breaking up a fight in progress between a homeless woman and her landlord—only to have the Chief drive by afterward and second guess that decision.

Once again, the Chief chose what was best for himself and dropped it. No apology, no explanation; it was just dropped.

The police department really didn't like our Chief; he constantly butted heads with everyone. He even refused to pay us during the Y2K scare.

We were required to be on call and had to make plans for our families to be taken care of should the power grids fail and civilization as we knew it fall; seriously, they really overreacted to this, and we were on 12-hour shifts and on call.

We were required to be reimbursed for being on call, as well as for the overtime for the 12-hour shifts, but the Chief refused to pay us out of his budget. He wanted it come out of the city's budget.

He called a mandatory meeting—which we had to be paid for as well—and told us all point blank that he wouldn't pay us for the extra time.

He said, "If you don't like it, then sue me. I don't care; I'm not paying."

This was his idea of employee relations.

We did start a class action lawsuit, after which the city wisely decided to pay us.

To make matters worse between the Chief and me, I ran into another Chief I knew from another department.

The chiefs have a yearly meeting where they all get together, and in this meeting my Chief was bragging about what good shots his officers were. He asked me if it was true that one of the guys intentionally shot a guy's dick off...I was speechless.

I'd made that shot on purpose, yes.

Being sixty feet away, I thought I was missing Jack Converse during the shooting; so, I lowered my weapon's aim to the groin area, thinking that I was shooting high because that's common at night. Jack had suffered the consequences.

To hear that the Chief was bragging about this in a Chiefs' meeting somewhere, I was shocked, angry, and now disliked him even more.

He never even so much as acknowledged me in the hallways at work, but he'd take credit for my work at Chiefs' meetings as if he were in some way responsible for anything I did.

THIRTY-FOUR
SHOPLIFTING A RAP BAG

ONE NIGHT, I WAS CALLED to a large grocery store that was in the central part of the city.

Store security had observed a man shoplifting and had detained him; they said they had a shoplifter in custody who had stolen a rap magazine.

I arrived and contacted security, and they took me back to their office in the rear of the store. It was about eight feet wide by ten deep, just big enough for a desk and a couple chairs.

They introduced me to a stocky muscular guy who identified himself as James Gray.

I asked Gray for identification, and he said that he had none; he claimed that he had no identification at all.

That was a problem for me because I couldn't release him on a misdemeanor citation if I couldn't positively identify him with legitimate identification.

I wrote down all the necessary information from the security guards and Mr. Gray, then asked him to stand up and turn around.

He stood up but didn't turn around; instead, he said, "What the fuck is this?"

I explained to him that without identification I couldn't give him a citation and that I had to book him into jail for the $2 magazine.

He said, "Fuck that. I ain't going to jail, motherfucker."

I told him again to turn around and tried to turn him, but he refused—and the fight was on.

He was really quite strong; I'd later find out that he'd just gotten out of prison and knew that this theft would violate his parole—and he was willing to do almost anything to avoid going back to prison.

We fought pretty hard for some time.

I slammed his head into the walls, destroying the drywall and really making a mess out of the security office.

Finally, I managed to call for back up, and I heard a couple officers acknowledge and claim that they were en route.

We were then back at it, fighting and wrestling, until finally I was able to get him cuffed.

We were both covered with the white powder from the dry wall, and we looked like hell.

The security officers had just backed out of the room when the fight broke out.

They were scared of Gray; he was pretty buff and very intimidating.

I cleaned up, and when I'd rested up enough I asked Gray what the hell the problem was, why the hell was he fighting so hard over a stupid shoplifting charge?

He then told me that he was on paper and would violate his parole and he would most likely be sent back to prison.

Then I understood at least why he acted the way he did.

I talked to him for a few minutes and found out that his family was outside in the parking lot, waiting for him.

Even though he was cuffed and had lost the fight, he was still combative, angry, and trying to get away.

He kicked at me a couple times and tried to head butt me—and finally I had enough.

I grabbed him by the head and slammed it into the wall a couple times—hard.

This broke the drywall, punching a hole in it through the other side; his head was now sticking out in the storage area of the store.

I pulled him back out of the hole and told him that he had a choice to make: he could either leave the store walking, or I'd drag him out like a fucking dog in front of his kids and everyone else.

This struck him hard; he didn't want his kids to see him that way, so he quit fighting and asked that I clean him up and let him say goodbye to his sons.

I agreed but made it clear that if he changed his mind, I'd embarrass him as much as I could in front of his family.

I cleaned him up as much as I could, and he did cooperate, so I let him say goodbye to his sons.

When we got into the car, he thanked me and apologized for fighting me.

He said that he thought that he could take me since it was just him and me fighting.

No other cops had shown up and helped out.

They'd shown up in the parking lot and signed out on the radio claiming that they were there, but they never got out of their cars; instead, they waited in the parking lot in their cars while I was fighting inside the building.

Two units were in the parking lot...so much for the thin blue line.

Years later, I was training a new guy on the midnight shift.

He told me that he was a security guard at that same grocery store in central city and that he'd "seen it all" working there.

He then started to tell me this incredible story about a shoplifter who had refused to submit to arrest.

He said that the cop was smaller than the shoplifter and that he destroyed their store's security office arresting him.

He said they talked about it for months, about how it had happened and how the guy's head went into the drywall.

He told me the whole story from his point of view, recalling how terrified he was of the shoplifter, then later how afraid he was of the cop.

I never told him it was me.

It never ceased to amaze me how others saw the things that were just a normal part of the job for me.

THIRTY-FIVE
BURNING HOUSE ENTRY

ONE NIGHT, I WAS ADVISED by dispatch that there was a report of a house fire in my area.

Dispatch would often give us a heads-up on medicals and house fires so that we could help out with traffic control and securing the scene before medical arrived.

Usually, we were too busy to help out unless it was really bad; however, this night had been slow.

When I arrived, there were a couple cars already there.

The cops were out of their cars, watching the fire.

The building was a house that had been remodeled, and it was now a duplex, one apartment up and one apartment down.

The downstairs apartment was fully engulfed by the fire.

Everyone knew the upstairs was occupied by a group of ten to twelve Mexicans, most likely illegal immigrants working to support their families in Mexico; we'd been to that apartment several times on loud parties.

I got out and asked the group of cops that was there if anyone had exited the upstairs apartment.

They said that no one had come out since they'd been there.

I was a bit anxious; I wasn't going to sit back and watch while a bunch of people burned to death.

I asked, "Well are we going in?"

They said that they "weren't going in to rescue a bunch of Mexicans."

I started towards the house, and they yelled "we aren't gonna save your ass for a bunch of Mexicans either…you're going alone."

I kept going.

Another officer ran up to me and said, "What the hell are you doing? You're gonna die in there!"

I turned to him and said, "I'm not gonna sit out here and watch while they burn to death when I could have done something. I won't live like that; I won't have this shit on my conscience."

He grabbed my arm and said, "They're just Mexicans."

I broke free from him and started up the stairs to the apartment above the fire, and he started to cry.

He was scared to death but said, "Wait! Then…OK…I'll go with you."

We went in and got the people out long before the fire department arrived.

I was really scared that the fire had burned out enough of the floor in the top apartment that once we entered we'd fall through to the fire below.

He cursed me the whole time we were in the burning house; it was hot and smoky and really hard to see, and we were coughing hard while we searched on our hands and knees to make sure they were all out.

When we finally got back outside, I left.

The other officers shook their heads, watching us exit the house; they weren't impressed at all at what they felt was my stupidity.

Later, the guy who went in with me would approach me.

He was still mad, and he said to me, "You are fucking crazy. I heard this about you—that you do this stupid shit! You could have gotten us killed!"

It was days like this that made me feel like I lived in a different universe.

THIRTY-SIX
JOE'S PERFECT CAMARO

THERE WAS A GUY NAMED Joe in the inner city who had a really sweet '68 Camaro.

He'd put a lot of work into it, and it was amazingly nice.

I used to stop and talk to him while he worked on it.

He was married and had a couple kids. His wife wasn't as excited about the car as I was, and she didn't like me showing up and praising the work he did.

One day, I caught a call for a car that had driven through the front porch of a house, then crashed into a tree.

I arrived, and there was Joe's Camaro wrapped around a tree—completely totaled. It was a sad thing to see.

I started to interview people and found out that the driver had been Joe. I couldn't believe it.

Witnesses said that he'd come out of his apartment, got into the car, and started it, revving the motor. Then he drove it through the front porch of a neighbor's house.

He continued down the driveway and across the street into the tree, then got out and ran back to his apartment.

I went to the apartment and knocked on the door.

His wife answered.

She was beaten up and just pointed into the apartment and said, "He's in there. Get him the fuck out of here."

I went into the apartment and found Joe.

He was covered in sweat and drooling. I'd never seen him that way. I put him in handcuffs and walked him out of the door.

His wife denied medical treatment for her injuries; she just wanted him out of their apartment.

I took him to jail, and on the way he started to hallucinate.

While in jail, he started seeing bugs crawling on the walls and screamed that they were on him; I couldn't complete the paperwork with him wigging out next to me.

The other officers in the booking area were really uncomfortable with him acting this way as well, so I decided to put him into a holding cell and asked the booking officers to open one up.

I put him in the cell as he ranted and raved about the bugs on him, then closed the door, sat back down, and went back to work on the paperwork.

About ten minutes passed, and I was almost done—when it became really quiet in the holding cell.

I looked up, and the other officers also stopped and we all looked at each other, waiting, listening.

After a few seconds, I got up and went to check on Joe.

I looked through the holding cell door window, and there was Joe. He was on his knees, his head in the steel toilet, hands still cuffed behind his back. I thought that he was trying to kill himself.

What I did not know was that the holding cell plumbing had been inoperable for several days. Someone on one of the floors above the cell had flushed rolls of toilet paper down the toilet.

It is a way that inmates try to fight back against the system. (Minor passive aggressive actions that cause disruption for the correctional officers.)

Anyway, the toilet had not been working for several days. It had filled up with shit, piss, and vomit during those three days and Joe had his head buried in it.

I yelled at the booking officers and told them to open the holding cell.

I went inside and yelled at Joe.

As I entered the cell yelling at him, he pulled his head out of the disgusting muck in the toilet.

Shit and chunks of vomit running down his face and in his teeth, mouth and nose.

I said "What the hell are you doing?"

He turned and looked at me and said, "I was thirsty!"

This was by far one of the most amazingly disgusting things I had ever witnessed.

The correctional officers came in and hosed him off and I finished booking him into jail.

I was amazed at his behavior. It is shocking what tweekers are capable of doing after a couple of weeks without sleep.

THIRTY-SEVEN
BAT SHIT CRAZY

IT WAS NEVER MORE APPARENT that I was not like the rest of the guys I worked with than when we went to training.

Guys who are proud to display on their office walls the certificates of expertise they have earned usually conduct training for Law enforcement.

They have impeccable resumes, and impressive credentials. Basically mirroring academia in the belief that certificates, public accolades, and successful course completion equates to valuable real world experience. It does not.

The expert on the street is the guy who survived the previous night.

Every night is a challenge to adapt to an ever-increasingly hostile and complicated series of obstacles. The fact you continue your employment and survive the battles on the street both mentally and physically is a testament to your expertise.

Not the trophy wall, not the resume proudly displayed on line. Your resume is a series of successful returns to your home and family.

Regardless, the law requires that cops be trained in the "latest" techniques thought up by Law enforcement "experts".

In our state a minimum amount of training was required by Law and it was a budget challenge to figure out how to keep the training hours up and costs down.

The idea should have been to get the most bang for your buck. Instead for a period of time it was to get the cheapest training possible. This made for some interesting classes, taught by the "I love me" cops.

One option our department tried out for a time was a televised network of training classes. We would be required to pile into the department's training room and listen to the latest self proclaimed expert teach us the latest "critical skill".

One day I was sitting in class listening to the latest most amazing important skill I was supposed to master and trying desperately hard to not fall asleep.

The classes were tedious as hell and if you were a critical thinker at all you could see huge faults in the training logic.

I had been taught many years ago by one of the best cops I had ever met to challenge anything and everything you were taught. If it made no sense or if you could not modify it or make it work for you, dump it and move on.

His mentoring me would be a huge influence on my survival in the field.

The idea of 'questioning everything mentality' would rub a lot of people I worked with the wrong way and I would always be on the outside of the "good ole boy network" looking in.

The cop who mentored me was Robert Suggs. He will get his own story much later on in these books.

Today's class was about surviving a hostage situation as a cop.

If you were ever taken hostage as a cop what would your plan of survival be? Basically planning for the worst situation possible.

The scenario was spelled out like this; you were handcuffed and disarmed and being held hostage. How would you escape and overcome your captors?

The televised training went on and on about mentally preparing your self for this unbelievable eventuality.

One of the questions asked in the class was if you were ever in a situation where you were told to surrender your weapon or the bad guy would shoot another officer what would you do? The situation actually did happen occasionally.

One guy I worked with had been held hostage, he and another cop were tied up and told they were about to be shot in the head.

Somehow they escaped and physically survived the situation.

Mentally though he was damaged. He was scared for the rest of his career and would never respond to dangerous calls with the same sense of urgency.

He was terrified of being held hostage again.

I don't know what happened, I was not there, but I saw how it affected him.

The trainer did not make any recommendations about what your course of action should be, he just asked that we consider what our choices would be if it did happen.

The guy who was instructing the televised class said that he recommended that all cops keep several hand cuff keys on them at all times. He thought this was a good idea whether you were on duty or off. He then detailed the six different places he kept a handcuff key on him at all times.

Usually I kept my opinions about the training to myself. I had made comments before and I had been harshly rebuked and told I knew nothing, I was a rookie and I should keep my mouth shut.

I could not keep it in any longer though and finally erupted in a tirade against what I felt was not only stupid training but dangerous training.

My personal opinion is to always be on the offensive in any situation, not planning how to survive a seriously stupid mistake.

Don't make the mistake in the first place and you don't have to be a walking poster boy for a key fetish.

I voiced this opinion and immediately I could see the guy next to me was offended, His name was Tim Mathues.

Tim Mathues was a mystery to me and I admit I never really got my head around how he thought about being a cop.

He had been raised in a rural environment where I had been raised in the city. He was a strict rule follower, I mean to the letter. He followed every policy the department had in place to the letter.

I took great joy in breaking as many rules as I could.

Tim was one of my FTO (Field Training Officers) and he taught me everything I would never want to be.

Sometimes training was like that as well. You learned what you did not want to become.

Anyway one day while I was riding with Tim I made the mistake of calling him Tim.

He stopped the car in the middle of the street abruptly, hands gripping the steering wheel in a white knuckle death grip, while his breathing reached an alarming rate.

I thought he was having an anxiety attack. I was wrong.

He was having a temper tantrum.

He looked at me, red in the face and gritting his teeth, said "NEVER CALL ME TIM!"

He said, Tim was his father's name and he was named after his father.

I said, "Ok Tim what should I call you then?"

Rage, pure rage exploded from Tim and he screamed, "TIMOTHY! I AM TIMOTHY, NOT TIM!"

I was sitting next to him in a full size car.

I could hear him clearly.

I could also see that he had a serious need for some extensive dental work on his molars. His mouth was open that wide as he screamed this in my face.

I realized at that moment Tim was BAT SHIT CRAZY and could probably be the next character in a Stephen King Novel.

I quit tormenting the mentally unstable officer and started to watch him, trying to figure him out.

I was never able to. He was erratic and emotional and never had the same response to any situation.

So I was sitting next to Tim in training and he turned to me and said, "You don't see the value in this training? Do you know why that is?"

I said, "Ya, this is stupid! Do you really think that hiding handcuff keys all over your body is gonna save you? Hell with that! How about making sure that you are never in that situation to begin with?"

He said, "You don't see the value in the training because you don't see the danger in this job. For you this job is just that, a JOB.

"To those of us who take the job seriously it is more than that, it is a calling, a profession, something to be proud of.

"I listen to the ideas presented in these classes and take them to heart. I want to learn from others and better myself. I plan to be the best cop I can be."

His face was turning red as he talked.

I said, "Look, if you want to hide keys all over your body great! What if you get tied up with zipcuffs, or rope, then what?"

Tim was getting pumped up and the wind was definitely in his sails.

He went on and on about how being prepared for the unexpected was the most important thing a cop could do to survive.

By now our conversation had followers, several of the administration were listening and Tim knew this.

He was sure they agreed with him and I think that he was right.

He started to explain to me that he had hidden keys on his uniform and in his shoes for years now, just in case he was ever taken hostage.

I saw several of the older guys nod their heads in approval.

I asked "How many keys do you carry?" Curious how deep this fear went for him.

He said that he carried seven keys at all times.

I said, "Seven? No shit? Where do you hide all of them?" Pretending to be interested in the way he hid them. Really I was interested in where and why.

I had an idea I would learn more from that information and how he had thought this through than the actual number of keys he kept.

Tim detailed each location and as he did he explained why he kept the key there.

The administrators who were present listened intently to his explanation and I saw several heads nod with approval and smiles were exchanged in agreement with Tim's logic.

Tim reached Key number six and stopped. He just stopped and looked at me.

I said, "Ok that was six, where do you keep the last one?"

Tim was quiet.

I said "Well?"

Tim said, "I get a piece of tape and tape it to my body."

I could tell there was a lot more to this than met the eye.

His body language and demeanor told me that he felt proud of the thought put into the location this taped key.

Tim said that he figured that if he was ever to be taken hostage the only way to defeat his preparations and placement of hidden keys all over his body and in his equipment was to take him hostage in the nude.

He said that he had thought this out and that if he ever was taken hostage and stripped nude he would want to be able to escape.

He also felt that most likely the incident would include another cop also being taken hostage.

He felt that he had to take his preparations seriously, as both of their lives would depend on his planning and forethought.

The administration was extremely impressed by this depth of planning and Tim's commitment to tactical survival.

I was not, but I said nothing.

I said, "Ok, I see what you are getting at. Why would you go to all of this preparation to have it all defeated by simply removing the places you hide the keys? So where do you hide it?"

Tim stood tall in the training room and began to detail the thought process behind this.

He said he pictured himself and another cop naked and hand cuffed in a dark and dirty room. (Really? Seriously?)

They would be handcuffed behind their backs and being naked limited their ability to both hide keys and recover and use them.

He said that he finally figured out that he had to hide a key where it could not be seen but you could access it.

I was thinking to myself, here we go! Bat shit crazy is about to emerge again.

Tim said that he taped the seventh key to his scrotum.

I was speechless, I looked at the administration who were listening, their eyebrows all raised simultaneously in surprise.

I said, "What, you tape it where?"

He said, "You heard me!"

Louder now, and proudly, he said, "I tape the key to my scrotum. That way if I was ever handcuffed behind my back and was with another officer all I would have to do is bend over and the other officer could reach the key if his hands were behind his back."

The room was silent.

I could see the image playing out in the administrator's minds. Furrowed brows emerged as veterans became uncomfortable with the images starting to develop in their minds.

I burst out laughing.

I could not believe the level of paranoia Tim lived with.

This disclosure about his perceived planning for the worst seemed to incorporate more dark hidden sexual fantasy than real fear.

I could not stop laughing. The more I laughed the madder Tim became.

Then I said, "So Tim," knowing this would push him over the edge, "you have a key taped to your nuts right now don't you? I mean we are in training and there is no threat here, but when you came to class today you had a key taped to your nuts right?"

Tim unleashed the I am not Tim, call me Timothy speech I had received before.

Screaming at the top of his lungs, red in the face with veins popping out all over his neck and forehead.

In this context however it just did not sound the same. The administration suddenly had a different perception of Tim.

Looks of surprise and shock replaced their looks of approval.

Tim was bat shit crazy and a great example of the guys I worked with.

People have often asked me why I didn't feel like I fit in with the other cops. I tell them this story and ask, "Would you?"

BOOK TWO
STREET CREDS

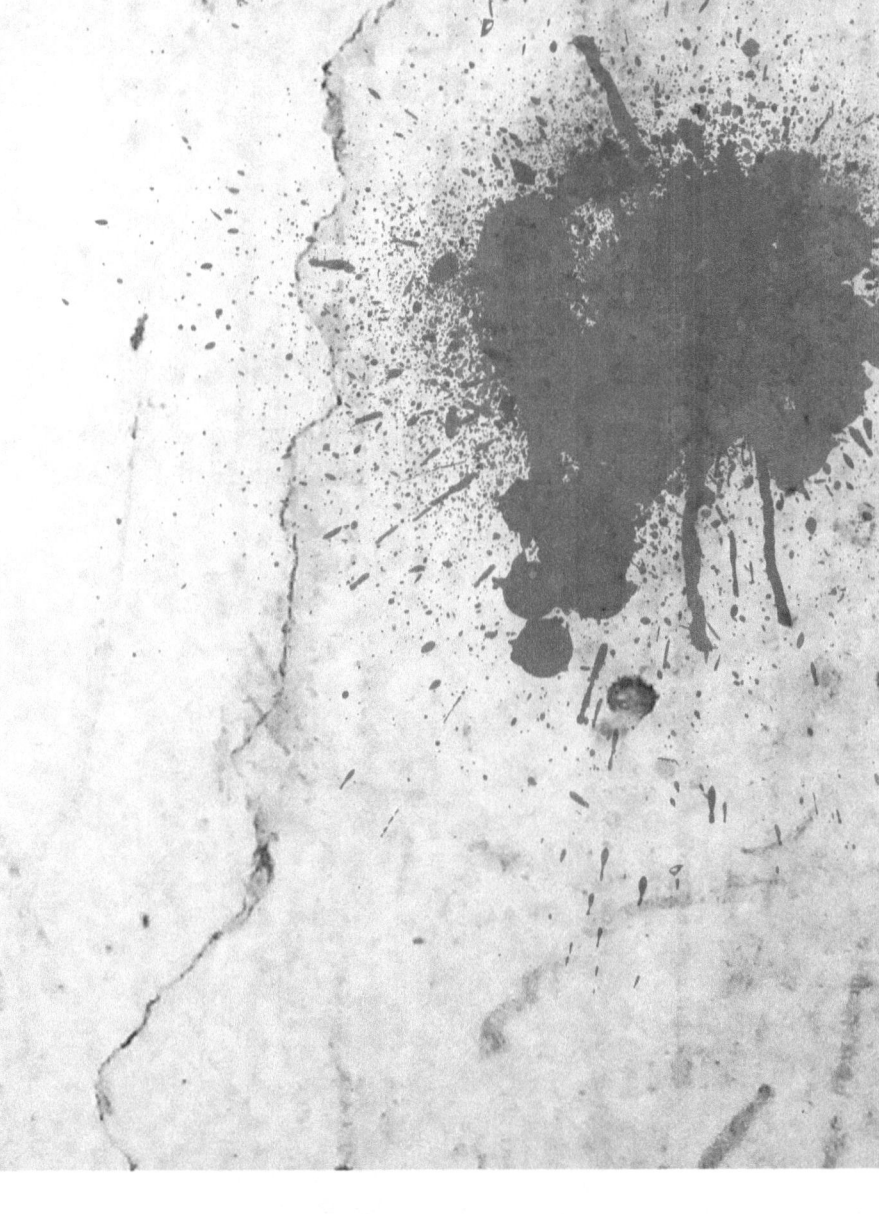

STREET CREDS

"Earning or possessing a high level of respect on the street. A reputation gained by repeated experience on the street or in the penal system."

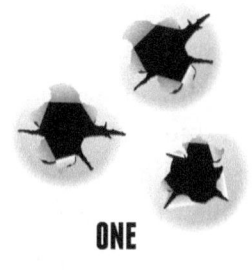

ONE
INITIATION RITES

MY FIRST WEEK ON THE Gang Task Force, I was attending a Gang Seminar in Dallas.

I was pretty excited to attend; I thought that we were going to meet a lot of experts from across the nation and hopefully get some new insight into how to make an impact on the gang problem.

But the reality was quite different; instead, we were surrounded by academics who were only concerned with studying philosophical, obscure theories about gang behavior.

There was no representation from anyone with actual practical expertise.

For example, one presenter felt that gang members joined the gang due to a lack of being able to play when they were younger. She felt that if gang members were allowed to "re-experience" childhood *(playing on swings, merry-go-rounds, and teeter-totters)*, they'd properly develop psychologically and no longer be interested the gang life.

This was typical of the bullshit that various researchers presented in an effort to validate their work.

I went from seminar to seminar, looking for anyone who had something valid and useful to teach me; I found very little.

Meanwhile, the crew that I went to the seminar with was only interested in playing hooky in the hotel rooms, sleeping and hitting the strip clubs at night; they could've cared less about trying to learn anything— but of course, they'd report back to the department that the seminar was well worth the expense and that they'd returned with valuable tools and insight.

I was transferred to the Gang Task Force to replace Detective Jim Smally, who had joined the task force about a year-and-a-half prior with some knowledge about gangs.

He knew a few gang members and was really excited that he might be able to make a difference.

One night after I was selected for the task force, Smally asked me, "Where do you think that the Gang Task Force needs to concentrate the majority of its efforts?"

He was eager to make an impact in an area that no one had addressed before, make his mark and carve out a new trail, so to speak.

I think he wanted to change the way the task force was perceived and have people in the department take it seriously.

I told him that I thought the previous group on the Gang Task Force had neglected the 18th Street gang and that they were a big problem that really needed to be addressed.

The previous guys working gangs had dismissed the 18th Street members as wannabes and saw them as no real threat.

What we were dealing with on the streets of St. Pauls was an offshoot of the original gang in L.A., where they are considered to be the largest and most active of transnational criminal gangs.

When I had expressed my disagreement with them regarding their position, I was ridiculed for it.

I told Smally about how I'd noticed that gang members were especially susceptible to praise and kindness, tempered with a hard edge.

I told him that this was the technique that I used to earn their trust, and I suggested he try it.

Jim took that suggestion and ran with it, and for the first year in gangs he did exceptionally well in the intelligence-gathering portion of the job.

He collected an amazing amount of information on 18th Street: who the members were, how the internal structure worked, and who the leaders were, and he even learned that there was more than one subset of 18th Street; he found out that there were at least two subsets represented in St. Pauls: West Side 18th Street and South Side 18th Street.

He also found out that they weren't always on friendly terms with each other, having different leadership and different goals.

He accomplished all of this in a really short period of time.

Surprisingly, though, his weakness was the same as the gang members—and they exploited it.

He was considered an outcast in the police department.

He and I had been on SWAT together, and he'd been forced to resign because he didn't fit in with the "in crowd" *(the Leeds, Divot, and Peabody crowd)*.

He was a former Marine, and they liked the bragging rights that gave the team, but they didn't like that he was an independent thinker who wouldn't blindly follow orders that didn't make sense.

When he went to gangs and started to befriend the gang members, they accepted him and actually liked him; as a result, he started to lose perspective and started hanging out with them off duty—even going to an 18th Street gang member's wedding.

He had his picture taken at the wedding and made the mistake of showing it to Mike Vetere, his partner in gangs.

Vetere had made a career out of making himself look good to the brass by being their snitch; he'd back channel information to them on what was going on in whatever unit he was associated with at the time.

He was instrumental in getting Dave Session and Rob Rinker removed from the task force, which he accomplished either by exaggerating things that they did with gang members or describing their activities to the brass in a way that was less than complimentary.

Meanwhile, he made himself out to be the sole person on the Gang Task Force that had a handle on the street and what was going on in the gangs.

He also frequently made things up and claimed to have information on cases that he never closed or made arrests on.

Whenever he was questioned about this, he'd claim that the other detectives had ruined his credibility on the street or had warned a witness that he was coming.

He played Jim Smally hard and had him believing that he could trust him and that they could work together, even stating to Jim that he finally had a partner in gangs who understood what needed to be done.

I warned Smally about Vetere, but he didn't listen.

He told me that he and Vetere had an understanding, a partnership, and that they were "in the fight together."

I wouldn't associate with Vetere, and I told Jim that, making it really clear that I wouldn't help him with Vetere in the conversation.

If he wanted my help, he'd have to come to me alone—or not at all.

He thought I was being paranoid *(I heard that a lot)*, and he told me that he and Vetere had hung out together off duty, had parties with each other's families and children, and that he trusted Vetere above anyone else in the department.

When Vetere saw the picture of Smally at the 18th Street wedding, he finally had the hard evidence he needed to take Smally off the task force—once again making himself look like the only one that the brass could trust to get things done.

He went straight to the brass and told them that "Smally had been compromised by the 18th Street gang" and that he needed to be removed from the task force.

He then showed them the picture of Smally at the wedding—and it took about three seconds for the brass to decide to remove him.

Smally finally came to me one night and told me, "You were right; Vetere has screwed me."

This was partially true; Smally had lost perspective as well.

He started out on the task force convicting gang members of the crimes that they were committing, but toward the end he was letting them slide, making cases drag on and on until the victims lost interest and covering for the gang members with whom he'd formed friendships.

It became so blatant that a deputy county attorney contacted the police department and complained that none of the cases being filed by the Gang Task Force were being won in court—and it wasn't because they weren't winnable; it was because the task force was incapable of turning in cases of conviction quality.

Vetere sidestepped this accusation by claiming that he'd done everything he could to make the cases conviction quality, but that Smally had been running interference and sabotaging his cases.

This did happen in detectives a lot.

Your fellow detective can be your worst enemy; it was a very competitive, dog-eat-dog environment, so it wasn't an outrageous claim.

Feeling betrayed again by the department, when he was told that he was being removed from gangs, Smally sabotaged the gang files.

He removed the pictures of gang members that he wanted protected, and he purged the gang lists as well; so, when I went in as his replacement, the gang lists were incomplete, the files were in shambles, and several hundred pictures of gang members were missing.

When I was selected for the task force, Vetere came to me and did the same thing that he'd done to everyone else in the unit: he claimed that he wanted to work together and collaborate on cases.

He praised me for my knowledge of gangs and the street and asked that I show him what I'd learned.

I made it very clear to him, though, that I worked alone.

I'd witnessed how he'd fucked over his partners—and I would *not* be his next victim.

I told him exactly that, using those exact words and letting him know that from that point on he'd be on his own.

I'd help him on other cases that he'd been given if he asked me to, but I wouldn't work with him in any other fashion—period.

This really pissed him off, but he ended up leaving the unit about three months later, along with his record of zero cases closed with an arrest and conviction of a gang member.

During my first week, while I was at the seminar in Dallas, the Sergeant came to me and said, "Zach! I have your first case. Councilman Young's house was shot at in a drive by, and it's all yours."

I didn't mind getting the case, but I thought that this was stupid.

I was in another state, at least a week away from being able to do anything meaningful on the case; meanwhile, there were other detectives on the task force who had stayed behind and hadn't attended the seminar.

They had the background experience and could've begun working on the case immediately. It just didn't make any sense.

Later, I found out that there had been a big battle over the case and no one wanted it, and if it wasn't solved there would be political fallout between the city council and the police department.

Councilman Young had never been a friend of the police department, and he'd complain nonstop until an arrest was made.

Giving me the case would make the task force look like it had done nothing to solve it for some time.

This was how it was managed: it was a group of people who didn't like working gang cases and didn't understand gang members—but all wanted the title of "Detective," the schedule, and the perks that came with the job.

So, I was stuck with a case of "give this one to the new guy."; no one else wanted it, and several flat out refused to work it.

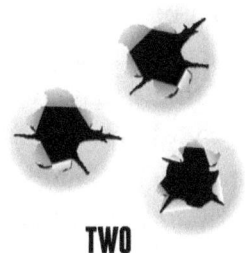

TWO
COUNCILMAN AT LARGE

I ARRIVED BACK AT THE department a week later, and during my first hour back the Lieutenant called me in and wanted to know what I'd done on the case.

I replied that I'd just gotten back from the seminar and that I hadn't even been in the building twenty minutes—what did he expect me to have done?

He told me not to make excuses, that he wanted results and expected an arrest by the week's end.

This was ridiculous; he'd let the case sit for a week-and-a-half already with absolutely nothing done on it—and NOW he wanted results.

I didn't want to end up like Smally, losing perspective, or like Vetere with no cases reaching conviction quality; yet, here I was faced with the culture of a task force set up for failure.

It made me realize that it wasn't as simple as becoming too close to the gangs or being accepted by the gang leaders.

With all the criticism that the Gang Task Force received in the department, I could understand that this wasn't hard to fall victim to.

Nothing was ever good enough; the more you accomplished in arrests, the more the other detectives hated you and were jealous of you—and the less you accomplished, the more you were seen as too soft and incompetent.

It was a no-win scenario.

So, I came in and decided to try to make a statement.

I'd be a friend to whoever worked with me, inside or outside the department, but I wouldn't compromise when it came to shooters.

I made that commitment for two years, doing whatever it took to get the shooters off the streets, then after two years I'd bounce. *(Two years was the most a "working" detective had survived in the Gang Task Force; after that, they'd been kicked out and discredited, having fallen from grace in the latest purge of the unit.)*

I made it a personal goal never to lose a case I made an arrest on; I had to get the conviction, not just the arrest.

If they were in a shooting or thought about doing a shooting, I had to make bangers realize that I'd be coming for them, arrest them, and convict them—no matter what.

As for the other detectives, they were either friend or foe, with no in-between—and there were very few friends.

I printed the case and read the facts.

Officer Dave Stils had written the original case.

He was a former military guy whom I disliked immensely; he had a very annoying habit of always finishing your sentences for you when he talked.

Additionally, regardless of the subject you talked about, he always knew more than you and had already done more than you could ever possibly do yourself.

He'd written a very basic case, having taken whatever Young had said at face value.

He'd collected evidence and obtained some witnesses' names, but he'd taken no pictures or statements.

Additionally, he'd shown no relationship between the suspects and the Young family; in other words, there was no apparent reason for the shooting.

It was reported as "random," but the Youngs knew who the suspect was and what car he drove.

There were a lot of unanswered questions, and after working on the case for about a week, here's what I found out:

First, the entire Young family had been heavily involved in gangs.

The sons and daughter were all members of the WSP *(West Side Pirus)*, which had been rolled into the SPVG *(St. Pauls Violent Gangsters)* under Jessie Afuvi's leadership.

Young tried to present himself as in touch with the streets, a "people's councilman" in touch with the needs of his area of representation; but, the reality was that he was the father of gang members, and on the weekends he drank beer and had barbeques with gang members in the park—not as a politician trying to keep in touch with his constituents, but as a friend and colleague.

The legitimate citizens didn't attend his parties and cookouts; they didn't like him or trust him.

His daughter had been dating a South Side 18th Street gang member secretly for some time.

The family had the guy over to their home several times and had no problem with him—until his rival gang membership had been discovered; then, they opposed him and told the girl that she had to end her relationship with him immediately.

According to the daughter, her dad had told her that the "people on the streets" wouldn't allow the 18th Street gang member to come to their home without consequences and that she could no longer see him.

So, due to pressure from her father, she ended her relationship with the guy.

The 18th Street gang member couldn't understand why the relationship had ended, and he needed closure.

Like most men, he wanted to understand what had happened; one moment things are going fine and smooth, the next it's all over for no apparent reason.

He tried to talk to her, calling and stopping by their house, and eventually his attempts to see her became threatening.

The men in the family told him not to come back or he'd get his ass kicked, but he wasn't about to back down.

He showed up trying to talk to her, and they piled out of the house, ready to beat his ass.

The official report was that he'd driven past and shot several times into the house, then sped away.

The Youngs were hiding in the house, fearing for their lives and calling the police for help.

Bullets lodged in the interior walls of the house were recovered by CSI. That was Stils' report.

The reality, though, was entirely different.

All the men in the Young family had piled out of the house, ready to beat this guy's ass.

He'd brought a gun and flashed it, showing them that he had it and warning them to back off; however, he was outnumbered *(it was now a testosterone contest)*, so he got into his car and left the area.

He returned a short time later and shot into the house, and the Youngs returned fire, shooting at him as he drove away.

They then piled into their own cars and gave chase, shooting at him and his car as he tried to make his escape; they weren't hiding in their houses and waiting for the police to arrive.

When the initial units arrived at the Youngs' house, the brass from the family's weapons had been mostly cleaned up.

I was able to get neighbors to provide me with an account of what had really happened, but they wouldn't give a written statement; they were too afraid of what the family would do.

They also didn't trust the police to do what was right.

They felt this way because they said they'd overheard Officer Stils talking to Young, asking him to explain the expended brass he'd found in the front yard.

Young told him that his sons had fired back at the suspects from the porch—of course, leaving out the parts about the vehicle chase and firing from them.

The witnesses said that Officer Stils told Young he'd omit the part about them shooting from the porch from his report and that he'd given the brass to him and told him to get rid of it; Stils had suppressed the evidence, then wrote his report to reflect the incident the way that Young wanted.

I found the suspect, and he gave me a written confession admitting everything that the witnesses had told me.

He also told me that his younger brother had been with him and could verify everything that had happened.

I obtained a confession from the younger brother as well, and then arrested both the boyfriend and his brother.

Both were illegal aliens and were to be deported after they served their sentences.

That was one thing about the 18th Street gang that I respected: they were incredibly honest.

They admitted and owned up to everything I ever questioned them about; it was a strange characteristic unique to them.

I was able to get photos of bullet holes in the trunk of the suspect's car, as well as in the right rear quarter panel. The holes were all new and the same size.

When I asked Young point blank if he'd fired back in response to the drive by or if anyone in his family had, he became very defensive and started to attack me, stating that I was trying to damage his good name *(as if he ever had one)*.

He said that he wouldn't stand for any slander and that I and the police department had better be careful—or he'd sue us.

When I spoke to the Sergeant in charge of gangs about the case and the suppression of the evidence, he closed the door to his office and said to me, "You've got the arrest; move on. About the suppression of evidence...welcome to Detectives."

I didn't want to think about what he meant by that comment, so I talked to the county attorney handling the case and explained the suppression of the evidence.

They felt it was an internal issue that needed to be dealt with by the PD, not them, so I had no choice but to drop it.

This was my first real behind-the-scenes look at how things went in Detectives and in the county attorney's office.

It was also the first of two gang incidents I'd investigate that directly involved Councilman Young.

After I closed the case with confessions and arrests, the two suspects were easily convicted.

The Sergeant made sure that the guys who had refused to take the case while we were in Dallas were aware of that, chastising them for their refusal *(not that they cared in the slightest what he thought)*.

This didn't make me very popular with the rest of the unit.

Soon, most of the others left and went to other specialties; it wasn't easy for them to claim that their cases weren't solvable when I was solving mine.

THREE
RIGHT AND WRONG?

RIGHT AND WRONG AREN'T AS obvious as some would have you think.

Looking back now, I see that more clearly.

My childhood was never ideal.

My father worked hard to provide for us, working two and sometimes three jobs to keep ahead of the constantly growing pile of bills my crazed shit storm of a mother would produce.

He wasn't a wealthy man and had only a GED, the bare minimum of education.

He wasn't stupid, though; he just had no idea what he'd married.

Quitting anything wasn't in him.

He should have walked away from the nightmare he married and taken us with him—but like I said, he had no idea how to quit.

For him, quitting was the same as failure, and he couldn't accept either.

It was really too bad because he also had no idea what went on when he wasn't at home.

I grew up being taught that it was only wrong if you got caught.

Stealing, lying, cheating—whatever fucked up thing you decided to do was fine as long as you didn't get caught. That was the value system my mother lived by and had ingrained in us, and I had no idea that it was wrong—and even less of an idea that it wasn't how the rest of the world lived.

I really had no idea that any other way even existed; I just knew how it was in my world.

Violence in the home was constant.

I remember several days when I was sure my parents would kill each other—and maybe even us.

With no moral compass to guide me and no example of what to do, I was lost—much like the people I'd run into on the street much later in life, working as a cop on the same streets I grew up in.

My mother pitted my brother and me against each other from the time we could first make a fist; I never understood how she got some sick satisfaction from the constant fighting and chaos.

Being the "wiser" and older matriarch, she'd then break up the fights and deliver our justice and punishment.

The problem was, she had a very intense need to be needed; the more she needed us, the more she provoked fights—and by the first grade, it was all-out war in our household.

We fought with weapons, hand-to-hand, and whatever we could get a hold of. Like the dogs that Michael Vick was recently arrested for fighting, we were raised to provide for her entertainment.

We were nothing more to her than those dogs were to him: mini-gladiators. In my mind, the picture seems funny; the reality, however, was not.

Here's an example of how she really was: I found out that when I was an infant *(and maybe even before I was born)* my brother was left alone with our mother.

She was evil and sadistic and would later admit to me that this incident occurred—after she'd beaten the living shit out of my brother in front of me, smashing his face into the floor repeatedly during an argument.

We were both still kids and had no idea there was anything wrong with this. It was how we grew up.

Anyway, she was kicking the hell out of him, and he said something about "remembering her smiling when he was little."

He didn't want me to know what he was talking about.

In spite of our intense hatred for each other, which was cultivated by her loving manipulation, we knew it was us against them and that they were older and stronger.

After the fight was over, I couldn't let that go...the smiling comment; I had my own fleeting memories of her smiling as well, ugly memories that I tried hard to forget.

Eventually, under the pressure of my constant questioning, she started to open up; you know the questioning that only a kid can get away with: the "Why? Why? Why? Why?"

You either get punched, or you get an answer—and I got an answer I couldn't believe...actually, I did believe it, but I didn't want to.

Turns out that when my brother was young, my dad would go to work and leave an innocent three-year-old with the woman he married. *(Nothing wrong with that in my dad's mind—what could go wrong?)*

Well, "Mary Poppins" had other ideas; she didn't want to be a mother to this child.

She was a walking nightmare of a human being, and as an adult I'd never let her spend one damn second alone with my own children until they were able to defend themselves.

Three-year-old kids are a handful, energetic, full of life, and happy. Exploring the world is what they do *(everything is new and amazing)*, and they can wear any parent down.

My mother had the coping skills of a rattlesnake: move, and she'd strike.

I don't know what my brother did; something horrendous, I'm sure, like eating too many cookies or maybe wanting a snack in the middle of her favorite fucking soap opera.

Who knows? I never asked because it didn't matter; nothing he could have done should have caused her to resort to her idea of discipline.

Years later, she admitted to me that she turned on the gas burner on the stove and lit it, then held his tiny three-year-old hand over the flame repeatedly 'til he got the message.

The comment about her smiling...well, that's what a sadistic fuck does when they harm little kids: they smile while they watch you scream in fear and pain as your flesh burns.

I listened to this and thought about the fight that I'd just witnessed. As I watched his face being smashed into the floor, nothing had changed in my mind.

My brother was just bigger now, and she could no longer burn him into submission; now, she had to *beat* him into submission.

The chaos was constant, and we never knew what to expect from either of them.

Sometimes you were praised for doing well, then the very next breath you were cautioned not to get too cocky, reminded that you were nothing without their constant guidance and approval.

I realized early on that I was very much on my own.

If I were to survive this nightmare, I'd have to find another way without any help from my family.

Eventually, I realized that I could find other people who would mentor me and guide me through the tricky maze of learning about the world without any real guidance.

One night, I remember my dad asking my mom to hem some pants for him.

She didn't want to do it, and after much arguing she picked up a pair of scissors and came walking down the stairs; my mother with a weapon in her hand wasn't a thing to be taken lightly.

She had my immediate attention, and I was ready to bolt for the door, focused on her and watching her every move.

I didn't know how she'd fare in a fight against my dad; to me, it was a toss-up.

Instead of open combat, though, she picked up the pants he wanted hemmed and cut one leg completely off at the crotch.

She then said, "There you go, you son of a bitch! Now they're hemmed!"

She picked up another pair and did the same thing, then another before he finally got to her and grabbed the pants and the scissors.

They proceeded to hit each other several times, yelling names and insults, then later hugged and told each other how much they "loved" each other...this was our life.

Dad was no saint either; he had his own demons, I guess.

I never understood this incident, but it happened:

We lived in a two-story wood and brick house.

In the heat of summer, it was easily 115 degrees in my bedroom on the second floor.

At six years old, I was trying to stay cool and had stripped out of my pajamas to just my briefs.

I'd been up and down to the bathroom to wipe a wet washcloth on my chest to try to cool off and go to sleep, but it wasn't helping.

Lying in bed with nothing but a sheet, I was suddenly aware of my dad staring at me; he was smiling, but not in a happy way.

Real fear was all I felt. I'd seen this look before.

He came in and sat on the bed, then asked me what the hell I was doing *(still smiling)*. I said I was trying to keep cool.

He said, "Uh huh...sure," and pulled back the sheets. I was nearly naked underneath, so I tried to cover up.

He said, "What's the matter—are you ashamed?"

I wasn't ashamed; terrified was more like it.

He became more and more aggressive, fighting with me to try to get the sheet off the bed—but I refused to let it go; I knew it was my only protection from the attack that was about to occur.

Finally, enraged, he stood up and pulled off his belt; he'd perfected a method of getting his belt off in one move, and he was very proud of it.

Anyway, he yelled out that "no son of his was gonna be a God Damned Queer!" then proceeded to beat me with the belt until he was tired.

My mom was at the bedroom door, watching all of this—and smiling her fucking smile. Finally, even she had enough and told him to stop.

I kept the sheet tight between my hands and feet to absorb the blows; true, my hands and feet stung when they were hit, but it was all I had.

Meanwhile, I was screaming and pleading for him to stop.

Finally, exhausted, he stopped.

My mom, who had been staring at me, then shrugged her shoulders and said, "You should have known better."

At the time, I didn't know what a "queer" was, but whatever it was it had made him pretty pissed off.

A few weeks later, we got air conditioning in the house…I guess "queers" didn't like the heat.

At an age that most kids are learning about colors and numbers, I learned to swear in a way that continues to make most people gasp in shock.

Fighting was daily, either with my brother or people he set up to fight me.

I really hated fighting; it made me feel sick to be that out of control, so I also learned to run.

Later—much later—that skill would take me to the High School State Cross Country championships my senior year, where I'd place 6th in the entire state.

I wasn't a runner by any stretch of the imagination; however, I had an enormous reservoir of rage to tap into when the pain started to flow through my body during the all-out-fast-as-you-can-run race.

The coach *(one of many mentors)* must have recognized this early on.

He took me aside before our first real race, away from the squeaky clean church boys I ran with, and told me, "I see that you go out way too damn fast at first, and you're running in oxygen debt for three quarters of the race. Hold back 'til I tell you to go, OK?"

I said that I only knew one way to run.

It was true.

I'd learned to run to survive: flat out, haul ass, then hold on and outlast your enemy. Endurance has been a gift my whole life.

He held me really firmly by both shoulders, stared at me a moment, then said, "I know how you run, and I know why. Do what I tell you. Wait for my word, and then you can run like you want to. Deal?"

We stared at each other for a few seconds.

I didn't know what he knew or how he knew it, but I agreed. It would be hard, but I could try it.

I started the race last man on Junior Varsity.

I was our worst runner by far; I was way too big and heavy to run with any of those clean cut, skinny church boys. They read scriptures, and I cut class.

I had long hair past my shoulders, and they had their short missionary haircuts.

Needless to say, I wasn't one of them, so I have to admit the idea of beating their church-going asses made me really happy, only I hadn't been able to—yet.

Anyway, the race started, and I did what the coach asked, holding back and feeling like I was gonna die.

Running like that caused me a lot of anxiety, whereas running was usually freedom for me; the faster I ran, the better I felt. *(In my mind, it meant I didn't have to fight—and I liked that.)*

As I was holding back and waiting, I started to have adrenaline dumps like crazy.

This had been my survival mechanism for years, and now I was crawling, hanging back in the pack with the slowest guys.

At the mile mark, I was suddenly aware of the coach running next to me. Barely breathing, he said, "Are you ready now?"

I said, "Ya."

He said, "OK. Open it up slowly, then let go and fly. I'll see you at the finish line."

I looked at him, and he smiled and said, "Go, Zach, go!"

Two miles later, with pain raging through my body like I'd only experienced in a real battle for survival, I crossed the finish line—coming in third on the team.

Even though I was 25 pounds heavier than anyone else on Varsity, I'd smoked the entire team except for the two absolute best runners.

One of them would become a world-class distance runner in college, the other was to be a good friend all through high school.

I've heard that Malcolm X once said, "Anger is a gift"; well, I've carried this "gift" my whole life—that and an intense desire to make shit that's obviously wrong, right again.

Why do I tell you all of this?

Because all of these experiences made me better on the street.

I learned early that nothing is what it seems. Leaders rarely have your best interests at heart.

Just because people go to church and put on smiles for the neighbors, it doesn't mean they're good people.

Not all parents "love" their kids.

Kids are products of where they come from; they don't just become killers—they're made into killers.

I used my life, my experiences, and my rage to relate to the people in the streets.

The gang members, hood rats, and drug dealers—the shit of society, all came from one form of dysfunction or another, and so did I.

Maybe some of them did truly have good families, but they themselves had a mental illness. I'd witnessed that as well, from day one of my life.

Sometimes a person from a bad parenting environment could survive and become more than their surroundings, excelling *in spite* of their environment and parents.

I tried to find those people and help them like I'd been helped.

I had the debt of surviving my childhood to pay forward to someone else, and I did what I could do...sometimes I succeeded.

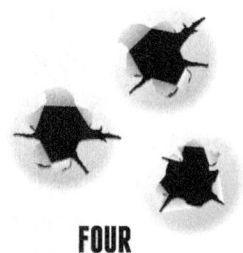

FOUR
SPEAK ENGLISH, DAMN IT

ABOUT MID-BLOCK ON 38TH STREET, just above Adams Ave. on the north side, was a dead end street.

It had several rundown rental units that populated the inner city; landlords would rent them out to people who were just shy of being homeless: the throwaways of the city, the disposable people.

They're there in every city; maybe you see them, maybe you don't. They're the people whom no one wants or they try hard to ignore.

Anyway, it went back in about halfway into the block, ending in an overgrown field. There was a family there that rented one of the units. They were Hispanic; they'd come from Mexico with their kids and were trying to start over and build a better life.

The parents both worked two full-time jobs, each at a fast food restaurant, while the older kids took care of the younger kids.

Theirs was a typical immigrant story in America: one generation after another working hard to make a better life for their kids.

One day, their son Alex and his cousin Jose had taken the family's only car for a joy ride. The parents were unaware of this.

The boys, each fifteen years old, were on an adventure; however, when they returned home they'd been the victims of a drive-by shooting, having been ambushed at an intersection while they waited for the light to change by two guys they knew from high school.

Alex and Jose had been heading southbound on Field Ave. when they came to a stoplight at the corner of 34th. Arturo Laredo and a friend were driving in the area and saw the Ornelas driving.

According to the Ornelas, they were enemies; they were rivals in school and on the street.

I didn't know it at the time, but the Ornelas were South Side 18th Street. I knew that Laredo was St. Pauls 13.

So, as Alex Ornelas was stopped at the light, Laredo told his friend Manuel Moncada to slowly pull up alongside him, driving in the oncoming lane.

He then hung out of the passenger side of the car and shot at the Ornelas several times, hitting Alex and narrowly missing his cousin.

Laredo emptied the gun into the driver's side of the car, shooting through the driver's open window at point blank range, then left the area.

Afterwards, Alex and Jose went home as fast as they could. This was all done in broad daylight, close to noon, just outside the struggling St. Pauls City Mall.

I was sent to the dead end street to assist the rest of the Gang Task Force in investigating the shooting.

When I arrived at the half street, I found the Ornelas family in a frantic mess. The parents spoke very little English and were trying to tell dispatchers that their son had been shot.

I arrived as Sergeant Gus, the Gang Task Force Sergeant at the time, Mike Vetere, and Noah Clark were also arriving.

We all got out and tried to sort out what had happened, unaware that this was to be a quick reality check of why the Gang Task Force wasn't solving cases.

Being the alleged leader of our group, Sergeant Gus asked the parents what had happened.

He didn't speak Spanish, and he didn't believe that they didn't speak English.

When they tried to tell him what had happened, he became really confrontational and told them that he knew they spoke English and that this "Yo no hablo bullshit" wasn't going to work with him.

He yelled at the parents and repeatedly told them that we weren't going to help if they didn't start speaking English—and fast.

Meanwhile, their son was bleeding and going into shock, and Medical still hadn't arrived.

I listened to Gus, Clark, and Vetere berate and insult these people for about two minutes, then I'd finally had enough.

I said to Gus, "Who's taking this case?"

Gus looked at me and asked what I meant, so I said to him, "Who are you gonna assign this case to? Because I'm outta here if all you're gonna do is talk shit to these people. I still have the Young shooting that I need to work on; if you aren't gonna get anywhere with these people, then I have shit to do."

Gus glared at me, then said, "OK then, smart ass, *you* get the case. It's all yours."

He then asked me in a really condescending tone, "What would you like us to do, Detective?"

This just pissed me off even more.

I said, "I want you to leave before you fuck this up worse than you already have. You can't insult the fucking victims and expect them to cooperate in your case."

While Vetere and Clark started glaring at me, giving me dirty looks, Gus thought this over for a minute, then smiled *(one of those "plotting against you" kind of smiles)* and said, "OK. What can I do to help?"

I needed the car processed for evidence, as well as the names of the people who were present, and he tasked Vetere and Clark with those jobs.

In turn, they did the bare minimum that each task required and handed the information over to me.

The Three Amigos then turned and walked away from the scene, their fat asses wobbling down the one-way street, returning to the world where drive-bys didn't occur—and if they did, no one talked about them.

Evidently, their help in this case was done.

As they left, I heard Gus say to Vetere, "We'll see how cocky he is after he gets his ass reamed for not solving this one."

Vetere laughed in agreement, saying, "Those fucking Mexicans are gonna make him look stupid. Everyone knows they can speak English, and besides they probably caused this damn shooting themselves. You know they're lying about this shit; they just hide it to get one over on us."

The injured Alex Ornelas was transported to the hospital for treatment.

He had a bullet wound in the leg, but it wasn't life-threatening.

I asked him if he knew who had shot him, and he said that it was Arturo Laredo, who he'd known from school; he was positive it was Laredo.

I knew who Laredo was, and I went back to the office and started to try to throw together a photo lineup.

Since he went straight to surgery, it would be several hours before I could run the photo lineup past the boy.

I called dispatch to get the time that the incident was reported, as well as the case number.

They told me that just as the shooting had been reported at the residence, another shooting had been reported by a woman who said she'd witnessed a drive-by shooting at the mall.

They sent patrols to the scene, but they'd found nothing. She'd left her name and information, and they'd assign it to me if I thought the shootings were related.

I wrote down the woman's information and called her.

It seemed unlikely that the shootings *wouldn't* be related; however, shootings happened often enough in the city, and quite often more than one shooting or incident was going on at the same time.

It was never safe to assume anything...ever.

I arranged to go to her house and meet with her.

When I arrived, she was a wreck; she was crying and sobbing and had really been traumatized by the incident.

She said that she'd been going to the mall with her daughter to spend the Saturday shopping and hanging out; they'd planned to try on clothes and have a nice Mother-Daughter day.

They turned the corner at 34th and Field, just as Arturo Laredo had started to hang out the passenger side of the car he was in.

She said that she saw everything.

She recalled every shot, as well as the "evil" look on Arturo's face as he shot into the Ornelas' car; she described the look as "filled with hate and rage," and she'd never seen that look on anyone in her life.

She said that she was in the way of Arturo's escape from the scene.

Since he'd pulled up alongside the vehicle the Ornelas were in, he was in the northbound side, blocking her lane.

They stared at each other for a few moments, and she was terrified that Laredo was going to get out of the car and shoot her and her daughter as well.

The driver of Laredo's car, however, did find a way past her, and they drove off and left the area.

I asked her if she had a description of the car, and she recalled it well. It was a small white car, and she'd written down the license plate.

I couldn't believe it. In any incident, it's really rare that a witness has the ability to remember to get real, useable information; usually, they're in such a state of shock that any memory is gone in moments.

I took the paper that she'd written the plate down on and asked her if there was anything else that she could remember.

She said, "Yes, the two boys in the other car, the car that was shot at, did nothing to provoke this shooting. They were ambushed by this evil man."

She would be an incredible witness.

I went back to the police department and announced the information I had on the radio in an ATL *(attempt to locate)*.

Sergeant Gus then approached me and told me that he'd assigned to me a guy named Dave Magnum; he was on loan from the County Sheriff, and we were supposed to go out and patrol the central city area, look for possible gang parties, and break them up.

I asked him, "What about the active shooting case I'm working on?"

As if he were surprised, he said, "Oh yeah…you can work on that, too, I guess!"

I was starting to get into a slow, burning mental rage.

The lack of desire by the rest of the unit to work these cases to an arrest and conviction was really getting to me; there was no sense of urgency or ownership to any of this.

I went out with Magnum and began to look for the shooters; fuck the parties the Sergeant wanted us to hit.

I'd worked with Magnum at the county when I was there.

He was a really nice guy, but he wasn't forceful and definitely had no feel for the street.

He was the kind of guy you wanted as a neighbor, not as back up in a fight; he'd wilt like a flower in the glaring sun at the first sign of confrontation.

We drove around for about half an hour, with me seething about the stupid shit I was seeing in the unit; I was mumbling to myself about how fucking dumb it was to send me out to look for parties when people were in armed combat at the mall in broad daylight.

Magnum took this personally and said that I could take him back to the station if I wanted; he didn't want to disobey an order from the Sergeant and was passively telling me that he wanted to go back to the station if we weren't going to do exactly what we were told.

I was considering taking his candy ass back when we pulled up to the intersection of 59th and Orchard.

I sat there for a minute, looking east and west; I don't know why I sat there, but I did.

This would happen a lot to me when I was in gangs.

I'd suddenly get an overwhelming feeling that I needed to go somewhere, or sometimes—like this day—just sit and wait. Call it a hunch or a gut feeling; I just felt I had to wait.

We sat there for a few moments, then finally Magnum said to me, "Hey man, are we gonna go?"

I said, "Ya, ya...in a second."

After a minute of waiting at the stop sign, a car pulled up behind us and honked.

Still, I sat...something was coming; I could feel it.

Then I saw a small white car coming towards us down the hill, and I said to Magnum, "Look what we have here: a small white car."

As it got closer, I could see two occupants, then the license plate; it was a match to the plate that I'd been given by the witness to the shooting.

Magnum looked at me in disbelief, his jaw dropped open with a "WTF" look in his eyes.

I told him that this was the suspect vehicle in my shooting case and that we were going to pull it over.

Swallowing in fear, he almost whispered, "Shouldn't we wait for back up?"

I said, "Fuck that! Surprise is on our side."

I then called out on the radio that I had the vehicle in the shooting at the mall and gave out our location.

We did a felony stop, my way. *(My way of a felony stop wasn't the typical tactics you're taught in the Academy. I like to get up close and personal; I want to see what's going on in the car and be sure that if I have to shoot someone—I hit them.)*

I approached any car with my gun out and aimed at the driver's head, letting them know in no uncertain terms that I'll kill them if they get stupid; this way, I'm able to see everything they do and every move they make, and there are no surprises.

This is not at all what you're taught in the Academy; however, as most cops who have been in the shit storm that's the streets know, the Academy is just a frame of reference. It isn't the end, but the beginning of your tactical training; you must always keep learning and adjusting to your environment.

Magnum wasn't happy about this.

As we approached, I had my weapon out and pointed at the driver, calmly telling him that if he made any move that I didn't tell him to make—today would be his last day; meanwhile, Magnum was doing the usual "Hi, I'm Officer Dave Magnum, may I see your ID" routine that we use on the mom-and-pop traffic stop.

I yelled at him to wake the fuck up and get his gun out on his suspect.

These two guys were wanted for a shooting and would kill him in a second if he slipped up. They'd already shot one guy that day, and they were probably still armed.

Magnum finally realized that he wasn't in the "green acres" anymore and geared up as much as he could.

We removed the two suspects and put them in cuffs, then searched them for weapons and found none.

Just then, Vetere and Clark showed up.

They offered to help out, so I asked them to process the car and impound it as evidence; I wanted the car searched for the gun as well. They did the impound sheet while Magnum and I went to the station with the suspects.

I interviewed the two suspects, but I wasn't able to get a confession from either one; I was, though, able to establish an alibi that was very easy to defeat.

The two men claimed that they'd been at Arturo's house, watching "The Untouchables."

They said that they'd been there for a few hours, watching the movie. They'd planned an alibi, but when separated neither one could recall what the movie was about, who the characters were, who died in the movie, or what the ending was.

I yelled at them out of frustration, telling them, "How fucking dumb can you two be? You come up with an alibi of watching this movie—and you pick one that neither of you has ever actually watched? You're fucking idiots!"

I booked them both into jail for the shooting, basing the arrest on the positive identification by the victims, as well as the identification of the car and Laredo by the woman going shopping at the mall.

The failed interviews of the two men took several hours.

I had to deal with constant interference from Vetere and Clark, who cracked jokes, talked about what they ate for dinner, and did their best to make sure that I couldn't get a confession.

The idea in interviewing is to keep up the pressure on your suspects, allowing them no way out and nowhere to hide from the facts that you're presenting. Eventually, they see they have no choice but to confess, and when you get them to that point, you offer an alternative, a way for this to "not be all their fault."

It doesn't have to make sense; it just has to allow them an escape from the emotional pressure that you're putting on them.

It really works well; however, it doesn't work at all when there are distractions that deflect the focus of the suspect from his troubles to anything else.

Having learned my lesson on this case, from then on I interviewed alone in a small plain room with no one else and nothing but the suspects and me; this allowed them nowhere to hide and nowhere to go.

It was really late, nearly 3a.m., when we had it all wrapped up for the night.

As we sat in the gang office, we breathed a sigh of relief.

The gang unit was looked upon as a joke; they couldn't solve cases, couldn't get convictions, and the poorest detectives ended up there—not by their choice, but by their failures.

Unlike the rest of the guys in the unit, though, I'd chosen to go there; I liked working gangs.

Anyway, Gus was our Sergeant, and he was debriefing us, making sure he had all the details of the shoot and the arrests before he called the Duty Lieutenant, who had just gotten off about two hours before. He made some notes and then made the call.

Gus thought of himself as an efficiency expert.

He had all kinds of phone lists miniaturized and laminated in his wallet, and he pulled one out and showed it to us, making sure we saw how efficient he was.

We all rolled our eyes and waited for him to finish while he called the number.

He thought he was calling his friend Lt. James, the Duty Lieutenant, but instead he'd called Chief James—and they were most definitely *not* friends.

Chief James and Gus had competed for the Chief spot when it had come open about eight months earlier; Chief James had won, and Gus had lost.

They'd been adversaries within the department for years.

Gus thought of himself as the intellectual, whereas Chief James claimed to be a "military man" by way of his Army reserve experience. They couldn't have been more opposite in their outlook or approach to police work.

Chief James hated Gus, who was overweight and a prankster, never serious and always joking.

He even moonlighted as a comedian at a club on Elm Street.

Chief James never laughed…ever.

So Gus called who he thought was Lieutenant James and started his usual joking and shit talking, saying that he was surprised that Lt. James was asleep—and already referring to him as "James."

He made several comments about James "banging his new girlfriend, and that must be why he's so tired," asking if she was as hot as she appeared to be.

He made comments about how he imagined she was in bed (*Lt. James had recently divorced his wife and was seeing a dispatcher, who we all heard was very wild*), then he proceeded to talk shit on Chief James—still not realizing that was, in fact, who he was talking to.

He said, "At least you're not at home with a ball gag in your mouth, taking it up the ass like the Chief; his wife runs that fucking house. You know she has to have a strap-on in the drawer by the bed. Probably never uses Vaseline either—just the way the Chief likes it."

Gus was laughing at the picture he painted, thinking it was quite funny—then all at once his demeanor changed, and he sat right up and said, "Yes, sir,," then "Yes, sir!" again and gave a quick brief of the shoot, apologizing for the inconvenience.

Gus then hung up, went completely pale, put his head down on the desk, and said, "Fellahs, I am so fucked! Oh God, I am so fucked!"

He was always pulling pranks, so we didn't believe his change of demeanor.

Seeing that we weren't buying into this, he stood up and yelled, "This is *not* fucking funny! I'm serious."

Still not believing him, we asked what had happened, and he said that he'd mistakenly called Chief James instead of Lieutenant James.

We all looked at each other in shock, thinking about what he'd said in that conversation—then we burst out laughing.

We laughed so hard, we started to grab garbage cans because we were throwing up.

Gus just stormed out of the office, pissed off.

He left us there, dry heaving with tears running down our faces, laughing and gagging.

Gus and the Chief had many funny conversations, and Gus' sense of humor got the best of him many times.

When this case went to court, the driver, Manuel Moncada, pled guilty and was convicted easily.

Laredo, on the other hand, didn't go down without a fight.

He requested a jury trial, and his parents mortgaged their business and house to ensure that they could get him cleared of the charges.

After three days of trial, the jury returned a guilty verdict in a few hours.

His family went crazy and began yelling at me that I was fucking dead and was gonna get mine.

A few weeks later, they accused me of tampering with the jury, claiming that I had contact with one of the jury members.

I had to go back to court and try to figure out what the hell they were talking about.

The allegations weren't true; it turned out that I'd been talking to the victims' assistance coordinator, and they thought she was a jury member.

The conviction held, and Laredo went to prison.

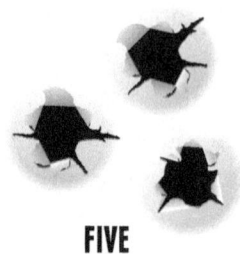

FIVE
CAPPED IN THE ASS

YOU KNOW HOW YOU HEAR about bangers always talking shit about "bustin' caps in some fool's ass"? Well, sometimes they mean it!

Doughboy from St. Pauls 13 had just come home on a home visit. He'd been in a Proctor home in San Marcos by court order, and he was allowed to go home on rare occasions to see his mom.

He'd been home in the city less than twenty-four hours when this shooting happened. *(It's also noteworthy that while he was in San Marcos, they had numerous drive-by shootings and gang activity increased noticeably...hmm...wonder why that was?)*

Anyway, Doughboy met up with Roberto Vega, another SP-13 gang member who had been in another "rehab program" back east.

They hung out at Vega's house, playing video games for a while, then decided go for a walk to another friend's house.

Both Vega and Doughboy had been out of the city for several months, so they went out walking in their old neighborhoods, talking about the girls they'd met during the time they'd been gone and comparing notes on their latest sexual conquests.

Suddenly, they ran into several South Side 18th Street gang members, Neto Arredondo and his cousins.

Arredondo was South Side 18th Street and had it tattooed on his chest. He was very proud of his gang membership, but his parents hoped it was a phase that he would soon outgrow.

This particular day, his family was having a wedding. His sister was getting married, and he and his cousins had come to the house to get wedding decorations.

They were standing in the front yard of Arredondo's house, taking a smoke break from loading their truck.

As Doughboy and Vega walked by, the two groups exchanged words.

It started out with "Whatchu claim, man," then went downhill fast from there. They were sworn rivals who hated each other by their gang affiliations.

Doughboy was a huge kid; at sixteen, he looked like a 35-year-old man. He was 5'8" and easily 250 lb.—and he feared no one on the streets.

He was one of only two Black kids that claimed St. Pauls 13 at the time; the other was already in prison for a shooting.

Black kids in St. Pauls 13 were rare since it was a Hispanic gang homegrown and unique to St. Pauls.

Most Black gang members in the city ended up as Crips or Bloods; Dough, however, had grown up hanging out with the homegrown Hispanics and felt an allegiance both to them and the Blacks in the city. He was a very unique guy in a lot of ways.

Anyway, Doughboy jumped the small fence in the front of the house and called the Arredondos out to fight.

St. Pauls 13 called the 18th Street gang members "in-betweeners" and sometimes "sewer rats"; 18th Street, on the other hand, called the SP-13 members "Chochas," "Dirtheads," or "Fakers."

So, Doughboy challenged the "sewer rats" to a fight.

The South Side 18th Street members outnumbered him, but he was huge—and he could fight.

The 18th Street members kept talking shit to him as they backed away, telling him to get the fuck off their property and get the fuck out of there.

Meanwhile, Arredondo went around the back of the house and went inside to get his father's 44 mag.

He then came out the front door of the house and confronted Dough, telling him to "get the fuck off of his property" or he'd kill him.

Doughboy called his bluff and stood his ground, talking shit back to Arredondo and telling him that he was going to kick his ass for trying to scare him with some fake ass gun.

That was a huge mistake—because Arredondo wasn't bluffing.

He shot one round at Doughboy's head, narrowly missing it; the round ended up burying itself deep into the telephone pole behind Doughboy and to his left.

At that point, Doughboy quickly realized that maybe it was time to leave, so he turned and tried to run, jumping the short fence with Arredondo in pursuit.

Doughboy took a couple steps, and Arredondo shot again; this time, he hit Dough right in the ass, the bullet driving deep into the muscle of his right ass cheek.

The bullet's impact was so forceful; it knocked Dough right out of his shoes.

Still, he continued running as fast as he could, limping now and bleeding.

Arredondo shot one more round at Dough as he ran past another telephone pole, again narrowly missing his head; the third round also got buried in the telephone pole.

Meanwhile, Vega was in high-speed "get the hell out of Dodge mode," running as fast as he could from the area.

He wanted nothing to do with the fight; he was on probation and nowhere near the soldier that Doughboy was on the street.

Vega never looked back, leaving Doughboy wounded, bleeding, and running for his life.

Asshole and elbows was all Doughboy saw; Vega was gone, leaving him to live or die on his own.

After yelling out threats and challenges to the neighborhood, Arredondo put the gun back in the house, announcing, "No one had better fuck with 18th Street!"

He then continued on to his sister's wedding like nothing had ever happened, feeling satisfied that he'd made his point, shooting one of the St. Pauls 13 gang bangers and sending the other running for his life.

As far as he was concerned, he'd shown—for that day, anyway—that South Side 18th Street is not to be fucked with. His cousins began praising him for his shooting of the "fakers," and for the time being he was the hero.

Doughboy, meanwhile, had run down the avenue away from the gunfire and eventually got some help from an elderly Black man who saw him limping and bleeding, trying to escape from Arredondo.

The man brought him into his own home, then drove him to the hospital to be treated. He didn't call for the police; calling the police in that neighborhood wasn't even considered an option.

I got the report of the shooting in the area, and when I arrived nothing was there and no one remained.

No one waved me down; people just stared, watching and saying nothing.

I had to walk the neighborhood and search for people willing to talk to me. Finally, I started to get witnesses talking and put together what had happened.

I was there for some time, winning back the neighborhood.

I found the shoes that belonged to Doughboy, and with the witnesses' help I had a pretty good idea of what had happened—I just didn't know why.

Then I got a call that a Black male had arrived at a nearby hospital, shot in the buttocks, so I headed up there to see if the call that I was on and the injured male in the hospital were related.

I met with Doughboy in the Emergency Room.

I'd known him for several years already, and we had a really good relationship. He knew me from patrol, and I'd picked him up for previous gang detectives many times.

I'd always treated him with respect and often took him to get a soft drink and say goodbye to his mother the times that I picked him up; this meant a lot to him and his mom.

I asked Doughboy what had happened to him, and he told me all about the incident.

He told me about Vega and Arredondo and the 18th Street bangers in front of the house. He was completely straightforward about what had happened.

I obtained a statement from him about what had happened, then went back to the scene.

Before I left, I teased him a bit about the gunshot to the ass, and we laughed.

Usually, bangers would be proud of the scar a gunshot would produce and would show it off to their friends at parties. I joked with him that he'd be showing off his ass at SP-13 parties and that no one would wanna see it.

We laughed about this for a while. Then I left the Emergency Room.

I went back to the scene and talked to Arredondo's parents, who had just arrived home from the wedding, and explained what had happened.

The said that they didn't know where Neto was, but when he returned they'd bring him to me. They were very upset about the situation and said that he'd brought shame to the family name.

To make matters worse, he'd done this at their home and on their daughter's wedding day. They were very upset by the incident.

I gave them my phone number and asked them to call when he returned, then left the residence.

I returned to the station and briefed Sergeant Gus about what I'd found out, telling him that the Arredondo family said they'd call when Neto came home.

He rolled his eyes and said that I was "stupid to believe a bunch of fucking Mexicans."

He then said to me, "Man, where the hell have you been the last few years? Working in fucking Mayberry?"

I tried to explain to him that the Arredondo family was old school Mexico and that they had the old school Mexican values. I believed them when they said they'd be in with Neto when he came home; this was a point of honor for the entire family.

Gus shook his head and said that I "had a lot to learn about Mexicans."

I was getting pissed, so I replied, "If I'm so fucking dumb about the street, how come I've solved the past two cases you gave me with arrests—while no one else in this unit has solved shit for months?"

He got up, mumbling something about "smart ass rookie," then left the office.

I started on my case report, and a couple hours later when I was almost done, the entire Arredondo family showed up with Neto.

They'd told him that he'd better confess to everything that had happened, or he'd be banished from the family and no longer considered a part of them.

He did confess to everything and told me the same story that Doughboy had recounted in the Emergency Room.

His father came to me afterwards and wanted to make sure that I was satisfied with the confession. He personally apologized for his son's behavior and said that he hoped that I'd call on him if I needed anything else for the case.

He said that he wouldn't have his family name tarnished by this incident and that his son would make this right or be forever banished from the family.

This was impressive shit to me, but not uncommon with families coming from Mexico that had the "old school" value system.

That was how every old school family I ever met from Mexico was; their family name and honor was everything to them. I had tremendous respect for the Arredondos.

Neto was just a juvenile at the time, but he was eventually certified as an adult and sent to prison.

When we went to court on the case, Doughboy was brought back to St .Pauls from San Marcos, where he'd returned after the shooting.

He didn't know who the guy was who had shot him, but when we went to court and he saw Arredondo and heard his name, he recognized him from high school and middle school.

Doughboy was shocked; he told me that he'd been friends with Arredondo in school for years.

He said, "Damn, this shit is stupid! We were friends in school. I didn't recognize him that day, and now we're in court."

He was genuinely upset, but not enough to leave the gang life.

As for Neto, though, I heard through the 18th Street members that he swore off the gang life and totally left it.

In letters from prison, he told them that he wouldn't be a member anymore and that he had to get his life back on track. He had to choose between his family and his gang—and he chose family.

He was lucky that his family was so strict in their belief that he had to make this right.

I never saw him again, even after he got out of prison. As far as I know, that was the end of his gang affiliation.

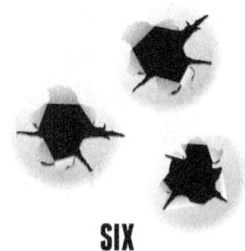

SIX
ST. PAUL'S TRECE GANG

I FIRST MET DOUGHBOY, THE Laredo brothers, and the majority of the peewee St. Pauls Trece gang members at Sam Ochoa's house in the 2200 block of St. Pauls Ave.

Sam and his older brother Jim were the nephews of the alleged leaders of St. Pauls 13. They claimed that their uncles "Getback," "Kickback," and "Shady" started SP-13 from CCL *(Central City Lobos)*.

From what I could figure out through interviews and filling in the blanks, some of the CCL gang members had gone to prison and met up there with other gang members from Sureneos 13.

In the prison system, the number 13 stands for the 13th letter of the alphabet: "M" *(for Eme, meaning the Mexican Mafia)*.

The southern California gangs have a huge influence on prison culture, and soon all the Sureneos gangs identified with the number 13.

The incarcerated CCL members came out of prison and adopted the 13 to their gang, adding the city name or initials.

They then spread the word and started St. Pauls 13. CCL was now only the older guys, and St. Pauls 13 was born.

I don't know for sure that the Ochoa family started SP-13; it's complicated because SP-13 is made up of several families and is organized more like a terrorist organization than a typical gang with a tree-like hierarchy *(leaders, captains, mid-level leaders, gang bangers, and peewees)*; instead, SP-13 has cells, families that are aligned with each other—and in some cases, rivals.

It's unlike any other gang in St. Pauls.

SP-13 gang members will fight each other and snitch on each other if they're from rival cells, and its gang membership isn't limited to members who live in St Pauls; they live all around the surrounding areas.

Additionally, SP-13 members don't have to be from one of the original families or from a specific race. Their membership includes blacks, whites, and members from other states who have moved into the city.

Another thing unique to SP-13 is that none of the junior members have any idea of the history behind their name or how the gang is organized; they're culturally unaware of the beginnings of the gang or the symbolism of the "13" in the name of the gang.

There are six main families that I could identify in the gang, and they're each unaware of what the other family cells are doing. It's a loose organization, and that's why it's so hard to defeat.

The police department has never addressed the cell organization; it treats the gang like a unified organization—which it is *not*.

If they addressed each family cell and organized their investigations based on that, the gang would quickly disappear.

I wrote an intelligence case to keep this knowledge of the structure of the gang in the database of the police department, but I doubt it's ever been viewed or acknowledged; that kind of intel wasn't seen as useful by the department's leadership.

I met a lot of the peewee SP-13 gang members at the Ochoa house. They initially didn't like me because I was a cop—and the feeling was mutual; I hated gang members with a passion. Since their mom worked, the Ochoa boys were unsupervised in the daytime.

I had no idea where their father was, and I never asked. It was obvious he wasn't in the picture. All I knew was that they never mentioned him, and he was never around.

The other peewees would show up at the house in the summer and raise hell with the neighbors, throwing rocks at cars and flashing gang signs.

They'd often try to pick fights with the Job Corps kids, who were let off at an office building across the street that was an annex for that program.

It was a really good idea for me to hang close to the Ochoa house when I was in patrol and stop fights and criminal mischief before it got started.

This was where I developed the strategy that would enable me to close the majority of my cases, develop informants, and get gang members to testify against each other in court.

One day while talking shit to the peewees at the Ochoa house, exchanging insults and name-calling, I noticed one of the kids was listening to the exchange; laughing but not angry, he had a lonely look in his eyes.

I watched him intently and noticed that he was really interested in the way that the police car was arranged inside. He was always looking in the windows, smiling and looking around, but he never said a word.

Eventually, I asked him if he wanted to see how the lights and sirens worked.

He said nothing, but his eyes lit up.

I turned them on, both lights and sirens—and the spell was instantly broken with all the peewees; in a single moment, they were transformed from hateful, spiteful, angry wannabe gang members into happy, laughing, normal acting kids.

They all came running and commenting on how cool the lights and sirens were, asking if they could turn them on, how it all worked, and what it was like to be a cop.

I was completely shocked at the transformation, and I had a hard time talking to them as the children they now were, remembering the hateful looks I was being given just moments before.

But the spell was broken for them and for me, and I let them take turns turning on the lights and sirens. Later, I even took the Ochoa boys for a ride in the car.

This was an epiphany, a turning point, as I realized that gang members had a real weakness.

The streets had hardened them.

They'd been twisted and screwed up by bad families, poor parenting, and the feeling that no one cared.

They were programmed to be able to defend themselves against anger, rage, and violence, but they had no defense against kindness, respect, or friendship. This formed the basic principals I used to develop informants and solve cases.

I treated all of them—no matter how much I disliked them—with respect and kindness, praising what I saw they took pride in, no matter how insignificant it appeared.

They all craved attention like every other person, maybe even more so.

Most cops treated them harshly, but they were able to defeat that; the more harshly they were treated, the stronger they were against the attack. But they had no defenses against kindness.

The younger kid who wanted to see the lights and so badly needed attention was a pivotal moment for me.

At the time, the group at the Ochoa house were just kids; they later grew up to be hardcore gangbangers, very capable of crimes and killing.

This group of kids would later be huge in the gang culture of the city. They included Arturo and Juan Laredo, Steve Costa, Sam and Jim Ochoa, Doughboy and Andrew Lucero *(li'l man)*, and Anthony Green.

Green, the only other Black kid in St. Pauls 13, was sent to prison at eighteen for an aggravated robbery. He lived with his grandmother, and she seemed resigned to the fact that he was gone forever when he was locked up. I tried to talk to her about him, and she gave me this look that said she was done with him, then closed the door on me.

He joined a Blood set just before he went to prison; being Black, he believed he couldn't belong to St. Pauls 13 in prison and have any protection, so he "jumped sets."

I asked the St. Pauls 13 gang members I knew about this, and they didn't deny that he'd jumped sets or that he'd have no protection.

This proved to me more the reality of what I saw in gang membership: the loyalty they claimed to feel for each other and the gang was fleeting at best.

A few years later, I saw his obituary in the summer; he was dead at an age when most men are just starting their own families.

Gangbangers live fast and hard, and they almost always die early.

SEVEN
GANG LIFE: THE PAINFUL REALITY

I FIRST MET STEVE FLOREZ Costa in the Gang Task Force office.

He'd been arrested for aggravated assault by Det. Dave Sessions, who'd survived the second "purge" of the gang unit by the Police Administration.

Purging the detectives from the task force was the administration's way of dealing with the gang problem; they purged the unit, removing all officers they felt were ineffective—whenever the prevailing political winds started to heat up.

City Council members who had absolutely no idea of the street, police work, or gangs would decide to flex their muscle with the Police Chief, asking what he'd done to increase gang suppression. Instead of finding a real fix for the problem, like adding more officers motivated to deal with the issue intelligently, or programs to help kids out with alternatives to gang life, he'd bring pressure on the Sergeant and Lieutenant to make personnel changes in the unit.

This was a quick fix that looked good on paper politically, but it did nothing to address the issue. It happened time and time again, usually every two years or so.

Anyway, Costa was the typical angry gang member; he was pissed off, abusive, and talking shit to Sessions and any other cop who came in to the office.

As I watched him and tried to learn about him, I saw that he was acting just like the peewee gang members and that he had the same defense mechanisms. He lashed out at everyone, and he was angry and spiteful to anyone who walked in or was nearby.

Sessions had called his parents, and they came down to say goodbye to Steve; he was going to jail, then most likely to prison after trial.

Sessions liked the parents and had developed a good relationship with them, so he left the room and let them have a moment alone with Steve. I stayed in the room to make sure he didn't escape, so I overheard their conversation.

Unhappy with his gang membership, they were basically telling him that he was on his own from now on.

His stepfather told him that Steve had wanted this life, that he had a choice and could have chosen another life—but didn't. Now he'd have to face the consequences of his decision.

His stepfather said that he was embarrassed to have called Steve his son and that as long as he maintained his membership in the gang, he wasn't welcome in their home. They were cutting ties with him as I listened.

Crying and furious, Steve told his stepfather he'd never understand what it meant to be a "soldier." He said that he was going to be a part of something bigger than his stepfather's piss poor life; he'd be a legend in the prison system, respected and admired as an OG *(original gangster)*.

He said that when they heard about how respected he was by the inmates and gang members on the street, they'd beg for him to return to the family. He'd show them they were wrong.

He told his stepfather to go fuck himself, then he let his mother hug him goodbye. They left the room, and Sessions came back and booked Costa into the jail.

Costa was released from prison in the late 1990s, being let out on parole.

I met him again when I was sent as a backing unit to a burglary alarm at Big O Tires.

It was in an affluent part of town with nice homes and clean parks, and gang crime wasn't supposed to occur in this world.

We never received alarms from the businesses in the area that weren't legit, so we approached this one with caution.

The business had been broken into; when we arrived, we were able to find the broken window that had been used to enter the business.

We surrounded the place and waited for K-9 to arrive.

As we were waiting, a guy jumped out from a large bush in the manicured landscaping near the business and broke into a run.

We chased him down and pepper sprayed him, and he went down fast as the spray took effect.

It was winter, and snow was on the ground, so we treated him with the snow until medical arrived to treat the effects of the pepper spray.

Once he calmed down and sat up, I recognized him as Costa.

He was much older looking, severely tattooed, and he was still just as angry and spiteful as he'd been before—perhaps even more.

After getting him calmed down, we found out he was on paper *(parole)* and that he was intoxicated; this alone violated his parole.

We had CSI process the scene at the business, and in the meantime we took Costa to the station for interviewing.

Costa's story was that he'd been at a SP-13 party.

He'd been invited as an OG who had just been released from prison and had arrived expecting to be admired and respected; instead, he was challenged, insulted, and belittled.

He didn't know what to think.

The junior members had shown him absolutely no respect at all, challenging him to a fight and talking shit about him being an "old man" and having no heart.

To prove his continued loyalty to the gang, they challenged him to participate in the business burglary.

He eagerly agreed, and when they arrived Costa took the initiative in entering the building.

What he didn't know was that things on the street had changed since he'd entered prison.

Senior gang members like Costa were no longer respected for what they had been; they had to re-establish their position in the gang.

When Costa entered the business and the alarm went off, the junior members left him there. Having no loyalty to him, they just drove off, not really caring about what happened to him.

His gang had abandoned him. He couldn't believe it.

He was in tears. All that he'd lived for and built his life around was a façade.

I talked to him for about an hour and told him that the streets had changed; he had to realize that and change himself, get a job, and go "legit."

He screamed in my face, saying, "Look at me, bitch! Look at me! I'm gang tattoos, head to fuckin' toe—no one will fuckin' hire me! Do you think I haven't tried to get a fuckin' job?"

He then became sullen and said, "I'm in this shit for life. I made a mistake—a *huge* fuckin' mistake—but it's too fuckin' late to go back now."

I noticed that he had a set of scars on the back of his neck. They looked really nasty and deep, so I asked him about them.

He told me that he'd been stabbed in a gang fight in prison and was nearly killed.

Now he was shaking and crying at the reality of what his life had become.

This wasn't what he'd envisioned years earlier, not what he'd hoped for—and now he'd been abandoned and betrayed by his gang, despite the fact that he wore "St. Pauls Trece" tattoos all over his body.

He was booked into the jail that night, and I never saw him again.

He did the rest of his time and got out of prison.

He attended another St. Pauls 13 party when he got out, but at this one he was stabbed again in the back of the head.

This time, he died at the hands of one of his own gang's members.

He lived the reality of being a gang member.

There is no golden age of respect later in life, and you'll never be a respected street soldier; you simply die angry, early, and alone.

Unfortunately for the senior gang members, this was a common story. I heard many variations of this same theme from the elder gang members I spoke to.

Not all died, but all weren't happy at the lack of respect that the younger generation had for them or the work that they'd done in the name of the gang.

This wasn't unique to a specific family cell of SP-13 either; it was across the board.

In the Ortiz family, "Bird" Ortiz told me this same thing.

In the Lucero family, it was "Bear" Lucero who told me this as well.

Juan and Felipe Gallegos also commented on this lack of respect by the peewees; it seemed that it spanned across the entire gang.

The old days of respecting the senior OG members were over; no one would listen to them or cared about what they thought.

The new breed of gang members lived for the moment.

They were only concerned about today, and they held no respect for anyone but their immediate circle of homies.

This was the reality of gang membership, and even that little bit of respect and loyalty was fleeting.

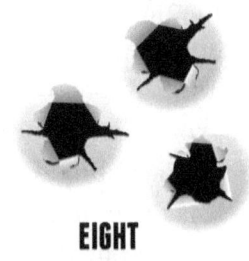

EIGHT
FAMILY REUNIONS

I FIRST MET BIRD ORTIZ in the 4000 block of Adams.

He'd just gotten out of federal prison for dealing drugs *(mostly cocaine)*, and he was at his brother Waldo's house, drinking beer and checking out the new motor that Waldo had just dropped into an old Chevy Impala.

While they were talking and getting re-acquainted, Bird saw the same guy who had ratted him out and sent him to prison.

The guy was walking down the street, so Bird confronted the snitch and they had words.

Bird pulled out a gun and shot at the guy, missing him but making his point that he wasn't happy about being ratted out to the cops.

I assisted the patrolman who'd been assigned the case, and we took Bird into custody.

I spoke Spanish and had overheard Bird asking his brother to take responsibility for the shooting so that he didn't have to go back to federal prison.

But Waldo refused to take the credit; no way was he doing time for his brother's mistakes.

While we sat there, Bird's mother came up and was yelling at him about being arrested already. She was really furious, and I had to get out and keep her away from the patrol car; she wanted to beat his ass big time.

I found out from her that Bird had three children she'd been raising while he'd been in prison. She'd hoped that he would get out, end his life of crime, and be a father, but with him being arrested again so soon, she knew that he'd be going back to prison and that she'd be forced to continue raising his children. She was *really* not happy about this.

I told her that she could bring the children to say goodbye to their father, but that was about all I could do for her.

She brought out two very young boys and a little girl to give Bird a hug goodbye.

He was crying and begging me to let him go, and he kept telling me that it was his brother that had shot at the guy—not him.

He said that he'd write a statement against his brother and "swear to it on a stack of Bibles."

I didn't tell him that I understood the conversation between him and his brother.

When the other officer investigating the shooting had the witness statements he needed and enough information, he came to the police station and took Ortiz to jail.

The next time I saw Bird was after I'd left the Gang Task Force and was working in the schools.

I'd been assigned to a school that had a mix of inner city kids and rich kids from well-to-do families. Both sets of kids had identical problems.

The inner city kids had parents who worked hard to survive, sometimes working two jobs over eighty hours a week; they were from broken homes and had poor parenting at home.

The rich kids had similar problems; their parents were rarely home, working eighty hours a week and making a lot of money—and they were never around to be parents for the kids either.

It was an eye-opening experience to see how similar the problems are between the really poor and the really rich.

One day, the principal called me into her office and explained that a guy had arrived fresh out of prison and demanded to see his children. He'd just been released and had come to the school with his parole officer's permission to see them.

She described him as very angry and extremely intense, and she wanted me to stand by while she called the school district administration for guidance.

I went to the office—and there was Bird Ortiz.

He'd grown considerably. He was heavily muscled and obviously still very much in the prison mindset.

I asked him to come to my office.

He asked why, saying that he wasn't going anywhere until he was able to see his children. We talked for a few moments, and he became more and more hostile.

I cut him off, saying, "If you wanna see your children, it's through me."

He said, "What the hell does that mean?"

I said, "That means if I say it doesn't happen, it won't happen—so you better start fuckin' workin' with me, Bird."

He was shocked that I knew his street name and who he was.

He asked how I knew him, and I told him we could talk in my office because it was more private there. He agreed, and we went to my office and talked for several hours. I let him vent and tell me about how he'd lived in prison and missed his kids.

I explained that I was there when the last shooting had occurred and that we'd talked back them. He didn't remember me at all.

I told him that if I could, I'd get him to see his kids, but that he had to be patient.

He said he just "wanted to see his baby girl"..he kept repeating that over and over.

I could relate to that. I was estranged from my own daughter at the time, and I knew the hurt he felt.

I told him that I'd see what I could do about speeding up the process, but that he had to calm down and try to be less intense and angry.

The people in the school weren't street soldiers; they were civilians not familiar with the street—and they were terrified of him.

He agreed to try to calm down, and I left him in my office and checked in with the principal.

She said that they'd made the decision to allow him to see his kids and that each had been asked if they wanted to see him.

The boys had said "No," they didn't want to see him; their mother had done too much damage to the relationship that they had with their father, constantly badmouthing him to the point where they had no desire to see him.

Besides, they barely remembered him. I could relate to this also.

I told him that the boys refused to see him but that his daughter was on her way down.

He was clearly shaken up by this.

He said that his kids were all that kept him going in prison; he couldn't imagine why they wouldn't see him.

He was getting pissed off again, so I had to settle him down and told him that I'd walk his ass out of the school in handcuffs if he didn't calm down. He still had his daughter on the way down, and at least that was a start.

I told him that he could see her in my office and have some privacy there, so he calmed down a bit—but he was still really anxious.

When his daughter walked in, he completely fell apart.

He started sobbing, then he grabbed her and started hugging and kissing her.

He was talking but making no sense at all, babbling nonsense. He then picked her up and held her in his arms like a baby and sobbed loud, gasping sobs.

She was just as emotional, crying "Daddy, Daddy."

I left them in the room alone for about an hour.

It was a very moving scene, not what you'd expect from a hardened federal prisoner just released from the joint.

Finally, they came out of my office and she went back to class.

He then came up to me, tears still in his eyes, and thanked me over and over, saying that he owed me one for that time alone with his daughter. He then left the school and went back to the halfway house.

I dealt with him many times over the next few years as he struggled to re-establish himself back into "normal" life.

His daughter and sons eventually did form a relationship with him, but they got into trouble a lot, and when I'd write cases on them he'd plead with me to try to keep them "out of the system."

He repeatedly asked that I "keep their jackets clean and free from paperwork," but I told him that that was his responsibility—not mine.

He couldn't understand how to be a parent.

He could lead gang members to survive in federal prison and on the street, but he had no idea how to parent his own children and keep them from following him into the penal system.

As he expected me to make exceptions for his kids that I wouldn't make, our relationship continued to be tense.

Finally, I grew tired of his complaining, and I told him that since he was an OG and had **"Street Creds"** he should be able to control his own kids.

He said that he couldn't and recounted the lack of respect for older gang members that I mentioned earlier; in response, I told him that he had to reach his kids as a father to his children—not as gang members.

He couldn't understand that; to him, there was no difference... that's how ingrained the lifestyle was in his mind and family.

The entire Ortiz family was deep in SP-13.

The boys had a cousin named NaNa, and both of her parents were also serving time in prison for dealing drugs. She was living with her grandfather, and he really hated her.

At thirteen, she was openly a lesbian, and he felt that was an affront to God and regularly beat her if he caught her engaged in any lesbian activity.

She was tough as hell and as much a leader in the new crop of peewee gang members coming up in the city as any male.

She also hated cops, and I was never really able to develop a relationship with her.

I did get her to talk to me eventually, though; she opened up a little bit after I arrested her grandfather for beating her up with a phone.

He'd caught her having sex with one of her girlfriends and beat her with the handset of an old style telephone, badly bruising up her face.

Eventually, she'd even play basketball with me on occasion. She was really likeable and tough.

Last I heard, she ran away from foster care, and I never heard from her again.

NINE
SNOOPY MEETS SNOOPY

MARK SOUTHWICK, AKA "SNOOPY," BELONGED to the 8 Ball Crips.

He was married to a sheriff deputy's daughter. They had a one-year-old son and were on their way to a friend's house to celebrate his first birthday.

When Southwick pulled into the apartment complex at 610 Redwood Ave, he said he immediately knew that it was a mistake.

He had to drive through a bunch of SP-13 gang members standing in the driveway of the apartment complex, and they started talking shit to him as he drove through the crowd.

Southwick said that he went to his friend's apartment to see if he was home. He was, and they talked for a few minutes.

They each decided that maybe that night wasn't a good night to have the birthday party since the SP-13 members were there at the complex, acting very aggressive, throwing up their hands, and challenging Southwick and his friend whenever they happened to look over.

Southwick said that he got into his car and told his wife to roll up the window.

He then told her to lock the door and that they were leaving the complex.

As he started to drive down the driveway to exit the complex, though, the SP-13 group split up, approximately half on each side of the driveway.

Southwick could tell that one guy in particular looked really angry, and this guy came up to the driver's side of the car and told him to roll down the window.

Southwick did, later saying that he did it to "avoid looking like a punk". He didn't want to appear to be afraid of the SP-13 set.

The angry guy asked Southwick what gang he claimed, and Southwick replied 8 Ball Crips.

The SP-13 gangster replied, "This is big time St. Pauls Trece, fool!" then pulled out a gun and shot Southwick point blank in the chest.

Southwick hit the gas and drove out as fast as he could.

After he pulled out of the area, he eventually pulled over and stopped. He had his wife drive because he was starting to pass out and go into shock.

She quickly drove him to the nearest hospital Emergency Room.

When he arrived at the Emergency Room, I received the call and went there to investigate.

I got the basic information from him about what had happened.

He thought that the shooter had been Pedro Lechuga; he said that he'd met Lechuga once before.

I told him that I knew who Lechuga was and that I'd go find him.

I then asked Southwick if he'd be willing to provide written statements and look at a photo lineup.

He said that he'd cooperate with the investigation, so I asked him to call me when he left the Emergency Room.

Amazingly, his injuries weren't critical or life-threatening. He'd been shot in the chest, but he was really lucky. The bullet had hit a rib and traveled up to the sternum. It stopped there, never entering the chest cavity or hitting vital internal organs. He was out of the Emergency Room in a few hours.

I hit the streets, looking for Lechuga.

I knew that he wasn't an SP-13 gang member; he claimed the "West Side Pirus" at the time.

I went back to the apartment complex and found no evidence of the shooting, nor did I find anyone that would admit to seeing anything.

I was left with no witnesses, and no one would cooperate.

The only information I could gather was from a woman who would talk to me briefly, only to tell me that the police department had abandoned them *(the occupants of the apartment complex)*. They'd called over and over again to report gang shootings, loud parties, drug dealers, and everything else you could imagine, and the cops would come and take reports and leave—doing nothing else.

She said, "You won't get any help here from any of us."

This was typical of the responses I received on most gang calls, so I had to prove to them that I meant to stay and deal with the shooting until I solved it, earning back the people's trust. It was a long, hard process, and it took a lot of time.

I checked the apartment complex and found no West Side Piru graffiti. There was absolutely none; however, I did find a lot of SP-13 graffiti.

I figured that Southwick must have been wrong about his identification of Lechuga as the shooter, but I had to prove that before I could move on to figuring out who the shooter was.

I went to Lechuga's house and contacted his family. They told me that he wasn't at home and that he was at a wedding of a client.

The family had a band that they all played in, and they'd been booked for the wedding.

So, I went to the wedding to confirm if Lechuga was there.

The wedding was being held in the Hampton Inn.

It was for a gang member that was SP14, a Nortaneos set—and it wasn't a friendly environment.

SP14 was a Hispanic gang that claimed red as their color. They were a very small and very quiet set.

There were some really hard-core gang members at that wedding, and they weren't happy to see me there at all.

But, I found Lechuga's parents and explained the situation, telling them that I'd be willing to let them continue playing in the band for the wedding as long as they'd give me their promise that they'd bring Pedro to the police station after the wedding. If they wouldn't agree to do that, then I'd have to take them out of the wedding.

They agreed to come to the station when the wedding was over; as a result, they had some very angry people at the wedding that they had to calm down.

The Nortaneos were very upset that the Lechuga family had told the police that they were at the wedding in the first place; needless to say, they were really pissed off.

Eventually, Pedro and his family arrived at the police station.

After much coaxing by me, they allowed him to give me a statement and take his photo for a lineup.

I then had a patrol unit run the photo lineup past Southwick, and he verified what I already knew: Pedro was *not* the suspect.

I advised the Sergeant, about this, and he told me that Southwick was duping me. He was sure that Southwick was lying and that he'd now know what Lechuga looked like and would go after him on his own.

I thought that was ridiculous and made no sense, but it wasn't our first disagreement, so I just ignored him.

I went back to the apartment complex night after night, trying to get someone, anyone, to talk to me.

Finally, I had a guy approach me and tell me that he knew who had done the shooting and that the guy lived in Smithtown.

The shooter claimed SP-13 and went by the nickname "Snoopy," but he thought his real name was Anthony.

I accepted his help and gave him my pager and cell phone numbers. I then worked the apartment complex nightly for two weeks, asking patrols to meet with me there.

I'd walk around the complex from all different approaches, trying to win back the people who lived in the area.

I handled any cases that came up while I was there, and eventually people started to talk to me and greeted me with smiles and waves.

One night, I got a call from the informant.

He called himself Tony, and he said that he was throwing a party for a bunch of the gang members who had been in the area that night and that Snoopy would be there if they showed up.

It had been two weeks since the shooting.

He said that Snoopy had stayed in Smithtown until things cooled off and had cut his hair, hoping to disguise himself.

Finally, that Saturday night he sent a message to my pager that Snoopy was there.

I arrived and had a patrol meet me there.

I briefed them on what we were going to do, then went up the back stairway and had patrol approach from the front.

The occupants of the party saw patrol arrive, but by that time I was already in place.

As patrol came up the front steps, Snoopy went out of the apartment and tried to go down the back steps; I met him there, blocking his escape.

I asked him who he was, and he claimed to be Xavier Lechuga.

Xavier was a minor gang member associated with SP-13. I'd met him once about a year earlier, talked to him, and knew that he had a really bad stutter.

This guy, though, had no stutter at all—so I knew he was lying.

Additionally, he had newly shaved hair.

So, I placed him into custody and put him in my car, then instructed the patrol unit to break up the party, acting like we'd been called out to a loud party.

The patrol unit did just that while I transported Snoopy to the police station.

It took me less than two hours to get him to confess.

I had a photo lineup made up with his picture in it, then sent it to Southwick with another patrol unit; he immediately picked out the suspect I had in custody.

I informed the suspect of that and told him that his only option was to be honest with me.

I told him that we *(the police, the judges, and the jails)* were sick of all the gang members coming into the city from other places. We were loyal to St. Pauls as well, and I understood his disgust at all the gangs coming into St. Pauls.

I asked him to help me. Of course, this was a ruse—but it worked.

He caved and told me the account that Southwick had recalled, except for one small detail: he said that after he'd shot Southwick in the chest while he sat in the driver's seat of the car, he reached back into the back seat and tried to fire one shot into the chest of their infant; saying he "wanted that fucking dirty kid dead with his poser father."

He said that the gun jammed, though, and he didn't know why.

I had him read the statement that he'd given me and correct any mistakes I may have made. *(I made mistakes on purpose so that he'd have to read it and fix them. It was a trick I learned from another detective; this technique made sure that the suspect could read and that they couldn't claim that the statement was forged.)*

I booked the suspect Anthony Mascarenas *(Snoopy, SP-13)* into jail. He went to court and pleaded guilty to the shooting.

His mother claimed that he'd been forced to sign the statement, stating that he couldn't read at all; however, the corrections he made to the written statement proved that she was lying, and I advised his attorney of those facts.

Later, Southwick would tell me that his nickname for the 8 Ball Crips was also "Snoopy"; he thought that was a weird coincidence.

After I told him about the disclosure that Mascarenas had made about trying to kill his son, Southwick was really shaken up and started to withdraw from the gang life.

He sold his car and changed jobs, and he quit hanging out with all the 8 Ball gang members except for his closest friends.

This was the end of his active gang membership.

He didn't quit the set completely, but he did withdraw from the active gang life, parties, and fighting and drive-bys.

This was good for a period of time, but then his wife got bored.

She liked gang life, and she wanted it and the excitement that went with it.

They ended up divorcing, and she started dating another SP-13 member. This drove Southwick into a rage, but he still didn't go back to active gang life.

I later asked Southwick about how he came to be in 8 Ball and not any other set. He said that he'd wanted to join 8 Ball and liked the name and what he felt they stood for.

He and a few of his friends drove to Denver and met up with some 8 Ball members there.

When they asked to be jumped in *(to be made legitimate 8 Ball members)*, the set did jump them in, then Southwick and his friends brought 8 Ball back to St. Pauls.

I asked him how they met the 8 Ball members, and he said that they'd met them at a concert in Denver.

Later, he'd help me on cases that involved people he knew as long as they didn't require him to give up anyone in his set.

He gave me another set of eyes on several cases, which saved me a lot of time.

Anthony Mascarenas did end up in jail, then went on to prison.

I was told after he'd been there about a year he stabbed a guy and tried to kill him, extending his stay in prison for some time. He was only nineteen when I arrested him.

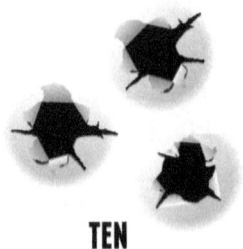

TEN
IT'S ALL ABOUT FAMILY

PEDRO LECHUGA WAS A WEST Side Piru.

He came from a family that had been in St. Pauls for generations and had associated themselves with SP-13. They claimed as a family to be members, or associates of St. Pauls 13.

One day, a few months after the Snoopy shooting case, they called me to report that Pedro had been beaten up badly at a party in west St. Pauls.

I talked to Pedro, and he wouldn't tell me what happened, only that he'd been at a party with some friends and that they jumped him.

I went to some of the guys that he hung out with and asked them what happened; from their response, it was obvious that they'd changed their opinion of him. They didn't speak highly of him, calling him a "punk" and a "bitch."

It took a while to figure out what had really happened, and I ended up going to his girlfriend—who now claimed that she was his *ex-girlfriend*.

She said that Pedro had been at the party and had been drunk.

He got into an argument with her and beat her up badly. She was really well-liked in the WSP set, and the guys in the set got pissed off, telling Lechuga to knock it off or face the consequences.

He told them to fuck off, that she was his girl and he'd beat her ass if he wanted to.

They told him again to stop, and he didn't, so they beat him up, making a point of ensuring that he got the message.

They beat his ass pretty good, and he was no longer welcome in WSP.

He was out on his own with no one covering his back.

I verified this story with some of the guys at the party without telling them where I'd heard it.

They just assumed that he'd told me, and they were even more upset that he'd told the cops what had happened.

I then told his parents what had happened and why, and they made a point out of telling him *(with me in the room)*, "You wanted to go with these guys. You said 'red was cool' and to give it a chance. They are *not* your family, Pedro—which is why they beat you up. You need to come back to the family."

A few months later, I heard that Pedro had been jumped in to St. Pauls 13; his family had wanted him out of the WSP and in with SP-13.

As an adult, I saw Lechuga.

He'd taken his family's advice and joined the "family gang".

Another generation of gang members was rolling down the assembly line.

This is a hard inheritance to break.

The wealthy families have their traditions: college at top tier schools like Harvard or Yale, membership at "exclusive" social clubs—all to keep a reputation among the elite.

The poor have them as well: gang membership, prison sentences, a "jacket" in the system—all to keep a reputation on the street.

It never ceased to amaze me the similarities between the two groups and their kids...neither group seemed happy to me.

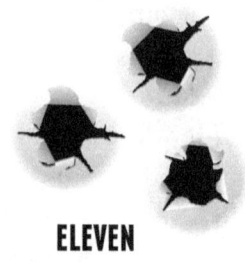

ELEVEN
TRUST NO BITCH

I WAS AT HOME ON my day off, playing basketball with the kids, when the phone rang.

I checked the Caller ID, and it was work calling again. I sighed and picked up the phone.

There was a guy in the hospital who had been stabbed at a party earlier that morning. He was a suspected gang member, and the circumstances made it seem gang related...so goes another day with my kids shot to hell.

I said goodbye to them and went to work.

After I arrived at the hospital, I spoke to the victim, who had just come to the ICU from the operating room; he'd been in the OR for several hours, having his abdomen literally pieced back together.

His name was Rene Ruiz, and I recognized him from working patrol.

He was really in a lot of pain, so as I tried to get a statement from him I was barely able to ask questions and get him to answer. It would be some time before he was out of the hospital, though, and I needed his statement to get on the case immediately.

He said that he'd been invited to a party in the basement of 2351 38th St.

He showed up and was talking to this girl who had invited him. He liked her a lot, and while they were talking he said that four other guys showed up. He didn't know them, but he could tell that they were SP Treces.

He was 7th Street Mafioso, but no one said anything to him, and he felt relatively safe for a while.

The four SP Trece guys left, and he stayed and talked to the girl and some other people at the party.

An hour or so went by, then the four guys returned.

They'd been drinking Tequila, and their mood had changed drastically.

People started to clear out of the party immediately, leaving only him and the girl who lived in the apartment.

He said he thought that the guys from the SP Treces had left the party as well, but he waited for a while to make sure they were gone.

What he didn't know was that they weren't gone at all; instead, they were waiting for him just outside the apartment.

When he finally did leave, he said these four big dudes immediately surrounded him.

He was only about 5'6" and maybe 145 pounds; the SP Treces—all four of them—were well over 250 pounds and strong.

They got in his face and started to push him around. He tried to run, but they had other ideas for him.

They beat him up a little bit, then each one grabbed an arm or a leg.

Then, while they spread him out on the ground, a fifth guy appeared out of nowhere and pulled out a knife, opening up Rene's jacket and shirt and telling him, "We're gonna carve your ass up for messin' with one of our bitches."

The fifth guy was Jose Costa.

He stuck the knife into Rene's abdomen and slowly started to cut, gutting him like a fucking fish—literally spilling out his intestines and internal organs while he screamed frantically for help.

The victim could do nothing but watch his stomach be cut slowly open by the drunk Costa.

The other four guys were huge, and they had him pinned while they, too, watched him being cut open.

When I later talked to the girl who had the party, she said that she heard him screaming but wouldn't open her door in fear of what would happen to her or her child. She claimed not to know who the suspects were and gave me a very vague statement.

I still believe that she set Rene up.

It was very common in the gang world for the women to invite dudes to their apartments or to parties, promising to "hang out" or set them up with some girl who had wanted to meet them.

The gangsters have a saying: *"Trust no Bitch."*

It's for a reason; women can get you killed really quickly in the gang world.

I worked several stabbings and homicides that were obviously caused by women setting guys up from rival sets.

Anyway, I didn't have much to go on in his statement; Rene couldn't remember who had cut him up as he struggled to stay awake while we talked.

I went back to the office, and the Lieutenant in charge of the gang unit told me that I'd have to work with Det. Liptrap on the case.

The brass assumed that I was out of my league (*according to whom, I don't know*), so he said that Liptrap would be in the next morning and that I'd brief him and follow his lead.

I was pissed. I hated Liptrap.

He was well known on the force as a liar who took credit for others' work. He also didn't know shit about gangs.

I worked until the leads ran out, then went home.

The next day, I came in early to try to get somewhere on the case.

Rene was awake, so I went to talk to him at the hospital.

He said he was feeling better, and he did remember one name. He was able to recall that the name of the guy with the knife was Jose Costa.

He said that he'd known Costa for years, in high school, middle school, and from the neighborhoods they grew up in.

He was absolutely sure that Costa had been the one to open up his stomach so mercilessly.

I knew Costa as well.

I went back to the station and made up a photo lineup, then took it to Rene.

He picked out Costa with no hesitation; he couldn't identify who had held him down, but he knew for sure that Costa had cut him open.

I left the hospital and went to Costa's house, but no one was there, so I left and went back to the station to do some more background work on him.

As soon as I arrived, Det. Liptrap came up to me and said, "Hey bud, I hear that we're working together on a case. What can you tell me about it?"

He was smiling in that typical, passive aggressive, fucked-up slimy way he had, knowing I was going to be doing all the work and that he'd be taking all the credit; this was his typical method of operation.

I thought about it and made a decision right there.

I looked at him and said, "I can tell you that I don't need or want your fuckin' help, so go back to your side of the room and stay there."

The smile disappeared from his face instantly.

He was one of the Golden Boys; he could do nothing wrong in the eyes of the brass and wasn't accustomed to being treated this way.

Instantly pissed, he stormed off and got on the phone immediately (*probably calling my Lt.*).

I left the police station, thinking my time remaining on the Gang Task Force was now down to a few hours; Liptrap would want payback for not giving him his due respect.

I went back out to Costa's house, and this time I caught him at home.

I told him that I needed to talk to him and that I needed him to come to the station immediately.

He was watching his kids and didn't have a sitter, so I waited at his apartment until his wife got home.

It took about an hour for her to arrive, and I was there the whole time, pretending that nothing was wrong as I talked to him and his friends—but I was still on edge.

On the inside, I was thinking that they'd try to shoot me or stab me at any moment; however, on the outside I was laughing and joking with them.

I was really pissed about how they'd carved Rene up, and I didn't want him to have any way of setting up an alibi, so I stayed.

After listening to him tell his wife that everything was fine, I drove Costa to the station; six grueling hours later, I was finally able to get him to confess to the stabbing.

He started out admitting only to being a driver in the car that they used to drive to the party.

I kept at him, though, and he eventually caved in step-by-step, first admitting to having got out of the car when he heard screaming.

Later, he was in the stairway when the stabbing started. Finally, he was holding a knife and standing over Ruiz.

He admitted that he and four other guys had held Ruiz down and that he'd taken the knife and slowly slid it into his abdomen.

He said he liked the way it felt slicing Ruiz' abdomen open and watching the terror in his eyes.

He hated Ruiz and felt that he was less than human because he was 7th Street Mafioso, and not one of his homies.

For some reason, he felt like he'd go home after this confession, and he protested loudly when I told him that he was under arrest.

He got up and started to try to fight, telling me I was fucked up; I reminded him quickly that he didn't have his four fat friends with him and that I had no problem beating his ass for what he'd done, then booking him into jail.

He backed into a corner with his fists up, but he gave up after a very brief struggle.

He then whined and cried about not being able to see his kids, ultimately claiming that he'd confessed in order to take the blame for his homies.

"Billy bad ass" with a knife had disappeared; the real Costa had shown up. It was late, and I booked him into jail.

I had a note on my desk to see the Lt. in the morning at 8:00 am sharp. I usually came in at 1:00 pm, so I figured I was being sent back to patrol for not appropriately kissing Liptrap's ass earlier in the day.

When I came in the next day, the Lt. called me into his office.

He said that he was going to fire me from the Gang Task Force until he found out that I'd made the arrest; he didn't appreciate me talking to Liptrap the way I did.

I told him that I wasn't going to work with Liptrap ever—period! If that was a prerequisite to being in the task force, then he might as well kick me out now.

He stared at me with his one eye for a long time. *(He'd lost an eye in the Korean War, and it was unnerving to have him stare at you; he knew this and used it to his advantage.)*

Finally he said, "You're a cocky li'l fucker, aren't you? Liptrap can teach you a lot, but if you don't want to work with him, then fine. Get the hell out of my office!"

As I got up and began to leave, he said, "Good job on Costa."

I still had a lot of work to do on the case, and I spent the next few days tying up the loose ends.

I'd successfully made a statement: from that point on, Liptrap and I were sworn enemies—but I handled my own cases.

TWELVE
SPVG RAN THE CITY

BY THE TIME I ENTERED the Gang Task Force, SPVG had been decimated by the detectives who had been assigned at the time of the gang's rise on the street.

Jessie Afuvi headed SPVG at that time, and in my mind he was the single most charismatic and dangerous gang leader that the city of St. Pauls had ever seen. He was an excellent tactician, manipulator, and leader.

He'd lead by whatever method worked, using diversions, planning, and communications to successfully pull off several crimes, drive-bys, and armed robberies.

Under his leadership, the gang outmaneuvered the police almost nightly; he did this by using his brain and planning out everything that the gang did with military-like precision and tactics.

Eventually, though, Detectives Session and Rinker took SPVG apart and arrested Afuvi.

I was in patrol at the time, learning the ropes of battling the city's gangs.

I watched as the two detectives played gang members against each other, creating internal strife and external pressure on the gang.

They used rivals and women who hung on the gang members to get information on what was going on and who the players were, then went after them.

It was an education in full-scale urban warfare.

My part in SPVG began when the gang was at its highest point. From my perspective, they ran us ragged.

The patrolmen were running all over the city, putting out figurative fires that SPVG had lit.

It was night after night of shootings, drive-bys, gang fights, robberies, and aggravated assaults; they kept us busy trying to keep up.

They fought with one SP-13 family cell one night, then would drive-by another SP-13 house the next. It was intense street combat.

Eventually, Afuvi was caught and imprisoned, and leadership fell to a lesser leader, Leland Afuvi.

He'd been dealing drugs and running the streets since he was little; now he was an adult, and he tried to step up and fill Jessie Afuvi's shoes—but he couldn't.

He was a thug, but not nearly as smart or as driven as Jessie Afuvi.

I began working on him like I did the peewees in St. Pauls 13; I saw something in him that made me think he was vulnerable to the same kind of praise and kindness that the peewee bangers had been—and I was right.

I concentrated on him and him alone, paying special attention to him, praising his leadership and his ability to lead the gang.

Eventually, I was able to turn that and began to tell him that he was too smart for this street shit and should be thinking higher, towards school and a profession.

He ate that up, and in the space of about six weeks I had him to the point where he was ready to roll and give up the inside workings of SPVG.

He asked for a deal from the county attorney, giving him immunity for any crime that he'd done up to that date in exchange for information.

The county attorney agreed with a couple exceptions: they wouldn't grant immunity on any murders or rapes.

The deal was made, and one night I picked him up at home and brought him to the gang offices.

Before we left, I had to meet with his mother and convince her that I meant her son no harm.

I told her that the deal was real and that if her son wanted to start fresh, he could after that night.

She was in tears; she desperately wanted him out of the gang and drug life.

Their house had been subject to numerous drive-bys, and their cars had been vandalized over and over again.

The Afuvi family was right in the middle of the gang wars in St. Pauls.

Leland spilled it on the tactics and communications that the gang used, such as codes on pagers, checking in to make sure that everyone had made it back after a mission, and setting up alibis before ever committing crimes.

They used diversions to draw the police to one side of the city, then hit the other side after allowing for patrol response to the diversion.

They used pre-planned escape routes and relayed escape cars, meaning they switched cars along the way, both to and from the location that they attacked.

They'd use their girlfriends' cars, switching license plates—and they always had the women driving.

The police department thought of gang members as stupid and unable to function as an organized group; the reality was quite the opposite.

I learned a lot from this disclosure about how gang members worked together, as well as about their mentality.

I also learned how hard it was for members to leave the gang life.

About three weeks after the deal had been done with the county attorney, one of the central city cars got a report that a group of gang members had attacked a man in the middle of a gang neighborhood.

The man and some friends had been walking on the street late at night and had been jumped by another group of men who wanted to know who they claimed *(what gang)*.

According to the victims, they answered that they didn't claim anything.

The men then attacked them with knives and machetes, and one of the victim's arms was nearly severed; it hung by a few tendons and a small piece of meat, and the bones were completely detached after he'd been hit hard with a machete.

The patrol that was sent to the call put out a description of the suspect vehicle.

I had a reserve with me whom I'd let in on the whole deal with Leland Afuvi and his immunity.

He hated the idea and thought that it was a bad deal, and we were arguing that point when another unit picked up the suspect car in West St. Pauls.

I headed that way to help out.

The patrol car that had given chase to the suspects had ended up in front of a known SPVG gang member's house, and the occupants had bailed out and run, leaving the car running.

After the patrolman and one gang detective had stopped there, they decided not to chase them.

The detective was Mike Vetere.

I asked him where the suspects had gone, and he motioned toward the backyard of the house. I asked him if he was going to follow them, and he said, "Fuck that. I don't wanna get killed."

I replied, "To hell with that. *They* should fear *us*—not the other way around."

I then asked my reserve if he was up for the chase, and he said that he was.

We were off.

We tracked the occupants of the car down one-by-one, following their footprints in the fresh snow, until we ended up at a house.

The final set of footprints in the snow went in

to the house and never came out.

We surrounded the house, and after brief negotiations with the owner—explaining that we could get a search warrant easily and search the entire house or he could let us in to get the suspect—he let us in.

There was Leland Afuvi, his immunity shot; he'd been involved in the machete attack, and now he was about to be charged for aggravated assault—or at least I thought so.

As it turned out, the detective assigned to the case *(Vetere again)* had never once had a case make it through court.

This case would be no different; he'd dick around with it, go through the motions, and make it look really fucking difficult until the interest in the case blew over.

I asked about the case over and over again, expecting to get a subpoena—but it never came.

Vetere had excellent evidence, but he could not *(or would not)* get the case to the level needed for court.

Afuvi was never charged, and I never let Vetere forget it.

I found out two years later that the victim in the case was, in fact, South Side 18th Street.

He'd told the gang detectives at the time that he claimed South Side 18th Street, but they were in denial about the gang being in St. Pauls.

They claimed that the guys who were on the street who claimed South Side 18th Street were liars and wannabes.

This would be a huge, huge mistake on the gang detectives' part; in a few short months, South Side 18th Street would be one of the major players in the city' gang culture.

For some time after that, the police department would continue to deny that South Side 18th Street had arrived in St. Pauls.

The next time I ran into Jessie Afuvi, he'd just been released from prison.

I was called into the Chief's office and given a picture of him and his release date. The Assistant Chief assigned to detectives then told me that "as soon as I had a case on Afuvi, I'd better make it stick."

He said that he "didn't want this motherfucker running us ragged again."

I agreed.

He was a formidable opponent, and it was now my turn to go head-to-head with Afuvi and hopefully get him convicted and off the street as soon as possible...I didn't have to wait long.

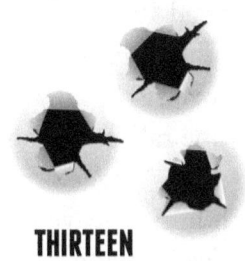

THIRTEEN
STREET RAP BEFORE FAMILY

JESSIE AFUVI HAD AN AMAZING reputation on the street. He'd worked hard to establish himself, and it meant everything to him.

When he initially got out of prison, he had to defend that reputation. He had a lot of people challenging him; like the St. Pauls 13 gang elders had learned, he found out that your reputation is challenged every day in the street. Gang life had changed; nothing was sacred in the gang world anymore.

As soon as Afuvi felt that he was forced into defending that reputation, I was given a case that involved him.

The complainant was Paul Ricos.

He was a member of WSP and had been in SPVG when Jessie Afuvi had rolled all of the smaller gangs in the city into SPVG a few years earlier.

He called to report that Jessie Afuvi had arrived at his house in West St. Pauls with his cousin Guy Dondo.

They'd come to his house after having a barbeque in the West St. Pauls Park.

According to Ricos, they said that he'd been talking shit about Jessie and that they wanted to "straighten things out with him."

Ricos went out of his house to talk with Jessie and Dondo.

He said that he told them that he hadn't been talking shit about Jessie and reminded him that they were cousins as well.

Jessie Afuvi then pulled a sawed off shotgun from his vehicle and grabbed Ricos' daughter, pointing the gun right at her head.

The discussion continued, with Jessie making it clear that he was out of prison now and back on the street—and he wouldn't tolerate anyone talking shit about him.

Ricos begged him not to harm his daughter, crying and pleading with him to leave her alone.

Jessie made sure that the entire family saw the incident and that he meant what he said.

He then told Ricos that if he heard anything else, he'd return and the girl would be harmed.

According to Ricos, Afuvi laughed at his concern for his daughter, then Afuvi and Dondo left the area.

I obtained statements from Ricos and his neighbors until I had enough information to get an arrest.

I then hit the streets and went out looking for Jessie Afuvi.

I went to his house, and his mother told me that he'd left in a brown Ford Crown Victoria with some friends to look for a job.

I hung around the area and eventually spotted the Crown Vic as it came across the 34th Street Bridge.

I stopped it and pulled Jessie Afuvi out of the car at gunpoint, then took him to the station and obtained a verbal statement from him.

We talked for several hours, and it was really interesting to see how much smarter he was than the usual suspects that I dealt with.

He was extremely bright and articulate; definitely a totally different animal.

He wouldn't admit to the incident, but he did say that he was struggling with how to stay out of trouble since being released from prison.

He said that since he'd been released, everyone was "talking all kinds of shit about him, knowing that he was on paper," hoping he'd be too afraid to confront anyone who talked bad about him.

He said that he had "not put in so much work to earn a reputation on the street to have it destroyed by the weak."

I told him I thought that he'd have to move from the area if he wanted to stay out of prison.

Reality was, he was now a target on the street, his reputation having made him one by both the gangs and the cops.

I told him that I'd been told that he was out of prison by the Assistant Chief and that I had orders to make any case with him stick.

He listened quietly but said nothing.

I then booked him into jail based on the statements I had from Ricos and other witnesses and waited for court.

When I finally did go to court, it was with charges of felony aggravated assault; I left with a conviction of misdemeanor assault.

Ricos refused to testify against Jessie Afuvi, neither would his family nor any of the other witnesses to the event; they all refused to talk in court, claiming they couldn't remember the incident and that they didn't write their statements—that I'd forged them.

I looked at Jessie Afuvi, and he smiled.

He'd told me that Ricos was a "bitch" and that he'd never testify against him in court.

After Jessie had threatened Ricos' daughter, I'd doubted that—but I was wrong.

I was barely able to get the conviction, but I did, and Jessie Afuvi was sent back to prison.

I had another case that Jessie Afuvi was named in, but I couldn't get anyone to provide a statement.

I did talk to some witnesses, and they all agreed that Afuvi was present and had participated. They wouldn't cooperate, though; they were too afraid of him.

The major crimes unit handled the case, and I was brought in as an assistant because it was considered gang-related.

SPVG was rumored to have had a coming home party for Jessie Afuvi. The party was in West St Pauls, and several people from outside the city were invited.

One girl was from Springdale and showed up to the party having no idea who she was partying with.

She started drinking and began talking shit to the party members, making racist remarks. She pissed off the SPVG guys' big time, so they coaxed her out of the house, then dragged her to a park near the railroad tracks.

Anonymous witnesses said that they could hear her screaming for help and that several men were repeatedly punching and kicking her as they took turns dragging her down the street towards the park. They repeatedly raped and beat her, then choked her to death.

They then dumped her body in the park in plain sight to make a statement: they would *not* tolerate disrespect.

This case was "solved" by major crimes; they were able to get JJ Jones to confess to being there and killing the girl.

In his confession, he claimed to have been the only person that had participated in the crime.

I had numerous people tell me that Jessie was there as well, and I approached major crimes with the information.

The unit wasn't interested, though; their idea was that they had Jones's arrest locked up and that to bring Jessie Afuvi in as well might impeach the arrest and conviction they already had.

I even had a "friend" of Jessie Afuvi tell me that she'd seen scratches on his chest and throat after the girl's murder and that she asked about them. He replied to her to forget she ever saw them—or she'd end up in the park as well.

She also wouldn't give me a statement about what she saw; she was too afraid.

Knowing about this case helped explain Ricos' fear of Jessie, as well as the witnesses' refusal to testify against him. If any of this is true, I still don't know; I was never able to prove it in court.

Afuvi was bigger than life on the street.

He'd built a reputation that made his life hell to live.

On the one hand, he was feared and respected by a lot of people; on the other hand, he was hated and blamed for a lot that he had no hand in.

This is another fact in gang life: your reputation can get you into trouble in many ways that you never anticipate.

FOURTEEN
HELL HATH NO FURY

WHILE I WAS IN THE Gang Task Force, I did have small breaks between the gang warfare.

During one of those breaks, one of the county attorneys called and asked me to investigate a claim by a 12-year-old girl who said that she'd been gang raped at an 18th Street gang party.

The girl, Amber Kilburn, was in the Juvenile Detention center called Pine Willow Bay. She'd been locked up for some minor charges and had been assigned a caseworker.

During one of the caseworker's many interviews, the girl broke down and began to talk about the incident.

The caseworker then called the county attorney, and the attorney asked me to look into it.

According to the attorney, the girl had identified known 18th Street gang members by their nicknames.

In addition, she also remembered the location where she'd been gang raped. It was an apartment complex, and she could describe it, but she couldn't remember the exact apartment number.

During the briefing the attorney said that the girl claimed to have been drugged and repeatedly gang raped by several men and boys at a party which was held in an apartment on 55th and Orchard.

I went to the apartment and checked the immediate area, looking for 18th Street gang graffiti; I found some graffiti, but not a lot.

I asked a couple women in the area if there had been any parties in the apartment complex in the past month or two, and they said yes, the men had had a party about a month earlier. One said that they had them every so often, but not frequently.

I advised the county attorney of what I'd learned, then went out to Pine Willow Bay to interview Amber Kilburn.

Initially, I thought that this would be a straight up interview; it turned out to be quite the opposite.

I had some difficulty just setting up the interview, having to call the attorney at home and get them to explain to the juvenile detention workers that I was there for the girl's benefit.

Juvenile Corrections is set up to protect the kids from the cops.

The people who work it usually take that idea to a whole other level and make it their mission in life to protect the kids; some even end up adopting the kids they run into.

After the prosecutor threatened to charge the workers with obstruction of justice, I was eventually granted access to a small interview room.

Kilburn was brought to the room after she'd eaten dinner, about twenty minutes later.

Initially, she started out acting like a little kid.

She was twelve at the time of the interview, and she acted like a normal 12-year-old kid: talking, acting nervous, and asking silly questions.

Interviewing techniques require that you set up the interview, watching the person you're interviewing, noting body language and eye contact, observing what's normal for them when they're relaxed and at ease; Kilburn wasn't relaxed and acting like a normal 12-year-old, though.

Every room in the facility was under camera surveillance, and the kids locked up there knew that; so, I had to talk quite a while to get Kilburn to let the façade drop.

There was no way the girl I was talking to would have been invited to an 18th Street gang party, much less actually attend.

Her body language eventually changed from a self-conscious 12-year-old to a slouching, much older streetwise female.

I then started to hit on the claims that she'd made, having her start from how she was invited to the party and by whom.

She claimed that she liked a "boy" and that he'd invited her to the party.

He hadn't told her that it was an 18th Street gang party; instead, he said that the party was just for some friends.

I asked her who the boy was, and she said he went by "Sleepy." She identified him by his gang name, not his real name, and this told me a lot about the "little girl" I was talking to. *(Everyone doesn't know gang names; in fact, the gang name is rarely known by anyone outside the gang culture. Most parents have no idea that their children have gang names and alter egos.)*

The 12-year-old girl was suddenly back, sitting up straight, playing with her hair, and smiling shyly.

I asked her to continue, and she outlined sneaking out of the house and going to the party with a girlfriend.

She said she was nervous about being at the party alone with "Sleepy," telling me how he'd coaxed her into a room and offered her a "blunt". *(She described a "blunt" using that term exactly.)*

I asked her what a blunt was, telling her that I'd never heard that term.

She laughed at me and said, "Really? Everyone knows what blunts are!"

She then laughed at my "stupidity" and started to relax.

The Juvenile Corrections workers had interrupted us several times by this point, telling me that I had limited time with the girl.

Finally, I had to remind them of the threat to be charged with obstruction of justice by the county attorney. I asked how their bosses would feel about them being charged and working there, alluding to the fact that their jobs were now at risk if they continued to interrupt.

Finally, they left us alone.

Surprisingly, Kilburn relaxed, and when I started to get into the details of the gang rape her body language changed.

It didn't change the way it should have, though; she became more relaxed, leaning forward and loosening up, rather than closing off and taking a more protected posture.

She made eye contact comfortably and kept her arms and legs open and relaxed.

She then recounted waking up on the bed with her legs high up in the air, saying that two men held them while two other men held her arms.

She said that a grown man *(she described him as maybe 40)* was raping her.

She said she was really out of it and looked around the room and saw that it was filled with men all chanting in Spanish, encouraging the rapist to "keep fucking her". *(Her words.)*

She said that she passed out, and then became conscious again several times.

Each time, a different guy was on top of her, and each time she heard the cheering and clapping by the onlookers.

She didn't know any of the men that she recalled raping her, so I asked about the claim by her caseworker that 18th Street gang members had raped her. *(I hadn't told her that I knew Sleepy and that he was 18th Street.)*

She said that when the men were done with their turn, the "boys" took theirs.

She described several 18th Street gang members by their gang names: Perico, Sleepy, Silent, Wicked, and Penguin.

She said they rolled her over and preferred to fuck her from behind.

While she was recounting this, her body language had changed drastically.

She was no longer leaning forward; instead, she started leaning back and making suggestive eye contact, tracing a line up her inner thighs with one finger nearly to her crotch while pulling down her T-shirt with the other hand.

Exposing her training bra, she looked at me without breaking eye contact, smiling and licking her lips.

The timid 12-year-old had disappeared. *(When interviewing, paying more attention to body language and the way something was said was always more important than the message that the person wished you to hear; this was a great example of why.)*

She went into great detail about each gang member and what he did to her.

I asked her what happened with Sleepy, and she started to describe how, when it was his turn to "rape" her *(her terms had changed again)*, he was reluctant.

She said that the men were laughing at him and telling him he was a pussy.

As she recalled this, she laughed as well, saying, "There I was on my knees, legs spread out, my ass in the air, pussy there for the taking—and his shit couldn't get hard!"

This was quite a change from the timid little girl that I'd met at the beginning of the interview.

I said nothing, simply staring at her as I watched her body language change and evolve.

I had her recount the story again, and the more she told it, the more streetwise she became.

Her language changed, her attitude changed, and by the last time she recalled the incident she described the alleged gang rape in almost pornographic terms.

She described men "nutting" inside her and forcing her to swallow their "jizz"; as I knew they monitored the interview, I wondered what the juvenile workers were thinking now.

I finally called her on the inconsistencies of the rape, and after about fifteen minutes of her calling me a piece of shit and a worthless cop and telling me I was covering for the 18th Street gang *(she also claimed over and over that we cops were covering up the crimes by 18th Street)*, she finally admitted that she'd made the gang rape up.

She told me that she'd been having sex for drugs since she was nine years old, claiming that she wasn't a prostitute because "whores did it for money" and she only "fucked for drugs."

I asked, "So you've been fucking for drugs since you were nine years old?"

She said, "Yes."

She didn't even show the slightest discomfort at the question or her admission.

She then said, "But I wouldn't fuck just anyone! They have to be 'fine,' and they have to have good drugs."

I asked her why she'd been so angry about Sleepy in the made-up rape story and recounted how she'd claimed he couldn't get hard.

She said that she liked him and wanted to have sex with him, but he refused because he knew she fucked for drugs.

She said he didn't want anything to do with her because, at one time or another, she'd fucked everyone in the gang for drugs; she was mad that he thought he was too good for her now.

She made the comment, "That limp dick don't know what he's missing out on!"

I said, "That's it? This whole story, all this time it was about him not wanting to have sex with you?"

She said, "Yes!"

That and he'd failed to pay her in drugs for a blowjob he'd finally let her give him.

She wanted her payment, and she wanted him to realize that he couldn't just use her and not pay what he owed her.

She was furious with me for seeing through the gang rape story and getting her to admit to the real story.

She called me a "lazy fuckin' cop" in one breath, then asked if I wanted to hook up when she got out of lock up in the next.

She was a mess.

After I terminated the interview and she was led back to her room, I began processing out of the facility.

The workers who were very cold and disrespectful to me earlier were now warm and friendly.

The senior supervisor even came out and said that he'd never seen anything like that.

He said the transformation that the girl went through from a scared, timid 12-year-old to a streetwise gangster bitch fucking for drugs was unbelievable.

He said that unless he'd seen it with his own eyes, he never would have believed it.

I smiled and said sadly that it was the nature of gangs. Hiding in plain sight from family and friends who weren't in the gang and having two distinct lives was normal for gang members.

I thanked him for letting me get to what really happened, then left the facility.

Kilburn was later released to foster care.

Meanwhile, her mother had been arrested for having sex with one of her underage boyfriends; sex crimes detectives later learned that she'd "turned out" her daughter at the age of nine to have sex for drugs, frequently telling her that she was better at sex than the girl and could steal her younger boyfriends whenever she wanted to.

As a result, they had an intense sexual competition for the little girl's boyfriends.

A few years later, I'd get a call from another juvenile case worker, who asked me to be a foster parent to Kilburn.

She said that Kilburn had specifically asked to be placed in my home because I was the only person that she'd never been able to lie to.

I refused the offer, and the caseworker became irate.

She said that I was a cop and that I needed to give back to the community and help this "poor little girl."

I told her that if she felt so strongly about it, *she* could take on Kilburn as a project; I refused to subject my kids to her.

She hung up on me.

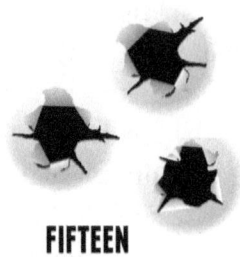

FIFTEEN
TRAVIS VICK AND PAT WALLACE

TRAVIS VICK (SANDMAN) AND PATRICK Wallace were both from smaller gangs that were rolled into SPVG under Afuvi.

Vick had earned the nickname "Sandman" for his ability to knock people out in a fistfight.

They were both very active under Afuvi, and both admitted to me that they feared and respected Afuvi immensely.

Wallace was a really talented cook and even earned a scholarship to a cooking school back east based on his talents; however, he refused the scholarship.

When I asked him why, he said that he was too afraid to be in another city, away from his "homies"; that's how ingrained the gang mentality was into him: he had a way out, and either could not or would not take it.

Both men ended up working in the kitchen of the local elite St. Pauls Golf and Country Club.

We in the gang unit and patrol laughed hard about this: the rich country club members were actually eating food prepared by Wallace and served by Travis "Sandman" Vick, both from SPVG.

The humor in this was way more than we could stand.

We often joked about our arrogant Chief sitting in the dining room of the country club with his family, eating and talking his usual shit about "his guys" and "his department," bragging about how he was personally making a difference in lowering crime in the city—all while eating food prepared by and served by the very gang members he was so determined to run out of the city.

This was a hilarious picture to us.

Pat was even featured in the local newspaper on a full front page of the Food section. The country club was very impressed with his abilities as a cook.

We laughed hard when we saw that.

Then came the final straw: pipe bombs were being found in the country club itself.

The management of the club was perplexed; how did pipe bombs get into the country club? Why would any one of their members bring them into the club to hide them?

They must have finally figured it out because Vick and Wallace were let go.

The elite people in the club lost their talented chef, and Vick and Wallace lost their hiding place for weapons and pipe bombs.

We sat in briefing afterward, wondering if anyone thought to ask the Chief how he'd missed the obvious fact that the cook and waiters were known members of one of the most notorious gangs in St. Pauls.

I know that this is really petty, but we liked the idea of his arrogant ass being served by these two SPVG gang members and him not even being aware of it.

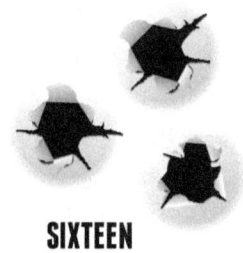

SIXTEEN
THE MAILMAN DELIVERED

I BECAME AWARE OF A small gang that had started to become very active in the city. They were Crenshaw Varrio Lobos 13, and they'd arrived in the city as a small family group.

The Romero family had moved into the city, and several extended family members had arrived with them. There weren't a lot of them, maybe twelve members deep, and they aligned themselves with West Side 18th Street, which at the time was the more violent of the two 18th Street subsets in St. Pauls.

CVL13 was very skilled in shooting people and drive-bys, substantially better at it than any other gang in the city.

I was determined never to let another gang enter the city unchallenged like 18th Street had a few years earlier, so I made an effort to meet and talk to as many of them as I could.

I asked patrol units to contact me if they had any contacts with them, and I took photos of them every chance I got.

I also recorded license plates and car descriptions of anyone that they associated with.

I'd learned from the SPVG interviews and experience with other gang members that associates' cars were often used in drive-bys, frequently without the owners knowing what was going on.

The bangers would borrow the car to make a "quick run to the store," then go out and do a shooting, returning the car when they were done.

I started building an intelligence file on the gang, trying to stay ahead of the curve on their activities. I also teamed up with a juvenile probation officer and began to accompany him on home visits with any West Side 18th Street gang members that associated with the CVL13 set.

I wanted to learn as much about them, their associates, and how they were structured as I could. They became part of my main focus for several months.

I visited one West Side 18th Street gang member with the juvenile probation officer who he said was one of the single most serious gang members he monitored.

The juvenile was nicknamed "Smoker," and the probation officer introduced me to him and his family.

As a result, I was able to see how he lived, his room, and his interaction with his family and their relationships.

This was really helpful later that summer.

One day, I came to work and received a case that detailed a shooting that had occurred in the 4300 block of Lincoln Ave.

A car had pulled up, and the occupants had called over a 14-year-old kid who was standing in the front yard.

There were three occupants in the car, and they made small talk with the kid, then asked him what gang he claimed.

The victim's name was Randy Choose.

He stated in the case that he claimed no gang affiliation and that the back seat passenger had yelled some gang name at him and the front seat passenger pointed a gun at him.

He said that he ran and that the guy with the gun shot at him repeatedly, finally hitting him in the ass as he approached his parents' car in the driveway.

He hid behind the car as the suspects drove off.

I went to interview Randy, and he said that he didn't know who the suspects were; he'd never seen them before and had no idea why they'd shoot at him.

I had no leads and no ideas of who the suspects could be.

The car they were driving was a red two-door, and Randy didn't get the vehicle's license plates; he wasn't much help.

I searched the neighborhood for witnesses of the shooting and found none. I had no leads, and the case was dead in the water.

A few days later, the gang secretary handed me some faxes that she'd received from the prison in the northern part of the state.

They detailed different gang activities in the city and had been sent to an inmate who had been a resident of St. Pauls, providing an inside look into the accounts of this particular gang member and what he told his friend in prison.

I had the secretary ask the prison to send me anything that was gang-related as soon as they got it, and they agreed to send whatever came their way.

A couple days later, they sent another batch of faxes.

One of the letters detailed an account of a shooting that had recently happened, talking about how the guy writing it went out hunting "Chochas" *(18th Street slang for St. Pauls 13)* with "Oso" and "Joker."

They drove several streets and finally located a dude in his front yard.

They pulled up to his house and called him over to the car, then asked him who he claimed because they wanted to make sure that he wasn't 18th Street; they didn't want to shoot an 18th Street gang member since they were aligned with them.

He said that they really didn't like hanging with the 18th Street gang members, but since they were such a small set, that was their only back up in the city.

The letter said that the kid told them he was "big time St. Pauls 13" and that Joker then came out of the back seat and pointed a gun at the kid.

The letter said that Joker told him, "This is Crenshaw Varrio Lobos Trece, bitch" and that he *(Joseph)* and Joker started shooting.

He said the kid ran and that they kept shooting until the guns ran out of ammo. He said they then drove off, laughing and calling the kid a pussy for running.

He went on to say in the letter that he wasn't sure if they hit the kid or not and that he watched the paper for the next few days to see if the shooting had been reported.

He said that it was reported that they hit the kid in the ass and that the police had no leads, laughing about that and telling his friend in prison that the cops would never catch them because they were new and no one knew them in the city.

He said that he was pissed that they didn't kill the kid, only hitting him in the ass.

He then said that they'd have to practice shooting so that they'd be better at hitting their targets.

The letter was signed "Alrato," then "Joseph," and it had no return address.

This was an amazing look into the mindset of the gang member.

From an intelligence-gathering point of view, it was unprecedented in the police department; no one had ever had this kind of intelligence on gangs before.

The key with intelligence, however, was to make it usable.

Intel for the sake of intel was worthless; I had to find a way to make this into a conviction.

The case resembled my unsolved drive-by case enough that I went to talk to Randy Choose again.

He denied being St. Pauls 13, and he said that he couldn't recall what the shooter had said to him about what gang he claimed; he said he was too frightened to remember much.

I asked him if he could identify the suspects if I showed him a picture of them, and he said he couldn't.

Meanwhile, his parents were getting pissed off that I hadn't solved the case, and they wanted to know what I was doing.

I told them that I was working on it but that I couldn't make arrests out of thin air; I needed their son's cooperation.

They said that he'd done enough and that they would do no more to help me.

They then said that it was well known on the street that the "Gang Task Force" was in the 18th Street gang's pockets and that no one could get a case against them into court.

This told me a lot about the family.

They were obviously very deep into St. Pauls 13, not realizing that their statements gave that away.

It also showed me that I had a lot more work to do to overcome the reputation of the Gang Task Force.

I told the father that he was opening his family up for more shootings by not cooperating, but he just said that they would "take care of their own."

I left the house, pissed off.

I had a pretty good idea of who had done the shooting, but I only had uncooperative witnesses and a letter written by some guy I didn't know, detailing what had happened; I still had a long way to go.

I went back to the office and wrote up what had happened thus far, then added it to the case file.

I then learned that I had some more faxes from the prison waiting for me.

The same guy, Joseph, had written another letter detailing a rape that he'd committed on the boulevard.

He'd been driving a car that he borrowed and picked up a girl on the boulevard.

He then took her to a park and started making out with her.

He said that he started to take off her pants and she told him that she didn't want to have sex with him.

He said he told her that she knew what they were there for and that she wanted to fuck way too much to back down now, then forced her pants down and raped her on a picnic table in the park on 37th Street just above Washington.

He said that she was screaming for help but that no one came, bragging about how hard his dick was from her fighting with him and that she cried out when he came inside of her.

He detailed how he loved that she screamed for help and that he just kept raping her, saying that he liked how it felt and planned on trying to see how many more bitches he could rape on that table during the summer.

From that point on, I made this guy a target.

No rapes had been reported, and I had no victim, but with this fucked up letter he'd gone straight to the top of my "to do" list.

His name was Joseph Lucero.

He'd written a return address on the letter and signed it "Alrato," then his name.

I put his name out in patrol briefing that I wanted to be notified of any contact that any unit had with him.

I had his name and an address, but I still couldn't tie him to the drive-by on Randy Chase with anything but his letter; I was getting closer, though.

I continued to monitor Joseph, getting frequent calls to meet him from patrol units that contacted him.

I had a case in the 3500 block of Madison that he'd been involved in.

Several witnesses had reported that a car had driven past an apartment house on the east side of the street and that the occupants of it had yelled at a guy who was sitting in the front porch area of the house.

The guy had exchanged insults with them, then they started to shoot at each other.

The car then drove away.

Witnesses later identified the occupant of the apartment building as Joseph Lucero.

I went to the scene.

Patrol had enough information to make the arrest on Joseph, and I assisted by them by taking statements from the witnesses.

From that point on, we started having a lot of contact with CVL 13.

From the letters faxed to me by the prison, I knew that the leader was known by the nickname "Oso."

The main nucleus of members was Oso, Cisco, Joker, Chucas, and Joseph.

They hung out with West Side 18th Street gang members Silent, Smoker, Speedy, Bomba, and Wicked.

Patrol had several reports at Oso's house on 2251 Cottonwood of parties and shots being fired.

They'd responded to the house and asked for permission to search for weapons; Oso gave it to them, and they found none.

They then had harsh words with the occupants but no probable cause to make an arrest, so the cases were forwarded to me.

Two days later, Joseph wrote to his friend in prison, detailing how they'd hidden the guns and the stupid cops couldn't find them.

He bragged about how easy it was to get away with shooting in the city and that the local cops were nowhere near as smart as the cops in California.

He also sent pics of the people at the party, and now I had nicknames and pics to tie to the names.

Very few people were at the party, and patrol had taken names on all of them; by process of elimination, I had them all figured out except one: I couldn't find out who "Cisco" was.

I still didn't have probable cause for an arrest, but I was building a case against the entire set.

The next day, I was reading a huge pile of faxes about some other gangs in the city that were communicating with inmates.

The secretary of our task force told me that Detective Clark had a shooting that he'd closed without an arrest.

He had a habit of pissing off the victims in his cases by blaming them for the shooting, a tactic he'd learned from Vetere; they'd been pretty good friends and had worked together on cases.

This enabled the officer to "exceptionally clear" the case and was looked on by the brass as a legitimate closure of it; they felt it wasn't our fault if the victim wouldn't cooperate, particularly in gang cases.

She handed me the case and another fax, then said, "I held this one for you. You're the only one who may be able to do something with it; no one else cares."

I read the case, which detailed a shooting that had occurred in the 5500 block of Grant.

The case reported that Randy Choose *(again)*, his cousin Paulo Lumina, and their grandfather had been having a barbeque in the front yard of the grandfather's house.

A car had driven past with three occupants, went up about a block, then flipped a bitch *(made a U-turn)*.

As the car pulled up, the passenger window rolled down, and the passenger held out a handgun and started firing at the three guys in the front yard.

They ran for the house, barely missed by several of the bullets.

Inside the house were several younger children watching television; the bullets narrowly missed them as well. It was really lucky that no one had been hit.

The faxed letter was an almost identical account of the shooting, only it wasn't an eyewitness account by Joseph. He retold it to his friend in prison but said he hadn't been there, instead claiming that "Smoker" and "Bomba" from West Side 18th Street had done the shooting.

I called the Sergeant in charge of the gang unit at the time and told him that I had information on another detective's case.

He'd closed that case "exceptionally," and I wanted to take a crack at it.

The Sergeant wasn't happy that it was Clark's case; they were close friends. He thought it over, and then gave me the OK to pursue the case.

I went to the house on 55th and Grant and talked to the grandfather.

He was really angry, saying that he was never going to cooperate with the police department on anything.

He'd called the police asking for help, then had some "asshole detective" blame him for the shooting.

He said we were all incompetent assholes and that he had ways to deal with it himself.

I argued with him for at least an hour, but he wouldn't budge, refusing to cooperate.

I left a card with him and told him that I knew who had done the shootings, as well as the shooting of his grandson, Randy Choose, a couple weeks before.

I could get the arrests of the guys, who did the shootings and lock them up, but I needed the family's help; without it, I couldn't get convictions. He just had to trust me.

He still refused to cooperate, saying that he had connections and would take care of the shooter himself.

He'd taken his grandchildren out of the city and had them live with their uncle Vince; he said they'd be safe with him.

I disagreed, but he said that I didn't know Vince; he had a good name in "the joint" and on the street, and he was respected. No one would mess with him.

I then told him to ask Vince if he'd allow me to talk to the grandchildren to see if they could identify the shooters and ask him to convince the family to cooperate with me.

I knew who "Vince" was; he went by the nickname "Shady," and he was one of the original Ochoa brothers who were rumored to be the leaders in St. Pauls 13.

I told the grandfather that I wouldn't let this go and that one way or another I'd try to get these guys arrested for shooting at his grandkids—with or without his help.

I didn't know it at the time, but his wife was watching our argument from inside the house, which would later prove crucial to the case.

I left the residence, pissed off; it seemed like I was always fighting an uphill battle in gangs.

That night, Smoker had a drive-by done on his house. He lived about two blocks away from the 5500 block of Grant. There was one round shot through the front door; no witnesses, no vehicles seen leaving the area. Most likely, the shooter was on foot.

With only one shot, no car seen leaving in the area, and nothing yelled out about any gangs, it wasn't a typical gang shooting.

I think the grandfather believed he knew exactly who was in the car shooting at his house—and the grandfather had sent a message himself. Fortunately for me and a lot of St. Pauls 13 gang members, though, the grandmother had different plans.

I called the county attorney who had handled my gang cases and set up a meeting, where I laid out what I'd collected in the CVL13 set. Side-by-side, the faxes and the police reports detailed cases we had on record of the two shootings and the searching of Oso's house.

I explained the nicknames of the people listed in the faxes and who they related to, as well as the fact that there was one person I didn't have identified, named "Cisco."

It was a very complicated case, and it took a lot of explaining, and then re-explaining.

Eventually, once the attorney understood the cases, I told him that I wanted to try to pick up the entire set in one shot. I had to put a stop to this immediately; this was open gang warfare on the streets, and it was out of control.

I asked the attorney if I had enough to make an arrest, and he said that I did have enough for probable cause, but not conviction; I'd have to get more from the families to convict.

They also weren't sure about the admissibility of the faxed letters, but they seemed legally safe for court use.

I decided to go for it.

I called the Sergeant and explained my plan to try to locate the entire set and take them down in one arrest.

As we were talking, Detectives Tony Gamboni and Clark called me and told me that they'd just been dispatched to another shooting, this time at 4400 Quincy.

The victims were St. Pauls 13 members, and they'd been chased in their car by another car, a red two-door.

They'd wrecked their car trying to get away, and they said that the passenger of the car had gotten out and shot at them several times, narrowly missing their heads as they tried to get away.

They recognized the shooter as Joker.

They knew him from school; he attended the same high school as they did.

I knew Joker was from CVL13, so I told Gamboni to get statements and that I'd be out to help him as soon as I could.

I then updated the county attorney on this latest case and left, telling them that I'd call and let them know what we did.

I met the other gang detectives back at the station and told them what I planned to do.

After we briefed, we set out in the city, looking for the CVL13 set— but they were nowhere to be found.

It was a Friday night, the warmest night of the year so far; I remember that the radio station I listened to said just that.

An hour later, I met back up with Gamboni and Clark, and we decided to set up static positions in the city to try to locate the CVL 13 set.

Each of us took up a position on one of the main roads and waited; about two hours later, I saw a car with Joseph Lucero from CVL13 drive past me.

I was in an unmarked car, and they didn't see me.

I called out to the rest of the units and let them know where I was, then informed dispatch that I was trailing a car that had suspects in several drive-bys.

I waited for back up, but none came; so, I followed the car for several blocks, then finally pulled out the "kojack" single light I had for the car and initiated the stop.

I approached the car with my gun drawn and made it clear to the occupants of the car that if anyone moved, I'd start shooting.

I then told them all to put their hands on the roof of the car and keep them there.

The driver was Oso, and the front seat passenger was Joseph.

Joker was in the back seat, along with Smoker.

I made sure that I could see their hands and that they saw that my gun was out and pointed at them.

I saw that they were all wearing gloves and ponchos, and I asked them why. They said that they were cold *(in spite of it being the warmest day of the year)*.

I understood immediately that they were planning to do more drive-bys.

They were out hunting SP-13 gang members, and the ponchos hid their clothing and the gloves defeated the "gunshot residue" tests we did at the time.

They started talking a lot of shit to me, trying to fuck with me and get me flustered; I ignored that tactic and just made sure I could see all their hands and that no one caught me slipping.

I knew from their reactions that I had them by the balls this time; the newest gang in the city wouldn't slip past me like 18th Street had done to the detectives before me.

Finally, back up arrived and I removed them from the car one by one.

I took Joseph to my car first, and then left the scene to be processed by the other units.

We recovered three guns from the car and ended up taking almost all the occupants to the station for questioning.

I'm sure that we prevented them from doing even more drive-bys that night.

I interviewed Joseph for hours before he confessed to being the shooter in the Randy Choose case.

I told him that I'd been watching him for some time and that I knew everything he'd been doing in the city.

I outlined all the stories that I'd read in the letters that he'd sent to the prison, and when I was done I explained to him that he was new to the city and had no idea who I knew and who had been talking to me.

He was furious and said that when he found out who the snitches were that ratted him out, he'd kill them.

After talking for over six hours, he gave me a full written confession.

I then came out from that interview and prepared to interview Joker.

We'd briefed that we would each close our cases and interview *all* the suspects we had, rotating until we were all done; no one was to be booked or arrested until we were all done—but that hadn't happened.

Det. Clark had interviewed Joker, and when he confessed to the case that Clark had *(the shooting earlier in the day)*, he took him straight to lockup.

He didn't let me know, and he didn't ask if I needed to see him; instead, he did everything he could to prevent me from interviewing Joker.

I was really pissed, but it was too late that night to do much about it. He was locked up, and I'd need parental consent or at least a guardian's permission to interview him.

I was pretty devastated by this; it was the most blatant in-your-face attempt to sabotage a case I'd ever encountered.

I continued on and booked Joseph into jail for the shooting.

I also interviewed him about the cases that had happened earlier, and he confessed to shooting at the suspects in front of his apartment about a month earlier.

Smoker had also been released before I could talk to him; it was done accidentally by a patrol unit at the scene of the stop on 3400 Adams.

I was really demoralized by these events.

It had taken a lot of work to get all the information together to make these arrests possible, and I hadn't expected to be so obviously backstabbed by another detective.

I returned to work the next night and went to Smoker's house.

I'd met his parents several times with his parole officer and had established a pretty good relationship with them.

I told them I needed to see him, and they agreed to let me talk to him.

I then took him to the police station and told him that I'd arrested Joker *(a lie)* and Joseph as well.

I had enough to arrest him for the shooting at 5500 Grant on Randy Choose, Paulo Lumina, and their grandfather, and his only hope was to confess and admit what he had done; that was the only way the judge would consider giving him any kind of a break.

Of course, this was a bluff; I had nothing tying him to the shooting except the rough description of the suspect vehicle, which matched his father's car, as well as the faxed account from Joseph of the shooting.

Smoker felt guilty about being left out of the arrests and not being locked up like his friends, and I used that against him; in one hour, I had a complete confession.

He wouldn't tell me who the other person was who was with him when he did the shootings; he claimed that he was alone.

I knew from the letter that had been sent to the prison, though, that the other person was "Bomba" from West Side 18th Street—but I couldn't find him.

I went to his house, and the family claimed not to know where he'd been for several months. They said that he'd gone to Mexico and hadn't returned.

I arrested Smoker and placed him into Pine Willow Bay Detention for the shootings.

I then told his father what had happened and why his house had been shot at.

He didn't say much except that his son had disgraced the family, then closed the door to their house.

I left, then went to Randy Choose's grandfather's house and told him that I'd arrested all the shooters in every single incident that had occurred to his family.

I told him that the suspects had done more shootings and had nearly killed two other kids the day before; they were getting ready to shoot more people, but we'd pulled them over on the streets and they'd been stopped.

I again asked him for his family's help.

I'd done everything I'd promised, and they were all locked up; now it was up to him and the family to cooperate with me. If they didn't, there was a very real possibility that the shooters would get out of jail.

He listened but didn't say a word, instead just glaring at me.

He then closed the door on me, and I left.

When I returned to work a few days later, Randy Choose and his grandmother were waiting for me at the police station.

His grandmother wanted to talk to me alone.

She told me that she'd been listening to what I'd told her husband, and she wanted me to guarantee that I'd made the arrests of the suspects that I'd told him about.

I showed her the cases and the arrest documents, along with the confessions.

She then showed them to Randy and told him to cooperate.

He was hesitant at first, but he eventually provided me with a statement and a positive identification of Joseph from a photo lineup.

She left, returning a short time later with Paulo Lumina and her husband.

They both provided me with statements, and her husband *(the grandfather I'd been talking with)* apologized.

He said that he appreciated what I'd done and that Vince *(the uncle with the great reputation on the street)* had told them all to cooperate with me.

I was quite surprised by this statement.

I went to court on all of the cases.

Joseph pled guilty and went straight to prison; he was eighteen years old.

He was straight up about what he'd done and was adamant about finding out whom I'd talked to that had snitched on him; he made it clear that he intended to kill the snitch.

It was pretty funny to me that he was the snitch; the letters that he'd sent to his friend in prison had sealed his own fate...I don't know if he ever found that out.

When I went to court on Joker, it was a real eye-opener for the county attorney.

Det. Gamboni had been able to get him to confess to the case that I'd started.

He'd been called to testify in Juvenile Court, and he was sworn in and took the stand.

He was then asked by the county attorney assigned to the case a few simple, basic questions to establish probable cause for the arrest.

He'd taken a gun from Joker in the traffic stop that I initiated at 3400 Adams; it was a *six-shot revolver*.

The county attorney then asked Gamboni how many rounds he'd recovered from the gun.

He replied, "Seven," then thought for a moment and changed his testimony to "Five."

The attorney dropped that line of questioning and asked him if he recognized the case number on the court docs as an SP police department case.

He replied that he didn't and also said that he had no idea what the numbers were.

He was losing the case through his incompetence *(or maybe on purpose? I never found out)*, and the county attorney was both furious and amazed.

He came to the desk where I was seated and whispered, "I don't fuckin' believe this idiot! I'm gonna have to call you to the stand to save the case."

He then did just that, telling me beforehand that "you have to salvage this case, or we'll lose it."

I testified and cleared up the confusion in the 5/6/7 shot revolver. I also identified the case number as one of ours.

Eventually, Joker was certified as an adult and sent to prison at fifteen years of age.

He had an extensive record that included aggravated rape and aggravated assault, in addition to the drive-bys and attempted homicides. Smoker was also certified as an adult and sent to prison. He was only seventeen years old.

SEVENTEEN
SCARECROW

THE WORD WAS OUT ON the street that CVL13 and West Side 18th Street were planning to retaliate for the arrests of their gang members.

I didn't know how serious the threats were, but I guessed at least one of my co-workers took them pretty seriously.

I was in front of the "Arcade Centre," a game arcade that used to be at the corner of 37th and Reynolds, talking to some 18th Street gang bangers; the business owner had asked that we make frequent stops at the arcade to keep problems with the gang members to a minimum.

I was talking to a group of about fifteen gang members with Det. Gamboni, who had been in the unit for about four months at the time.

I had my back to Tony and was talking to a kid—when suddenly the whole group started to laugh and point behind me.

I was surprised; the gang members rarely laughed at anything that wasn't dark humor.

When I turned around, I saw Tony hiding behind a car; he had ducked down behind my car and was hiding, scared and shaking.

I asked him what the hell he was doing, and he said that a red two-door had just slowed down across the street and he thought that the CVL13 gang was doing a drive-by on me to kill me for the arrests of their members.

He said all this out loud, so all the peewee 18th Street gang members heard him.

They all looked at each other, then at me, then rolled their eyes and started to whisper that he was a "bitch" and "what a fucking pussy."

I looked at the car he referred to and noticed that it was similar to the CVL13 car that had been used in several drive-bys.

"So when were you gonna tell me that they might be trying to shoot me?" I asked.

He didn't reply; instead, he just tried to ignore me while he got up from behind the car, then started trying to talk to the laughing gang members again.

They would have nothing to do with him, though; his true colors were now exposed.

I was pissed off as well.

Not only could he *not* count how many bullets were in a six-shot revolver, but now I discovered that he'd leave me out in the open without even a verbal warning that I might be getting ambushed.

I was done working with him.

I never let him ride with me again, and from that point on the gang members called him "Scarecrow."

EIGHTEEN
CEASE FIRE

SHORTLY AFTER JOKER WAS CONVICTED, Oso was hanging outside his house, drinking.

He'd been pretty upset by the conviction of his nephew, Joseph Lucero, and his brother-in-law, Joker. He was alone now with only a few members of CVL13 left in the city—and they weren't the hardcore members.

I was monitoring him closely, checking on his residence daily in the hopes of catching him doing something that I could arrest him for.

I had several letters faxed to me by the prison that had identified him as the driver in numerous drive-bys, but they weren't enough to get him convicted in court.

I'd done my best to paint him as a possible snitch to the members that I'd arrested, trying to destabilize the group with doubts about who they could trust.

This was a regular practice for me: make an arrest and allude to the information coming from within the gang, sowing the seeds of mistrust.

With each arrest, I tried to create as much internal damage as I possibly could.

Psychological warfare was as critical to my success as actual street combat—not to mention winning cases in court.

Anyway, on this particular day Oso was outside, brooding while drinking and sitting in a lawn chair.

His daughter, wife, and several family members were outside with him as well.

I'd stopped by several times to check on him, and he was getting drunker each time I came by.

I talked to the family and listened to their apologies for the arrested family members' behavior; they apologized over and over again, but they had a very angry edge to their apologies.

I listened, hoping to learn more about the gang, as well as the relationships within the family; maybe I could use this against them later.

The gang had been dealt a serious blow with the arrests, but they'd want to recover, and I felt I had to prepare for their next move.

Like I said, I made several trips to Oso's house that day, the last one of which would be the most noteworthy; it would prove to be a severe test of my ability to rise to the gang members' level on the street.

At about 2 am, I was on my way home when I got that creepy feeling again.

I've mentioned it several times in *CurbChek*, as well as this story.

Something was about to happen—something really fucked up—and I had a very overwhelming, intense feeling that I should stop by one more time.

So, I turned around and drove back in to the city.

Twenty minutes later, I arrived at Oso's house.

The majority of his family had left, and all that remained were his wife and daughter in the front yard.

Oso had sobered up a bit, but he was surly as ever.

He made some half-serious, half-joking comments about shooting me in my car in front of his house.

I laughed loudly and replied that he'd be dead before he took his first shot, telling him that I already had my gun out and pointed at him through the door of my car.

He said, "Bullshit, ESE!"

I told him I wasn't like the other cops; I'd kill his ass in a second, but I'd talk to him as well.

He carefully walked up to the car, looked in—and saw my gun pointed straight at him.

He then looked at me, smiled, and said, "Damn, Ese—you're fuckin' serious!"

He laughed and told his wife that I had my gun pointed at him.

She made no comment; just watched us, keeping their daughter close to her.

Oso looked at me for a long time and didn't say a word, the tension continuing to build between us.

Finally, he started talking quietly about being worried about Joker and how he'd be in prison, wondering if he'd be OK. He had a lot of heart, but at fifteen he was very small.

He asked me if I thought he'd be OK, and I replied that I didn't know. I knew nothing about what prison was really like; I was on the outside looking in.

I then suggested that it would be really important to write a lot and often *(setting up my next move, I hoped, with more intelligence gathering).*

While we were talking, a car pulled up.

It was Jose Osano from Chancellor Street 13; he was an ally of Oso's, and he went by "Chukas."

Oso went to his car, and I heard him whisper that he should leave because I was there, which he did.

I asked him why he told "Chukas" to leave, and he was startled that I knew who he was.

I told him that I'd been knee-deep in his ass for months; I knew everything about him—including the fact that he'd trusted the wrong people.

I said, "Coming to a new city, it was hard to know who you could trust and who you couldn't."

He yelled, "I knew it! Those fuckin' 18th Street bitches ratted us out! Fuckin' putos!" *(More head games and distrust successfully planted into his mind.)*

As we were talking, another vehicle drove past, this time a truck.

As it slowed down, Oso looked up.

I looked as well and recognized them as rival gang members: Juan Laredo and Roberto Quintana.

They were related but belonged to different gangs. Juan was St. Pauls 13, and Quintana was West Side Piru.

They started to yell at Oso, and he yelled back.

After they passed by, he said to me, "What are you gonna do about that? They just come by here and harass my family and me—and you fuckin' cops do nothing."

I thought this was funny: big badass gang member/leader wanted my help.

I didn't move, but I hung out the window of my car to watch them pass.

They stopped, and the passenger, Roberto Quintana, hung out the passenger window, looked right at me, then aimed a gun back towards us.

I thought he was aiming at Oso—but he was actually aiming at Oso's 2-year-old daughter.

Quintana shot and hit the girl as she stood on the side of the road a couple feet from me, and she dropped and started to scream.

I was really surprised by this, and for a brief moment I sat in disbelief; then, I felt this incredible feeling of rage surge through me.

I had to make a decision—and quick.

The truck was speeding away, and the girl was hurt, so I chose to chase the truck.

I was getting incredibly angry.

The edges of my vision were blackening, and tunnel vision started to creep in.

I remembered that a fire station was close to Oso's house, just around the corner, and that they had paramedics. I called out to dispatch and told them what had happened and to send medical to the house.

At the same time, I'd backed up my car and flipped around in a maneuver called a "J turn" to chase the truck.

I called out the direction of travel of the truck and tried to keep up with it in the hopes that another unit would intercept them; this, however, wasn't going to happen for some time.

Time slowed way down for me.

The chase seemed to go on for hours, but in fact it had only been maybe five minutes at the most.

I chased the truck though the city, running stop signs and crossing intersections at speeds hovering near 95 miles an hour.

I was raging, crazy pissed off; it was inexcusable to shoot a child in this gang warfare.

It made me even angrier that I knew both occupants of the truck and that they knew me and that I was present at the house—and in spite of that knowledge, they shot anyway.

I was furious.

I took this personally, wanting to fight and kill them both.

The law, the job, my family—it all went out the fucking window.

All I could think about was killing them both, but I'd have to catch them first—and I wasn't going to let them to survive this night.

They'd crossed the line and challenged me directly, doubting my response and my ability to rise to their level.

If I caught them, I was going to kill them...I was really fucking mad.

I was driving a small Chevy Cavalier, 4 cylinders, unmarked.

They had a GMC Sonoma pick up; needless to say, they left me behind with no problem.

When we reached an intersection at Reynolds and Jackson, they slowed way down, and I saw that they both turned to look at me as I approached.

I rolled down my window and yelled at them to stop and get out and fight; they looked at me, then looked at each other—and took off down Jackson.

I was out of my mind with rage.

I couldn't keep up in my car, and I called for any unit to help me catch them, but no one answered my call.

I was driving down Jackson Ave., running stop signs, gaining speed, and beating the hell out of my car.

Every intersection we crossed, the car slammed into the pavement, sending up sparks.

I could hear metal parts flying off the car and hitting the pavement, and I looked in the rearview mirror and saw metal parts flying up behind me; I hoped the car would hold together long enough to get me through the chase.

They never slowed down again, and I had a hard time keeping them in sight.

I called out again for another unit to help, but no one answered.

The truck reached the intersection of 43rd and Monroe, then went north.

Another police car was there, and it started to chase them as well—but the other cop was going too slowly, so I got on the radio and yelled at him to either get the fuck in the chase or get the hell out of my way.

He didn't respond, but he did speed up and gained on the truck, which then turned the corner at 43rd and Specker and pulled over.

I was out of my car immediately and approaching the shooter; in my mind, I saw images of me blowing his head off, then shooting the driver.

I walked up to the car and yelled at Quintana, saying, "Give me a reason to let you live, bitch."

He said nothing; he just looked at me and stared.

I wanted him to do something, say something, move—anything I could use for an excuse to shoot him.

But, he did nothing...he had no idea how bad I wanted to kill him right there.

I looked over at the other officer that had pulled the car over.

He was new; I didn't know him, so I had no idea what he'd say if I assassinated these two pieces of shit sitting in the car.

I was frustrated and angry.

I wanted the car stopped, but I also wanted to kill Quintana and Laredo.

I'd have to be satisfied with an arrest; that wasn't enough for me, but I had no choice.

I pulled Quintana from the car, still goading him, asking him to give me a reason to let him live; he said nothing.

I slammed him against the car and cuffed him, then walked him back to my car, dragging him by his hair and calling him a "fucking punk ass bitch."

I slammed him against my car and opened the passenger door, then put him in the car and cross-faced him while I put on his seat belt.

He started to complain, saying he'd have my badge for the cross-face move.

The stupid fucker had no idea I was way beyond that now; he was lucky to be breathing at all.

I grabbed him by the throat and told him I wanted to kill him right there, sitting in my car.

He was gagging and gasping for air; I had a tight hold on his throat, and he started to squirm and kick with his feet because he couldn't breathe.

His eyes were now wide with terror.

Inches from his face, I whispered, "What now, bitch? You gonna have my badge when you're fuckin' dead?"

I wanted to watch him die, and then I heard other cop cars approaching.

When I heard another cop say, "Hey, what's he doin' to that guy?" I knew I couldn't kill him.

I let go of his throat and slammed the door to the car with Quintana coughing and gasping for air inside.

I then called dispatch on the radio and checked the status of the little girl.

They said that she'd arrived at the hospital and was OK.

I was still out of control, though, so I just walked away from the scene.

I went about half a block, then grabbed a fence that was on the side of a construction site, holding on 'til I could think clearly again; screaming, cursing, and crying, I had nowhere to vent my rage.

Finally, I calmed down and went to the hospital.

I met with Oso there and told him that I'd caught the guys who shot his daughter and that I needed his help to convict them.

He was as angry as I was, pacing back and forth and screaming to the sky that he'd kill all the SP-13s.

I told him to stop, and after he saw how I was acting—how really truly angry I was—he stopped and listened.

I told him that I needed him to let me handle this, that there would be no payback until I got them into court and convicted; he could have his battle after the court dates were over, but not now.

He made no promises, but he said he'd think about it.

Meanwhile, his daughter would live.

She had injuries, but they weren't serious.

The bullet had punched through one arm, grazed her chest, and lodged in the other arm. She'd been really lucky; Quintana had aimed for a chest shot...he wanted her dead.

Oso called me on my cell phone a few days later and asked me to come to his house.

I met him out front; just as we'd been on the night of the shooting, my gun was again pointed at him.

He looked in and—seeing the gun—smiled.

"Sup, Ese?" he said.

I said, "Not much."

He said that he'd called a meeting with his set, CVL13, and Westside 18th Street. They talked over their options and decided that they wanted to go to war with the St. Pauls 13 gang for the shooting.

He said that he talked to them and convinced them to wait and see if I could get the guys who shot his daughter convicted; if I could, they'd take care of it in prison.

They weren't happy with him working with me, but they agreed to wait and see.

He asked me what I thought about that, and I told him I was cool with it.

"Just keep your ass off the streets so I can focus on getting them convicted," I said. "If I have one case cross my desk with your name on it, I'm coming after you—and the shooters will walk."

He glared at me long and hard, then finally said, "OK, Ese—you make that shit happen! You put those putos in the penitentiary; I'll do the rest."

Funny how quick we were able to become allies.

I still hated this guy, and he hated me—but we had an alliance now, a common goal...weird shit, how the street worked.

I was able to help convict both Quintana and Laredo of the shooting, and Oso kept his word and didn't start a gang war. I never had another case with him as a suspect again.

In the trial, I found out that Juan Laredo had a plane ticket out of the country to visit family in Mexico; he would have left early the next morning after the shooting.

He'd planned on doing the shooting, then leaving the country 'til things cooled off.

Roberto Quintana admitted that he'd shot at Oso's daughter on purpose, claiming that someone had shot at his kids and that he'd heard on the street that it was Oso.

He'd searched for him for some time and had finally found out that his cousin Juan knew where Oso lived.

They got drunk and went out that night, looking for Oso's house.

NINETEEN
GREEN LIGHT ON PACMAN

WHILE I WAS WAITING FOR trial on this case, I had an informant call me and tell me that West Side 18th Street was having a meeting at Speedy's house.

They'd agreed to hold off on retaliation for Oso's daughter being shot; they felt that since he wasn't directly one of their gang members and was only an associate of theirs, they lost no face in letting the shooting go.

They did, however, feel that Smoker's arrest required a response, and my informant went on to tell me that they felt that I had to be taught a lesson for arresting him.

They hadn't had a member of their set arrested by the PD in some time.

They felt they had an arrangement with other gang cops, and they believed that they were immune from us; however, my arrest of Smoker had made a statement to them that this would no longer be the case.

The gang's leadership felt that they had to take action to protect the gang from me and make a statement of their own.

According to my informant, they'd agreed to meet at Speedy's house and make plans to kill me.

They were planning alibis, getting the logistics down as to who would do what and where...in short, they were planning a hit—on me.

As I pulled over and listened to this information, my informant was scared and out of breath.

We'd worked together on a lot of cases, and he was seriously afraid.

He said they were serious about it and that "they weren't fuckin' playing." They'd even shaved their heads and dressed down. *(A statement meaning they were going to war.)*

They were serious and planned on doing the hit that day.

I still wasn't over the rage from the little girl being shot, and I have to admit I wasn't in my right mind.

This threat didn't make me afraid at all; instead, it only made me even angrier *(if that was possible)*.

I sat on the side of the road and tried to think of what to do.

If I told the police department, they wouldn't believe me.

No one believed the gangs were this organized and disciplined; the cops foolishly believed that they were immune from gang violence.

I had nowhere to go with the information that was legitimate.

I drove past Speedy's house, and the yard was full of West Side 18th Street gang members' cars.

I started getting really pissed off.

I couldn't depend on the cops to help; they were so stupid about the street, I could never count on them.

So, I decided to deal with it myself. I was getting more and more angry, less reasonable, and less coherent. I called my informant and told him that I was going to take care of it myself. I also told him to tell someone else about what he'd heard if I was killed.

He asked what I was going to do, and I told him that I didn't know yet. I drove around for about five more minutes, mulling over different ideas.

Finally, I decided, *Fuck this!*

I went to Speedy's house and walked in on the meeting—with my gun out.

Speedy tried to kick me out of the house, but I pushed past him and told them all that I heard they wanted me dead.

There were at least twenty gang members there, and a lot of them I didn't know and had never seen.

They all had shaved heads and were dressed down, and they were quiet; no one said a word.

I said, "Word is, you fuckin' putos want me dead. Well, bitches, here I am—who the fuck do I kill first?"

After I got no response from the group, I said, "You fuckin' want me? Here the fuck I am! You aren't gonna sneak up on my ass on the street, shoot me in the back of the head, and drive off. We do this right *now*, motherfuckers!"

Still nothing.

The house was silent; no one moved, and no one said a word.

I said quietly, "Who the fuck is gonna step up and face me one-on-one?"

No one moved; they just stared at each other, then started talking to each other in Spanish.

One guy said I was fucking crazy and that he wanted no part of this.

Another one said that they should all rush me at once.

When I heard that, I said in English, "I agree, you should fuckin' rush me—who's gonna die first?"

I then yelled, "Come on, motherfuckers—let's *do* this!"

I started waving my gun, aiming it from one gang member's head to another, finger pulling on the trigger.

I wasn't bluffing; I'd really lost it. No one moved.

Finally, after about five minutes of this, I said, "If it even *looks* like one of you punk ass bitches is close to me—I'll kill your fuckin' asses. There will be no warning...I'll blow your fuckin' punk ass heads off. You bitches come near me—and you're fuckin' dead. Plan *that* into your fucking plans!"

I backed out of the house and left, then called my informant and asked him to keep his ears open.

After I told him what I'd done, I asked him to let me know what they decided to do.

He said, "Jesus, ESE! Are you fuckin' *crazy?*"

Ya, I guess I was crazy.

The girl being shot had changed me; I was really angry all the time.

A couple hours went by, and my informant called me back.

Laughing hysterically, he said they changed their minds!

He said that they decided I was fucking loco, and if they didn't succeed in killing me the first time that I'd hunt them all down and kill them all one at a time.

They said that because I was a cop—and crazy as well—I could get away with anything, so they called off the hit.

He said I scared the shit out of them, that they could see in my eyes that I was crazy and meant it that I wanted to fight right there in Speedy's house.

He was laughing so hard, he could barely talk.

He said, "Pacman, you really scared the shit out of them...you *are* fuckin' loco, ESE!"

I guess he was right...I *had* changed.

TWENTY
TODAY A SUSPECT, TOMORROW A VICTIM

SOMEWHERE IN-BETWEEN THE CVL13 CASE, these cases happened as well.

I got a call of a shooting at the 7-11 that used to be on the corner of 31st and Washington.

The victim was Juan Laredo *(this was before the drive-by on Oso's house)*.

He was out with some girls and was pulling into the parking lot at a 7-11, which was popular to turn around in on the boulevard.

He was showing off his new car to the teenage girls there and didn't notice that there were several South Side 18th Street gang members in the parking lot.

He'd made several runs up and down the boulevard, showing off the car and getting noticed.

He then pulled into the parking lot to get some gas, going into the store to pay for it and get some food.

When he came out, "Evil" from South Side 18th Street was talking to the girls.

This really pissed Juan off, and he tried to pick a fight with "Evil," calling the South Side 18th Street gang member a sewer rat.

"Evil" got pissed off and shot at Juan, narrowly missing him.

Juan quickly left the parking lot in his car, and the store clerk called the police.

By the time I arrived, everyone was gone.

I took down the information from the clerk; he'd written down the license plate numbers of the vehicles involved and had told several witnesses to stay nearby 'til we arrived.

I took the statements from the witnesses and the clerk, then started to look for the suspect.

Initially, the scene had been very chaotic, and very few people actually knew who the shooter was or what he looked like.

Two girls said that they knew who the shooter was and identified him as "Angel"; he was a known South Side 18th Street associate.

I put together a photo lineup, and they both identified him as the suspect.

I went to his house, picked him up, and brought him to the station.

After several hours of interrogation, I determined that Angel wasn't the shooter; he'd been there, witnessed the shooting, and provided me with details of what had happened, but he wasn't the shooter himself.

He identified the shooter as "Evil" from South Side 18th Street, saying that until the shooting occurred, Juan was the aggressor in the incident and "Evil" had pulled out the pistol to protect himself from Juan because he was bigger than "Evil."

He did confirm, though, that Juan had no weapons.

The next night, I went to pick up "Evil" at his home.

Det. James *(the gang members called him "Powder")*, who was new in the unit at the time, accompanied me.

We went to the home and found no one there.

We got ready to leave the area, but I decided to wait *(that weird ass feeling again)*.

We sat by our cars for about five minutes, then "Evil" came around the corner in his parents' car; he was a passenger with his father and other family members in the car.

We stopped the car and removed Evil at gunpoint, taking him to the station.

I spent several hours with "Evil" but couldn't get him to confess; however, Powder took a crack at it and was able to get him to confess to the shooting in just a few minutes.

Evil was eventually convicted for the shooting.

During the trial, it was difficult to prosecute him because we now had cases pending with Laredo as a suspect as well.

This is one of the common problems with gang cases, and why it's so difficult to get successful prosecution: in one case, your victim is a cooperative—then a week later that same victim is now your suspect, and you're arresting them.

They're difficult and dynamic cases, and the gang world is constantly changing...your victim today is your suspect tomorrow.

TWENTY-ONE
GANG CULTURE

THE ASIAN BROTHERHOOD HUNG OUT primarily in a neighboring county. They liked to frequent a Buddhist temple in the region, and they also had connections with Asian gangs in St. Erie and networked into California. They were led by the Choi Family, which lived at 3600 Jackson Ave.

I had a couple informants in the gang and learned that they had an entirely different philosophy than the Hispanic gangs. For one, their initiation rite was totally different.

The Hispanic gangs had a process where prospective gang members were beat in; they had to face a group of fellow gang members that attacked them and beat them up.

Outnumbered, they had to show their "heart" and "toughness" by fighting the group until the allotted time had elapsed.

If they performed well, they were accepted.

The process was called being "jumped in."

The same brutal process was used to get out of the gang *("jumped out")*, only the beating was much more brutal.

For the Asian gangs, the process for prospective gang members to enter the gang was quite different: they were required to commit a crime.

The gang would choose a crime, usually either burglary, robbery, or rape, and the wannabe gang member would have to execute the crime as the gang described.

To me, this seemed to be a more intellectual approach to the gang banging life; show your ability to conduct crimes that would benefit the gang, such as enriching their monetary holdings or creating terror in a business owner to be "taxed" at a future time.

This difference spoke volumes to me about the Asian Brotherhood and their connections to other Asian gangs.

They had a culture and a "value system" consistent with Asian gangs all along the West coast.

They hadn't just randomly adopted a set of behaviors that seemed appropriate; they followed a well-established code of conduct.

St. Pauls 13, on the other hand, seemed to be a disorganized, chaotic mess.

Family cells were unaware of each other and frequently in direct conflict with each other; they each believed that "they" were the true St. Pauls 13 members and that the rest were just wannabes.

Each faction believed that they were tougher, smarter, and more "down" than the others in the set.

On the one hand this made them incredibly disorganized, but on the other it made them really hard to attack. They had no central leadership and no direction, and that made them difficult both to understand and defeat.

They also had no heritage.

They didn't know how the gang started or what the "13" meant in the name they yelled out so proudly.

They had no idea that it identified them as Sureneos *("Southerners")* when they entered the California prison system.

The California influence on St. Paul's gang culture is significant, and they seemed totally ignorant of this.

They professed to hate the Sureneos and referred to them as "sewer rats"; yet they carried the Sureneos identifier: "13."

They were a mystery to me.

Culturally, they were "poor" compared to the Asian gangs, unaware of their own gang's history.

On the other hand, 18th Street had some historical awareness of where the gang had originated and what the Sur 13 moniker meant.

Any 18th Street gang member I asked knew what the Sur 13 symbols meant, and they were just as baffled as I was by St. Pauls 13 gang members' ignorance of what the 13 in the gang's name meant.

I had several of them comment to me that "they call us sewer rats, but they're Sureneos just like us—what the fuck is wrong with them?"

South Side 18th Street was led by a distinct hierarchy.

The Gardenas family was the leadership of the set.

They were from California and were well known in the Hispanic community. The oldest, Brother Andy, was the leader of the set.

He was in and out of prison for drug distribution.

South Side 18th Street primarily focused on "making money."

They attempted to impose a street tax on residents in Central City, they were well known for drug distribution, and they had numerous connections to small, family-owned businesses that were rumored to be fronts for money laundering and drug selling.

West Side 18th Street was headed up by Jose Valencia, aka "Silent." They were a much smaller and more violent set than South Side.

South Side and West Side 18th Street had an uneasy alliance with each other; neither trusted the other, and both wanted to be in charge of the city.

TWENTY-TWO
GALLEGOS SPRAY AND PRAY

THE GALLEGOS HAD BEEN ONE of the dominant families in the St. Pauls 13 gang during the early nineties, and they'd suffered the consequences of being so heavily involved in the gang life.

The main Gallegos family faction of St. Pauls 13 had been led by Juan and Felipe Gallegos, who lived in a small, rundown house on the west side of the city.

They'd pretty much dominated the gang activities during the early 90s and had been victims of numerous drive-bys and gang fights.

First they fought with the SPVG gang, then with the Asian brotherhood, and finally with the 18th Street gang for dominance in the gang culture of the city.

After experiencing several negative incidents, the Gallegos finally withdrew from being the leaders in gang activity in the city.

First, Juan Gallegos attempted suicide then claimed to have been attacked by rival gangs when he survived.

He was in extreme depression from the toll the gang lifestyle had taken on his life, as well as the lives of his family and children.

Then, when it was discovered that he'd attempted suicide, he was thought of as weak and no longer a viable leader.

Also, the neighborhood gang members that the family had intimidated and threatened for years through their dominance of the gang became fed up with them, and they executed a very extensive drive-by on the Gallegos' home one day while the family was having a party in the front yard of their house.

There were numerous rounds fired, and well over forty casings were left in the street outside their house; using semi-automatic assault rifles and hand guns, the disgruntled gang members made a statement that they were no longer going to follow the Gallegos' lead.

I was assigned this case, and the family expected me to be able to solve it with no cooperation from them.

They'd developed a great working relationship with Det.'s Session and Rinker and expected that I'd follow suit and do whatever it took to make them happy, which was similar to the problem I had with 18th Street and the relationship that they had with Det. Jim Smally.

The Gallegos family expected preferential treatment from the police department, and they refused to cooperate with the investigation—yet still insisted that I "do something."

I was never able to get an arrest on the drive-by of their house, though, in spite of the fact that the entire family had been put at risk.

Surprisingly, no one was injured in the shooting; St. Pauls 13 was nowhere near as skilled at drive-bys as the CVL13 gang.

If CVL13 had done the shooting, I would have had several dead people in the front yard of the house.

TWENTY-THREE
ASIANS VS. TRECES

ANOTHER CASE I HAD WAS a gang fight between the Asian Brotherhood and members of the St. Pauls 13 gang that were aligned with the Gallegos.

The Gallegos were driving around the city one night and ran into the Asian Brotherhood.

The Gallegos had bought a yellow mid-80s Monte Carlo and had been showing it off in the city; the entire family was proud of the car and had been bragging about it to everyone they knew.

This particular night, the brothers Juan and Felipe had been out with cousin Jose Gallegos, aka "Batman."

While they were cruising the boulevard, they ran into the Asian brotherhood and began exchanging words and making comments about each other's cars.

The Asians would buy Honda or Nissan vehicles and work on the motors and body to make them into street rods. They didn't like Chevys, the Gallegos' favorite model of car.

The two groups ended up in the middle of the street, fighting in the middle of the night.

Jose Gallegos was stabbed several times and rushed to the hospital.

At the same time, an Asian kid named Diovanni Lee showed up with multiple stab wounds.

Neither group would cooperate with the investigation.

Both kids were injured with multiple stab wounds, but neither was seriously injured, and they went home after a few hours of observation.

Prior to this incident, Lee hadn't been identified as a gang member.

I went to his home and spoke to his parents, who had adopted him and his brother, David.

They confirmed that the boys had belonged to the Asian brotherhood, and they were at a loss as to what they should do; the boys had quit listening to them after joining the gang, and they felt that they had no influence over them.

No arrests were ever made in this case.

Without doing anything to help, the Gallegos again expected me to make arrests and get convictions.

They refused to allow me even to question Jose Gallegos, and statements were out of the question.

The Asians also never cooperated with the police.

They retained an attorney immediately for any case I had that involved them, or they simply refused to talk to me.

TWENTY-FOUR
BLACK GANGS

WHILE WORKING THE HISPANIC GANGS, like St. Pauls 13, CVL13, South and West Side 18th Street, and the Asian gangs, as well as smaller gangs like 7th Street Mafiosos and SPCC *(St. Pauls' Craziest Chicanos)*, I also had to work the black gangs in the city.

We had a couple local gangs: "Doggden," a mixture of Bloods and Crips that claimed they controlled the Fred Marshal Center, and a loosely tied group of black dudes who were criminals, dealing drugs and making money but with no name to identify themselves.

Then there were the California gangs represented by members who had moved to the area either through Job Corps or "business opportunities" *(drug dealing)*.

My first contact with a transplanted California gang member was a mall security guard at the St. Pauls City Mall.

His name was Ray Riggins, and he was introduced to me through another police officer who worked part-time at the mall.

I used to hang out in the vicinity of the mall on my work days since it bordered my area and a lot of gang members would hang out there.

We used to talk, and I started to notice little things that he said and did that implied that he had an in-depth knowledge of the black gang members in the area, as well as the black drug dealers.

I started spending more and more time talking with him and learning from him, and eventually he opened up and admitted to me that he'd been a gang member in California and had moved here with Job Corps, which he'd entered to try to get away from California and make a better life for himself.

He said that he claimed East Coast 190 Crip and told me that he was one of many California gang members in the area.

Technically, he was still a gang member, but he'd curtailed some of his activities since he'd moved.

As our friendship developed, he showed me home movies of his brothers and other gang members at gang barbeques and parties.

During the videos, the family members were constantly throwing up gang signs and making cryptic gang comments.

He refused to wear anything red in color—ever.

I was surprised at how ingrained this aversion to the color red was in his mentality; even outside of California and in an environment that was relatively free of black gang-on-gang violence, he refused to wear red.

He began to open up to me about what was going on in the black community.

I'd been unable to develop any informants in the black community, and I had suspicions that there were numerous gang members in the city who hadn't been identified.

Over a period of several months, he confirmed that there were several different California sets represented in the city.

He told me about a correctional officer who worked in the jail. The officer was also an East Coast 190 Crip that went by the AKA "Lil Capone"; his real name was Paul Pogars.

He'd been working in the county jail for about two years and had taken the job for two reasons: he needed a job and had been hired by the sheriff's department, and he wanted access to the records kept in the jail about who was in jail, who visited the inmates, and how they could be contacted; this gave him inside information into the things that went on between the inmates, their attorneys, and the police.

I was quite shocked at how easy it had been for any gang member to infiltrate the corrections and police databases and facilities.

As I gained more and more of Riggins' trust, he began to loosen up and told me a lot of amazing things about how the police department and local correctional departments had been infiltrated by California gangs and local drug dealers.

As my awareness grew of what was going on behind the scenes, a lot more of what happened on the street made sense.

I understood why people who were really familiar with the street didn't trust cops and didn't believe we had any clue what was going on; we had no damn idea what was going on right under our noses.

Meanwhile, Paul Pogars worked in the jail and had access to all their records and databases.

Also, Riggins and two other guys worked in the mall and were closely associated with the police officers who worked there, and they talked daily to the cops who worked there part-time and gained their trust and confidence.

They knew everything that was going on at the police department and frequently rode around with the cops on duty when they *(the gang banger mall security guards)* weren't at work.

This gave them insight into how we worked and how much each guy really knew about the street.

The department had a very loosely monitored ride-along program, so they rode as often as they could to learn about the police.

TWENTY-FIVE
STEVE TREMMEL

RIGGINS TOLD ME ABOUT A local guy whom he felt was running the worst scam of all.

He was bitter enemies with this guy; they both liked the same girl, "Kiki," and had been in fist fights and gunfights over her on several occasions.

The guy's name was Steve Tremmel, and he worked at Lost Creek, a juvenile lock-up for the more serious juvenile offenders in the area.

Tremmel bragged about how easy it had been to get into the system and use his position to locate and cultivate kids to distribute drugs in the community.

He was in a position in the facility to closely monitor the children and pick out the ones who he could most depend upon to keep his secret drug operation going; as a result, he cultivated a network that made him very rich.

I tried over and over again to get someone in Narcotics to listen to the information I had about Tremmel, but no one would listen.

I heard over and over again how impossible it was for the Juvenile corrections system to have been infiltrated so easily and that if that were true, their informants would have advised the Narcotics agents of it.

It was frustrating how stupid my peers were.

Riggins laughed when I told him about how Narcotics refused to look into Tremmel.

He said to me, "See! And you motherfuckers wonder why no one on the street trusts the cops?"

Finally, I mentioned Tremmel to Dirk Wiser.

He'd been recently assigned to the Narcotics section and had asked me if I knew of anything that had been missed by the previous group.

He spent a lot of time trying to get to Tremmel, and eventually he did; this was, however, years after the disclosure that Riggins had made to me.

TWENTY-SIX
T-BONE AND LOLLIPOP

RIGGINS ALSO TOLD ME ABOUT a California gang member who he said was the single biggest dealer of cocaine in the area.

His real name was James Bellweather. He used the alias "James McElroy" and had the gang name of "T-bone."

He was a Santana Block Crip from California and had formed an alliance with a local black drug dealer named "Sam."

I started to look into "T-bone" and began to monitor him closely.

I'd developed a pretty good understanding of who he hung out with and his pattern of behaviors.

I also checked with the Narcotics unit, and they'd heard of him.

Det. Mike Slacker had several cases pending on "T-bone" and had an informant who had made several buys of narcotics from him.

He hadn't been able to identify "T-bone" definitively, though, and without complete and correct identification he couldn't get an arrest warrant.

So, he asked me to keep an eye out for him.

T-bone liked to hang out at the American Legion at 38th and Aspen. It was a pretty much a "Blacks Only" bar with very few white people trusted and allowed inside.

He was very careful about who he sold to and did his business with a pager.

If you paged him, he called you back IF he recognized the number; if he didn't recognize the number, he wouldn't call you back.

He was very low profile and had made a name for himself on the street as a mellow, easygoing guy—as long as you didn't cross him.

He was also very likable and was trusted by a lot of people, which made him even harder to work my way into.

One night there was a shooting at the bar, and several cars were reported to have been leaving the area at a high rate of speed.

I was working the Central City at the time of the reported shooting and continued slowly towards the area.

I saw T-bone's white Chevy Monte Carlo approaching me at a high rate of speed; when he saw me, he slowed way down, dropping the nose of the car as he slammed on the brakes to drop speed.

As he turned the corner, I pulled him over.

This was the first time I actually had probable cause to stop him; he was leaving the scene of a shooting, traveling at a high rate of speed through a residential area.

I approached the car with my gun out and calmly told T-bone to keep his hands on the steering wheel.

I saw that he had his girlfriend in the front seat of the car and another drug dealer named Lollipop in the back seat.

"Lolli" was a little guy and was learning the "tricks of the trade" from "T-bone"; in effect, he was his apprentice—and he was armed, which I didn't find out 'til I was well into the stop.

Not that it mattered, though; by this time, I'd learned to treat every single person I ran into as if they were armed, no matter what the circumstances.

I asked T-bone to get out of the car and follow me to the rear of the vehicle.

He had no identification.

I knew that he never carried any; that was how he kept himself anonymous on the street.

No one ever knew his real name: "James Bellweather"; "T-bone" was how his closest friends knew him—and that's all they knew.

I played dumb with him, not letting him know what I already knew about him.

I told him that I needed to know who he was and that since he was driving, I needed a valid driver's license.

He admitted to me that he didn't have one.

I searched him for weapons and found none.

He did have a pager *(the pager he used to conduct his business)*, so I asked him the number to it and warned him that I'd call it to verify whether or not he'd been truthful.

He gave me the number to the pager, and I called it from the cell phone that I kept in my car. He'd given me the correct number; we were establishing trust.

I asked him if he'd been at the Legion bar, and he said that he had been, but "all kinds of drama had busted loose," so he left.

I told him that was the reason I'd stopped him; he was traveling away at a high rate of speed from a report of shots being fired at the Legion.

He replied that it made sense to him.

This all went into my report to justify the stop.

I asked him if there were any weapons in the car, and he said that no one had weapons in the car.

I told him that, due to the nature of the stop, I'd have to search the car.

He agreed and even gave me permission to search it.

I did find a Lorcin 380 in the back seat where Lolli had been sitting, and I approached "T-bone" and said, "What the fuck is this, man?"

He instantly transformed from calm "T-bone" to angry "T-bone" and confronted "Lolli," saying to him "I told you no guns, motherfucker!"

"Lolli" was a prick and said, "Fuck that shit, man! Quit kissing this cop's ass; he can't prove shit."

"T-bone" quietly turned to me and said, "I didn't know he had a gun, and I apologize for it."

I didn't know what to think of him.

There he was, mellow as hell to me and angry with his friend for having a gun.

I didn't expect that from him; I was ready to go to war with the guy, ramped up to battle with his drug-dealing ass.

I could see why he was so trusted by the people on the street; he may have been a drug dealer, but he was very real.

Criminal? Yes. Asshole? No.

Regardless, I told him that I'd have to book him into jail because I couldn't verify who he was.

I told him that if he had a driver's license I would have been able to release him on a citation, but that it was state law that if I couldn't identify him I had to book him into jail.

He said that he understood and asked that I release his car to his girlfriend.

It wasn't legal for me to do that, and if things had gone differently I have to admit I would have fucked him over any way that I could, impounding his car and digging for some way to make his life more miserable.

To me, attitude was everything. Treat me with respect, and I'll return it; treat me like shit, and I'm gonna find any way possible to make you hate the day I was born.

So I did release the car to T-bone's girl after I checked "Lollipop's" gun to see if it was stolen.

It wasn't, and it also wasn't loaded.

I had no reason to keep it or arrest him, so I let him leave with "T bone's" girlfriend and car.

I then transported T-bone to the jail, and we talked on the way.

I have to admit, I liked the guy; he was very likeable, and he was the biggest dealer in the city for a reason: he was very smart and articulate.

I booked "T bone" into jail and specifically asked that he be fingerprinted; that was unusual for a no driver's license charge, and I had to explain why to the intake officer.

I asked that the card be forwarded to Det. Slacker in the hopes that "T-bone's" real identity would be discovered.

They agreed and fingerprinted "T-bone," then released him on bail to his girl.

The information I'd been given by Riggins was correct, and I began to rely heavily on him for more.

I told him about my stop of "T-bone," and he said that "T-bone" had told him about the stop as well.

He said that they played video games together often and that "T-bone" told him about how he'd been doing business *(dealing drugs)* in the city for several years and that the cops had never caught on to him because he was careful and smart.

He said that "T-bone" made the comment that the cops in this area were really stupid compared to California and that it was easy to stay out of jail.

He laughed about the stop that I'd made, bragging that he'd gotten away again without being identified.

He laughed and said, "That cop booked me under my fake name! They'll never catch me!"

A few days later, Slacker got a hold of me and thanked me for the stop.

He'd positively identified "T-bone" as James Bellweather.

Having pulled his record and found that he'd done time for a murder in California, he was able to convict Bellweather for the drug deals that he'd done in the city and sent him to prison.

I ended up using "T-bone's" opinion of how stupid the cops in St. Pauls were to my advantage.

I hung out and started to push my contact with him, tailing him in my area and stopping to talk to him whenever I could.

I learned a lot about him and who he hung out with, as well as how he continued to sell drugs right up until he was sent to prison.

"T-bone" started to trust me and even asked that I write a letter to the parole board to help him get an early release; I did whatever it took to cultivate informants, so hell ya, I wrote the letter.

"T-bone" later confided in me that his attorney had tried to pick up on his girlfriend after he was incarcerated. He felt really betrayed by that; he hired the man because he was highly recommended.

"T-bone" found out the hard way what we cops already knew: attorneys were no one's friends. It took a very "special" kind of person to be an attorney.

Anyway, after that "T-bone" asked that I keep an eye on his girl while he was locked up and let him know if she was seeing someone else. I did look out for her, and when I saw her going frequently to "Sam's" place to buy cocaine, I let him know.

He sent her a letter telling her that I was watching and that she needed to quit going to the drug house; I knew all of this from the faxes I was getting from the prison.

He told her that he was gonna go straight and that they'd move from the area when he got out.

They kept in touch, and he was given an early release from prison.

I met him in the mall later, after he'd been released.

He walked up to me and shook my hand, thanking me for what I'd done for him.

I don't know what he thought I'd done to deserve that; I had been the one that had identified him and ultimately enabled him to be imprisoned—but like I said, we clicked.

TWENTY-SEVEN
RON RON HUBBARD

RIGGINS TOOK ME UNDER HIS wing and tried to explain the streets to me from his point of view.

One day, he told me about a guy he respected tremendously, Ron *(Ron Ron)* Hubbard.

He described Ron as another drug dealer in the area who was an L.A. gang member. He said that Ron claimed Palm and Oak Crips, and that he had quite a reputation on the street as a drug dealer and a fighter.

He told me about an incident between Ron and a local dealer named Perry Willer, which occurred at the American Legion.

Perry had been talking all kinds of shit on the street about Ron, saying that he was a "punk" and a "bitch" and that he *(Perry)* was gonna take over his drug trade.

Ron had gotten word of this and confronted Perry in the American Legion, choosing the bar for a reason; he wanted to make sure that no one doubted who he was and what he was capable of.

He confronted Perry and beat him up badly, making sure everyone in "his world" saw it. *(He didn't want anyone thinking he was a bitch.)*

After beating his ass down, Ron made Perry apologize to him and call him "Sir" in front of everyone at the bar.

Having made his point, he then walked away.

Riggins told me about this and laughed about Perry and how Ron had called him out on his shit talking.

He admired Ron for his toughness, and he said that when he wasn't beating your ass, Ron was really cool.

I started to look into "Ron Ron" and found that he lived on the west side with his father, who was a heroin addict.

"Ron Ron" watched out for him and tried to keep him clean.

His father rented the house from a local church, and I started to keep an eye out and waited for a call or an incident to occur there so I could have a reason to get in and talk to Ron.

Several months went by, then one night I heard a call dispatched to patrol to report that a man had called the police to claim that he'd been beaten up.

The address was Ron Ron's, so I took the call, jumped in, and headed down to the house.

I cancelled the back that was sent so that I wouldn't have anyone screwing up this rare opportunity.

I met with the victim, who identified himself as Andrew McElroy.

He claimed that he'd been beaten up by Ron, then thrown out of the house.

He said that he'd lived in the house with Ron and his heroin addict father for several months and that Ron had kicked him out for disrespecting his father.

Andrew said that he knew his rights and that he was a victim of domestic violence; he'd been a co-habitant with Ron and had been physically beaten up by him, so he wanted Ron arrested for the DV assault.

I did see that Andrew had a minor cut on his lip, and it appeared that he might have been hit in the mouth.

So, I checked with Ron and heard his version of the story.

It was my first meeting with Ron, and I was sizing him up to see if he measured up to what Riggins had told me.

Ron was very straightforward about the incident, saying that he'd kicked Andrew out for calling his father an addict and for not paying rent.

He said that he asked him to leave several times, but that had Andrew refused; so, Ron said he picked him up and forced him out of the house.

He said that Andrew tried to hit him, and he blocked the punch and "popped him once in the mouth to get his attention"—and that was the end of the fight.

After that, Andrew ran off and started to cry.

Ron called him a "whining bitch," and I had to admit that he was a whining bitch; he was literally crying as well—and he was really getting on my nerves.

I talked to Ron a little longer and noticed that he had tattoos on the backs of his arms; there was a "P" and an "O" in dark black ink.

I asked him what the tattoos were, and he said that he was a Palm and Oak Crip from Los Angeles.

I suspected that he'd been telling me the truth from the beginning, and now he was admitting his gang membership freely.

I was starting to like this guy!

Honesty and an "I don't give a damn attitude" always made it easy for me like people.

I decided to check on Andrew and see if he had warrants.

After I found out that he did have one, I arrested him for it.

I added what he'd told me about the assault into the report but didn't arrest Ron for it.

I told Ron that I'd heard about the incident at the Legion Club and was well aware that if he wanted to beat Andrew's ass, he could have.

I also told him that I agreed that Andrew was a whining bitch and that I wasn't gonna arrest him *(Ron)* for the assault.

Ron was alarmed that I knew about the assault at the club and asked me what I'd heard.

I told him that I knew someone who had witnessed it, but I didn't tell him who had told me about it.

He asked that I come back after booking Andrew into jail and talk to him some more, and I did just that.

When I returned, we talked 'til morning *(several hours)*.

He freely admitted that he dealt drugs and that his father was a heroin addict.

He also told me that he and a few other gang members from California had been in the area dealing drugs for some time.

I told him that I was mainly interested in gangs and had no interest in his drug trade.

He told me all about "Doobie," "T bone," "Lollipop," and a guy named "Boo Rock," saying that they were all "businessmen"—meaning drug dealers.

He said that his real name was Ronald McElroy and that he'd used the name Ron Hubbard because it was easy to remember; the real Ron Hubbard was famous, and that would confuse the cops if they ever heard anyone talking about him.

It was a really interesting night; he was quite upfront about his business and what he did.

He said that it was getting tougher and tougher in the street for the black dealers to make money dealing drugs; the reason being, the Hispanics had moved in and taken over, which made it harder for the blacks to maintain dominance in the drug trade.

He specifically named 18th Street and EME *(The Mexican Mafia)* as being present in the city.

He said that he had drug charges pending and that he knew he was headed to prison and would probably never see his father again.

He said that he wanted me to know that the 18th Street gang was taking over the streets and that they'd been running restaurants and small stores.

He also knew that they had large sums of money buried in the yards of houses that they owned.

He went on and on about them, how they worked the drug trade and laundered money, bringing drugs into the country when they bought supplies for their stores and restaurants from Mexico.

He was amazingly open and upfront about his gang membership and drug dealing; he wasn't ashamed at all of what he did.

He said that he was "a gang banger and a thug and that dealing was only about money."

It was a business to him.

He had the old school value system of gangs and street behavior; they had a code that they lived by, a distinct value system.

This is now gone from the street, and the only value system is centered on the value of money and surviving the moment.

When I left that morning after talking to him for several hours in the front yard of his house, I was in a daze; it was always a trip to talk to someone that you should hate and really despise—but instead find yourself identifying with them and liking them more than your fellow cops.

I had more in common with Ron than I had with 95% of the cops I worked with.

The next time I saw Ron Ron, he was in court; he was there to get sentenced and saw me in the courthouse on another case.

He came over to me and shook my hand, then told me to take care. He said that the next time he'd be free, we'd both be old men and that we'd go get a beer and talk about the streets when we were younger.

The reaction this caused in the people in the courtroom was comical because he did it right in front of a bunch of cops.

They all looked at me with their eyes wide open and jaws dropped.

"Ron Ron" didn't talk to anyone—much less a cop in uniform; however, he'd shaken my hand and openly talked with me as a friend.

This was another one of those priceless moments where it was painfully obvious that I didn't fit in on either side of the alleged thin blue line.

TWENTY-EIGHT
DOOBIE

DOOBIE WAS AN L.A. GANG member who came into the city in the early nineties.

He'd been dealing cocaine and eventually was caught and sent to federal prison.

He had quite a reputation on the street as a scrapper, and he came back to St. Pauls after serving his time and made a real attempt to stay straight.

I got a call to his house one night.

He'd been working a job as a semi-skilled laborer for a company in the industrial area in Widefield, and his boss had been really impressed with his work ethic.

Doobie showed up for work one night, and the boss told him to go home, saying that since they were way ahead of their projected output, he was giving him the night off.

He also said that Doobie had been the biggest reason for that output and that he'd be providing Doobie's parole officer with this feedback.

He was really impressed with the job that Doobie was doing, and he was one of the best—if not *the* best—workers that he had.

Doobie was really happy; finally, his life had started to turn around.

He'd bought in to the whole "work hard to get ahead, stay clean" philosophy, and it was working for him.

Maybe he could make this new life work for him (*his words*). He came home happy, "sincerely happy," for maybe the first time in his life.

He was living with and/or married to his girl, who had stayed with him through prison.

She had his children, a boy and a girl. They'd gotten back together when he got out of prison, and he was trying to be a father and a husband.

This was new territory for him, and for the first time in a long time, he liked how he felt.

He was excited to tell his girl about his latest success and spend an extra night with the kids; however, when he pulled up to his house and walked to the front door, he said he looked through the glass in the door and thought that he'd mistakenly gone to the wrong apartment.

Why? Because he saw his kids watching TV on the living room floor—and his wife in the same room with his two best friends.

She was giving one a blowjob while the other was fucking her from behind.

He said that he was stunned; he couldn't believe what he was seeing.

All this was happening in the same room as his children watching TV. They were on the floor in front of it while their mom was being tag teamed by his two best friends.

He walked through the door and beat serious ass.

He beat the shit out of his two "friends"—I mean *really* beat them up bad—then he went to work on the wife, beating the hell out of her.

He was in a rage; he'd been in prison and had been a real gangbanger from L.A.—and he knew how to fight.

I got the call from a neighbor who heard the fighting.

When I arrived and tried to ask the wife what had happened, she wouldn't tell me anything.

Doobie just sat on the front porch and said nothing.

The wife had been beaten up, and finally he said to me, "I beat her ass."

I asked what had happened, and he wouldn't say.

I then arrested him, and he went with me quietly.

On the way to the station, he was in shock and really acting weird, so I pulled over in the vacant parking lot of a place that had recently gone out of business.

I started to talk to him, and he started to cry; at first it was just a little bit, then he sobbed and really broke down.

He told me what had happened, how he'd bought into the whole "work and live right and your life will turn around" …he was totally devastated, an emotional wreck.

I let him sit in my car and cry for several hours.

He told me all about his life, selling drugs and prison life, and how he'd tried to turn it around, "do the right thing," and "come correct."

I listened, and after a while I knew I wouldn't arrest him; I'd probably get fired, but instead I wrote the assault up as a minor assault so that I could release him on a misdemeanor citation.

In my report, I minimized the beating and didn't fully explain his wife's injuries.

I told him that he was doing the right thing, that he was living the right way—but that he had to realize a few facts.

He had changed, but his wife had *not*.

I'd seen this often while I was in gangs: the guy (*gang member*) would change and expect that the wife or girlfriend would be OK with it—but they weren't.

The women who are attracted to gang members have a whole different set of issues of their own.

Most liked the element of danger when it comes to being around a gang member; the constant chaos and danger were addicting.

When that thrill was gone, they turned to sex, drugs, and betrayal of the gangster.

If Doobie wanted to go back, they had a lot of shit to work out.

I asked him if he wanted to go back, and he said that he did.

So, when he was ready, I took him back to the house, met with both of them, and told them what I was gonna do.

The wife then went to a friend's house, and Doobie stayed in the apartment.

I told him that I didn't know what his P.O. would do, but I wouldn't put him in jail because that would violate him for sure and he'd go back to prison.

I don't know what happened to him; I never saw him again.

I never regretted the decision I made not to arrest him, though, and I never went to court on the ticket, nor did I ever get a call from his P.O.

TWENTY-NINE
BOO ROCK

ANOTHER NIGHT AT THE LEGION, and another fight had broken out.

This time, I arrived at the Legion and found that there were several people still there, milling around.

Two guys had been seriously injured and were about to be transported from the scene to the hospital; one of them had received a severe stab wound on the side of his head and was bleeding profusely.

I spoke to the girl who was helping him and asked her what had happened.

She refused to talk to me, but she did follow him to the hospital.

I knew that her name was Sandy Stafford and that it was well known in the black community that she dated only black men and was one of the few whites trusted and allowed in the American Legion club.

I followed the ambulance as well and hung around the Emergency Room in plain clothes, minus my gun and badge, to see what I could learn.

Sitting in a chair and reading a magazine, I listened to what was going on.

I soon overheard three people talking to Sandy in the hallway.

She told them that "Bobby," "Ebony," "Bay," and Gary Wright had arrived at the club with several of their friends; they'd come to fight with several of the California Gang bangers who had recently moved into the area and were trying to expand on their drug trade.

She said that they'd told "Boo" that he wasn't in California any longer and that he needed to show respect to the "brothers" who were here.

She said that Boo had gotten into an argument with Bobby and that Bobby broke a bottle and stabbed him in the head.

I had all I needed to go talk to "Boo."

I took the back way through the Emergency Room and went into his room, where I introduced myself and told him that I was there to check the facts of what happened.

I asked him if he was OK.

He replied, "Yes, sir, I am."

California gang bangers are almost always incredibly polite.

This was my second clue that he was, in fact, from California.

I recounted what I'd heard in the hallway and used the name "Boo" when I referred to him.

He acknowledged that he'd been in a fight with Bobby Snyder.

He didn't react to me using his street name, "Boo"; this was so much a part of his identity that it was second nature, and he hadn't realized what had just happened.

He said that Snyder had jumped him at the Legion, and I asked if it was about "business and respect."

He said it was.

He said, "Damn, man, how do you know all this?"

I played like I'd been watching him for weeks and knew all about him.

I told him that I had informants in the Black community and knew that he went by the name "Boo rock."

I also told him that I was aware that he was a "businessman" and that this fight was about business.

He nodded his head in agreement to both facts; he didn't deny he was "Boo rock," and I continued to refer to him as "Boo" as he gave me the complete story of what had happened.

I asked him if he wanted to press charges, and he rolled his eyes at me and replied, "niggah please."

I said, "Hey, I have to ask."

He said, "Hell no, I will *not* press charges. I ain't no bitch. I'll deal with this in my own way."

I said, "OK. Anything else you wanna tell me?"

He said, "No."

I said, "If I need to get a hold of you, will you be staying at Sandy's place?"

He just stared at me and said, "Damn, man—you *have* been watchin' me! Ya, that's where I stay."

I knew that "Ebony" was the street name for Doug Croates and that he was a known associate of Bobby Snyder. "Bay" Stewart was Will Stuart, and Gary Wright was an 18-year-old kid who had been hanging around them lately.

I was able to get a copy of the name that Boo rock had given the Emergency Room and ran him for NCIC warrants.

He had a hit out in California; he was wanted for an Aggravated Robbery. I used that to gain Sandy's trust later when I went to her house.

I tried to follow up on the case but couldn't get anyone to cooperate.

I went to Sandy's house a few days later and talked to her and "Boo rock."

I told them that the case was dead but that I'd done some checking and that he was wanted in California on an Aggravated Robbery charge.

They tensed up, and I told them that I'd keep that on the down low for now; I was mainly interested in gang information and wanted to know what they could tell me.

They didn't tell me anything, claiming that they didn't know anything about the local gangs; that was a mistake. I'd been straight with him and had given them both breaks—but I would *not* be played like a punk. Work with me, and I could be a friend; cross me, and you're in deep shit.

I left, then called the Narcotics Strike Force and told them about "Boo Rock," telling them that I had an informant that gave me his real name.

I also said that I'd checked and that he had a warrant as well. I told them that I'd heard that he was a major dealer and lived with Sandy Stafford.

They'd been working him but didn't know his name, so with the information I gave them *(his name and the place he was staying)* they arrested him a few days later on a search and arrest warrant.

When I went to see Sandy a few days later, she was crying; Boo had been arrested, and she was alone again. She talked to me for quite a while, telling me her life story.

From that point on, she waved when I drove past, and if she was at a scene involving the Black community and I saw her, I'd later go to her house and she'd give me information on what had happened. She never knew that I was the one who gave up Boo Rock and that I got almost all my information on him from her.

THIRTY
BANK ROBBERIES

ONE NIGHT, RIGGINS GOT A hold of me and wanted to meet somewhere away from the mall.

I was immediately on guard and started thinking that I needed to cover my ass; was he gonna try to get stupid with me?

I didn't know what he had planned, but I went prepared to kill him if necessary; I was sure he was setting me up.

That's the nature of a cop's relationship with informants; it's based on a twisted kind of trust that can dissolve in a heartbeat.

I arrived at a car wash in a nearby city where he wanted to meet.

He was alone and really agitated, and he said that he'd heard some shit that he wanted to get off his chest.

He told me that he'd been at a party at Snyder's house the previous week and had overheard some kid talking about doing bank robberies.

He'd thought the kid was full of shit and blew him off until he saw on the news that a bank robbery had, in fact, happened.

He didn't know the guy's name and didn't feel like he could ask around since he was "an out of town niggah" *(meaning, since he was a gangbanger from California, he had only limited trust in the local community)*. He felt sure that the kid had done the bank robbery, saying that he was "fucking crazy" and was "waving a gun around at the party," calling himself "Superman" and saying that he was "bulletproof."

The kid had really gotten him upset.

I listened to him, but I was suspicious.

I'd arrived there at the car wash expecting to get into a gunfight with him and whoever he was with; instead, I found him alone and wanting to talk about a bank robbery.

I asked him why the secrecy and he said that the kid had really shaken him up.

He said he was really worried that the kid was gonna kill someone and that he truly believed the kid thought he was invincible.

I asked another informant about the kid, whose street name was "Dazzle."

He said that he'd been at the party as well and was surprised that I'd heard about it.

He admitted that there was a kid there who was bragging about doing a series of bank robberies that had occurred in the past few weeks.

He said that the kid hung out with Bobby Snyder and had recently bought one of the new Toyota Land Cruisers, claiming that he paid cash for it.

He said for me to keep my eye out at the Center City 7-11, and I'd see him there; he liked to go in there and show off the car.

I asked if "Dazzle" had seen the Land Cruiser.

He said that he had and that it was nice.

I asked him if he knew what the kid's name was, and he said he only knew that he went by "Gary."

I started to hang out at the 7-11, waiting for Gary to show up.

A few days later, he did—and he did have a really nice Land Cruiser. I complimented him on the car and asked him if I could look inside.

He said, "Sure, go ahead. I'm goin' inside the store to get some grub."

It was immaculate, and while I admired it I wrote down the VIN so I could run it to see if it was stolen.

He came back out and told me, "You in the wrong line of work, PoPo."

I said, "No doubt, man, this is nice! How much did you pay for it?"

He said, "Fitty large," meaning 50 thousand.

I asked, "How the hell can you afford this, Gary?"

He didn't bat an eye that I'd called him Gary.

He said, "Gary Wright has his ways, Po Po…he has his ways."

He then smiled and left the parking lot.

I ran the VIN and license plates, making sure they belonged to each other. I then checked the car to see if it was stolen. It wasn't; in fact, it was registered to Gary.

I contacted the detectives in St. Pauls who were working with the FBI on the robberies.

They were working with the SPCAT (*St. Pauls Criminal Apprehension Team*) as well.

SPCAT was a multi-jurisdictional unit that worked with the FBI in tracking down only the most serious criminals.

I advised them of what I'd been told by Dazzle and Riggins—but I didn't disclose who had told me, only that "informants" had put me on to it.

They told me that I was out of my mind if I thought some fucking 18-year-old kid could have done these robberies; they'd been "professionally done" and couldn't have been the work of "some stupid fucking kid."

I wasn't surprised at their arrogance; I was getting used to how incredibly stupid my peers were, and this wasn't gonna be an exception.

I dropped it, and a few days later when I heard Gary was arrested by the FBI for the robberies, I wasn't surprised.

I later talked to Dazzle, and he said that Snyder had given the kid up to the FBI.

He also said that Snyder was "in their pockets" and "had been for some time."

A light went on in my head. Snyder had done an ass load of crimes in the area; he'd been caught in sting after sting, selling stolen property, stolen cars, and drugs—but he never served more than a month or two before he'd be back out of jail.

He never went to prison for anything and now it made sense: Snyder was a snitch who would give up his friends to keep himself out of jail.

This was exactly what his father had done to stay out of jail as well.

Now that I thought about it, it was painfully obvious.

I don't know if it was true or not; I was never able to confirm it.

I was, though, able to confirm that Gary was arrested for the bank robberies.

THIRTY-ONE
THIS DJ AND DIRTY LEFT

ONE NIGHT, I WAS HANGING out at the mall talking with Riggins and Pogars.

When they mentioned going to a party with Snoop Dog's stepbrother, "Dirty Left," I thought they were full of shit—and I told them just that.

They were both really offended and said that they weren't lying.

I said, "OK, you show me a picture of motherfuckin' 'Dirty Left' and you together, and I'll believe you."

Pogars said that he did have pictures of him and "Dirty Left," but even more than that, he'd been invited by "Dirty Left" to go to Snoop Dog's house in about a month and hang out.

I said to them, "OK. You show me pictures of you at Snoop's, and I'll believe it."

Pogars had never talked to me about anything.

I waited for him to leave, then asked Riggins about the claim to know Left.

He said that Pogars was really the one who was friends with "Dirty Left" and that when Pogars had told him that he was hanging with Snoop's brother, he hadn't believed him either.

Pogars introduced Riggins to "Dirty Left" at the Legion one night.

Initially, Riggins didn't believe that this guy was Snoop Dog's brother, but then he started to listen to the guy's story.

According to Dirty Left, he was Snoop Dog's half-brother.

They'd grown up together, and when Snoop became famous he'd asked Dirty Left to move away; the whole East Coast vs. West Coast rap thing was getting really heated in California, and Snoop thought rival gang bangers might try to kill or kidnap Dirty Left to get to him.

So, "Dirty Left" moved to Pine Valley, a city near St. Pauls.

He was arrested for an Aggravated Robbery there and did some time. After he was released, he stayed in the state and occasionally went back to California to visit Snoop.

Riggins said that Dirty Left had shown them pictures of him and Snoop together in Snoop's house, standing on the "Dog Pound" logo in the carpet.

Riggins said that he then believed Dirty Left's claims.

I heard these stories about Dirty Left for a few weeks, then one day Pogars showed me his own pictures.

They included him, Snoop Dog, and another guy in swim suits hanging out at a pool.

He said the third guy was Dirty Left.

He then showed me a picture of all three of them and the "Dog Pound" logo in Snoop's carpeting.

I was amazed; again, I'd found more information linking the gangs in St. Pauls to the gangs in California—and now big names in California—and had no one to tell who would believe me.

As far as casework was concerned, this had no law enforcement value, but it did show a significant connection to major gangs on the West Coast.

A few weeks later, Riggins gave me a calendar.

In it were pictures of two Long Beach gangs.

One was a set that included Dirty Left, Snoop Dog, Nate Dog and Warren G; the other was another gang that they were rivals with.

The two gangs had called a truce, agreeing not to kill each other, and they made a calendar to try to spread the peace of the truce to other gangs in the area.

The different months of the calendar showed pictures of gang members in each set whose lives had been affected by the gang life.

There was only one picture of Snoop and Dirty Left.

They were identified in the picture by gang name—and they were the same two faces I saw in Pogars' pictures of him with Snoop by the pool, as well as in Snoop's house.

I asked Riggins if he could get me "Dirty Left's" real name, and he said that he'd try.

A few weeks later, he came to me and told me "Dirty Left's" real name, and I looked it up and did a "III" check; as a result, I found out that there was an aggravated robbery charge in Pine Valley City assigned to that name.

I then looked up the name "Dirty Left" on the Web and found that there was a song by Warren G that referenced "Dirty Left"; it was called "This DJ."

This was the kind of amazing shit that went on right under the police department's nose, but no one would believe it or have any idea of what it meant for the gang culture in the city.

By way of Pogars and Riggins, legit hardcore California gang members were hooked up to our databases and knew the way we operated.

THIRTY-TWO
DOGGDEN VS. SOUTH SIDE 18TH STREET

I HAD VERY LITTLE CONTACT with Doggden.

I theorized that they were a collection of local Black criminals who dealt drugs, sold stolen property, partied at the American Legion, and hung out at Bobby Snyder's house—but I was never able to prove that; I just didn't have the time to devote to gathering that kind of intelligence on them.

The only significant activity I had with them involved South Side 18th Street and the Fred Marshal Center.

The Fred Marshal Center was a youth center named after a cop who had been killed during a hostage situation.

Having grown up in the city, he was a "home grown cop" and was thought of very highly in the community.

To the best of my knowledge, the center was never clearly claimed by any gang.

It had very strong ties to the Black community, and the police department felt like they were welcome there as well; reality was, the cops were just tolerated.

The people who ran the center were very leery of them, and after I became more aware of how deeply we'd been infiltrated by criminal elements, as well as how many dirty cops there were, I understood this fear.

We were completely stupid and unaware of what was really going on in the streets.

Some time during the summer of that year, South Side 18th Street made a push to take over the Fred Marshal Center.

They started by showing up in groups and hanging around, which made the people who frequented the center uneasy.

Then 18th Street started being more aggressive, throwing up gang signs and writing South Side 18th Street gang graffiti on the benches and basketball courts outside the building.

Finally, they started to harass women and children in the area.

I was made aware of all this when shootings started to occur.

It turned out that two to three South Side 18th Street gang members had walked up to several Doggden members and told them the center was theirs; the Doggden crew, though, had no intention of letting the 18th Street gang take it over.

18th Street gang members then started doing their usual show of gang signs and shit talking to the "Doggden" members, but the Doggden members weren't impressed or afraid of the 18th Street gang members, instead pulling out guns and starting to shoot.

No one was hit, but the point was made.

A few days later, the 18th Street gang retaliated and shot at several Black guys and their families who were hanging out in the park; again, no one was hit.

The 18th Street gang yelled out their gang's name during the shooting to let the whole area know that they meant to take over the center and that their gang was responsible for the shooting.

Doggden retaliated immediately—and much more dangerously.

They weren't fucking around; they made it really clear that if 18th street wanted a war, it would be an all-out, no holds barred event.

They targeted an apartment complex near the center where several 18th Street gang members lived; instead of targeting the gang members themselves, though, they went after the women and children—including infants.

This was getting out of hand.

Within a day, I received word through an informant that the mother of the Gardenas family wanted to talk to me about the incidents.

So, I went to her home and spoke to her.

I was expecting her to ask me what I planned to do about the shootings and why hadn't I arrested the Doggden gang members; instead, she asked me in a very roundabout way if there was anything I could do about the shootings.

I wasn't on good terms with the Gardenas family.

They were very full of themselves as a group and didn't like me as a detective in the gang unit.

It took some time for her to get to the point that she was trying to make. In a nutshell, she asked that I contact the members of Doggden, preferably their leadership, and negotiate a truce; I couldn't believe what I was hearing. *(This was a true "WTF" moment.)*

I told her that I had no idea who the leaders of the group were.

I then said, "From what I understand, your guys set this bullshit up and tried to take over the Fred Marshal Center. Why the fuck should I help you out now?"

She said that one of the infants that was nearly killed in the previously mentioned attack was a friend's child and that she didn't want any children injured.

She again asked that I talk to the Doggden gang members and call off the fight.

She claimed to be able to guarantee that South Side 18th Street would withdraw from the center and that no more graffiti or shootings would occur from their set.

I told her that if I and my name were gonna be involved, she'd better be able to do what she claimed.

She again said that she could guarantee that the activities would cease.

We looked at each other long and hard.

Neither of us said a word; there was lots of nonverbal communication going on, but nothing being said.

We hadn't had the kind of relationship that would warrant this kind of trust; we didn't like each other at all, and neither of us pretended that we did.

I decided that I had nothing to lose in trying to get the fight over the center stopped.

So, I agreed that I would try—but I offered no guarantees.

I told her that I'd let her know what I found out and that she needed to get the word out beforehand to stop her side from doing anything while I tried to locate the leadership of Doggden, if there was any.

She said that she'd already made the calls and that everything had stopped; this was a surprising admission to me, that she had that kind of control and that the family was indeed in charge of South Side 18th Street.

I spent the next two days talking to anyone that would listen, trying to get the word out that I was looking for someone—anyone really—who had leadership in the Doggden Gang.

Then one day I found a very cryptic message on my voicemail.

I was told to talk to a woman in an apartment in the inner city; the message left on my office phone named an address and an apartment number, and it said to contact her about the shootings at the center.

I went to the apartment, and after verbally dancing around for about a half an hour she finally came to the point.

"I understand you want to talk about the shootings at the center?"

She hadn't admitted anything, but her eye contact and nonverbal communication said a lot.

She was talking about the truce that I'd been asking around about on the street.

I told her that I'd been asked to communicate a request for a truce and that South Side 18th Street would withdraw from the center if the shooting stopped.

I told her that I had a guarantee from their leadership that this would occur; they simply wanted the shooting to end.

She argued that they'd started the fight and that the "muthafuckin hood had responded."

I agreed and told her that they hadn't anticipated the reaction that they'd received.

The center wasn't worth the fight to the 18th Street gang; they wanted a truce.

She said that she couldn't promise anything, but she'd talk to some people and see what she could do; she was a spokesperson, not a leader.

I saw inside the dark apartment that there were several large black males milling around, anxious and listening to the conversation; so, I made it clear that I'd been approached by South Side 18th Street and asked to deliver the message, and that I felt that they were serious.

I told her that I needed an answer that day, but she said that she couldn't give me one.

I pushed the point, saying that I needed an answer from whoever would make that decision that day and that I'd wait 'til I got one.

If the group of men in the house didn't want me to find out who they were, they'd be trapped there—and I was hoping that that alone would be enough to push a decision.

I waited thirty minutes outside the house, nervous as hell that at any moment they'd get tired of this candy ass shit and come out of the house shooting.

Arms crossed and leaning against my car, I tried to look relaxed; however, my hand was on my Glock in my shoulder holster the entire time, unsnapped and ready to go.

Finally, she came out and walked up to me and said, "It's done, motherfucker—but you better be for real, or your ass is in deep shit! One black brother gets a cap in his ass, and we'll come for you first, motherfucker, then we'll go after the Mexicans."

Laughing, I said, "OK, I'll deliver the message." *(Laughing is what I do when I'm starting to get angry.)*

I then gave her my card and said, "If you have any more problems, call me, and I'll take care of it myself."

I left and went directly to the Gardenas' home, telling the mother of the family about the exchange.

I made it clear that if anything happened at the center, I'd hold her personally responsible and target her anyway I could.

I knew that she worked for a local Mexican restaurant and that if the owner found out who she really was, he'd fire her.

I also made it clear that, if she was lying to me, I'd do anything I could to destroy her and her entire family.

She just closed the door.

A week went by, and nothing happened at the center; life returned to normal.

I checked the center frequently, looking for South Side 18th Street graffiti or gang members, but there were none.

The shootings stopped, and both sides kept their word.

I was amazed.

Had I really just negotiated a truce between two street gangs?

No one would believe this shit; I barely did myself.

The street was always very educational...and unpredictable.

THIRTY-THREE
"LEVI" AND EME

I WAS ALWAYS REALLY INTERESTED in taggers and had spent a lot of time collecting pictures of tags done by artists in the city.

One tagger in particular became a frequent contact, and I developed an uneasy relationship with him over a period of several years.

I'd noticed a pattern that most every tagger developed: they liked to tag either near their house, or somewhere they'd see the work that they'd done on a very frequent basis.

Taggers are very proud of their work and see themselves as street artists, and some *are* very talented.

They have a very different motivation than the usual gang member, although they can morph quickly into a gang if they're threatened as a group.

This particular tagger was a scribe, or a writer. He had some artistic ability and did do some murals on buildings and walls, but his passion was tagging his moniker all over the city.

He'd done a couple murals near his house, and I took a wild guess that he was the tagger "Levi" who had written the tags and murals.

I approached him on it, and initially he denied it.

He had quite a reputation with the cops and didn't trust any of us *(not that I could blame him)*, so it took several months to gain his limited trust.

I kept at it, though, and eventually one day I was driving past and he came out of his house and waved me down.

He started off with small talk, then he got to the point.

He said, "Hypothetically speaking, if I was 'Levi', what would you wanna talk about?"

I told him that I was interested in tags and the process that went into making a mural, as well as why the tagger chose the moniker; honestly, the whole subculture was an interest to me.

There are taggers worldwide, in every culture and nation, and they range in age from little kids to older grownups.

There are also tagger magazines, publications, and websites.

He listened and watched me for several minutes, then said, "I may be able to help you learn a thing or two, but I'm not this 'Levi' person—what did you call him, a tagger?"

A big smile grew across his face, then he said, "Come back in a couple days, and maybe we'll talk."

Another example of how listening to what *isn't* being said is more important than what *is* being said.

I returned a few days later, and we did talk.

I got to know him and his family really well.

He dated the daughter of one of the SPPD records clerks, and they had a baby together; the clerk hated him with a passion, though, and I had to agree never to talk to her about him or share anything I learned about him with her.

He said that he just wanted to get along with her as well as he possibly could and didn't want to cause problems.

I'd talked to the clerk on several occasions, and she admitted to being a female gang member in California and always carried a knife.

She bragged about stabbing two Black guys who had tried to rape her when she lived in California and claimed that she was a member of Sur 13.

She'd earned the nickname "Mad Dog" in the police department because she was one crazy bitch.

She was one of the brass's favorites and had a lot of pull with the senior members of the administration through three Police Chiefs' administrations.

As time went on, the tagger admitted that he was, in fact, "Levi," and he began to trust me on a limited basis.

He was frequently arrested for various minor things, and each time he was locked up, I had to start over rebuilding his trust.

One night I stopped by his house, and he was installing hydraulics in a car.

He had a reputation on the street for being able to install the hydraulics exceptionally well, and gang members from several different sets would pay him to do work on their cars.

He sat down and explained the install process to me one night, going into great detail about what was required to make the cars do what he wanted them to do. It was really an education; he was quite skilled.

He told me about several cars he'd done for different guys in the city. I'd seen a few of them, and they were very impressive.

I returned a few days later and found him depressed.

His girl had broken up with him and taken their son, and he was angry.

He asked me if I knew what the EME was.

I replied that I did; they're the Mexican mafia.

He said that he knew of a certain records clerk at a Police Dept. who had been living with a Mexican Mafia member for many years.

He said that the clerk bragged about how she'd manipulated the senior administration of the police department for years and had them fooled thinking that she could be trusted.

She bragged about how she'd provided her boyfriend with information on drug dealers and arrests that the police had made, who the police informants were, and how they worked cases.

I asked him why he was telling me this now, and he said that a certain records clerk had talked her daughter into leaving him and taking their son—and he was pissed off.

I then told him about all that I'd found out about how the jail, the juvenile correctional system, and the cops had been infiltrated, saying that I really doubted I could do much with this information to help him out; no one ever believed me, even when I showed them proof.

He was drinking beer and stopped talking for a few minutes.

He then looked up at me and said, "Doesn't that bother you that you know all this stuff and no one listens?"

I said it did but that I'd found out that most cops were really stupid about the street and were more concerned with their egos, thinking they knew what was going on instead of really learning the streets.

The brass was also to blame for this stupidity; they "encouraged" (*"demanded" was more like it*) ticket writing to increase the city government's revenues—which damaged our relationships with the people in the street; no one liked the unofficial tax that writing tickets really was.

I left that night and wondered about what he'd told me.

Meanwhile, the clerk he was talking about quit the department less than a week later and left without notice; she just disappeared.

I asked him about it, and he said, "Maybe a certain records clerk found out a certain detective knew her secret?"

I never confirmed what he told me—but I did believe it. We had huge leaks of information within the department.

Narcotics would get ready to do a bust, and twenty minutes before they'd hit a house the occupants would vacate the building, running to cars and leaving the area.

Informants would be found out, and entire blocks of information on certain people would disappear from the computer databases... *someone* was doing that stuff.

I had informants telling me that someone in the Narcotics Strike Force was trading information for money and drugs.

Girls who worked the streets constantly told me stories of cops who had traded them being arrested for sexual favors, and in some cases cocaine for painkillers.

I was getting really jaded.

I didn't trust anyone that I worked with, and no one in the system seemed legit.

I trusted my own informants more than any cop I worked with; at the very least, I knew that I could prove they were honest, and I felt I knew what their agenda was about.

THIRTY-FOUR
CRAZED NEGOTIATOR

AFTER THE DRIVE-BY AT OSO'S house, the armed confrontation at Speedy's house, and the truce negotiated at the Fred Marshall Center between Doggden and South Side 18th Street, the Matriarch that led South Side 18th Street called me again and left a message on my cell phone.

She asked that I meet her at their new place.

It was on a short, out of the way street that had been having frequent drive-by shootings the past few weeks.

There would be reports of shots fired and people screaming, but when we showed up there would be nothing but silence...dead silence.

She asked that I come to the house after work.

She still worked at a local popular Mexican restaurant and would be home about 12:30 or 1 a.m.

I arrived early and watched the house.

The conversation I had with the West Side 18th Street set was still fresh in my mind, and although they'd been nowhere near me, I didn't believe for one second that the hit was called off; I thought they'd just wait 'til I relaxed, then try something.

So I watched and waited, but I saw nothing to make me more paranoid than I already was.

I idled in, lights out on my unmarked car, slowly rolling down the street, windows down, listening.

When I arrived at the address, I quietly got out of the car, gently pressed the door closed, then started to walk towards the house.

The mother of the family came out of the front door with her oldest daughter.

They began to talk to me, making small talk and asking about the rumors they'd heard about the West Side 18th Street meeting and my talk with them.

I ignored their questions, but they persisted.

The mother made a comment that she'd heard that I'd lost my fucking mind and had gone totally crazy.

She was looking at me, trying to size up my reaction.

She said word was out on the street that I'd gone crazy and was totally fucking loco.

The entire time, she was watching me, looking for a reaction; she just kept repeating the same thing over and over again in different ways, watching me for a reaction.

I said, "So why did you want me here? No way in hell you're concerned for my fuckin' welfare. So what the fuck do you want?"

She eventually cut to the chase and asked if I'd heard about all the shootings on their street the past few weeks.

I said that I had.

She said that there had been problems with the Nortaneos family that lived on the opposite end of the street; they didn't want a South Side 18th Street family on their street.

She said that when she moved into the house she didn't know that Nortaneos gang members lived on the street, and now she couldn't afford to move.

She then asked if I could talk to the family down the street for her.

This was getting really weird.

I didn't expect more negotiations.

I was worried about being set up, watching my back constantly with the bangers on the streets and the cops I worked with.

Detectives are intensely competitive, and I'd made even more enemies with my success on the recent cases, in spite of the interference by my fellow gang detectives.

I explained to the woman that my only contact with the Nortaneos hadn't been positive.

I had no rapport with them as a group. They weren't like the rest of the gangs in St. Pauls; being outnumbered, they were very suspicious and just wanted to be left alone.

I explained that after I'd showed up at the wedding, looking for Pedro Lechuga about a year and a half earlier, on the Snoopy shooting, they hadn't warmed up to me at all.

While I was explaining this to her, a car came around the corner at the opposite end of the street.

We were standing by my unmarked car in the street, away from a nearby streetlight; basically, all three of us were talking in the dark when the car came around the corner and turned its lights out.

The car quietly rolled to a stop, and I could hear it idling; it was late and dark, and the sound of the engine carried to where we were.

The woman I'd been talking to asked her daughter, "Who is that? Do you recognize the car?"

The daughter was also as deep in the gang culture as you could possibly be. *(Gangbangers pay serious attention to the cars and people around them; their situational awareness is much higher than the average person.)*

She was pregnant with the child of a subordinate Lt. in the gang and knew as much as any member did, possibly more.

They watched for a minute, and when the windows rolled down on our side of the street they cried out in a panic and ran towards their house, screaming, "Get the fuck down! They're gonna do a drive-by on us!"

I didn't move.

The woman ran behind the house, and the daughter ran inside.

They were both large women who slowly ambled when they walked. It wasn't easy to move all that body weight; their usual gait reminded me of elephants at the zoo, rockin' back and forth and taking a step every now and then as they breathed loudly—and talked even louder—their huge breasts resting on huge folds of fat, which rested on even more folds of fat.

They were very large women; however, when the windows rolled down on the mystery car and they realized that they were about to get shot at—all that sloth began to move with a purpose.

They were amazingly fast, crossing the front yard and flying up the stairs and into the house in a few short seconds.

Left alone in the front yard, I watched the car and realized that they still hadn't seen us, nor had they seen the women's rapid escape.

I could see movement in the car, though, and that arms were coming out of the open windows.

I had another huge adrenaline dump.

As I pulled my gun from the shoulder holster, I heard the mother yelling to me, "Pacman, get the fuck outta the street! You're gonna get killed!"

I still wasn't sure that she hadn't set me up.

I thought I'd watched the house long enough and was processing in my mind if I'd missed anything, anything in the conversation, their behavior—had they set me up?

I didn't know for sure.

Regardless, I was here.

The car was here.

The windows were down—and it was painfully obvious what was about to happen.

I pulled out an extra clip from the shoulder holster and held it so I could do a combat reload when the shooting started.

I then stepped into the streetlights.

I was really calm, but very intensely pissed off as well; this shit was starting to piss me off.

I was *never* gonna run from this shit.

I wasn't gonna go through another high-speed chase or be worried about being ambushed.

Whoever it was, if they wanted a fight—I was gonna make it really easy for them.

I was armed and I was gonna kill as many of them as I could.

As I waited in the street, there was movement inside the car that sat at the opposite end; windows down, an occasional gun coming out of a window, then going back inside the car.

I started to get more pissed off and yelled out, challenging them and holding up my arms in typical gangbanger fashion—gun in the right hand, spare clip in the left—screaming, "Come on, bitches! Let's *do* this!"

We had a standoff there for what seemed like a very long time; it was probably only seconds, but it seemed like forever.

The car finally shifted into reverse and slowly backed up, lights still out, then pulled away.

I waited for them to come back, expecting them to return from another direction at any moment to finish the drive-by; they never came back, though.

Eventually, the women came back from the house.

The mother was laughing and crying at the same time.

The slow ambling gait had returned, and they were still breathing hard from the rapid sprint across the front lawn.

They called me a "fuckin' lunatic" and said that they "had never seen some shit like that."

I was barely listening.

Still in a rage, adrenaline still flowing—and still not convinced that they hadn't set me up—I got in my car and left them standing there.

I don't know what became of them after that…I never saw them again.

THIRTY-FIVE
LAST GASP

MY LAST ATTEMPT TO GET the administration at the department to listen and deal with the gang problem proactively—and not reactively—was over some gang graffiti I found in a city park.

I was driving around, looking for new graffiti, and I got out and checked a restroom at the park.

I found a bunch of gang graffiti there that was for a gang I'd never heard of before; it appeared to be gang graffiti mixed with satanic symbols.

I had no idea who they were and had never heard of them, so I took a few pictures and went back to the office to decipher them.

I found the graffiti to be a Sureneos gang that went by "MS" and "Mara Salvatrucha 13."

I'd never heard of them, so I asked if anyone spoke more fluent Spanish than I did—and everyone referred me to Maria, the Major Crimes Detectives' secretary.

She and I didn't get along, though, and I didn't want to go to her for help of any kind.

So, I looked for a few days for anyone else who might help, but no one had heard of the group on the street, and none of the people I knew who spoke Spanish knew what the words meant.

I'd called a contact that I'd developed in the Los Angeles CRASH unit to ask if he knew about the gang, but I hadn't heard back from him.

Finally, as a last resort, I asked Maria if she knew what the word meant.

She looked at them and said, "Trucha is 'trout' in Spanish."

She looked at it a minute longer, then said, "I think that what you think is gang graffiti is really some trout fisherman!"

She laughed and laughed, making a point of telling everyone that some guy that had been writing about his fishing trip on the bathroom walls had duped me.

Jesus, she was an annoying fucking bitch; I really hated her.

The problem again, though, was that she also had the ears of the brass and went so far as to tell them that I was stupid and paranoid and had been duped by the "trout fisherman."

Finally, my friend in the Los Angeles CRASH unit called me back.

I told him about the MS13 graffiti, and he said that they were one of the most violent gangs in the United States.

They had their roots in the El Salvadorian revolution, and they weren't only Sur 13 gang members—they believed in satanic worship as well. *(That fit the graffiti I found.)*

He recommended that I get a hold of my administration immediately and make them aware that we had this particular gang in the area.

He said that they made 18th Street look like little kids in the park playing baseball by comparison.

I thanked him for his help and hung up.

I then wrote up a memo and sent it up the chain to the brass.

I don't know how far it got, but I got it back a few days later with a yellow sticky note on it that said, "We don't have the time or the resources to investigate trout fishing."

It wasn't signed.

I'd received it through the department interoffice mail, so it had at least gone to the Assistant Chief.

After that, I turned in my resignation from the gang unit, asking for a transfer back to patrol.

The Sergeant called me into his office, asked me to close the door, then proceeded to rake me over the coals.

How dare I desert the unit and him?

He'd counted on me to carry the unit and had structured it around my continued presence.

He said I needed to think about more than myself—what would the rest of the officers in the unit do without my help?

I plainly said that that wasn't my problem.

My two years was up, and I wasn't going out on the department's terms; I'd leave on my own terms.

I'd set a timetable, and I intended to keep it.

I'd learned why it was so hard to be successful in the unit: it was structured to fail.

Just like in my childhood, though, I succeeded in spite of my surroundings.

The feeling was all too familiar; it was time to read the writing on the wall: time to go.

I left gangs a short time later.

I was fried, burned out, and paranoid, and I didn't trust anyone I worked with anymore.

I continued to be called upon to help out with cases that involved gang members, but only as a last resort.

I was seen as an outsider; when the detectives had no other option, they'd ask for help.

THIRTY-SIX
JOKER GETS LOST, THEN FOUND

I WORKED SECURITY PART-TIME AT a department store for six years.

I got to know a lot of people there, one of whom was Dan Sears.

He worked in the men's clothing area, and when it was slow he'd ask me questions about what it was like to be a cop.

He'd always end the conversation with the comment that he was glad he wasn't a cop because he didn't think he'd want to be exposed to that life.

I told him that it was my opinion that you couldn't hide from "that life"; I thought it was better to be aware of it than ignorant of it.

He disagreed.

He was very religious and felt that as long as he lived by the teachings of his church, he'd be protected; he had no need to learn of any other life.

One day I went to work, and he wasn't there, so I asked around about him; I thought that he'd probably quit because the store had an extremely high turnover rate.

The girls that I asked, though, said that he hadn't quit.

They then looked at each other quietly—their eye contact speaking volumes—and one asked me, "Didn't you hear the news?"

I said, "No, what news?"

"He was killed by a group of gang members on the street near his house. They stabbed him in a fight."

I didn't know where he lived, so I looked into it.

Turns out, he lived near my house *(I'd just divorced my second wife and had been forced by finances to move into the city)* and had, in fact, been stabbed by gang members as he sat in his car.

I was working in schools at the time and was glad I wouldn't have to work that case.

A few months went by, and I'd tried to forget about the stabbing.

I had to check in with my boss at the time, and I'd stop by Detectives to see what was new with the few people left that I liked in the department.

On this day in particular, I overheard the Lead Detective assigned to the Sears case asking his Lieutenant if he could ask "someone" for help.

The detective said that he'd talked to everyone he knew and asked everyone he could for help, but he couldn't find this last guy involved in the murder of Sears.

The last guy that he couldn't find had gone deep; he'd been the killer and had to most to lose.

He said, "You know I don't wanna ask him for help, but if we're gonna get this last guy, I have to try."

The Lt. was Leeds, and he and I didn't get along at all.

The Lead Detective was Skidmark, and we didn't get along at all either.

Leeds yelled at Skidmark, "I don't fuckin' like this! You know I don't like him! If you get any information, you keep it quiet. We can solve our cases without his help. This is bullshit! He won't find him anyway—and if he does, you don't tell anyone he helped, you understand me? You tell no one!"

Skidmark said that he did understand, then left Leeds' office.

As he came out, he looked around and saw me, and his shoulders dropped; it was then that I realized they were talking about me.

I smiled, turned around laughing, and left Detectives.

That night, Skidmark called me at home and asked for my help.

He said, "I know you overheard the conversation in Leeds' office, but I need your help. I'm looking for Joker from the SP Treces. Do you know him?"

"Don't insult me," I replied. "Of course, I fuckin' know him. What did he do?"

Skidmark said that he was the killer of Dan Sears, that he stabbed Sears in the chest while Sears sat in his car and asked Joker and his friends not to talk to his girlfriend.

Turns out that Joker and company had talked some trash to Sears' girlfriend.

He'd just left to go to the store or something, and while he was gone they walked by his house and said some sexually explicit remarks to his girl.

When he returned, she told him, and he felt it was his duty to ask them not to talk to his girl that way.

This was the way Sears was: honorable, but naïve.

Anyway, so they stabbed him in his chest in the car.

Skidmark wanted me to help him, and Leeds was pissed that he even had to ask for my help.

Skidmark even had the balls to ask me to give him information on my informants.

I laughed; there was no way that was ever gonna happen.

I had an understanding with them that I *never* disclosed who gave me information—no matter what—and I made it really clear to him that he'd never get that information, ever.

If he wanted my help, I'd ask around, and if I got information on Joker he'd have to guarantee me that no matter what time of the day or night, he'd come.

If he couldn't make that promise, then I wouldn't help him. He agreed and said that he could pay my informant if they produced.

I told him that they all worked for free, but that if he wanted to give me money to pass along, I'd do it after the fact; no one who worked for me worked for money.

Skidmark wasn't comfortable with this, but he agreed.

He wanted control of everything—but that was too fucking bad.

I called my most dependable informant in the gang involved, SP-13, and asked what they knew about Joker, such as where he'd been or if he was still in town.

The informant asked why I wanted to know, and I told them about the stabbing and what had happened—AND that SPPD's finest couldn't find him anywhere and the detectives needed the help of "two fucked up wannabe thugs like us to get this dude."

He laughed, and we exchanged insults about who the wannabe really was.

Finally, he agreed to ask around and see what he could find out. I never had any doubt that he'd ask around; he loved the fact that he could make a difference in the city and outperform "the man" *(cops)* when it came to hunting down bad guys.

I told him to call day or night, which was our standard practice; whenever I asked for a favor, it was always big and always 24/7.

He knew that I'd never give him up.

Two days later at 10:30 pm, I got a call.

My informant said that Joker was in an apartment in Central City.

He'd been there for several weeks without leaving, and he said that he knew for sure that he was there now—but he didn't know for how much longer.

I wrote down the address, then called Skidmark at home.

He was reluctant, complaining that it was late and he was tired.

I said, "Look, motherfucker, you wanted this dude—he's there now. I'm on my way, and this isn't my fuckin' case, so get off your fuckin' ass and get in here—or I'll arrest him myself and let Leeds know you had a shot at him and didn't take it."

He changed his mind quickly and got on his way.

We coordinated deployment prior to arrival: I took the back door, Skidmark took the front.

In typical Skidmark fashion, he tried to bully his way in rather than talk his way in, accompanied by a patrol unit; I was alone in the back, listening and thinking to myself that some people will never learn.

Then the back door opened up—and there was Joker.

He stepped out of the apartment and slowly walked down the stairs.

Hidden in the shadows with my gun pointed at his head, I spoke up and said, "'Sup, Joker?"

He turned to me and said, "'Sup, Pacman?"

"Not a thing," I said. "Just out to get some fresh air."

He says, "Ya, it's nice tonight."

I said "So? What's it gonna be? You tired of running? We gonna fight, or do we do this like men?"

He said, "Ya, I am tired of running."

I asked him to turn around, then I cuffed him.

No fight, and no disrespect; it was over.

I told him that Skidmark was upfront and that he (*Joker*) gave him a run for his money, "but in the end the motherfucker had to come to me to find you, so you keep your head up. You didn't go down like a bitch."

He said, "Alright. Thanks, man."

We walked to the front of the apartment where Skidmark was still trying to bully his way in, and I turned Joker over to him.

He said thanks to me, then immediately started in on the guy about what a piece of shit he was.

I went home and called my informant.

He had a perfect record for finds and information, and I gave them feedback on what happened, every detail and every word.

I also mentioned that they might get some money this time, if he was interested; he was, so I passed the money along.

The next time I saw Lt. Leeds, he wouldn't even look at me; the mutual dislike continued to grow between us.

No one ever knew that I found and arrested Joker—with a lot of help from a really good informant.

THIRTY-SEVEN
THE ALEX MASCARENAS' HOMICIDE

I NEEDED TO BE OFF the streets, so I volunteered to go to schools; I saw that as a way to unwind a little bit and hopefully get out of the street mentality.

I'd been in schools about a year when I got a phone call and was told to go to the Major Crimes unit; they had a case involving a child who had been shot in the park in Central City in the middle of the day.

The shooting appeared to be gang related, but the scene was confusing; they couldn't tell what had happened or why.

The entire case was confusing; there were several things that had gone on simultaneously, and they needed any help that I could provide with the interviews of the kids involved.

I was originally brought in because the victim was in my school.

I didn't know him at all; he was a Special Ed kid, and I'd seen him in the halls but had spent no time with him.

He'd been sitting with his family, watching a baseball game in the park, and had been shot in the head for no apparent reason.

He died in his mother's arms.

The investigation revealed that there had been a fight between St. Pauls 13 and South Side 18th Street at the park about a half an hour earlier.

The fight was over, and patrols had stopped several kids in the area and FI'ed *(field interviewed)* them.

The kids had then gone on their way when the cops were done.

Then another fight had broken out about two blocks south of the park; this fight involved adults and a car.

The occupants had fled the area, though, so even though the neighbors had called the fight in, by the time cops arrived the fight was over and everyone was gone.

Shots had been fired in the fight, and it appeared to detectives that one of the shots had missed its target and traveled two blocks up the street and hit the victim, Alex Mascarenas, in the head—killing him instantly.

I didn't want to be involved in this case in any way, shape, or form; nonetheless, I was brought in as a possible link to the first fight that had occurred.

Some of the kids in my school had been in that fight, so I went to talk to them.

Riqo Luna was one of the kids involved in the fight, as well as the Ortiz brothers, Andrew and Joseph.

I spoke to all of them, and I remember that Luna was really shaken up by the shooting.

He knew who Alex Mascarenas was and had liked him; his death hit Luna hard.

I talked to him for some time but he had nothing to offer me about the shooting.

So, I spent some time trying to help him cope with the bad news rather than gathering anything meaningful to help in the investigation.

I returned to the police station and briefed the lead detective—Skidmark again *(lucky me)*—on what I'd learned, which wasn't much.

The two incidents appeared to be unrelated.

Skidmark told me that he thought the shooting was gang related.

He said that several witnesses saw that there was a car driving around in the area of the 38 and 3900 block of Ellis.

The car had four occupants, and a woman was driving.

There was also a Black dude in the front seat, and they'd been trying to start a beef with South Side 18th Street gang members in the area.

They were there looking for a fight, coming back time and time again and calling out "St. Pauls 13!," trying to get the 18th Street gang members to come out and fight them.

I told them that the only Black gang member in St. Pauls 13 that I knew of that wasn't locked up in prison was Doughboy.

I had a really good rapport with Doughboy and had talked to him many times over the years.

I'd handled the shooting in which he'd been shot in the ass several years earlier.

So, I volunteered to locate Doughboy and interview him.

At the time I volunteered, I really hoped that I would have been refused.

I didn't want any part of this case, or working with anyone in Detectives; I knew how notoriously sloppy they were when it came to protecting informants and keeping their mouths shut about cases.

Unfortunately, I was asked to locate and interview Doughboy, if he would talk to me.

So, I picked up Doughboy's last known address from the department's database and started there.

After a series of contacts, I eventually ended up at his mother's house in Widefield.

I'd met her several times over the years I'd spent at SPPD, and she invited me in and asked me what had happened this time.

I told her that I didn't know if he was involved or not but that it had to do with the boy that was shot in the park.

She started to cry; the years of his gang life had taken their toll on her.

She'd been contacted numerous times in his short life for fights and stabbings and his being shot, and now she wondered if her son had murdered this young boy.

She was really upset.

She told me that he wasn't home but when he did come home, she'd call me.

I told her to remind him of who I was; he knew me, and we'd been on good terms.

She said that she would and that she remembered me as well, then thanked me for trying to help her son over the years.

She did say, however, that she felt he was beyond help.

I left the house, and a few hours later I got a call from Doughboy's mom, telling me that he was home.

I went and picked him up and asked him what had happened, and he gave me the basics.

He said that they'd been driving around the area, looking for "sewer rats". *(South Side 18th Street gang members.)*

He was the passenger in the front of the car, they'd been drinking, and they'd decided to go pick a fight with any random 18th Street gang member they could find.

They ended up in Central City, yelling out challenges to anyone they thought might be 18th street—and that's when a guy had come out of his house on the west side of the street with a rifle.

Doughboy jumped out of the car and "called the guy's bluff"; he didn't believe that he'd shoot him with a rifle. *(It was amazing to me that Doughboy hadn't learned from the first shooting.)*

The South Side 18th Street guy shot at Doughboy, then at the car as he jumped in and they took off to get away.

Doughboy said that his group hadn't fired a shot.

I tried to get him to give me statement about the incident, and he nearly did and started to write it out.

Then he stopped and said, "No, I can't. I'm going to prison; I know it, and you know it—and I can't go as a snitch."

I had to respect that.

He'd at least given me a start: he'd admitted to being there and had confirmed witness accounts of the fight.

Detective work is a series of steps.

Doughboy had given me much, and at that point a lot of detectives would call their witness names or belittle them; I never did this.

Anything they said was better than nothing, and in my mind even an outright lie at least told me what did *not* happen.

Doughboy had a warrant and was definitely gonna be locked up, but I let it go and just talked to him.

I asked him how he'd been and how his ass had healed from the shooting years earlier.

He laughed about that; we both did.

Then I took him to the jail and booked him.

As we walked in, he passed an inmate being released.

He told the guy to call him and yelled out a local phone number.

I pretended not to pay attention, but I memorized the number and wrote it down when he wasn't looking.

He knew he was gonna be locked up a long time, and he wouldn't get any phone calls—so the number he was giving out was most likely someone who had been in the car, letting them know that he'd been locked up; it was a warning to his gang that we, the police, were onto them.

I left the jail, then got on my cell phone immediately to dispatch and had them look up the address associated with the phone number; it belonged to a woman who lived in West St. Pauls.

I went to the house and found that no one was home.

There was mail in the mailbox near the door, so I pulled it out to see what was there.

There were bills, ads, and a letter from Doughboy to the occupant, a woman *(I thought most likely a girlfriend)*.

The driver of the car involved in the incident had been a woman, and I was hopeful that this was her.

I had dispatch search the address and the girl's name for previous cases, but we had very little on the occupant or the address.

So, I parked a few blocks away for a while and watched the house; nothing happened.

Feeling hungry and needing a break, I went to get something to eat, then returned.

When I did, a woman was in the yard feeding her dogs, pit bull puppies.

I took off my gun and badge, got out of my car, then walked up and approached her.

As I started talking about the dogs, she was noticeably nervous; she talked to me, but she watched me carefully.

I said to her, "I'm not gonna bullshit you; I'm a cop, a detective with the city—but I'm also a friend of Doughboy's. He sent me out here to talk to you."

She asked about him and what had happened to him, and I told her that he was locked up for a warrant and that he'd asked me to come and tell her just that; he'd told me that she meant a lot to him and that he wanted her to know what happened.

I told her that Doughboy had said that he couldn't be a snitch but had asked that I talk to her and that maybe she could help me out. *(This was all a lie.)*

She was quiet for a long time and just petted the dogs.

Finally, she turned to me and asked, "What do you wanna know?"

I asked her what had happened, and she told me the same story that he had—only she included who was in the car, their names, and the fact that they were her cousins.

They were also previously undocumented St. Pauls 13 gang members, and I didn't know them at all.

When I asked about the car and where it was, she said, "In the garage behind you."

I asked her to show me, and she did.

It was the car that they'd used to escape the gunfight.

I asked her to give me a written statement detailing all that had happened, and she agreed to do so.

She did, however, want to take care of her dogs first.

I agreed that it would be no problem and told her that I'd wait for her in my car.

While I waited, I called Skidmark and told him the names that she'd given me.

I also told him where the car they'd driven was located and that she'd agreed to give me a statement.

I said that we'd be on our way to the police station in a few minutes and asked him to wait 'til I had her there at the station before he went to pick up the other two occupants of the car.

I explained *(very slowly, using small words)* that we needed her statement; she controlled the car and had the most control over where they'd been and what they had done.

I did get her statement, and she outlined everything that had happened; she was very cooperative.

When I gave Skidmark the statement—in typical Skidmark (*stupid motherfucker*) fashion, he read it, then started in on her.

He called her a "piece of shit" and told her that she was responsible for the death of Mascarenas; he didn't have the case locked up by any stretch of the imagination, yet he was already alienating his witnesses.

Jesus, this was frustrating.

I wanted no part of this stupid shit.

No way would Skidmark ever close this case with an arrest doing this stupid shit; it was a long time before he'd ever be in court, and the case was a long way from him being able to make an arrest of the suspect.

I left the station, leaving him to his "police work."

Before my help, they didn't have a thing, but I was able to get him all the people in the car identified, the location of the car itself, and statements from the suspects and witnesses—just by talking to people and treating them with respect.

Skidmark couldn't understand that gang cases are a process of gaining trust and that you have to treat your witnesses and suspects with respect or you'll never get a successful prosecution.

The case never made it to the inside of a courtroom; the suspect fled to Mexico, and the witnesses refused to cooperate.

Once again, my assistance was minimized to the brass, so I wrote a very short supplemental report and was done helping with this incredibly fucked up case.

THIRTY-EIGHT
TRANSFORMATION

TO GIVE YOU AN IDEA about how jaded and angry I'd become, here are a couple great examples of how I'd changed.

From the green rookie "Can I help you, poor citizen who has lost your way?" in Chapter 6 of *CurbChek* to this:

After I returned to patrol and had been through the shootings, I was an FTO *(field training officer)*.

I was tasked with teaching new officers how to complete paperwork, write reports that would get convictions, and try to teach them the street.

One day, I was driving around in Central City; actually, I was the passenger, the trainee was driving.

I looked over into the car next to us and saw Adam Medina.

He was an SPVG gang member, and his brother, Johnny Medina, was an SPVG gang member as well; the whole gang lifestyle permeated their family.

Several gang bangers had told me that Adam Medina was looking for me, meaning that he wanted to shoot me and was putting out the word to the rest of the gang members that he was "gonna put a bullet in my ass."

I'd also heard from one of the guys in the gang unit that they'd been told the same thing.

Medina had been talking a lot of shit on the street, saying how he was gonna "bust some caps in my ass."

I didn't know what the reason was that he'd suddenly taken an interest in me; I'd been out of gangs for some time.

Apparently he had though, and there I was looking over at him in the car next to me.

I told the guy I was training, "That's Adam Medina next to us."

I kept watching, and it appeared to me that he'd seen me as well and that he was looking down at something in his hands; it looked like he was manipulating whatever was in his hands while pretending to be unaware of my presence.

I started to get pissed off.

I thought he had a gun that he was preparing to shoot me with, and if the fucker wanted to shoot me—I was *not* gonna be ambushed.

I told the trainee to pull in front of the car and pull it over.

He said, "What"?

I said, "Pull the fuck over *now*, goddamn it! Right fucking *now*!"

He looked at me like I was fucking nuts, but he did what I told him.

I then jumped out of the patrol car, gun out and pointed at the passenger of the car we'd stopped, and yelled at the guy in the car that I thought was Medina, "What now, motherfucker? What you got to say to me now?"

Then I told him to "get the fuck outta the car," pulled open his car door, and pulled him from the car; it was then that I noticed that he had a cell phone in his hand—not a gun.

I slammed him against the side of the car, my left hand on his throat and my right hand holding my Glock to the side of his head.

I said, "What now, bitch? You want me dead? Here the fuck I am! Go ahead, bitch—show me what you got!"

I wanted to kill him right there on the spot.

I didn't want to be ambushed like I'd seen so many gangbangers do, sneak up and shoot an enemy while they aren't looking; I wanted to make damn sure they fucking knew that if they came after me, I'd fight them and kill them—not thinking twice about it; so I was in this guy's face, hating his ass, wanting to kill him.

There I was in Central City in the middle of the day on a Saturday, seriously thinking about blowing his brains out.

Just then, I heard a voice that most definitely was *not* a gang banger's say, "Sir, I'm sorry for anything I've done. I don't know what I did, but I'm sorry."

There was real fear in that voice; no anger, nothing that sounded even remotely streetwise.

Everything slowed way down.

The sound of the street disappeared, and everything became quiet, like the way it sounds in the middle of a forest when the snow is falling: not just quiet, but sounds seemed to disappear.

I looked at who I thought was Adam Medina, and his face morphed in front of me: he was *not* Adam Medina; he looked nothing like Adam.

I had pulled some kid out of his car, gun to his head, and held him by the throat and scared the shit out of him—ready to kill his ass for nothing.

He had a cell phone and was driving next to me; that was all he'd done.

He didn't look or act like Medina in the slightest.

I released him and apologized, telling him that I thought he was someone else and that I was wrong.

I got back in the patrol car and told the trainee to get us the fuck out of there.

I thought about everything long and hard, the way I'd seen what I'd seen, the way the guy's face changed when he spoke from what I thought I saw to what he really looked like.

I was really fucked up; dangerously so.

I didn't know if this was what a flashback was like or if was I just losing my mind—but either way I'd nearly killed a guy for nothing.

I needed to get off the street before I hurt someone.

THIRTY-NINE
PERMANENTLY CHANGED

ANOTHER INCIDENT OUTSIDE OF THE department occurred at home.

I lived in a rural area; I'd moved my kids there to protect them from the shit I'd seen in the street. I didn't want my children to grow up like I had and like I was seeing these kids growing up.

I felt somewhat safe at home; my guard was dropped.

I was walking down the hallway of our house, and my daughter was in the bathroom.

I looked in and watched her for a moment.

At the time, she was the single most amazing thing in my life.

She meant the world to me; now, we can barely speak to each other civilly.

I was watching her through the crack in the door as she pulled her hair up, doing the hairstyle changes that girls do, seeing how different styles look.

Then she put her fingers up to her chest.

She had two fingers on the right hand pointed out and one on the left, elbows out, looking in the mirror.

I was enraged instantly: my baby girl was throwing up gang signs for "2-1," the latest gang in St. Pauls, another transplant gang from California.

In spite of all that I'd done to try to protect my children, my worst fears had come true.

She was hiding that she was in a gang and was practicing throwing up signs in our fucking bathroom mirror.

As ridiculous as this fear sounds, I'd handled cases where girls younger than my daughter had been gang raped by their own choice as an initiation into the gang.

I'd talked with several parents who were lost as to what to do to get their kids out of the gang—and their children were younger than my daughter.

I burst through the door and said, "What the fuck are you doing?!"

She said, "Nothing," then dropped her hands.

I went off, cursing and swearing.

I told her that I wasn't stupid and that I knew what the fuck she was doing.

I was the sworn enemy of *every* gangbanger in St. Pauls and I would *not* have this shit in my house.

I said, "If you think you can bring that shit into our house and get it past me—you are fuckin' wrong. I will be in your *ass*! Don't lie to me! What the fuck were you doing?!"

She started to cry and said, "I was looking at nail polish in the mirror to see how it went with this shirt! I'm sorry!"

I grabbed her hands and looked: each finger had a different color.

I was shaking with rage and fear that my baby girl had become one of them.

I looked in her eyes, and I saw nothing there that was streetwise, hard, or defiant; instead, she was afraid of her father, scared of what I'd become.

I'd never be able to make this right.

I apologized and tried to explain, but I saw fear in her eyes when she looked at me.

I'd never talked to her like this; she was the most precious thing in my world.

I had two boys as well, but they were boys, rough and tumble, growling and wrestling.

She was my first child and more beautiful than anything I'd ever seen, and now I'd shown her a side of her father that she never should have seen—and I couldn't change that.

I hated what I'd needed to become to survive the job I worked.

BOOK THREE
CURBCHEK
RELOAD

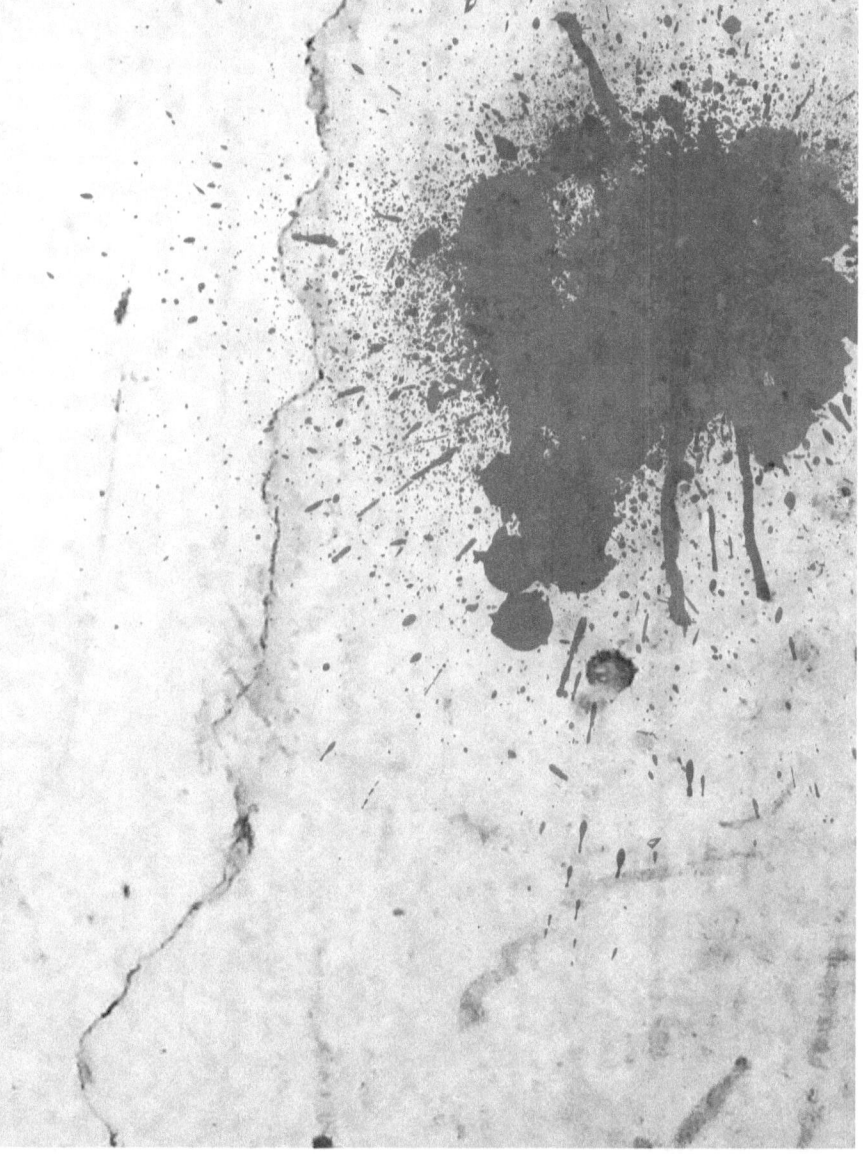

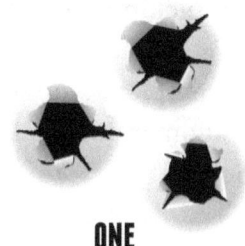

ONE
WE WERE MADE FOR EACH OTHER

PEOPLE TALK A LOT OF trash about cops and all night donut shops and 24-hour convenience stores. I've heard it my whole career: if you want a cop, go to the nearest 7-11 or donut shop, and there they'll be. There's a reason for that; several, actually. Midnight shift is long, and you get tired. The more fatigued you are, the more you crave sweets.

I ate an amazing amount of gum and candy bars. They'd keep me awake and somewhat sharp after the rush of calls had ended at about 4:30 a.m. and we were left with the early risers, Daywalkers beginning to exit their homes and retake the city.

Some cops ate donuts, some candy, some fruit, but we all craved sweets to fight the fatigue. We all had a store that we staked out as ours. Sometimes it was that the coffee was better at that store or the clerk was someone you could talk to that wouldn't ask stupid questions. But we all took a store as ours to protect and watch over.

That, too, was the reality. We were there to keep them safe. Shit could break loose at an all-night store fast. The clerks weren't able to defend themselves against the predators of the night. You never knew what would walk through the door, or when, if you were a clerk at one of the stores.

The clerks often offered free food or coffee if we'd hang out at the store. Sometimes guys abused the offers, and sometimes they didn't.

The clerks were a wealth of information as to what was going on in my area. They could tell you the latest drug trends or who the newest hookers were in the area, and I'd frequently ask them questions, picking their brains about what was going on.

People came into the store all night, talking trash, drunk, high, and completely unaware of the information they spilled in front of the anonymous clerks. I took their input into my area's trends very seriously.

Train the clerk to watch out for who you were looking for—or better yet, find a clerk that was already aware of the street—and you had a relationship that would benefit you both.

I learned a lot from the clerks. One guy explained to me why they were always out of the antifreeze testers. He said that they ordered them in by the hundreds and they'd be sold out in hours. I had no idea they went through so many.

He said that the testers were made of tempered glass, able to withstand heat. Crackheads and tweekers would buy them and empty the glass tubes, modifying them into glass pipes to smoke their drug of choice. (Street people referred to them as the "glass dick" and said that tweekers and crackheads were slaves to the "glass dick," referring to a look of relief and enjoyment that porn stars, crackheads and tweekers all shared during their oral relief).

I was amazed. I knew that they used the glass pipes, but I had no idea where they got them. Any automotive shop or 7-11 carried the testers, and they were always running out of them in my area. The clerks taught me a lot, upping my street IQ. I was always happy to learn from anyone who would teach me.

One night, we came out of briefing and hit the ground running. The calls were stacked up, and none were small or minor. The city was rocking, and we had to step it up to meet the challenge. We couldn't gradually step into the street tonight. It would be a strange night.

Normally, we all met at an all-night convenience store and hung with Sergeant Duke. He was one of the few sergeants we all liked. He was one of us, and not admin. He took a special pride in his squad and made us feel like what we each did mattered.

This was a direct contrast to the Chief, who repeatedly told us we could be replaced by anyone and at anytime. He admitted to us that he was a "bean counter," and it showed in his management philosophy.

We, too, were nothing but beans to be counted, and nothing we did mattered or was special. The man was an idiot.

Anyway, this night we couldn't meet at the store for our regular bullshit session before we hit the streets. It was a case of fate, and I wonder how things would have turned out if it had been slow that night instead of so frantic.

Meanwhile, the clerk wondered where we were. She had the coffee ready, freshly brewed. Minutes ticked past, and still we didn't show. We were so busy, I wouldn't hear about the incident that was about to occur 'til the next day.

Some nights, it seemed to us that the city was infected with an evil disease, like on one of the popular zombie movies.

The city was alive with crimes in progress; shootings and stabbings. You could hear the sirens screaming and the patrol cars' motors gearing up as we bounced from call to call, putting out fires and keeping the dark side of the population in check.

Tom Miller was a frequent client of the store, and we saw him nearly every night we were there. He was on Social Security and lived on a small amount of money in an apartment near the store.

He was one of the night people that Daywalkers are barely aware of. He was mentally disabled, but he appeared to us to be harmless. He'd often stop and talk to us as he stopped in on his nightly quest for a large Mountain Dew and candy. He never said one hostile word to us or to the clerk. We were aware of him, but he wasn't perceived by any of us as a threat.

What we didn't know was he was schizophrenic. As long as he was on his medication, he did really well; but for some reason, the voices got to him one day. They were a little louder.

Maybe he forgot to take his medication, or maybe he needed the dosage to be increased; I don't know.

He started to hear the voices again, and they told him to quit taking his medication. He did quit taking his medication, and the downhill spiral was rapid after that. He became worse and more paranoid. He quit coming to the store at night and stayed in his apartment.

The night we were running throughout the city, trying to keep the chaos from getting out of hand, he was at his worst. The voices had spoken to him for days, telling him to go to the store and kill us all.

He had a shotgun, and he loaded it up and waited for the time we normally showed up at the store. He left his apartment, walking the two or three blocks to the store then walked in, shotgun loaded, finger on the trigger, safety off, ready to go.

We weren't there. The clerk saw him and immediately dialed 911. He walked through the store, looking for us—but saw no one. He went to the clerk, who was on the phone, and started shooting.

He had no intention of robbing her or us. The voices were clear: kill them all! He shot the woman at point blank range, blowing her shoulder and left arm completely off. He reloaded and shot her again, then set the weapon down on the counter and waited for the cops to come.

Who knows what would have happened if we had been there? Maybe he would have killed a couple of us, maybe not. Maybe we would have killed him and the clerk wouldn't have been harmed.

The "what if" shit drove us crazy. We felt responsible for her injuries, feeling guilty for not being there when she needed us. We had a relationship with her as a squad. We took care of each other.

Again, there was a feeling that we'd failed. You couldn't be there every time, every place, everywhere you were needed. No matter how you tried, no matter how much you educated yourself in the ways of the streets, there was always random shit like this that was brutal and life altering.

We tried to go back to the store, but the guilt was too much. Our bullshit sessions were over, and no one said a word, but we all felt like we'd failed her.

The clerk somehow survived, but she'd be forever handicapped by the shooting. We started to meet at other stores and in smaller groups. We couldn't face the feelings of failure that being in that store brought us.

We failed all night long every night to win back the streets. As hard as we tried, we barely kept the shit in check. We had to have someplace to go and feel that we didn't fail, even if it was an illusion.

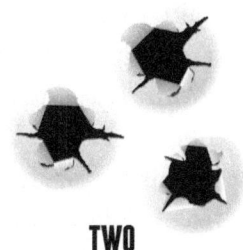

TWO

HERO TO ZERO: A RUDE AWAKENING

ONE SATURDAY, WHILE WAITING IN line to go to lunch behind the list of other officers that had beat me to the punch and got on the lunch list, I was dispatched to an unknown 911 call at a facility that took care of severely handicapped patients.

The caller had whispered to come quick, that he was being beaten by the caregivers, and then he hung up.

Dispatch had called back and reached a caregiver in the home, a male adult. He said that one of the patients had been able to get a hold of the cordless phone and made the call. He said the patient did not want to be there but that he was all right and no police response was needed.

I went anyway. Calls like this never happened; not once had I been to a nursing home or care facility for a 911 call, so I was suspicious. The dispatcher agreed, saying the whispering voice sounded sincerely afraid and could possibly have been crying.

I arrived at the facility and located the caregiver. He was a huge man and I later found out he was a college football player, one of the defensive linemen. He had taken this job because it was easy and fit into his class schedule; he could study at night and get paid for it while he was at work.

The college had arranged for the player to get the job as part of his "agreement" to play for the school.

Anyway, this dude was a mountain, 6'5," well over 300 pounds, and solid. I was talking to him, and he seemed fairly at ease. I asked to look around, and he said, "Sure, go ahead."

Nothing seemed out of the ordinary, so I asked which one of the patients had called. He told me that a middle aged man who was in a wheelchair had called. He called him Mr. Robins. I asked to speak to Mr. Robins alone, and again the Mountain agreed and let me have the room to speak in private.

Mr. Robins was confined to a wheelchair. He had a neurological disorder that had left him crippled and barely able to move the chair. He had these really thick glasses, and his eyes were huge behind them while we talked.

I asked him if he had called, and if so, why? He asked me if the Mountain had left the room, and I said that yes, he had. Mr. Robins started to cry and detailed to me that the Mountain had abused him for months. He said that the Mountain had repeatedly degraded and humiliated him, calling him "cripple" and "vegetable man," and sometimes referring to him as "V-8" for the vegetable drink.

He had tried to ignore the abuse and said that eventually, when he did not react, the Mountain had started to punch him. He said the mountain never punched him when anyone else was in the room.

He was sobbing as he told me this. He said the Mountain would pick him up by the shoulders, completely out of the wheelchair, then shake him and threaten to throw him against the wall.

He was hysterical while telling me his story. I asked him if he had any marks or bruises that he could show me to help support this claim.

He said, "Oh, hell yes!"

Mr. Robins had me unbutton his shirt and pull his arm out of the sleeve. Obvious deep bruises covered his arm and chest; in my mind, there was no doubt that he was being abused.

I told him not to worry, that the abuse would end today; I would make sure of it.

I called for another unit to assist me on the call.

While I waited, Mr. Robins told me that the Mountain was only one of several caregivers that abused him in the facility and that he would have to be removed from the facility to be truly safe.

He said, "I beg you, please don't leave me here; there is no way I will survive the night if you do."

When the other unit arrived, I left Mr. Robins and began to question the Mountain. He readily admitted abusing the wheelchair-bound man, stating that he was a piece of shit and sometimes just needed his ass kicked back into line. After he had been slapped around a bit, he was less mouthy and did what he was told.

The Mountain said that he never really hit the man too hard; just enough to scare him and intimidate him into compliance—that way, he could get back to studying.

The Mountain made a point of telling me that he was protected by the college and that that they would back him up on his statement. He was one of the stars of the football team, and they needed him to win; that was his twisted logic.

This kind of arrogance is not that rare. Everyone believes that they are exempt from the law for one reason or another. Everyone thinks that they are special, that they can speed through school zones, smoke meth, drive drunk, beat their spouse—whatever they wish—and when we show up, they respond just like the Mountain.

When I told him he was under arrest for abusing a disabled person and that there was an enhancement because he was a person of trust, he came unglued. He stated the same old standby you hear over and over again: "Why don't you go out and arrest some real criminals and leave me alone?"

The Mountain went down without a fight. The back up unit took him to jail for me while I worked on finding the manager of the facility.

I couldn't locate anyone, so I left messages and called the state agency that was responsible for licensing the home; I was going to make sure this abuse was stopped today.

I called CSI and had pictures taken of Mr. Robins' injuries, advised the Sergeant of what had happened, then called DFS (Division of Family Services) to get Mr. Robins temporarily placed in another home.

I had a worker on the way to pick him up and was feeling pretty good about the work I had done. The bad guy was locked up, and the helpless victim was free from continued abuse. The bruises were real and serious.

The Sergeant told me I had done a great job and to let him know when it was all cleaned up—then the phone rang; it was the facility's director.

I told the director what had happened, and at first he was in disbelief. I told him that I had personally seen the injuries to Mr. Robins and that the Mountain had admitted to me that he had slapped Mr. Robins around, 'but only when he needed it.'

The director was very upset about this, saying that this was horrible and that he would be right in. I told him that would be fine but that I had called DFS and that Mr. Robins would be removed from the facility that night for his protection.

The director became really quiet and then said, "Officer, you need to listen to me very carefully: do not remove Mr. Robins from that facility under any circumstances."

I told him that I had no choice. Mr. Robins was in danger, and I had to ensure his safety before I left. He said, "Mr. Robins is not what he appears to be; he is a very dangerous man. Do not take him out of that facility."

I turned and looked at the wheelchair-bound man, noticeably relieved that he was safe from further abuse.

I then said, "How in the hell is he dangerous? He is helpless!"

The director told me that Mr. Robins was a violent pedophile that preferred to abuse infants. He had been arrested and convicted for nearly killing two infants that he had raped.

He had played the helpless invalid in his family and had gained the trust of one of the family members. He then took advantage of a moment where he had been left alone in a room with two infants and had brutally raped both of them, causing severe internal damage to the babies.

I looked at the handicapped, meek Mr. Robins and thought no way this could be true.

I told the director I would wait for his arrival and that he needed to be prepared to show me the court documents placing

Mr. Robins in the home. Meanwhile, I called our records division and had them run Mr. Robins.

While they checked him out, I knelt down and quietly asked him about the allegations. He said nothing for several seconds, then responded. It was like a switch had been thrown in his mind: the meek and mild Mr. Robins was gone; suddenly, he was like a rabid dog, spouting, "Fuck you!" and "I was almost out of here, you stupid mother fucker!"

He said, "Why did you have to go and call the director? You stupid fucking cop! I was almost gone! I could have buried my dick in some more sweet, tight ass before they caught up with me if you hadn't called, you fucking idiot!"

I said, "By 'tight ass', you mean little babies. Is that what you mean, Mr. Robins?"

He glared at me and spit out, "Fuck Ya! Best ever! You can tell they want it! You should see their faces when I slide my dick in!"

I stepped back, amazed at the transformation; this was the real Mr. Robins. It was no wonder the Mountain had wanted to beat his ass.

I was shaking with rage and feeling sick.

Robins continued to spew venomous shit in my direction until the director arrived.

He walked in and looked at us, saying, "I see you have met the real Mr. Robins. Do you still need to see the documents?"

I said that I did and that he should show them to me.

He said that Mr. Robins had tried to escape many times and that he was one of their most difficult patients. He was sad about the abuse Mr. Robins had received and would make sure that it did not happen again.

I left the facility with my head spinning. I wrote up this surprising turn in the case and explained to the Sergeant what had happened.

He looked at me in disbelief as well. I cleared the case with dispatch and was told that I could now go eat; it was six hours later.

I had no appetite; I passed and went on to the next call, trying to put some distance between the sick, angry Mr. Robins and me.

THREE
LET ME HELP YOU OUT OF THAT SHIRT

THE POWERS THAT BE HAD made a decision, and I was on day shift; apparently, they needed to break up the "cliques" that had developed in the department. (Meaning the different squads were getting too close, too vocal against the administration's current botched attempts at management.) Sergeant Duke had been on mids (midnights) for years, and he was now on the other one of the two day shifts.

I was sent to straight days with the old timers, good dudes that had survived many administrations and many purges of personnel; solid old timers who had done their time on the street and had finally gravitated to day shift to finish out their tours, waiting for retirement.

They had forgotten more about the street than most of the new guys would ever learn. I was fortunate to have been "banished" to this group.

Like I have said before, the daylight hours are full of "Daywalkers," the people that spend their lives going to work, watching *Dancing With The Stars* at night, and driving minivans full of screaming kids to soccer and dance practice. They are not night people. They actually believe your job as a cop is to answer their questions, make their lives comfortable and safe. They drive me insane.

While I was sitting there one day in my patrol car, a guy rolled up and waved. Smiling—actually smiling—he got out of his car and walked towards me, not realizing, of course, that I was not a day cop.

I had already unholstered my gun, just in case the smile and wave were a ruse.

At night, no one walks up on a cop car—*never*; they know better.

At night, my windows are always down, and I am always listening. If I park, it is in a large parking lot or backed up to a fence in the corner of a vacant lot; no one is going to sneak up on me and put a bullet in my head without me having plenty of warning.

At night, that is the reality. In the daytime, all the lots are full, there is nowhere to park where you're safe, and the Daywalkers are out smiling and waving, unaware of the shit storm that surrounds them, walking up to ask you a question they feel must be asked—and naturally, you're there to provide the answer.

Anyway, Mr. Used Car Salesman approached, and my gun cleared leather. I waited, watching his hands and body language as he approached.

"Hi, officer, I'm wondering if you can answer a question?"

That's usually how it begins: smiling, wanting to shake my hand. He was baffled why I wouldn't return the gesture.

Watching his hands, I saw no calluses; there were manicured nails, gold jewelry proudly displayed, a nice watch, and a masculine gold bracelet worn on his wrist; a walking robbery victim begging to be robbed and beaten, if this were a night shift.

I relaxed a little bit, realizing that he was obviously soft, very soft—the kind of guy that folds up and shuts down if he's present during a robbery of his favorite jewelry store.

Later, though, he'll be in front of a camera, telling the reporters how he wanted to stop it, but couldn't, while the robbers raped the girl behind the counter. Every night cop knows the type.

The question he has to ask? It could be any of the following: "I need a battery for my cell phone—can you tell me where I can get one?"

"Do you know where the closest pay phone is?"

"Can you recommend a good restaurant?"

"Where is the nearest Laundromat?"

"Can you recommend a good mechanic?"

Seriously this is what Daywalkers think you're there for, a walking almanac of information at their disposal.

If he makes the *huge* mistake of telling me that he's the Chief's or Mayor's best friend?

Well, he's about to get directions all over the damn city, finally ending back at the nearest drug house or the worst neighborhood in the city that's nearby.

Never tell a street cop your BF is an administrator in the department, and then ask a question; just a bit of advice, take it or leave it.

Anyway, I was on days, and Mr. Soft Hands had been sent on his way. I was checking an apartment complex parking lot, looking for stolen cars that may have been dumped.

I saw a Chevy Tahoe approaching from the opposite direction, dark windows, two occupants. I could see immediately from the way they were sitting and acting that they are not civilians. Looking closer, I saw the hidden red and blues in the grill; law enforcement of some kind.

I pulled up and rolled down the window, then recognized the occupants: probation and parole officers hunting their lost sheep. We exchanged greetings. I knew the driver, who said to me, "What the hell are you doing off nights? I never thought I'd see you out in the sunlight." I muttered something about it's a long story and to drop it.

I asked them, "What's new? Who are you looking for in the area?" The driver handed me a picture of a 14-year-old girl who has been on the run for some time. They had been trying to find her for months. She was being "taken care of" by her boyfriend/pimp, and they were trying to get her locked up and cleaned up. They had heard from informants that she was staying in the apartment complex, but they didn't know exactly where.

They told me her history: abusive parents, drugs, sexual abuse by her brother and uncles.

They asked me to keep an eye out and if I saw her, tag her big time, then call them anytime and they'd come pick her up. They wanted to get her off the street before she ended up dead.

They also warned me that she's a runner.

I looked at the picture for several minutes, memorizing her face. The driver said I could keep the picture if I needed it. I said thanks, but no.

Once I have the face, it's locked in memory; I won't forget it. A few more looks at the picture, and I handed it back.

I asked them to tell me her name and DOB, this I had to write down. Faces are a lock, but names and dates of birth never; I can barely remember my own.

I got their cell numbers and told them I'd be on the look out. We then parted ways after exchanging a few insults about each other's departments.

Three weeks later, I was trolling the apartment complex. It had become a daily part of my routine. I had found three stolen vehicles in the lot and recovered them.

Day shift is clean up work, and this is the best I can hope for. Today I found no new stolen vehicles, and as I left the complex I saw a soft top jeep approaching.

I checked the driver to see if I knew him, and I didn't. Then I looked at the passenger: the lost and wayward 14-year-old girl was in the passenger seat. We made eye contact; it was definitely her.

I let them pass and enter the complex. I then pulled out of the complex and watched in my mirrors. They were watching me as well, making sure I pulled away.

Once they were no longer able to see me, I made a hard U-turn and accelerated; I was going to catch up to them when their guard was down.

Calling out the plate on the jeep as I turned, I told the dispatcher where I was and that I was out of the vehicle.

They had pulled into a parking place in the complex parking lot, so I pulled up fast and quiet. I blocked the jeep's escape and exited the patrol vehicle, locking the doors.

I then approached the passenger side of the jeep and started talking to the girl, telling the driver to keep his hands on the steering wheel.

He was about twenty-five, and probably a customer of the girl's. I explained to her that I knew who she was and that she was coming with me. She pretended to give up and unbuckled her seat belt.

As I opened the jeep's cloth passenger door, though, she was up and trying to go out the driver's door—over the top of the driver.

I reached in and grabbed her shirt, and it tore right off her; this is not what I had hoped for at all.

She was out of the vehicle and running, and I was thinking *Shit, I hate day shift.*

I started chasing her. I'm an armed officer in full uniform, chasing a shirtless, braless 14-year-old girl through an apartment complex common area.

The girl was wearing really short nylon shorts, pink and white tennis shoes, and her breasts were flopping in the wind.

To make matters worse, she started yelling for help and screaming, "Rape! Help me!"

Can things get any worse? Oh, hell yes they can!

Dudes started piling out of their apartments to see what the hell was going on, and women were yelling at me to leave the poor little girl alone.

Then I heard on the radio that dispatch was sending all available cars to the apartment complex on a report of a rape in progress.

There was a man in a security uniform chasing a naked girl through the complex. She said he'd raped her. That's the dispatch.

Now I was really pissed; no way this kid was getting away.

She ran all through the complex screaming rape, and when I didn't give up, she crossed the road and jumped into the nearby river.

By this time, I had a group of men chasing me as I chased her; guess they're gonna save her from the security guard rapist.

I jumped into the river as well, and I heard the patrol cars coming with sirens screaming and motors wound up. I'll never live this down! The old timers are ruthless in their pranks.

I waded across the river, which stops the crowd that was trying to get to me. The girl was already across the river and up on the bank.

She stopped to catch her breath, turned around, saw me, and started running again.

Fortunately, there was a guy on a mountain bike nearby. He rolled up as I crawled out of the river and said, "Do you want me to chase her down?"

I said, "Yes! Please!"

He asked what she had done, and I told him that she's on the run and being used as a prostitute by her boyfriend to make money and drugs; I was trying to get her out of that mess.

He was off and had her stopped in moments. I ran up and took her into custody.

I took off my uniform shirt and put it on her to cover her up. She turned and spit on me; so much for being a hero today.

I started to walk her back and explain to the responding units on the radio that I was the rapist security guard and that I had her in custody.

I had to walk her back across the river while the other units dispersed the crowd of "do-gooders" that had gathered to kick my rapist ass. (They wouldn't get wet and cross the river, however).

The duty Lieutenant walked up to me, pissed off and spewing venom. He said I had a lot of explaining to do and that I was in deep shit.

That was it! I lost it.

I replied, "Hey, do you know what the fuck you're talking about? Do you know what happened here? No, you don't have a fucking clue. You don't know shit! So why don't you man the fuck up and find out what happened before you decide I was in the wrong. Oh—and by the way, I'm fine, no injuries; thanks for asking." I walked off.

The Lieutenant had no comment—and the old timers?

Like I said, they'd forgotten more than this idiot would ever know. They all started laughing and jumped back into their cars, clearing the call.

I completed the paperwork, retrieved my shirt, and tried to dry off.

The Lieutenant made sure to get a statement from the half naked girl, asking over and over again if I'd tried to touch her in anyway that was sexual. To her credit, she said, "No."

The next day, the old timers bought me lunch, saying I'd earned it for putting the Lieutenant in his place. Day shift really sucked.

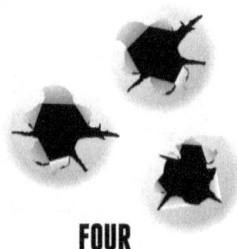

FOUR
COLD HEARTED SNAKE

I WAS WORKING CENTRAL CITY again, day shift, and finally had an in-progress call. It was just a domestic, but still, at least it was in progress.

The caller said that he was walking past a house in central city and could hear a woman and man fighting in the upstairs apartment. He said that he actually saw the man punch the woman in the face while he stood on the sidewalk outside the building. The caller then hung up, not wanting to be involved any further.

I arrived at the house, and all was quiet. My back up was a few minutes out, and I went in. The house was one of the older and larger homes that had been bought by one of the city's many slumlords. It had been renovated and was comprised now of several small apartments being let out at prices that drew the poor, elderly, and underachievers.

I entered the front door and listened. Nothing; not a sound.

Then a door opened upstairs, and an elderly woman looked out at me. She pointed at the apartment across the hall from her, nodded, then closed the door.

I advised my back up that the fight was in the apartment upstairs on the right, then quietly walked up the darkened stairs.

I waited outside the apartment, and I could hear people talking inside; several voices, no anger, just conversation.

I knocked on the door, and a voice said, "Come in." I opened the door and found I was in the living room of the apartment.

There were three couples sitting on the two couches in the living room, three men and three women.

One guy had his arm around a woman who was bleeding heavily from her nose. The blood was really flowing down her face and shirt as she sat there, her head down, and his arm was gently brushing her hair back out of her face.

The tension in the room was thick as I watched the others for their reaction. No one acted like anything was wrong with the situation; they just kept on talking as if this were normal. I asked the woman what had happened, and she didn't reply. I asked the man stroking her hair what had happened, and he said, "She fell down."

I asked her to get up and speak to me in the other room. She did this and told me that he was her husband and that he had regularly beaten her. She was afraid because he had threatened to kill her this afternoon when she told him she was leaving. She said that he told her he would never let her leave. Never.

I asked her if there were any weapons in the house, and she said that there were none but that all the people in the room were his family members, his cousins and their wives. She was afraid of what would happen if I tried to arrest him. I told her to let me worry about that and to stay in the back room while I talked to him.

I went back into the living room, and the guy was gone. The other couples were still there, talking as if nothing had happened.

I heard a noise in the bathroom and forced the door open; the guy was trying to force his fat ass out of a 1x1 window in the bathroom. No way that was gonna happen—he was way too big.

I stopped and watched while he tried and tried. I noticed he had a tattoo on the back of his neck that said "Cold Hearted Snake."

I finally said, "Hey, man, you aren't gonna ever get out that window. Just give up." He stopped and climbed out of the window and stepped out of the bathtub.

Then he tried to push past me; bad idea.

The fight was on right there in the hallway. I had him in a chokehold pretty quick and told him to stop or I'd choke him out.

He stopped fighting but started yelling in Spanish to his cousins to come in and kill me.

Things were getting interesting. He wasn't gonna go without a fight.

One of his cousins appeared in the hallway, and they had a conversation in Spanish. The Cold Hearted Snake was telling his cousin that they could kill me and dump me in the alleyway behind the house. No one would know or tell on them. I was alone, and they could take me out. I clamped down on the chokehold and told him to shut the fuck up.

I spoke directly to the cousin and told him I knew who he was and asked how his uncle Maldo was doing.

I told him that he'd better think it over before he decided to enter into this fight. He disappeared into the living room.

I figured that was a bad thing and that I had only a few seconds to get ready.

I had the Snake almost unconscious by then, and I dropped him to the floor, gagging and coughing. I cuffed him fast, then drew my gun and faced the direction the cousin had left.

He immediately reappeared, this time with a large knife in his hand.

I was calmer by now; this kind of combat was becoming the norm for me.

I talked to the cousin, calling him by his name.

"Remo, you need to think this over, ese. You know me, and you know I know you; no way you walk out of here alive if you take one more fucking step."

As I aimed at his head, he made eye contact with me and paused. He then dropped the knife on the floor and stepped back, hands up.

He said, "We cool?"

I replied, "Ya, we're cool, but this bitch is going to jail for beating his wife. You gotta accept that. You interfere, and I'll fuck you up."

I lowered my gun.

Remo began to talk to his cousin again in Spanish. He told him that he couldn't stop me from arresting him. He said that I knew him by name, and his uncle as well, and that he wasn't going to risk it.

He apologized, saying. "You're family, man, but I can't do this."

I holstered my handgun and picked the "Snake" up from the floor.

I started to walk him out, telling the cousin to get back in the living room. He did what I asked and backed into the room.

I made my way to the doorway of the apartment, watching every move made by the two remaining couples in the living room. They were agitated but not aggressive towards me.

The Snake was starting to get his wind back and started to resist me again.

I opened the door to the apartment, and the Snake yelled out in English that he had a thousand dollars for each of them if they stopped me from arresting him.

Then he said, "Kill this motherfucker now!"

I'd had enough. I looked at the two dudes on the couch, and they had an excited look on their faces; they were actually thinking that they could do this for money. Things were about to get real ugly as they quickly got up. Time to stop being so fucking polite.

I threw The Snake down the stairs, telling him to shut the fuck up. He screamed all the way down, tumbling and rolling head over heels, hands cuffed behind his back as he went down.

I turned and faced the approaching men and pulled my gun. I said, "Who's first? Who wants to die first, motherfuckers?"

They stopped. I was mad now. I said, "Bring it, bitches. A thousand dollars if you can take me. Who's first?"

They backed up. Remo said, "Hey, man. You just misunderstood, Pacman. We got no problem with you. Go ahead, ese, do your thing; arrest the bitch." They both wisely sat back down on the couch.

I heard the radios of my back up outside, then the front door of the house opened up.

The Snake was still lying on the floor at the base of the stairs, moaning. The back up officers drew their weapons, stepped over him, and rushed up the stairs.

The first officer there asked if I was OK. I replied that I was fine and that there was a woman inside who needed medical treatment.

They asked what happened to the guy at the bottom of the stairs. I told them he slipped and I couldn't catch him. I asked them to get statements while I transported the suspect to jail.

I went down the stairs and picked The Snake up from the floor. He was still fighting me, calling me a fucking punk and telling me he'd kill my ass when he got out of jail.

I told him I'd look forward to it as I put him in the car and took him to jail.

He wasn't done fighting, and I had to get help from the correctional officers to get him booked.

A couple days went by, and dispatch got a call from the old lady in the apartment next door to the Snake and his wife. She asked if I was on duty. They said I was, then she said that the Snake was back at the apartment; he was hitting the woman again, and she'd like it if I responded.

I was just around the corner when the call came in, and I asked dispatch to check and see if there was a protective order in effect for the couple. They checked, and there was an order; the Snake was violating it just by being there, and he was hitting her again.

I rolled up as he came running out of the house. He stopped, saw it was me, and took off behind the house.

I was out of the vehicle and chasing him. We jumped three fences and ended up in the alley that he wanted to dump my body in.

He took off down the alley, and as he was about midway to the street, another officer stepped into the alley and started walking up it.

The Snake was caught. He stopped, put his hands up, and said, "I give up! I give up!"

He put his hands on a nearby wall and said, "Just don't beat me up like last time."

The other officer overheard this and said, "What's he mean by that?"

I said that I didn't know; he must have me confused with someone else. I asked him to take Snake to jail while I went back and checked on the woman. He said that he would.

I went back to the apartment and found the woman inside. He had hit her again, and I obtained a statement from her and had CSI take photos of the new injuries.

As I was leaving, the old woman came out of her apartment.

She said, "Excuse me, officer."

I said, "Yes, ma'am?"

She said, "Aren't you the officer that was here last time?"

I said I was. She said, "And did you get him today?"

I said I had and that he was on his way to jail…again.

The old lady smiled and patted me on the arm. She said, "Young man, I like you! You have spunk! We need more police officers like you. Please come back and say hello some time."

I said, "Yes, ma'am."

I was stunned.

You forget working the street day in and day out that mixed in with the nightmare that is the street there are good people living in fear of shit bags like The Cold Hearted Snake.

She smiled at me and repeated, "Spunk!" making a tiny fist with her bony little hand and a little sparkle in her eyes.

I left and booked the Snake into jail. I never saw him again.

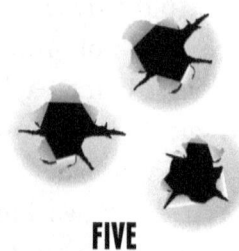

FIVE
CAN I GET YOU A CUP OF COFFEE?

I WAS SITTING IN AN all-night restaurant one evening, eating and writing reports. I usually ate alone unless one of the very few cops I got along with was working, and then we might eat together.

Usually, you need the time alone to process the night, to try to make some sense out of the chaos and stupidity that seemed to be the norm. It almost never happened that you could get through an entire meal without the dispatcher asking you to clear for an in-progress felony or a bad accident; so, moments of peace and quiet are valued.

Still, if dispatch doesn't call you out, there's always at least one guy who sees you in the corner, backed against the wall, watching the door as you eat and write reports—hoping to never be caught unaware should all hell break loose right in front of you.

This guy just knows for sure that you're his newest long lost buddy, and he has a story to tell you or a really important question to ask.

Every cop knows exactly what I mean; the guy waves, smiles, and starts walking over to you, not noticing that your hand has quietly slipped to your gun and unsnapped the holster, clearing leather, just in case the smile is a ruse and this guy thinks he can get his face on CNN by killing you.

Usually, though, it's just a friendly question about some incident that happened or a guy that wants to know how he can get hired at the department; then he moves along.

This night I was writing reports, and I noticed an old guy walk in. I thought he looked familiar, but I couldn't place him.

I categorize people by threat in my memory, and this guy raised no alarms. He just seemed familiar.

Finally, after he saw me and headed over, I recognized him as a co-worker from another department. His name was Jake.

We used to work together before I went to the city and we'd stayed in touch. He had a wicked sense of humor, and we shared many funny stories about calls on the streets.

He sat down, and we started to talk and laugh. It was rare to laugh anymore; we'd both seen a lot and shared the camaraderie that you can only share with someone who has seen the same battles and knows what you feel and think without saying a word.

He kept shaking his head, and I knew that something was on his mind and waited to see what he would eventually spill; I didn't have to wait long.

He started by telling me that he'd been in a lot of trouble lately and thought for sure that he'd lose his job.

I thought this was an exaggeration, but he assured me that it wasn't.

He said that he had really "screwed the pooch" this time, staring off into space, chain smoking and drinking coffee.

I said, "Ya? So what did you do?"

He said, "Well, you knew I was promoted, didn't you?"

I said that I did know that and replied, "Why you ever wanted off the streets, I don't know. Now you're in the Administration and hating life, I bet?"

He replied that yes, he was now in admin as a Lieutenant and that he hated every day of it. He was on his last five years and took the job to increase his retirement income.

He went on and on about how he hated his boss and that he was constantly taking shit from the guy and keeping his mouth shut.

This was hard to imagine because he'd never been one to be silent about anything. I just listened and shook my head, thinking it wasn't worth it to promote in our field.

Then he lowered his voice and said, "Well, I'll tell you what I did—but you have to promise not to tell anyone!"

I said I would.

He paused for a few moments and continued. He said, "You know how I hated the son of a bitch before I was promoted. He was an asshole when you were at the department, and he's only gotten worse." Jake said, "I just had to do something to fight back."

I was quiet, thinking, *Wow, this could really be bad.*

Jake continued, "Well, you know how he used to come in every morning and get that same old coffee cup and get a cup of coffee, then start in on the people around him? Always complaining and talking down to everyone? No matter how bad the night had been, you could always do better in his eyes, and he felt it was his mission in life to point out every officer's mistake?"

I did know. The guy was a real prick, and no one liked him.

Jake said, "So one day after he was really riding me hard and calling me a fucking idiot, I'd had it! I made up my mind I was done taking his shit without doing something back."

Jake had my attention now. I could picture any number of scenarios going down, and he was capable of anything when he was pissed off.

I stopped eating, quit writing reports, and listened…Jake was really agitated. This was going to be good! He said after the incident where the boss really chewed his ass, he came in early the next morning and picked up the Chief's coffee cup.

His beloved coffee cup hadn't been washed in years; he drank out of it every day and just rinsed it out, putting it back by the coffeemaker.

Jake said he took it to the bathroom and cleaned it out really good so that it looked like new.

I was puzzled. *WTF?* I said, "You got back at him by kissing his ass and cleaning his coffee cup? You really have gone to the dark side and joined Admin!"

He laughed and said, "Noooo, I cleaned it out good and shiny, spotless as a matter of fact, and then took out my dick and rolled it around the rim of the cup—after taking a piss, of course! That way, every time the cup went to the Chief's mouth, I'd know his lips were touching where my dick had just been!!"

I burst out laughing. I hadn't laughed that hard in a long time. He laughed as well, and the entire restaurant stopped to look at us. We laughed hard and loud for a long time, both of our faces red, tears running down our faces.

I said, "So how long has this been going on?"

He said, "Three years!"

"Oh my god!" I laughed.

Finally, after I caught my breath, I said, "So what happened that you almost got fired?"

He said, "Well, I came in one morning and went to get his cup and headed for the bathroom to do my daily ritual, clean the cup, piss, and then swab the cup with my dick. I was almost done, and the door opened to the restroom. I'd always locked the door, but that day I forgot—and I looked up and there was the Chief!

"He looked at his cup in my hand, my dick still inside of it. He just stared at me, I looked back at him, and then we both looked at the cup.

"It was a really weird feeling knowing that we were both looking at my dick in the Chief's cup. No one said a word. He looked at me again then left the restroom."

I was barely able to breathe, I was laughing so hard!

Jake said, "I didn't know what to say, so I said nothing! We both stared at each other, and then at my dick in his cup. It was weird!"

After I caught my breath, and he stopped laughing as well, I asked what happened next.

Jake said, "Well, he didn't drink out of the cup that day—I can tell you that!" More laughter and tears.

Finally, he said the boss called him in and asked him how long he had been "cleaning his cup" that way. Jake said he lied and told him about a month.

Jake said that they came to an understanding. He, Jake, had to promise never to tell anyone this story; the boss didn't want anyone knowing that he'd been drinking out of a dick-swabbed cup.

Jake agreed, saying that he felt like he wasn't in a place to negotiate. (He had a wicked sense of humor). He said that as long as he agreed to keep his mouth shut, he could keep his job. He was given two days off without pay, and that was it!

I couldn't believe it! I said, "That was it? That's all you got?"

Jake said, "Yep, that was it."

Funny thing, though: now the boss treated him a lot different—and kept his coffee cup in his desk!

I laughed again. This was too funny not to share, but I'd promised never to tell.

The waitress came over and said to me, "I have never heard you laugh in all the years you've been coming in here, not once. I saw you smile once, but never laugh. What's so funny?"

I couldn't tell her—and if I did, she wouldn't think it was funny anyway. She just shook her head and walked off.

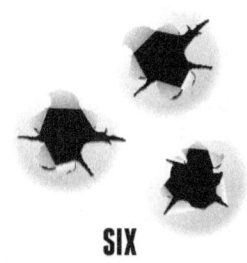

SIX
FEELING NO PAIN

ONE NIGHT, I WAS SENT to a domestic in an area where we never got those kinds of calls.

The area was an affluent one, where most of the residents competed with each other over who had the biggest boat or newest jet skis. They never called the cops about anything, so I knew it had to be pretty bad.

I arrived with a back up this time. We'd coordinated prior to arrival and arrived together, pretty much simultaneously. We walked up quietly, listening for any sound of a fight or disturbance; there was none.

After listening outside the front door for a moment I knocked, and a woman came to the door. She was beat to shit. She was bleeding from several wounds on her face and had a couple bald spots where her boyfriend had pulled her hair out. I asked her what had happened.

After several attempts to hide the truth, she told me that she and her boyfriend had been dropping acid and drinking. They'd gotten into an argument, and he'd just beat her up. Simple as that. She said when she got free from him, she grabbed the phone and called 911.

When he saw that she'd called, he took off.

She didn't want medical assistance and asked that we not call the paramedics for her. She said that she'd seek medical treatment on her own.

I asked her where her boyfriend might have gone. She said, "I don't know; he was so high, he could be anywhere."

Then we heard a noise in the basement, a loud crash.

I said, "What was that?" The woman said that she didn't know.

Both my back up and I went to the basement. After turning on all the lights, pretending that we had a dog, and announcing that we were going to send it in if the boyfriend didn't come out, several moments of silence passed—but nothing happened.

Finally, we decided we had to clear the basement and started down the stairs, guns drawn.

Before we went down, we asked the woman what her boyfriend's name was. She said his name was James Peebles, but that he thought of himself as a reincarnated James Dean. She said he'd only answer to 'James Dean Peebles'.

Great, we're going after an acid-dropping woman beater who thinks he's James Dean. Another typical night of weird shit.

We cleared the basement and found nothing. There was nothing out of place, no sight of the James Dean wannabe.

Then we heard a sneeze; soft and faint, but definitely a sneeze.

Shit! We looked at each other and thought, *what had we missed? Where could he be?* We looked around again and found nothing.

I called upstairs to the injured woman and asked her if there were any hidden areas in the basement. She came down the stairs and looked around and said, "Well, things have been moved. That large couple of boxes used to be over there, and now they're covering up the entrance to the crawl space."

I tried to move the boxes and found that they were very heavy; no one was in them, they were just heavy. It took a lot of effort by both me and the back up officer pushing them to move them.

Sure enough, there was a crawl space hidden behind the boxes. I saw that there was a light switch just inside in the dark and reached in and turned it on.

The crawl space lit up, we looked inside, and at the opposite corner all the way on the other end of the house was Mr. Peebles.

He was huddled up in a corner, facing away from us, pretending he wasn't there, I guess. We called to him several times, threatening to send a dog; he didn't budge.

Finally, we entered the crawl space, literally crawling on our hands and knees to get to Peebles. We were pissed off.

This was tactically dangerous, and besides that we were covered in dirt by the time we reached him. He didn't move until we were right on him—then the fight was on.

We outnumbered him two-to-one—and he was kicking our asses. He was high as hell and feeling no pain at all. Nothing worked; all the arrest control tactics we're taught as cops only work if the suspect is feeling pain—and Peebles felt nothing.

I had his arm behind his back in a wrist lock, and he didn't even notice. I cranked on the wrist until his hand laid flat against his forearm, palm laying flat against his own arm—and got no reaction at all.

I looked at my back up, and he looked at me, both of our eyes wide with surprise! We had to pull out all the stops and just brawl with Peebles until we had both hands cuffed. That only limited his ability to fight back.

We started to drag him from the crawl space, and he kicked and spit the entire way, slamming his own head into the floor joints above us.

About ten minutes later, we arrived at the opening of the crawl space, covered in dirt, sweat, and Peebles' blood and spit. We dragged him out of the crawl space—but he wasn't done yet.

He kept fighting as we pulled him out, growling like an animal and thrashing back and forth. His head went back and forth against the roughed-in 2x4 framed walls of the basement like a stick across a picket fence. He just didn't care. He felt nothing.

He continued to fight all the way to the patrol car.

Finally, we dropped him on the ground and shackled his feet. Grabbing a dog leash that everyone carried in their cars, we tied his feet to his wrists and dropped him in the back seat of the patrol vehicle. This was the only way to transport him at the time.

Years later, this tactic would kill several people, causing positional asphyxia; that night, however, it was the only way to control the acid-dropping Mr. Peebles. I booked him for the domestic assault and resisting arrest.

Two weeks later, I got a subpoena to go to court on Peebles. I arrived at court, expecting a brawl. I was beat to shit affecting the arrest of

Peebles; he wasn't a big dude, but he felt no pain. To make matters worse, I had to take my two-year-old daughter to court with me.

My wife at the time was convinced that I never did anything but write traffic tickets and help old ladies cross the street. She had an appointment to go to lunch with a friend and didn't feel that she should have to take our daughter with her.

She left me with the baby and said, "You'll be fine; you exaggerate so much! You big, tough man."

I walked in with my baby girl in my arms and asked the clerks to watch her. They said they couldn't.

I had to go into the courtroom with the crazed Mr. Peebles and my baby girl. I was on edge, ready to kill him if he even touched her.

I sat down, and the crazy fucker came right up and sat next to me; this was my worst nightmare.

I said nothing, and when they called the case, he stood up and said that he was present.

The prosecutor called me up, and Peebles turned to me. He said, "You're the one that arrested me?"

I said yes.

He looked at me for a moment, and I was sure we were gonna fight right there, but then his face changed.

He said, "I'm very sorry about that night. It must have been one hell of a fight, huh?"

I said, "Yes, it was."

He said that he didn't remember a thing, but the next day when he woke up, he could barely move.

He said to me, "What happened to my wrist? Jesus, it still hurts!"

I smiled and said again that it was a hard fight, all the while keeping my daughter behind me. He said again that he was sorry and that he just wanted to apologize.

He pled guilty to the charges, and I got the hell out of there, keeping myself between him and my baby girl.

When I finally did arrive home, I was still mad.

I began to argue with my wife about leaving me with our daughter.

She said, "Oh, you're just such a tough guy in your head, I know, but we both know your job isn't that dangerous!"

SEVEN
SESAME STREET

THE DRUG DEALERS IN THE city had a street they referred to as "Sesame Street."

It was a dead end street off a main drag that was known for its drugs, prostitutes, and crime. It was well known that everyone was high as hell, and if anything happened you were on your own. None of the people who frequented the street would help anyone else. It didn't matter what it was that happened; you'd better be able to handle your own business.

Sesame Street was a dead end in more ways than one for a lot of people. It earned the nickname 'Sesame Street' from the theme song from the kids show, referring to the magical place where everyone was nice and the air was clean. Our Sesame Street was the exact opposite.

One evening while working night shift, we got an anonymous call of a fight that had broken out on Sesame Street. If we did get a call about the street, it was always just like this: anonymous, and almost always very bad.

Two cars rolled to the street to see what was up. They arrived and went to the address reported by the caller. One guy was focused on the house, the other was his back up. We were running short on manpower, as usual.

If the citizens knew how thinly spread we really were at that time, they would have freaked out.

Late at night, most every night, we were cut back to six guys for the entire city; amazing, but true. We could barely keep up with the in-progress felony calls, much less do anything preventive.

Anyway, the two cars arrived and went to the house and found Bubba Johnson and his elderly father in a fight.

Bubba had beaten up his dad pretty bad. Dad was no slouch, though. He'd put up a good fight, and the two of them had destroyed the house, breaking furniture, glass tabletops, and windows.

Our biggest problem was that they'd broken the natural gas-fueled wall heater that heated the house.

The two officers removed the elderly father to awaiting paramedics, then went back to go get Bubba.

He was barricaded in a bathroom and refused to come out. They finally coaxed him out.

He was high (as usual), and when they tried to arrest him, he fought back. He beat the hell out of the two officers, throwing them around the house, ripping the badge off one of them and stabbing him with the pin on the back of the badge.

They managed to call for more units, and I was available and went in immediately.

When I arrived, the fight was still in full swing. Bubba was a good-sized dude and was feeling no pain. He wasn't going to go without a battle. He kept trying to get to a gas oven that was in the house and light it; he wanted to kill us all.

To make matters worse, he had full-blown AIDS. He'd contracted it sharing a needle and knew his time was limited. He just didn't care about living or dying.

I jumped in, and being fresh and not fatigued from the battle, I was able to get him at least pinned against a wall with both arms behind his back.

The other two officers were injured, and the gas was still pouring out into the house; any spark at all, and we were all dead.

I told them to get out and get treatment.

I had Bubba off the ground with his arms behind his back and his toes barely touching the ground, pinned against the wall. The shift Sergeant arrived and began to help me arrest Bubba.

As soon as I let his feet touch the floor, the fight was back on; this time, however, I was fresh, and the Sergeant was an old timer, Kenny Duke. He had been in the department a long time, and he knew how to handle himself. He was older, but tough and not afraid to mix it up with anyone.

I wrestled Bubba to the ground and was able to get one hand cuffed, but not the other. The Duke came at him from the other side, trying to get his arm to where we could cuff him; Bubba wouldn't give in.

Duke looked at me smiled and said, "This is why they call it Sesame Street! Are you having fun yet?"

That's how he was: calm as hell in the middle of a battle and joking, even though at any minute the house could blow up from the gas leak and kill us all.

Duke said, "Time to quit fucking around with this guy."

We were on the floor on our knees, leaning over Bubba. He drove his right knee deep into Bubba's ribs.

Bubba cried out, but he wouldn't give us his hand. Duke kneed him again, harder this time. I heard a rib snap, but still Bubba wouldn't give in.

Duke looked at me, with surprise on both of our faces; Bubba was really high and feeling nothing.

Duke pulled his leg as far back as it would go and drove it deep into Bubba's ribs. I heard many snaps and pops that time, and Bubba finally had a change of heart and gave in.

We cuffed him and got the hell out of the house.

Once we were clear, we advised Fire that the scene was secure, and they came in and turned off the gas.

The other two cops had received several minor injuries from their fight with Bubba. One had to get the stab wound, that he received from being stabbed with his badge, treated.

Bubba's father had to be admitted to the hospital for his injuries as well. Bubba was transported to the hospital for the broken ribs and was later booked into jail for the incident.

Any call we went to on "Sesame Street" was always an interesting time.

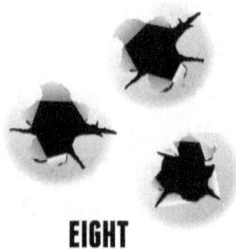

EIGHT
WARNED BUT IGNORED

ONE DAY, I GOT A call from a guy who wanted to talk to an officer. It wasn't a priority call. He called dispatch and asked them to send a cop to his house because he had a question to ask.

I went to his house at the very end of a dead end street. He was sitting on his porch, watching the neighborhood kids playing in the street. As I walked up, he never took his eyes off the kids; he just stared at them and spoke to me.

I asked him what he needed to talk to a cop about. He took off his glasses, and I saw that he had tears slowly rolling down his cheeks from both eyes. He said, "Officer, I need your help......I need your help right now before something bad happens."

I was expecting the usual: he had access to a secret plot by aliens to kill the president, or maybe signals from space were telling him of an impending alien invasion. This was how those kinds of calls usually started out.

I told him, "Sure, I'll help you in any way I can, sir," already noticing he had no weapons and that his hands were in plain sight. I had him stand up and checked all around him; no weapons.

I let him sit back down and prepared to listen to his story about the aliens; I was wrong, though—this was no story about aliens.

The guy told me his name was Rory Adams. He was on disability and living in a small trashed apartment. He says that until recently he had been fine, nothing had been wrong, and then one day he started to have "uncomfortable feelings." He was quiet.

I said, "Uncomfortable feelings? About what?" He didn't answer me for some time. He just sat, breathing in large gasps and sobbing.

He said, "Please believe me. I'm getting really strong feelings that I'm going to harm someone."

I was paying attention. Serious attention. We rarely had a warning from someone before they went off the deep end and harmed others. This guy was asking for help, and he was seriously upset.

I told him that I would do whatever I could to help him. I asked him if he had any urges to hurt someone specific. He said that he really wanted to take one of the kids he had been watching in the street and "harm them."

I now realized why he was "target locked" on the kids playing in the street as I walked up, as well as why he was crying; he didn't want to harm them, but he was having some kind of psychological issue that made him want to hurt them. He was asking for help, afraid of what he might do.

This was a first for me. Usually, cops were in reactive mode, always going to a call after something had happened; here was chance to stop it before it happened, and I planned on making the most of it.

I told him that I would take him to the hospital and have him involuntarily committed. The laws at the time allowed a cop to commit a person who was suicidal to a hospital psych ward. I explained this to him, telling him that the only way I could get him any help was that I had to hear him say he was suicidal, using those words.

He reached out his hand to me, asking me to take his hand. (This was a major tactical *do not* do.) I allowed him to hold my hand, however, and while he cried, he said, "Thank you," and "Yes, I am suicidal."

We both knew that he was not suicidal, but that was the only way I could get him off the streets. He had broken no laws, and there was no facility for people who *might* break the law. The psych ward was all I had as a resource. I handcuffed him and took him to the hospital.

Driving past the children playing on his street, he breathed a sigh of relief. He said over and over, "Thank you, thank you."

We arrived at the hospital, and I explained in great detail the nature of his problem to the psych workers, adding that he had told me that he was suicidal.

It was not a lie; he had told me that after I had coached him. They agreed to accept him. They really had no choice; by law, they had to keep him twenty-four hours.

I left the hospital and felt pretty good about myself. I wrote up the report in more detail than I normally would, just in case something did ever happen, making sure I added in his request and his telling me that he wanted to harm the neighborhood kids.

I went on to the next call and forgot about Rory.

About a month later, I got a call at home. Detectives were working the case of a missing juvenile female. She had been abducted from the same street Rory Adams lived on. She had last been seen with Adams, and when the detectives pulled Adams up on the computer, they found my case report. They asked me if I felt he was a real threat.

I replied that he was and that I had believed him enough to commit him to the psych ward. I told them that I had explained everything to the psych worker that night and added his information to the report as well.

They said that they had read the report, contacted the hospital, and that they said Adams was no threat; they felt he just wanted attention. I strongly disagreed.

I was pissed off. In spite of all I had done, he still did not get treatment; instead, he was freed without receiving meds or therapy, given a stamp of approval by the psych ward and let loose. Now he had abducted a little girl, and they were gone. I was sick. This shit really sucked.

I went to work that night and spent the night looking for Adams in-between calls.

This was before Amber Alerts, and the Internet was still relatively new. Cops didn't use it yet; however, we got on the phone to the late night radio DJs and asked that they announce his car description, license plate, and his name on their radio stations. It would get us fired if we were caught, but honestly no one cared. We all felt we had to do everything possible to find this little girl.

Adams was found later the next day. He had raped the little girl repeatedly. She was found in his car, tied up in the back seat, about 150 miles away on a rural road.

He went a month later to court and told them he had asked for help repeatedly, recalling our conversation and the report I wrote. He had warned us, but no one listened. I was frustrated beyond belief.

This is what the street is all about for cops: trying to make a difference—and rarely do we really succeed.

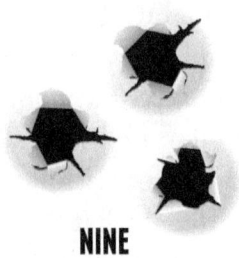

NINE
TAKE TIME TO UNPLUG

IF YOU HAVEN'T FIGURED IT out by now, I have never followed the rules. I thought I'd throw that out there.

One night I went to work, and the day started out like any other day: briefing on the latest stolen cars, people we were looking for, rapists and robbers, then we all sat down and discussed what had happened the night before. The Sergeant assigned was Leeds. (Again I was working for this dickweed.)

Afterward, we went out to hit the streets. First call out of briefing was a suicidal woman at the local hospital Emergency Room. She was being admitted to the psych ward and wouldn't go without a fight. The hospital security guards were having a hard time with her and needed help.

I arrived with the plan of stuffing her into a straight jacket and being out on the street in five minutes or less.

We had a saying on the street: "If you're talking about suicide, you're not serious."

The only people serious about suicide were those that were dead when we arrived; the rest we felt were just attention whores and pussies who couldn't cope in life. This call forever changed that in my mind.

I arrived to find a quiet woman about forty years old sitting in a chair. She refused to get up to go to the psych ward. She wasn't violent or abusive; she just wouldn't go.

The security guard was uncomfortable with her because she was pretty and she intimidated him. He didn't want to lay hands on her for fear of a sexual harassment suit.

The nurses didn't know what to do, so they called and expected me to make her go. I was briefed by them that she had been committed by her family because she was truly suicidal. We called it a "Blue Slip" back then: family members could commit her on a blue slip.

I started with the usual line that she could get up willingly or I would make her get up. The five minutes was ticking past, and I wanted to be out on the street.

She calmly looked up at me and said, "If you want to make me go, I have no doubt you can. It won't change a thing; when I leave here, I will kill myself—and there is nothing you or anyone else can do."

She wasn't afraid or emotional; she was very matter-of-fact, almost business-like. I looked at her long and hard. This was no cry for help. She wasn't upset; she was resigned, determined, and her mind was made up.

Rory Adams was still fresh in my mind. I had no confidence that the psych ward would be able to help her any more than they helped him.

Several minutes passed with us staring at each other, neither saying a word. Our eyes were locked in a staring match I have never forgotten.

Finally, I asked her if she'd walk with me and talk away from the hospital. I told her I'd give her my word that I wouldn't force her to go to the psych ward; I just wanted her to walk with me.

She stared at me another thirty seconds or so then quietly said, "OK."

We walked out the Emergency Room door, went to a nearby bench, and sat.

I pulled the radio I carried off my belt and told dispatch I'd be busy at the hospital and unavailable, then I turned off the radio completely.

I told her, "You have my full attention. I'll be in deep shit for this with my bosses, but I want to understand what it is that has you at this point."

She told me her story: her husband had killed himself about three months earlier, leaving her with three teenage kids. She was devastated by his death, and she felt betrayed by him. In the same breath, she felt terrible loss and wanted to be with him. She loved him dearly and felt that maybe if she killed herself they'd be together "somewhere else."

She said that her children didn't need her now; all they did was fight with her, and no one cared how she felt.

Finally, one day she decided that she'd just kill herself. Her parents and friends saw the change in her and elected to have her committed to the psych ward, where the experts would help her.

We talked for six hours. During that time the nurses came out to see if I needed anything. I asked them to leave us alone. After the first two hours had passed, they finally got the message and left us alone.

I told her that I agreed with her that no one could stop her from killing herself. If she wanted to do it, nothing would stop her. I told her about our rule on the street about suicidal people and that I had planned to stuff her in a straight jacket and move on. I changed my mind, though, when I saw her attitude was like a cancer patient that has no hope for remission. She had resolved herself to dying, and I couldn't let that just happen without trying to talk to her.

I told her about my life and the trials I'd experienced. Several times, I'd thought about blowing my brains out as well. The horrors of the street, several broken marriages, and now the estrangement I had with my daughter had taken its toll. I really didn't give a fuck about much.

I told her how I'd been hopping hot calls on the job, going from shooting to stabbing, hoping to get into some shit that would let me die on the job, hopefully in a battle.

I didn't want to die a frail old man, shitting myself in a hospital bed, surrounded by my children—who wouldn't want to be there to begin with. I wanted to go out on my own terms just like she did, by my own choice.

She was shocked by this. She took the offensive and told me I had no right to make that choice; I was a cop, and I was supposed to protect people.

I laughed hard at that.

I told her I used to feel the same way 'til a tiny baby girl was shot a couple feet from me in a drive-by shooting. I felt that no way anyone would try some shit like that knowing I was there—but they had. I hadn't protected anyone.

I told her about Rory Adams and how I tried to keep him from harming the kids on his street—but I couldn't; he still raped a little girl.

I told her about going into a blood-splattered apartment where a child had been beaten and kicked to death by a babysitter, seeing pieces of the infant scattered around the apartment—and not being able to do a thing to make that right either.

I told her about sitting in a parking lot at Christmas time, talking to a friend while a woman was beaten to death with a hammer by her husband a block away. I did nothing to stop that, so how could she think I protected anyone from anything?

She had no answer. She said, "What keeps you going, then?"

I told her, "For me, it's the battle, the possibility that tomorrow I might make a difference. I might stop a murder or a rape, I might make that day worth living."

That was the only thing that I looked forward to, the only thing that separated her from me.

We sat there sharing stories about our kids, and I told her about several of the more difficult emotional cases I had worked and how they'd impacted me.

We laughed about Sergeant Gus calling the chief by accident, and she cried about the girl who was raped by her boyfriend and cut up with a knife.

Finally, we stopped talking, both of us staring straight ahead.

I said, "I'm going to have to commit you to the psych ward just from what you've told me. I know they won't do a damn thing to stop you, but I'm required to do it by law. I just want you to know that up front. I appreciate that you've talked to me and told me about your life. If you do decide to kill yourself, I'll respect that. It's your life. You can do as you wish."

As we walked back in, she thanked me for talking to her for so long.

She said, "I hope that you don't get into too much trouble."

I said that I didn't care; the police department had forgotten long ago what this job is about. We're supposed to be here for people—that's everyone, not just the wealthy and sane, but the crazy and poor as well.

I suggested that she take it day by day…just make it through the next moment. That was what I'd learned to do on the street: survive the moment and then the next, 'til the shift is over and you've earned the right to go home to your kids.

She looked at me and said she'd think about it. I asked her to send me a card in a year or two if she made it through this hard time and let me know that she didn't kill herself and to tell me how it had turned out.

She gave me a funny look and walked away with the psych workers.

I went back to work. Sergeant Leeds was furious and called me a "sand bagging lazy fucker" for milking the call so long. He asked what the call was about, and I told him.

He rolled his eyes and said, "Jesus, you're not a fucking social worker!"

I told him, "Write me up, then!"

I'd given up on pleasing his ass long ago. I just didn't give a shit what he thought about anything.

About two years later, I came to work and an envelope was in my box. It had no return address and had a thank you card and a picture inside. It was from the suicidal woman at the hospital.

She said she was still taking it day by day. She enclosed a picture of her grandson, an infant maybe six weeks old. She said, "Without you, I never would have seen him. Thanks again."

Once in a very rare while, you felt like what you did actually mattered.

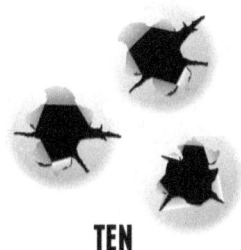

TEN

FISHING AT THE OLE FISHING HOLE

IT WAS ABOUT 7 P.M. ONE summer night when I got this call.

I was dispatched to contact the parents of a 10-year-old boy. They were homeless and living in one of the many low rent motels in the more rundown parts of the city.

The hotel had been built on the banks of a river, and in its day it was fairly nice. Its trademark was a huge water wheel, similar to the wheels that supplied power to saw mills and granaries using water power to turn the huge wheel instead of electricity. The wheel had long since quit turning and was now just for show.

I arrived at the motel and contacted the manager. I asked him about the occupants of the room I was being sent to see, trying to find out if he knew anything about them.

Being sent to similar motels had made me cautious, and I never went directly to the room anymore. I always checked with the manager first to see if the room was even occupied; I took nothing for granted.

The manager said the occupants were a family of four. They had been in the motel for about two months, and he never had any problems with them. He said that they had been ideal tenants.

I went to the room and contacted the parents. The father asked if we could talk outside the motel room, so we stayed outside.

He said that they were, in fact, nearly homeless. He had lost his job, and then their house; they had been forced to move into the motel while he looked for work. He said that his son had been frequenting the river bottoms and hanging out, fishing with some friends he had made with the "Bo's" in the area for the past 4 weeks. He said something had happened yesterday and that his son came home crying after spending the entire day fishing with his friends, the "Bo's."

I said, "By 'Bo's', you mean hobos? Transients?" He said yes.

I already knew this was not going to be good. People have been fed a line of shit by the media that there is no difference between hobos or transients and homeless people. There is a huge difference.

Transients are not homeless due to circumstances beyond their control; they choose to be that way. Most are severely mentally ill, dangerous, and a lot of them are on the run for crimes they've committed. Hiding in the homeless world is easy for criminals.

Anyway, the father asked that I interview his son and find out what had happened. He said that he was worried "something bad had happened" and that his son had refused to talk to him.

I spoke to the boy and asked him if he would talk to me in my car. His demeanor was very disturbing. He looked emotionally shattered, broken, and barely keeping himself together.

I could tell that I wasn't going to do the kid any good by forcing him to tell me what had happened. He was broken by whatever had happened to him, so I started out by talking to him about fishing, asking him what type of fishing he did.

"Have you ever fly fished? Are you a bait fisherman?" He brightened up and started to talk.

I then let him know that I was familiar with the river bottoms and told him about a fight I had with a huge transient about ten years earlier who had wanted to kill me.

I told him that I had always thought hobos were cool until that moment; I had been raised in an era where people thought of hobos as harmless simple-minded folks who wore patched clothes and were more like clowns than criminals. I found out differently when I started to work as a cop.

He was quiet listening to this.

I recalled how a clown had been at a birthday party when I was a kid. The clown was dressed as a hobo. So that was what I expected when I first met them: harmless happy guys who would do tricks.

(Of course, this wasn't what I really believed, but it made sense in a kid's world.)

He nodded and said, "Exactly!"

He started to tell me that he'd been befriended by a group of five or six men who lived in the river bottoms. They'd talked to him as a friend and treated him with a fatherly kind of attention.

He had fished with them and learned how to clean a fish after he caught it, learned to build camp fires, and he listened to their stories about living the life on the road.

I agreed that that sounded great. I asked how long he'd been fishing with them.

He said that he met them about three weeks ago and that they'd introduced themselves with their road names. (Cowboy, Boots, Whistler, Sticks, and Cookie.)

He recalled shaking each man's hand and feeling like the group accepted him. He said he'd spent every spare moment in the river bottoms and rail yards, hanging out with his new friends.

When I could tell that we'd established some trust, I started to pry into what had happened the day before.

I asked him, "So what happened yesterday? What went wrong?"

His demeanor immediately changed from happy 10-year-old boy to broken, damaged kid.

He was quiet for about five minutes, and I said nothing at all and let him work up the courage to tell me what had happened.

Finally, he started to talk.

He said that he went fishing in the morning and ran into his friends at about 10 or 11a.m. They were fishing as well and bathing in the river. He said he could tell something was different about them, but he didn't know what.

He finally asked, and they told him that they were going to leave that day and hit the road. They said it was time to move on.

He said he was sad and asked them not to leave, telling them that they were about the only friends he had.

They said that they had the "itch"; they'd been in one place too long, and it was time to go.

He said all five of the men were swimming in the water, and they invited him to join them. He stripped down and jumped in the water with them then a couple of them got out and started to break camp.

They then went into the woods nearby and brought back a large log to sit on. Finally, they all were out of the water, getting dressed. The two guys that had gotten out of the water first grabbed him.

He thought that they were playing with him; they weren't.

The three men took turns raping him anally while the two men held him bent over the log. He said they held a knife to his throat and told him that if he cried out for help, they'd cut his throat and dump him in the river.

They did cut him slightly on the arm, just to emphasize the point.

After they took turns raping him, they then made him sit on the ground on his knees and give each of them a blowjob while someone held a knife to his throat.

Listening to him sob and cry, I was sickened by what he'd been through. He said that when they were finished with him, they made him get in the river and stay there to clean off the blood, shit, and semen.

They then took his clothes and hid them, packed up, and hopped on a train.

They told him to wait 'til the train was out of sight before he got out of the river or they'd come back and kill him.

He did what they said. Then he got out of the river and searched for his clothes. Eventually, he made his way home, broken and betrayed.

His parents could tell something had happened; usually he was happy and had stories to tell them about the hobos and their exciting life, but he came home that day quiet and trembling from the day's events.

He said that he felt dirty, and he couldn't understand why they'd done that to him.

I spent the next hour helping him process the rapes, making him realize he wasn't to blame.

I told him I would have to tell his dad and mom and asked if that was OK with him. He eventually said that it was OK, but he knew they'd think it was his fault.

When I explained to his parents what had happened, the father threw up and the mom just sobbed.

I told them I wanted to have their son submit to a rape kit, but they refused. They didn't want a report made. They didn't want this to be recorded anywhere.

I told them I wouldn't be able to convict the men if they didn't cooperate. They didn't care. They just wanted to ignore the event, and they asked me to leave—now!

I left and went to the rail yards. I found the camp and the log that the boy had been raped on. There was nothing around, no evidence, no cans, foot prints—nothing.

I went back to the motel the next day to see if I could get the family to change their minds about cooperating with an investigation, but according to the manager, they'd checked out in the middle of the night. He said they couldn't pack fast enough and that they were very rough with the boy, telling him he should have known better.

The manager asked, "What did that mean? What should the boy have known better about?"

I said nothing; I just shook my head and got into my car.

This wasn't an event that they could pretend never happened. The kid had done nothing wrong.

I drove around for a while in a smoldering rage, wishing I could find the transients, but at the same time knowing I could never make this right.

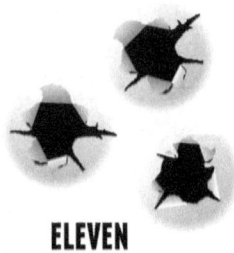

ELEVEN
NOBODY RIDES FOR FREE

BECAUSE OF MY AREA, I was in the Emergency Room a lot.

There was a lot of violent crime in the area, and like I've mentioned before, a lot of people with various mental illnesses.

Cops and ER nurses are like two prize fighters sizing each other up: each is able to land fatal blows, knowing the other is a shadowy reflection of what could have been. Both are adrenaline junkies, both think on their feet, and both play by their own rules.

I became friends with several of the ER nurses, and immediately the pranks started. We started out with small stuff, but eventually we were into some serious "destroy-your-life" stuff; no holds barred.

For example: one night, I brought a really combative suspect to be treated at the hospital before he was booked into jail.

The jail wouldn't accept injured prisoners, and this guy had put his fist through a window and nearly severed his arm. He was drunk, abusive, and bleeding like hell. I'd wrestled him down and contained him, then stuffed him into an ambulance.

They took him to the ER, and I followed them in case he got wild in the back of the ambulance.

While we were waiting, one of the nurses that I was in a constant battle with walked past and said, "That guy is a mess, was he a hard one to get here?" I said he was.

I was still a little bit shook up over the battle. He was feeling no pain and bled all over me.

She said, "Hey, I'm going to get a drink. Do you want me to bring you one?"

I said, "Sure, please."

I pretended not to be suspicious, but by now I trusted no one; anyone who was nice to me while I was in uniform was suspect.

She came back a few minutes later with an opened can of Coke. I said thanks and left it on the tabletop while I wrote reports. She came back two times in five minutes to see how I was.

If I were on "Lost in Space," Robot would have been yelling: "Danger, Will Robinson! Danger! There is a crazy woman nearby!" I heard the robot loud and clear.

I kept writing, and after she left I poured about half of it out in a nearby sink and moved the can.

She came back, I looked up, and she smiled and said, "Doing OK?"

I said, "Yes, thanks for the drink."

She smiled and said, "Anytime." She then left.

About twenty minutes later, another nurse walked past. She was a good friend. We'd sparred briefly and both realized that this would be a no holds barred death match.

Finally, she asked me to meet her at the ER one night and called a truce.

She said, "I'm calling a truce. I realized after your last prank that we're gonna end up killing each other; neither of us plays by the rules, and neither of us will back down. I'm asking you to stop. Truce?"

I said, "Sure, truce—but you cross me, and it's back on."

She never did, and we became good friends with mutual respect for each other's abilities as pranksters.

Her name was Tori. I called her Scary Tori 'cuz like me, she had an evil sense of humor.

Anyway Scary Tori said to me, "Did you drink that can of Coke?"

I said, "Absolutely not. Do I look stupid?"

She smiled and said, "I knew you wouldn't."

She told me that the other nurse had laced the drink with a diuretic and that had I drank it, I would have been peeing for hours.

I said, "Ya, well she was way too nice. I knew something was up."

Unlike my peers, I didn't think I deserved special treatment for being a cop and actually expected to be treated poorly. So when someone was nice (especially a beautiful nurse), the Robot came out waving his arms, and shields were up.

I got my payback, and the caring, concerned nurse also called a truce (wisely), apologizing and promising never to spike a drink again.

A few weeks later, the ER had a new clerk. I came in a few times, and she had heard about the pranks.

She was really cocky and thought of herself as a princess. She was out to prove that she could handle whatever I dished out.

She said one night, "I heard you're scary! You don't look so scary!"

The nurses around her started to scatter. I ignored her.

She said, "Yep, just what I thought—all talk!"

She then waddled away. I shook my head.

I went up to the cafeteria where the hospital workers ate and bought lunch, eating while I finished my report. When I returned to my car, it was buried in snow. I walked back in the ER, and Tori came to me and said, "I told her this was a really bad idea, but she wouldn't listen."

I said, "Where did she get the shovels to move the snow?"

Tori smiled a huge smile and said, "Well, I can't lie; I told her where they were. I think I'm going to like seeing the princess put in her place—but I did tell her not to do it."

I cleaned off my car and drove away.

No way this plump dairy princess would be able to hang, so I let it go. I parked in another lot the next time I went up to the hospital to eat. This worked for a short period, until one night I returned to my car—and it was covered in toilet paper. Seriously, this was her idea of a prank? Toilet paper? Maybe in 6th grade!

I had a reserve riding with me that night. (Jeff Mckell again.) I told him he should probably go home.

He said, "No, man—I heard about your pranks! I wanna see what you'll do."

I said, "Are you sure?" He said he was.

I said, "OK, no matter what—no statements; you didn't see anything. Understood?"

He said, "Sure!"

I went back to the ER and looked at the Princess' nametag. She smiled at me, and her double chin jiggled as she tried not to laugh. She had a little cat-shaped pin on her lapel, and I noticed the eraser on her pencil was also a cat.

The woman liked cats. Hmmmm. Tori saw the look in my eyes and raised her eyebrows. She held up her hands, said, "I'm out of this!" and walked away.

I went to my car and told Jeff, "Last chance!" He just laughed and said, "I'm all in."

Getting out of the patrol car, I called up dispatch and asked for the on-call animal control officer's phone number. I called her at home, waking her up.

Keep in mind, it's 3 a.m.. Did I care? No, this is all-out war now.

I asked the sleepy worker where they kept the dead cats after they put them to sleep. She said in a barrel, then when the barrel was full they'd burn them. She said the barrel was in the back of the complex and that the entire animal control complex was fenced and locked. No one was there.

I said, "OK, thanks."

She asked why I wanted to know, and I said, "Never mind. It's a dumb question. Good night!" The sleepy animal control worker went back to sleep.

I pulled two black plastic garbage bags out of the trunk of the patrol car and drove to the animal shelter. I got out, and Jeff saw the bags. His first thought was that I was going to burglarize the animal control shelter. He was really upset.

He had a pending job offer at a nearby police department, and now he thought he was witnessing a burglary-in-progress by another cop. He pleaded with me to stop, but I ignored him and jumped the 10-foot-high fence.

I went to the back of the complex and dumped out the barrels, picking out six of the most disgusting of the dead cats. I double-bagged them and came back to the car.

Jeff saw that the bag was full and put his head in his hands. I put the cats in the trunk and got in the car. Jeff was nearly in tears.

He said, "Zach, please! I don't wanna go to jail; just take the money back. I won't say a thing!"

I realized he was serious! I laughed. This was too sweet! Two pranks for the price of one.

I started the car and turned on the radio, and "Ratt" came blaring over the radio, singing "Nobody rides for free!" This was karma! I started singing the song and driving like crazy.

Meanwhile Jeff is watching his future go down the toilet; his degree will mean nothing now. In his mind, his dream of being a cop one day is over.

I hauled ass back to the hospital and found the dairy princess' car. It wasn't hard to find; when I was on the phone with dispatch, I had them run her name and got the plate for her car, a purple Dodge Neon. The personalized plate? It said PURR.

In five minutes, I had the car opened, the cats strategically placed near the floor heater vents (but out of sight), and the car locked back up.

I returned to the car, and Jeff was elated! He said, "It was just cats? No money, just dead cats?"

I said, "What the hell, man? You think I'm gonna burglarize the animal shelter?"

He laughed a giddy, nervous laugh, then said, "Zach, with you I never know what's gonna happen." Then he mumbled, "I get to keep my job; it was just dead cats." He was seriously traumatized.

The princess warmed her car up because she didn't like to be cold. She did this every night before she went home; so, when she came back to her car, the dead cats were thawed and oozing all over the car's carpet. She lost her mind when she found the first one, and six cats later she was crazy with rage.

Tori told me that she took her aside and said, "I told you don't mess with him. This is stage one; you don't wanna play this game. Stop now while you can."

She asked Tori to tell me she was stopping, that the game was over, no more pranks—which she did.

I went into the ER a few days later with another wacked out Tweeker to be treated, and while I was writing my report the princess sat down near me.

I made a soft "Meeoow" sound that only she could hear. She threw her papers at me and left the room.

The Princess eventually had to sell her car; she never could get the smell out of the carpet.

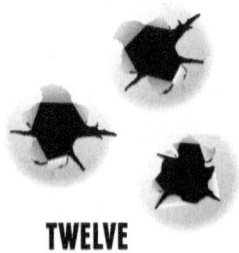

TWELVE
WANNA GO FOR A RIDE?

FOR MOST COPS, A RIDE-ALONG is a pain in the ass.

You get some college or high school kid that has taken a course or two and is now an expert in the law enforcement.

Even worse, if your luck is really bad, you get the Criminal Justice major—the expert in all things law enforcement—commenting on your every traffic stop, every interview, evaluating your probable cause, and critiquing your abilities as a cop.

During my career, I had a few ride-alongs. Most were short-lived and moved on to friendlier, more patient officers. You get in my car and change the radio station, adjust the heater or air conditioner, then sit back and begin to critique my work—and you will find your ass on the side of the road in a bad part of town. If you're lucky, I *might* at least take you back to your car before telling you in no uncertain terms to get the hell out and don't bother coming back.

In my mind, the whole damn concept of a ride-along is flawed. It's the police department's idea of public relations. They require the ride-along to sign a waiver, releasing the department from liability should anything happen to them, and then they hop in the car. Smiling, shiny faces hoping to see some real action, have some "cop" experience to brag about to their classmates or friends.

Reality is, every night the cop goes out, he is armed, trained, and wearing body armor.

Every night, he is on guard the entire night, watching hands, eye contact, looking for weapons on every person he meets; listening not only to what every person he comes into contact with says, but how it is said, acutely aware of nonverbal communication; seeing potential threats everywhere.

The ride-along is a severe distraction, and another helpless person you're responsible for.

To make matters worse, they think they know everything and talk to everyone you meet. They never shut the hell up.

One night, a ride-along went out with one of the newer guys. The officer felt it was his duty to take the guy from one hot call to another.

They started out the shift hitting the first domestic that came in. A man and his wife had been drinking and fighting, and the man had beaten his wife up. The scene was secure, and by the time they arrived it was pretty much just a peep show, walking the ride-along through the scene and explaining what had happened.

The ride-along was disappointed; he wanted to see some "real action," not a cold domestic, but the situation was all cleaned up and the fighting was already over.

Next call was a DUI. The officer went to help out and stand by while the FSTs (field sobriety tests) were being done, and fill out the impound sheet for the suspect's car after it was towed.

This is the reality of cop work: boredom and paperwork, helping the other guy out, hoping to keep each other safe and prevent a situation from going bad and becoming a "CNN moment."

The ride-along complained that "this was boring" and he wanted to see some real action!!!

If it was me, he would have been out of the car at that point, walking his candy ass back to the police station, mumbling about what a prick I was as he passed the drunks and transients that frequented the area.

Police work isn't a ride in an amusement park; you pay a fee for fake thrills and the almost-danger of going fast on something that you have to be "this tall to ride."

This is the real deal, not a ride, and there's no safety inspector to warn you when things are getting ready to go to shit and ask you if you are sure you want to stay on the ride.

The night wore on with the cop trying to get his ride-along to more interesting calls, and the ride-along complaining that he was bored.

They were on another traffic stop that was a carload of gang bangers. They had stopped the car because it matched the description of a car involved in a drive by.

The incident had happened a few hours earlier, and they were checking out the occupants of the vehicle, getting identification on each and looking for weapons.

For the cops, it's a tense moment. Any traffic stop can go to shit in a moment, and that moment passes so fast, if you're not watching everything and seeing it almost before it happens, you end up breathing from new holes in your chest or face that aren't supposed to be there.

This stop was going well, and while they were identifying everyone, the ride-along sat in the car. Another unit stopped by, and they began to help out in the stop.

The cop had a weird feeling, he said later, and it turned out to be right.

The two officers re-approached the car and began to remove the occupants one at a time. Finally, they got down to just the driver and the right front passenger.

The officer that started the stop was talking to the driver, and the back up was on the passenger side, watching the front passenger.

While talking to the driver, the first cop was also watching the front passenger.

It's a reality of the job that you have to be aware of everything going on at all times; impossible task, but you try.

Anyway, while he was talking to the driver, the passenger looked back and saw the back up cop watching his every move.

What neither of the cops knew was that the carload of bangers had recently done a home burglary, and the trunk of the car was loaded up with rifles and handguns stolen in the burglary.

They had been driving around with the intention of "putting in work," meaning they were looking to get into a gunfight or do a drive-by on rival gang members, hoping to at least kill some rivals and make a name for the set. They were jacked up and angry, and looking for a fight—with anyone.

The passenger is watching the cop on his side, waiting for the cop to make a mistake, look away, lose his focus just for a second.

Finally, the moment came, and the back up looked down—just for a moment. The passenger took the opportunity and pulled a gun from his waist, twisting around almost 180 degrees in the front seat and pointing the gun at the back up officer, who was still looking down.

When the back up officer looked up, he was staring at the barrel of a stolen Glock 40 caliber handgun pointed at his face. The banger pulled the trigger.

Simultaneously, the primary officer was watching, and he pulled his gun and shot. He fired three rounds into the passenger while the driver was still sitting in the car, holding the steering wheel, gunpowder burning her face and eyes; the gun was that close when the shooting started.

She screamed and exits the car, running as fast as she could, screaming the entire way.

She was later located after people called the cops to report a hysterical screaming woman in the hallway of a nearby apartment building.

She was so traumatized by the shooting, she had a breakdown and just sat in the hallway, screaming and crying that her boyfriend had been killed.

Meanwhile, the banger had pulled the trigger on his Glock, trying to kill the back up cop.

He was a recent parolee from prison and wanted to die a hero to his set, and he figured that killing a cop was as good a way to go out as any; however, Karma—or whatever power you believe in—had different ideas.

The bullet did not fire, and the cop learned a valuable lesson the hard way and was able to survive that moment.

The banger was shot several times by the primary officer and eventually removed from the vehicle. He somehow survived the shooting and ended up back in prison. His hero status was intact; his life, however, was destroyed. He was nineteen years old.

His attempt to shoot the backup officer was confirmed by the firing pin striking deep on the primer of the unspent bullet found in the chamber of the Glock.

The bored ride-along? He was watching all of this. Again, Karma is a bitch; be careful what you wish for—especially on the street.

When the shooting broke out, the bored ride-along went from entertained amusement park rider wishing he had some popcorn and a drink while waiting for the next thrill from the safety of the front seat of the patrol car, to terrified dumbass, hoping to survive the next few moments.

Survival instinct has two options for any animal in life or death situations: fight or flight. The "I am bored, I want to see some action" reality show wannabe exited the vehicle as fast as his ass could go.

No longer concerned with the thrill of watching real cops in action, writing paperwork and going to cold calls, he was on the front row of a real battle for survival – and life or death battles are wicked, fast, and brutal.

He sat, jaw dropped and eyes wide open while the ejected brass from the cops' weapons bounced off the hood of the patrol car in front of him.

He exited the vehicle and ran as fast as he could, not caring where he went or what else happened; he just knew he had to get the fuck out of there—and now.

Later, after the scene was secured and medical arrived to treat the severely wounded gang member, the cop sent out word about the missing ride-along, and units were sent out to look for him.

After about twenty minutes of searching, the now not-so-bored ride-along was found about a half-mile away, walking in circles in a parking lot, sobbing and in shock.

He kept repeating, "I just want to go home" over and over.

After going through an interview and completing a written statement for investigators, he was released. He elected never to ride-along again…imagine that.

THIRTEEN
YOU ARE IN OR OUT, NO IN-BETWEEN

COPS HAVE A WEIRD SENSE of who's in and who's out.

If you're in with one clique, you're usually out with another. I guess the old timers decided I was "OK" after I was in a couple of really messy calls.

They have a code that you have to have been baptized by fire before you're accepted by them. For the most part, this was cool with me.

I liked the old school cops as much as I liked the old school gang bangers. They all lived by a code; an old school unwritten code, but still a code. I understood that. I liked the way they treated each other. There was a sense of respect for who you were.

I was at the range, qualifying after the latest shit storm I'd survived. I was still a little shaken by it, and they put me back at the end of the qualification with the administration of the department.

I heard later that they did this in case I needed help qualifying, in case I'd lost my nerve. They didn't realize that I actually went the opposite direction.

I'd kept hidden from them some of the more serious incidents I've written about in the other books.

I wasn't about to lose my nerve; if anything, I was sharper than ever, too sharp. Edgy as hell.

So after I qualified, the administration was all gathered around, cleaning weapons and bragging about what they'd done back in the day when they were on the streets.

Funny thing about administration, they can't wait to get off the streets, feeling they're better than the rest of the street cops. Once they're off the streets, however, they can't seem to shut up about what "heroes" they were way back when. Legends in their own minds, I suppose.

I guess they felt like I belonged as well. They were trying hard to remember my name, patting me on the back while I cleaned my gun. I just wanted to get done and leave. The hair was standing up on the back of my neck.

I worked mid-shift to stay away from these guys. They weren't friends by any stretch of the imagination. They weren't the old school street cops; they were administration—and no one's friend.

So, while I was cleaning my gun, I overheard one asking the other to tell him about the guy above the river. They were all laughing about this.

Apparently, this is a story that was rarely told—and I'd soon know why.

As they whispered back and forth ("Do you think it's OK?," "Ya, he's OK; he won't mind"), I got the impression they were referring to me. I looked up, and they all looked at me; smiles from all these old dinosaurs as they looked my way. Yellow, old teeth; glassy blurry eyes... shit was creepy as fuck.

One of them started to tell a story about how he'd arrested this guy one night for being drunk at one of the bars in the city. He said that he was taking the guy to jail, then the guy started to talk trash to him in his car.

After a few well-placed insults about the cop's fat ass and potbelly, he was fed up and called another cop (who was now also sitting at the table at the range). They agreed to meet near the river that flowed through the center of the city.

They laughed as they recalled tying a rope to the suspect's feet and hanging him upside down from a large tree branch above the river. They then bragged about shooting at him with rubber bullets numerous times as he hung helpless from the tree.

I stopped and looked down the table, listening at the laughing elderly men. I didn't laugh; I just stared quietly at them, one at a time. This shit was unreal.

These are the same two-faced dickwads that would hang one of us out to dry at the slightest hint of breaking one of the department's policies. They'd let guys go for not being able to pass the PT test after being injured on the job. They strutted around the department with this holier-than-thou attitude, barely able to recall your name when they said hello.

Here they are, bragging about a clear violation of the law—not to mention the guy's civil rights.

I listened while they bragged about letting the guy go after running out of rubber bullets. They took him to the county line and dropped him off, telling him never to return.

They then began to recall how they'd been pretty scared when the FBI showed up and began investigating the claims of a man being hung over the river and shot at by cops with rubber bullets. They laughed about how they'd defeated the investigation.

I shook my head and made eye contact with another guy who had missed his first appointment to qualify and had to shoot with them as well. His eyes were wide in amazement, and he said under his breath, "Can you believe this shit?"

I replied, also in a whisper, "Ya! I can."

I finished cleaning my gun and began to leave the range. They called to me again—using the wrong name—saying, "Where you going? Hey, come back and sit with us."

I didn't reply; I just got into my car and left.

The next time I saw one of them in the hallway at work, the nonverbal communication was clear. Old eyes glaring at me now disapprovingly; I wasn't to be trusted, I wasn't one of them—and they now knew that. I was definitely out.

FOURTEEN
THE WITCHES OF CENTRAL CITY

AFTER YOU'RE ON THE STREET for a while, you get less and less excited about the calls. Your imagination is less involved, and reality is more what you gauge the threat and the intensity of the call by.

I went to a house on a report from an older woman that her schizophrenic daughter had become too difficult to manage.

The people in the neighborhoods of central city thought of the two women as witches. They were given a lot of room by the central city dwellers for fear that a curse or some other black arts magic might be thrown their way should they cross the witches.

Reality, however, was that both women lived very sad, lonely lives, struggling with mental illness and a lack of any real, healthy contact with their fellow city dwellers.

I arrived, and the mother said that her daughter had been off her medication since she broke up with her latest boyfriend.

He'd left when the schizophrenic illness became too much to tolerate, and she was devastated. Going upstairs to meet with the daughter, I heard her screaming out incoherently. She was definitely off her medication.

I had Jeff with me on one of his last days as a reserve on the department. He'd tested and made the list on several police departments, and he wanted to work in St. Pauls, but he'd been picked up by another larger department. It would be a great thing for him; not so much for me.

I opened the door, and we went into the daughter's bedroom. She was as feral as I'd ever seen her. The illness was in full swing, and she was in bad shape: raving, drooling, and screaming—clawing at the air one moment and crying and whimpering the next. It was a sad thing to see.

I tried to talk her into coming with me, and she lunged at me, stopping inches from my face and screaming at an all-out blood curding volume that should have made me jump.

By this time, not much phased me, so I looked back at her and told her to get her shoes on; she needed help, and we both knew it.

She glared at me for a while, then a small glimmer of who she was came through her eyes; it was a small moment of recognition. "Slick? Is that you?" this little child-like voice said.

I said, "Yes, it's me. Will you come with me?"

She said yes and started to cry. She told me about her latest boyfriend leaving and that she felt that she wanted to die. She looked at me and said, "If I died, would you care, Slick?"

I said, "Of course, I would care."

I told her I was here to help her. I could just leave and say her mother was crazy as well and not take her to get help, but I wouldn't do that; I wanted her to get help.

She smiled, then said, "Thank you, Slick."

As she started to get ready, I turned to Jeff and could see he was still amazed by the war cry she'd let loose just inches from my face. His adrenaline was pumping.

We talked later, and I told him that I'd dealt with many mentally ill people in the area. I found that most were manageable and were nothing to be afraid of—as long as they weren't armed. Had she been armed, this call might have gone a lot differently.

He smiled and said, "Sure, whatever!"

I took the daughter to the hospital and stayed with her during the intake process. She was singing a song that I recognized, and as she did, she started to get jacked up again, repeating the lyrics over and over, louder and louder.

The nurses and ER staff were becoming anxious and afraid.

I recognized the song; it was Bruce Dickenson's latest album at the time, Balls to Picaso. The song was "Tears of the Dragon."

When she stopped to catch her breath (after nearly screaming the lyrics out), I quietly repeated the next verse, and she stopped screaming, startled that I knew the lyrics.

She smiled and said, "You like that song?" in a quiet, little girl voice again. I said that I did.

She said, "Me, too; it makes me feel normal."

The ER nurse looked at me, surprised at the rapport that I had with the younger "witch."

It was really sad to see how tortured the young girl was by the illness and how hard she struggled to have some kind of happiness in her life.

As I was leaving, the nurse said, "You sure have a way with the crazies, Slick."

Another one of the last calls with Jeff was a report of three men fighting in a garage on the east side. I cancelled the back up since it was Skidmark and I had Jeff with me.

Jeff said, "Are you sure that's a good idea, Zach? I'm just a reserve, and there are three of them—and they're fighting."

I told him, "Ya, I'd cancel Skidmark anyway—even if you weren't here. With you here, the odds are better than normal."

On the way, we received more information from the complainant that the three men were definitely fighting. They were yelling and swearing, and the complainant heard one of them say, "How you like that, motherfucker?" after a loud crash came from the garage.

Jeff was getting really jacked up. He was breathing hard already in anticipation of the battle he was sure we'd be fighting in a few moments. I kept telling him that this was a bad idea, to arrive with an idea in mind of how the call would be.

I'd learned the hard way over and over again not to get caught up in the call and let emotion run my decision-making.

We arrived blacked out and coasted to a stop, parking down the street from the address we were given.

As soon as we got out of the car, we could hear the men's voices—and they were very loud.

I tried to calm Jeff down, but I could tell it was too late; he was in survival mode already, terrified of the battle he knew we were about to be in.

We walked up to the house and carefully looked around the corner to the detached garage.

There was a loud crash, and then someone said, "That's what I'm talking about, motherfucker!" and then "What? What?"

There was something familiar in that voice.

I stepped out and walked up to the garage, looking through the crack in the door.

The three guys inside were playing dominoes and slamming the tiles on the table where they were playing.

I recognized them immediately as the mall security guards I mentioned in *StreetCreds*. They were drinking Old English 800 beer and playing a very enthusiastic game of dominoes.

I called Jeff over and had him look in on the "fight."

He watched, and I could tell from his body language that he began to calm down immediately. He looked at me and rolled his eyes. "How did you know?" he whispered.

I didn't know anything; I'd just finally learned not to get caught up in the call. It only took me fifteen years or more,—I was a slow learner!

We opened the door and started talking to Riggins and Pogar and another guy I didn't know. I told them about the report of a fight, and they all busted out laughing.

They said, "Are you serious?" I told them I wouldn't be there otherwise.

I left after they promised to bring it down a notch or two, and we walked back to the car.

Jeff was still shaking from the adrenaline dumps. Dominoes can be intense like that.

FIFTEEN
DREAMING ABOUT LASSIE THE LAND SHARK

BEING IN K-9 HAD BEEN a dream for me for years.

I went into the military with the promise from the recruiter that I'd be assigned to K-9 once I completed Basic.

Like most 18-year-old kids looking at the contract to sign up for military service, I had no idea what the language meant. I trusted the guy (foolishly), and when I arrived I found out I'd never be allowed to be in K-9. I was in the wrong career field.

I was really pissed, and when I completed the training for Basic and tech school, I came back to find the recruiter. He was gone, of course, moved on to another assignment; meanwhile, I'm in a career where I get to watch K-9 handlers almost daily—but never actually handle the dog.

It was like being a fat kid in a bakery with no money; it drove me crazy. Eventually, I found the SAC combat competition and poured my frustration into that.

After I got out of the military and became a civilian cop, I was like a heat-seeking missile on the K-9 program.

I read everything I could read about training dogs. I talked to the old handlers and picked their brains about different techniques and practices.

A lot of what you read is theory; reality is a whole other thing.

It takes an amazing dog to be K-9. They're like world-class athletes, combined with the instincts of a MMA fighter and the intellect of a Nobel Peace Prize winner. Imagine Mike Tyson, Usain Bolt, and Albert Einstein rolled into one man. That's your *average* police dog! They're truly amazing.

The K-9 handler has to be pretty amazing, as well.

Picture being able to understand your spouse or best friend completely by their body language. Seeing their moods, feelings, and understanding exactly how they felt that day by the way they held their shoulders or ears or the eye contact they made.

It's an amazing talent to be a dog handler, and I truly believe that they're as rare as the dogs themselves.

When the Sergeant in charge of K-9 retired, we had an opening. The political powers had decided that increasing the K-9 unit was a good idea and decided to do just that.

I applied for a position in K-9 and was the number one selectee in my department.

The process was meant to weed out those who were just in it for the alleged glory of the position.

The job is incredibly challenging; you always have the dog with you, caring for it, training it, and socializing it so that you can have it in public in a large crowd without incident—but given the correct command, Lassie becomes a land shark! All teeth and attitude, ready to take out whoever you direct the dog to attack.

It's quite an accomplishment to take an animal as intelligent and driven as a police dog and form the team that makes the K-9 unit.

I thought I was up to the challenge…I wasn't.

A dog handler has to be patient beyond belief. They literally have to be able to project themselves into the dog's head and see what the dog sees, smells, hears, and sometimes fears.

They have to read all that in the body language of the animal. No words pass between them that don't come from the handler. They not only speak different languages, they're entirely different species. That's the reality of K-9.

I was assigned EMO, a sleek, black athletic dog fresh from the newly reunited country of Germany.

He was from the former East German side of the country and only "spoke" German; so, not only did I have to learn "dog language," now I had to learn German to speak his human commands.

No biggie, I thought, I'll learn German and "Dog," and he'll love me and follow me wherever I go, my loyal and amazing dog. My dream had finally come true.

Wrong! I was book smart; I knew everything I could read about dogs after eight years of watching from the outside, and finally I was in.

I failed as a K-9 handler miserably.

EMO was gifted. He had a nose like no other dog I'd ever seen. He could find one damn pot seed in a house within a few seconds and let me know it was there instantly by his body language.

I was able to read him pretty well after a while. He was an amazing dog when it came to dope. He loved it.

He had a prey drive that was amazingly high, "prey" being the desire of the dog to hunt. Cats, skunks, raccoons, dope—we trained the dogs to think of the dope as prey, and they'd hunt for the dope like they'd hunt in the wild for an animal.

EMO was the idiot savant of dope.

When the Narcotics strike force called me to do a search of a house, I knew immediately when I arrived at the door if there was dope in the house. Didn't matter where it was hidden or how it had been disguised, he smelled it and found it.

He seriously found a single pot seed in a heater vent after searching the entire house during one search.

I took the vent out, expecting him to have found a large stash; there was nothing. I looked and looked; I could find nothing. I brought him back to the vent, and EMO told me, "Dude, it's in there; I swear to God, it's there."

By this time, I knew to trust his nose, so I kept at it—and finally I noticed the round seed in the round tin heating duct and removed it. Holding it up, I thought, *Jesus, really? You can smell this?*

I had him check again, and the body language was "Nothing here; can we go now?"

I was amazed and proud of the piece of trash. (All K-9 handlers referred to their dogs as "trash"; it's meant as a term of endearment and respect. You realize early on how special the dogs really are).

EMO loved dope, but he was one moody ass dog.

He was dual certified, meaning he could do dope (which he loved) or he could do apprehension (which he tolerated).

He loved to search buildings and could fight if he had to protect me (if he decided to that day).

Here's an example of an average day with EMO:

I received a call to search a building that had been broken into.

Patrol had responded to an alarm and found the building open. One of the doors had been pried open with a crowbar, and the silent alarm had gone off. They'd set up a perimeter and felt there was a good possibility that the burglar was still inside.

I got EMO out, and he was his usual happy self (hoping to search for dope, I'm sure); however, when I made it to the door and told him to drop while I yelled out the standard warning (that I was the K-9 unit and we were going to search with a dog, come out now and you won't be hurt), EMO's body language changed.

If he was speaking my language, he would have said, "Man, I hate this shit. I really do. I thought we were gonna play dope."

Anyway, I did the call out and encouraged him, praising him and getting him jacked up and ready to search.

Then I gave him the command to search.

He started off fast, then about ten feet in he stopped, turned around, and stared at me as his ears went back.

Head up, chest out, his ears came back up, then he started to walk towards me; he was challenging me.

In a K-9 handler and dog relationship, the handler has to been seen as the Alpha dog. They're a pack, a unit, and the handler has to be—without question—the leader. In every pack there's a leader, and there are the dogs that challenge the leader.

EMO, being the moody ass that he was, challenged me constantly.

He was rank as hell, meaning he always felt that he should be Alpha dog and I should be doing what he wanted. He didn't like being told to do anything.

So, he was challenging me for Alpha dog right here in the middle of the search.

I said out loud, "Seriously, motherfucker? Right now?"

He growled and showed me his teeth, and my back up said, "Who are you talking to?"

I said, "Back out; the dog wants to fight."

He said, "What the fuck?"

I said, "Back out now!"

He backed out as EMO came for me.

I caught him in mid-air, snapping and growling, then rolled him into a subordinate position called an Alpha roll.

An Alpha roll forces the dog on his back, exposed to you, while you're over him, dominating him and looking into his eyes, showing your superiority and staring him down.

He'd challenged me this way many times, but never in a search.

EMO was growling and digging with his paws, trying to bite me. The backup officer was stunned, and I heard him say behind me, "Holy fuck—your dog is crazy."

After about five minutes, EMO submitted; satisfied that I'd earned the Alpha dog status, he relaxed and looked away.

As his body loosened, I let him up, then put him back in a ready position and called out the warning again.

He was on now, ready to do what I asked.

I gave the command to search, and away he went.

When I entered the building, my back up wouldn't come in.

He said, "Fuck you! That dog is fucking crazy; you're on your own."

Great news! Now I was searching the entire building without a back up.

EMO found nothing inside; whoever was in the building had escaped before the perimeter was set up by patrol.

He came out happy and playful while I praised him for his work. He was back!

"EMO the wonder dog" was always a challenge. The patrol unit, on the other hand, thought we were both nuts.

Since then, I've heard from many handlers that the dog always reflects the handler. Maybe that's true; I don't know.

I was a pain in the ass as well, always defying the brass and doing what I thought was best, in spite of what the "rule book" said.

We had many adventures, EMO and I, and I admit now that we were more alike than I cared to believe at the time.

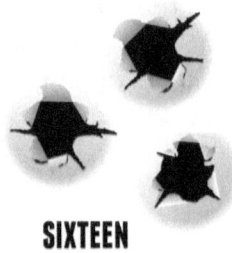

SIXTEEN

IT'S A BIRD, IT'S A PLANE, IT'S EMO THE WONDER DOG

ANOTHER IN-PROGRESS CALL AND ANOTHER search with EMO, the wonder dog.

Residents had called to report a burglary in progress at a house in their neighborhood. The neighborhood was well off, and the house was owned by some very wealthy people who had been on vacation. They'd asked a neighbor to watch the house, who said they'd been watching as a man had arrived and entered the house.

They were positive he'd broken in, and when I arrived, they told me that they believed he was still inside.

Again, I had no back up. We were short on personnel and had no available units.

This is the reality of police work. You try to be as safe as possible, but sometimes you have to enter a situation that can't be made safe.

Critics will tell you that you always have the choice; no shit, we all know that—but like EMO the wonder dog wanting to be the Alpha, cops are the Alpha dogs as well. We don't wanna bow down to anyone. Out numbered and out gunned, we still run *towards* the shooting when common sense would say to run the other fucking direction.

Don't ask me why that is; I don't know. I just know that for me to walk away from a fight, a real fight—especially where someone else might die if I don't get involved—is almost impossible. Criticize it all you want; it's who I am.

So anyway, EMO and I were at the open door left by the burglar. I put him in a down position and did the call out. I checked EMO's body language, and today he was on. He was going to search. I gave the command, and away he went. We were off searching.

One of the things about a rank dog that's really cool is that they're independent. EMO never needed my reassurance; he was positive that he was the toughest, baddest land shark on the planet.

Both he and I searched, me with my gun out. We crossed paths many times, me watching his body language as he searched.

I trusted his nose, and he was wind scenting, nose up high, checking the air currents in the house. His body language said, "No one is home, but I smell something."

I checked the house and found nothing.

EMO wasn't done yet, however; he was still searching, and his body language told me he was in prey mode, not fight mode.

Had he found some dope? I couldn't tell, so I watched…then out of nowhere, a cat bolted across the living room floor in front of us. Scared the shit out of me.

EMO was like a heat-seeking missile and chased the hated, evil cat.

Animal rights folks won't like this, but I'd learned by this time that EMO had a prey drive (a desire to hunt) that was uncontrollable. Two skunks and a raccoon later, I'd bought an electric shock collar to keep him in check, and he wore it daily. He had it on now, and I had the controller on my duty belt.

To keep him in check, it had to be on the highest setting. (That setting would send another dog into total submission, begging the handler to stop; EMO, on the other hand, was like me: stupid stubborn and crazy determined. When either one of us were in the hunt, there was no stopping us—short of killing us.)

He was after the cat, and I gave him the command in German to stop and lie down.

He heard nothing; there was a cat in the house—and for him, this was better than sex. Hunting was his sole reason to live.

The cat ran around the room, barely evading the pursing land shark, which was snapping, and growling.

I lit him up with the electric collar three times, and his body would contort from the electrical current running through his neck, but he wouldn't slow down in his pursuit of the hated cat. I was sure the cat was dead.

The owners had left a sliding glass door open and the screen locked. The cat ran right through the screen at full speed, punching a small hole in its fabric. We were on the third floor of the huge home, and the sliding glass door led to a balcony that surrounded the house. EMO hit the door a second later, taking the entire screen door out. I was right behind them, hoping to save the cat.

They circled the house once on the balcony. I lit EMO up twice more, and he barely reacted to the shock. He could sense the kill was within his grasp, and he'd finally have the wily cat!

The cat had other ideas. It was desperate and finally took the only out left: it hit the only chair on the balcony, then the ledge surrounding the balcony, and launched into the air.

Three stories up, the cat was flying, airborne.

EMO was about a half-second behind and hit the chair, then the balcony ledge as well.

His ears flopped in the wind for a moment, then I think he finally realized what the cat had done: it had drawn him in, then launched off the balcony. It was maybe six pounds and would probably survive the fall; EMO was ninety-five pounds.

I stopped at the balcony and he turned his head and looked at me as he fell.

For the very first time, I saw EMO the puppy; he was scared and had the "Oh shit! Help me, Dad!" look on his face.

About a second later, the cat hit ground and was off running. It had survived the gamble and was headed to the nearest tree as fast as it could go.

I didn't wait to see how EMO landed.

I was sure he'd have broken legs, at the very least, after he hit the ground. I was hoping that he'd just survive the fall.

I was running through the house, imagining him with broken legs and shattered teeth, lying in the driveway, whimpering.

I opened the door, and there he was, meekly wagging his tail. He was humbled for the first and only time I ever saw the entire time that I worked with him.

He hit hard enough to knock loose his pride, but that was all. He had a small cut on his chin, his teeth were all in good shape, and he had no broken bones. I was relieved he was OK.

Maybe I'm reading into it, but the way I read his body language was this: "I almost had him, Dad—did you see that? I almost had him!"

I told him to go to the truck, and off he went, head down, tail wagging low and slowly. The electric collar, scarred up from the impact after the jump, hung uselessly around his neck. We never found the burglar. He'd left long before we arrived, frightened off by the neighbors.

Looking back now, I think the old handlers were more on the mark than I ever realized. EMO and I had a lot more in common than I'd ever admit. We were both hard-headed, determined, and had our own agenda. To hell with what others thought about us; we did what we wanted to do, even to our own detriment. We both resented the hell out of authority, and we both loved intense physical activity.

I'd take him running, and he was my best bud. He loved to work out. Like me, he didn't like to fight and only did it if he had to—but when he had to, it was a thing of beauty.

The sleek, solid black dog closing on a bad guy trying to run away, trying to do the impossible and escape EMO and his amazing nose... that was a sight that only a dog handler can appreciate. EMO launching his body and hitting the guy, knocking him to the ground, and then biting if the guy continued to resist.

For some reason, he'd spit out a suspect as soon as I gave the command and back off, ready to attack again if I gave the command.

I know for a fact that if he ever caught that cat, there would be no spitting him out 'til EMO was satisfied he was dead. The cat, the hunt; that was his passion. The suspect? That was just work.

SEVENTEEN
NEVER JUDGE A BOOK BY ITS COVER

I WAS WORKING ONE NIGHT, and a guy came to me and asked me to take a ride-along. I rolled my eyes. *Jesus, really?*

He said, "I know you don't like them, but I told her she could ride along, and I forgot that I'd already told another guy he could come out. I can't take both."

Some guys were like that; they loved showing off the cop skills they thought they had.

Like I said before, I hated ride-alongs.

I said, "Look, man, you know how I feel about ride-alongs; if she gets in my car and starts talking nonstop, her ass is out on the curb."

He replied, "I know, I know. You know she won't last long—but I promised, so just make it look good, then kick her out so I won't get in trouble."

I agreed to take the ride-along. As I walked back in to the police station, he said, "Oh! She's a college ride-along, a Criminal Justice major." He then ran off laughing, knowing I was in for a very long couple hours until I could get her out of the car.

I walked into the station and went to the lobby. I looked around for the college kid, imagining the pimple-faced fat girl wanting to someday be a cop and cure the world of all that was wrong.

I could see the image in my mind: chewing gum, greasy hair, glasses. We'd start off with her telling me she knew all about police work and that she was Soooo excited. "Like, oh my God!" The acid was already pouring into my guts at the aggravation; fuck, I did *not* want to do this.

I looked in the lobby and saw no one resembling a college student. Several people were there, waiting for copies of reports or wanting to talk to the night detectives.

I went to the desk Sergeant who was dealing with the crowd and said, "Hey, Sgt., I'm supposed to meet a ride-along. Has anyone come in?"

He said, "Ya, one woman was here asking about that."

I turned around, and there was the woman he was referring to.

When I was at work, people registered with me mentally by threat. I'd looked at the woman and not even registered that she was there. She was dressed in business attire, not casually. She was *not* a college kid; instead, she was in her mid-twenties.

I said, "Are you supposed to ride tonight?" Still not sure that this was correct.

She smiled and said, "Yes." She then stood up and introduced herself.

I said, "OK, well we're outside and I have a call pending already, so we have to go."

Time to start this off on the right foot and make sure that she knew I wasn't going to be friendly.

We walked to the car, and I got in. She walked to the other side. We hadn't talked at all on the way to the car. I was already counting down the minutes 'til she'd fake a headache or stomach cramps to get the hell out of my car.

I'd noticed that most of the female ride-alongs liked to be coddled; flirt with them, and they'll never go away—so I was a royal asshole.

I backed out of the parking lot and was all business on the way to the call, with waves of hostility rolling off me. She didn't say a word.

When we arrived, I said bluntly, "Don't talk to anyone, don't answer questions; you get out and stay near me...you watch and observe. One comment about anything you've learned in school, and you're back at the station as fast as I can get you there. We clear?"

She said, "Yes, clear."

We got out and made it through the entire call without her saying one word.

I was disappointed, hoping for an excuse to get rid of her. I wrote reports in silence, and then went on to the next call.

Three calls later, we were at one of the houses of a Peewee gang member. His mom and her boyfriend had been drunk, and the mom wanted him out of the house for the night. They'd been in a pretty big fight. Neighbors were involved, and there were a lot of witnesses. It was a strange scene.

Everyone we talked to kept looking at the ride-along, staring at her.

I was frustrated.; she hadn't asked to go back to the station yet, and the two-hour mark was getting near. I was being a complete ass, and nothing was working.

To make matters worse, I couldn't get anyone—men or women—to stay focused on the questions I asked. They'd start to answer, then turn to look at the ride-along, watching her.

To her credit, one guy started to talk to her, assuming she was a detective; that's how professionally she was dressed. She told him that he'd have to speak to me only and said nothing else.

We got back in the car afterward, and I said, "Do you know them?" She said, "No."

I said, "Weird that everyone is staring at you."

We went on to the next call, and then the next. Finally, I said, "Do you wanna get a drink? Need to use the restroom?" She said, "Sure, if that's what you'd like to do."

This was weird; nothing like the usual ride-alongs asking to be pampered and coddled, talking to everyone at the scenes we went to, changing the radio station, adjusting the heater. She was quiet and respectful.

I went to the usual place I went to get a drink, checking the store before I entered to make sure that it wasn't being robbed. The area I worked was tough, and the store had been robbed many times at gunpoint.

I got out again, ignoring her, and entered the store.

I hit the restroom, then got a drink. While I was paying, I noticed the clerk watching her as well. She was looking at drinks, trying to decide what to get. He was fixed on her, staring.

I said, "Hey, man, can I get my drink?"

He said, "Oh ya, sure, brotha. Who is that?"

I said, "A ride-along."

He said, "Oh."

I asked, "Why?"

He said, "Jesus, she's beautiful."

I said, "Huh? Really?"

I hadn't even really looked at her, I was too busy focusing on the problem of getting her out of the car as soon as possible. I went out to the car and thought that was weird. I waited while she got her stuff, paid, then walked to the car.

The night wore on, and she never left; no matter how I tried to be an ass, she was still there. At the end of the shift, I took her to the station and dropped her off at the car, then she asked if I'd mind if she rode with me again. I thought it over.

She *had* been really quiet, and she hadn't asked any stupid questions. I guess it would be OK.

I said, "Yes, you can ride again—on one condition." Her eyes glazed over, her face became hardened, and her tone changed.

She said, "What's that?"

I said, "You're gonna have to change the way you dress. I work the worst area in the city, and you stick out like a sore thumb. Everyone was staring at you all night. If you're gonna ride with me, you're gonna have to fit in this area. You're too dressed up. Simple shit, really. If you wanna ride with me, those are my rules."

She was stunned. She stared at me and said quietly, "That's it?"

"Ya, that's it," I said. *Jesus, this is police work—not a business meeting.*

She relaxed and said, "What should I wear, then?"

I replied, "Really? I have to explain this? Wear some fuckin' Levis, a jacket, ball cap, and running shoes. Not slacks and pumps and a business jacket."

She stared at me in disbelief.

I looked back and said, "I'm serious! You come back dressed like that, and you're not going with me."

She agreed and asked if she could ride the next week.

I said, "Sure."

The entire time she was in the ride-along program, she ended up riding with me and turned out to be a real asset on several calls. She was quiet and smart, and she was the first ride-along I actually thought might be able to become a good cop.

EIGHTEEN
CLEAN UP ON AISLE 5

SUMMERTIME IS A BUSY TIME for cops. Kids are out of school, so juvenile crimes skyrocket.

In spite of what Daywalkers think, it isn't the hardened career criminals that make up the majority of our work; juvenile crime accounts for a huge percentage of the crime we deal with.

Summer also brings out the tourists, feeling they're entitled to special treatment because they're spending their money in "your city," demanding to be let go for whatever crime they've committed—or they'll never spend another penny of their money in this city again!

Summer also brings out my personal favorite: the transients.

Yep, summer keeps us cops hopping.

There's another downside of summer, as well, and that's the heat—but not in a way that you'd understand unless you were a cop.

I got a call in a large apartment complex in central city one night. The tenants weren't prone to calling us at all. It was the inner city; cops weren't welcome until the shit really hit the fan—and then it was a love-hate relationship: you were welcomed only for the moment.

"Please deal with this shit storm we've called you to fix, then please leave as fast as you came."

Anyway, the occupants lived in pretty bleak conditions. People pissed in the stairwells and left their garbage in the hallways for someone else to put out for the trash. The place smelled pretty bad on a daily basis, and in the summer the stench was horrendous.

When tenants called one day and complained about the smell coming from a specific apartment, I knew this would be a call I wish I never received.

I arrived at the apartment complex and was met in the parking lot by the man who called. Word had gone out through the hallways that the cops were on their way, and as I arrived cars were leaving the parking lot and people were suddenly remembering their New Year's resolutions to start exercising more. (Keep in mind, it's July now). There was a mass exodus from the building.

The caller said that there was something wrong in a third story apartment. An older woman rented the apartment, and she was always very quiet. He said no one had seen her in about two weeks and that now there was an odd odor in the hallway around her place. He was worried something bad had happened. He said he'd knocked several times, but no one answered.

I sighed heavily, then opened my trunk and pulled out some Vicks vapor rub that I kept for just such calls. This was really gonna suck. I dabbed the vapor rub on my upper lip and said to the man, "OK, show me where she lives."

The manager had arrived as I was getting the information from the caller, and I offered them both a bit of the Vicks. They looked at me strangely, exchanging odd glances, then politely refused the offer and rolled their eyes at the peculiar cop that had arrived.

We entered the building and headed up the stairs, and by the second floor I could smell the familiar odor.

By the time we reached the apartment door, I swear you could see the odor in the air. In my mind, the colors were a dark brown, black, and green swirling in the air, thick and toxic.

"Last chance for the Vicks." I said as I offered it to the manager and caller.

They were gagging and coughing, but said no.

The manager opened the door, and the stench of the most disgusting smells you can imagine being thrown in your face hit us like a wet curtain.

Both the manager and the caller threw up right there—several times—and I stepped aside to keep the mess off my clothes and shoes.

I went into the apartment and searched for the dead body I knew I'd find inside. I found the elderly woman lying on the floor of her bathroom, dead, naked, and lying in a pool of her own bodily fluids.

Her body had blown up like a balloon from the gases of decomposing flesh. Eventually, the body started to seep out fluid on the floor, and she was lying in that. I saw no signs that she'd died anything but a natural death at home, but in the cop world you have to prove that.

Detectives were called, as well as CSI. The scene was processed, the body eventually removed, and after a while your senses started to dull to the overwhelming stench.

The vapor rub helped dull the sense of smell. It is an old cop trick to use either vapor rub or a smoking cigar on dead body scenes.

I don't know if it's psychological or what, but after every dead body call I can never seem to get the smell out of my clothes, hair, and literally the taste out of my mouth.

I was late getting home that morning, and I went right to the bathroom, stripped, and started to brush my teeth. I put my uniform in the washing machine, then took a shower, scrubbing my face and the inside of my nose to try to get the smell out.

After washing my face half a dozen times, cutting the hair out of my nose, and shaving my moustache, the smell started to go away. It was disgusting.

The next day in briefing, Sergeant Duke asked me about the change in my facial hair. I told him that I couldn't get the woman's decomposing smell off me, so I shaved. He laughed; everyone did. We'd all been there at one time or another.

Dead bodies are the calls we all hated and never talked about.

He began to tell us a story that had occurred to him in his first couple years of being in the department.

He said one of the first dead bodies he'd been on as a younger cop was a very large woman who had died and fallen on the kitchen floor. She was wearing a housedress, at least, and wasn't naked when they arrived.

She lay there for a couple days 'til the smell reached the neighbor's house and they called. He said that he and another officer had been assigned the call, and when they arrived they did the routine investigative tasks and eventually called a mortuary to come pick up the body.

The morticians arrived with a gurney and placed it next to the body for a quick pick up. They stood at the head of the body, and because the woman was really large, they asked the two young cops to take her feet.

Duke said he should have known something was wrong, but he was young in his time on the force. He still believed people were basically good and meant you no ill will as a cop.

They counted to three, agreeing to lift the woman on three. Each man grabbed a limb: the two morticians grabbed the arms, and the two younger cops grabbed each of the legs.

On three, they all lifted.

Duke said that just before they lifted the woman, he noticed the dead woman was wearing no underwear (we all grimaced); it was about to get a lot worse.

Duke said instantly he and the other cop were sprayed in the face and chest with bodily fluids that came shooting out of the dead woman's vagina and anus.

He said she'd blown up with gases from the decomposing flesh and was like a balloon waiting to pop; when they lifted her, that's exactly what she did: "pop."

He said they each received a face full of the spraying fluids and dropped the body instantly—and the body hit the floor and sprayed all over them again.

We were all in tears, laughing as we sat and listened to the story. This was the single most horrible account of a dead body call that we'd ever heard.

He looked at me as he laughed and said, "Remember that no matter how bad it is, it could always—and I mean *always*—be a lot worse."

Duke always had a way of making the worst things we went through seem manageable and survivable, making us all share in the horrors of the street in a way that could make us laugh about the worst of what we had to do.

We laughed hard about this story and asked questions, laughing at his account of what happened next. It was an incredibly funny, disgusting story.

He said after that, he always made sure that if he picked up any dead body, he *always* had an arm.

NINETEEN

THE LOW DOWN ON THE LOW DOWN

CENTRAL CITY WAS A STRANGE collection point for the area.

For some reason, it seemed like everything came back to central city. All the crime, all the dark and hidden undercurrents of the area came back to the toilet bowl we called central city.

One early morning, I was patrolling the area; the city had finally fallen asleep, and the morning was slowly starting to brighten the horizon. Black changed slowly to dark blue, then lightened up and started to wake up the brighter side of the city, loosening the grip the night held on it.

It was the only peaceful time I ever saw in the city, a brief period between night and day where the dark and evil side retreated and the Daywalkers weren't awake yet.

I was winding down from a night of battles, double-checking businesses to make sure they were still secure and that there was nothing obvious that I'd missed during the night.

On this early morning, a call came in from an address I'd never visited. It was some type of business that was housed in a renovated older home right at the center of my area. It was an exception to the rule of my area.

The home was immaculate, the yard and shrubs perfect. There was a sign in the front yard that had the business name and logo, but no indication of what work they actually did inside.

Anyway, someone from inside the business called to report that someone was breaking in. We took calls like that often that turned out to be nothing. I went anyway to check it out.

When I was halfway to the call, the occupant called back, scared and screaming that the burglar was inside the business. The caller had grabbed the cordless phone and locked themself inside the bathroom, staying on the line with our dispatchers.

I picked it up, pushing the patrol car to its limits and arriving a few seconds later. I told the dispatcher to let the caller know that I was at the scene and to stay in the bathroom.

I saw that the front door to the business had a large oval decorative glass piece that had been shattered; the call was legit.

I drew my Glock and carefully walked through the broken glass, ready to fight it out with whoever had broken into the business. I searched the building quickly and found nothing, no one.

My back up arrived, and we did a more thorough search. We found a guy hiding in a utility closet on the main floor. He was covered in sweat and terrified.

After a few tense moments of talking him out of the closet at gunpoint, we placed him under arrest.

After a couple moments of conversation, it was plain to see that the guy was tweekin': suffering from the side effects of meth and several days without sleep.

He'd been hallucinating and thought that he was being shot at by several people with AK-47s and chased by pit bulls. He'd broken into the business as a last gasp attempt to escape the crazed killers he was sure were still just outside, waiting to kill him. He was almost as happy to see us as the worker at the business who was still locked in the bathroom, on the phone with our dispatch.

Once we made sure the rest of the house was secure and no other tweekers were inside the business, we coaxed the worker out of the bathroom, and I began to collect her information for the report.

Nothing had been taken, and the tweeker had harmed no one; he just wanted to survive his imagined attackers.

After I transported him to jail, I returned to the business and asked the worker what they did there. I'd worked the area for many years and always wondered what they did, but I was always too busy to think about stopping to ask what went on there.

It looked like a doctor's or lawyer's office; however, I noticed the lights were on twenty-four hours a day, and I never saw anyone ever enter or exit the business.

The worker felt indebted, I guess; I seriously doubt that I ever would have found out the true purpose of the business if I'd just stopped and asked.

The frightened worker was a woman in her early thirties. She said to me, "Are you sure you really want to know what we do here?" I said yes.

It always helped to understand what was going on in the area on many levels. Each layer I uncovered explained to me more in depth why what happened did happen, and the "why" was always important to me. Understanding the layers of the city and how they fit and affected each other could make the obscure and apparently unrelated events suddenly all fall into place.

Imagine a huge, complex Rubik's cube or puzzle that had many levels hidden below the facade you saw on the surface; the only way to solve crimes and make a difference in the area was to understand the puzzle on multiple levels.

Did I want to know what she did in the business? Definitely!

Another layer of the puzzle, another piece was about become clearer. She explained that the company was a messaging service. They were a place for the elite businessmen and women of the area to have their messages collected and sent to them while they were at home or at work.

They were very discreet, and because of that they'd earned a reputation with the wealthy business people in the area as a company that could be trusted with their secrets; personal and business secrets.

They kept files on who called their clients so that the "operator" was able keep the secret lives of their clients separate from their professional lives.

Basically, it worked like this: doctors, lawyers, and business men and women would have families with the spouse or partner that had gotten them to the position they were in. This was their surface life, the life the public saw.

On the "down low," they had sexual partners of both sexes that they spent time with on the side, and they'd use the service to keep their two lives separated. They'd give the men or women in both lives the service's phone number. It was a way to contact them.

It was the "operator's" job to keep track of where the client really was, as well as what the cover story was that they'd told the person who wanted to leave a message for their client; basically, they kept track of the lie, maintaining the façade for their client.

The Daywalker side of the city would never tolerate this kind of behavior, so they kept it hidden and on the "down low"; maintaining lovers on the side in addition to the spouses and families would be severely frowned upon by the business communities and religious culture that dominated the area.

I was fascinated. I'd come across this facet of the city a few times during my travels in and out of the many hidden layers of deceit that shrouded the city. Here was a focal point where the rich all came together with their dirty little secrets.

She showed me a room full of file cabinets that housed their clients' files. She said if the information in those files was made public... WOW! The local churches, government, and businesses would never be the same.

I laughed. We both laughed hard.

We both knew the secrets that the people in the city held close, living their double lives. This was a hidden secret that the elite kept among themselves.

The poor had their own secrets to keep, and the similarities of the two social classes were always so amazing to me.

I started to stop in occasionally and talk to the woman, picking her brain about incidents that happened in the city and surrounding areas. We started to develop trust in each other.

She could often fill in the blanks on many incidents that didn't fit or make sense: how certain people were selected for certain positions in government; elected officials who granted building zoning changes in certain areas in the city; doctors and lawyers that would be entangled in weird, messy incidents that made no sense on the surface.

All the stories would suddenly be made crystal clear when I knew the background provided by the woman. If I had been an investigative reporter instead of a cop, the local paper would have increased its subscription rate dramatically.

We shared many secrets, each of us filling in the blanks that occurred in the stories that went on in the city. The down low was always incredibly fascinating.

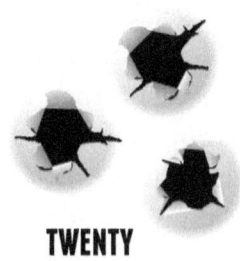

TWENTY
BEST FRIENDS FOR LIFE

JIM HAYES AND LARRY FOWLER were best friends.

They'd gone to high school together, played high school sports together, and even been the best man at each other's weddings. They had a close relationship, and when Jim was going through a divorce, Larry stayed at his house for a couple days to help him get through it.

Jim had caught his wife with another man and was heartbroken. He rented an apartment in my area and had started to try to rebuild his life.

One weekend, they started to drink early in the morning. They started out drinking a beer now and then, and as the day progressed they drank more and more. Neighbors said that they were listening to music loudly as they sat on the front porch of the house in which Jim had rented an apartment.

According to Larry, he and Jim had been competitive their entire lives, competing in sports, business, and in high school, seeing who could date the hottest women.

Larry said that Jim was always winning. It had bothered him his whole life that he never could seem to defeat Jim at anything, always being second to Jim's first.

Anyway, the two men were drinking, and sometime in the mid-afternoon they fell back into old habits, one challenging the other to various contests.

It started with arm wrestling; Jim was a lot stronger than Larry, and after several contests that Larry lost, they moved on to Bloody Knuckles.

Bloody Knuckles is a game that every boy knows. You stand facing each other, hands balled into fists, your fists barely touching your opponent's fists. The first one tries to slam his fists down on top of the other's exposed hand before the victim can pull his hands away. If you miss, you lose your turn, and now it's the other guy's turn to smash your knuckles.

It's a contest of speed and concentration. Jim won consistently, and Larry's hands were bruised and swollen from losing the contest so often. They moved on to Indian wrestling, and again Jim won. The more they competed, the more that Jim won, and the more they drank.

Larry said it really pissed him off that here he was being a good friend to Jim and supporting him during his divorce, and still Jim was beating him. Old resentment started to boil up in him, and the daylong drinking fest started to take its toll. The two men ended up in a fistfight in the front yard of the house.

According to neighbors, they fought for some time, wrestling, punching, sometimes laughing, and sometimes cursing at each other. They fought sloppily for some time, too drunk to really cause any real damage, and too drunk to stop. Finally, they started to get angry.

After taking some really solid punches to the face, Larry got in a lucky hook and knocked Jim to the ground. Larry was on top of Jim in a second, pummeling his head with blow after blow, the entire day's frustration finally being vented on his best friend's head.

Larry wasn't done when Jim was knocked unconscious from the repeated blows to the head; he climbed off Jim and picked up a large rock from a nearby garden.

He then carried the rock over to where Jim was lying unconscious and slammed it repeatedly into his head, crushing his skull.

We received the call when neighbors heard the cries of anguish from Larry.

They didn't call the cops in this area unless it was really bad, so we knew going in that this would be a bad call.

I arrived and found Larry in the front yard, crying and rocking back and forth. He was holding his best friend's bruised, battered body like a man holds a baby, with Jim's crushed and bloody skull oozing brain matter and blood down the front of Larry's shirt.

Larry told us the story about the day's events, and neighbors filled in the rest. They said that after Larry had finally defeated Jim by crushing his head, he yelled out a defiant primal scream, arms up in the air.

He'd finally defeated the amazing Jim Hayes—finally, after years of trying to defeat him, he had won!

Larry said that he held out his hand to Jim and tried to help him get up, repeatedly asking Jim to get up and acknowledge his victory.

Reality eventually set in, and he realized he'd killed his best friend, beating him to death in an alcohol-fueled rage.

It was a very sad scene.

I interviewed Larry and arrested him.

The case then went to court, and Larry pled guilty; both men's lives were destroyed that night. Central city moved on unaffected by the scene…just another horrible story among many.

TWENTY-ONE
THIS IS 911—WHAT IS THE NATURE OF YOUR EMERGENCY?

911 WAS INVENTED TO ENABLE anyone in an emergency to call the cops, fire department, or paramedics and get help immediately.

The state laws required our response to 911 calls. No matter what the call, we had to go; however, some people's idea of what constitutes an emergency is a lot different than what the people who invented 911 had in mind.

Here are a couple examples: Penny Steele lived in an apartment in the inner city. She was living with a man, and they both drank heavily. They fought bitter, brutal fights, and she would frequently call us to help her dig herself out of the latest mess she'd buried herself in.

She and her man were totally different people when they were sober; they were both nice, polite, pleasant, and easy going—mellow, even—when they weren't drunk. They were the stereotypical assholes when you added alcohol.

When I got the call to go to their apartment, it was always the scene of a brutal battle if they'd been drinking. I frequently took them both to jail kicking, screaming, spitting, and spewing venomous hatred at me all the way to jail.

One night, the dispatchers called me on the radio and asked me to call them on the phone. This was frequently done when the call required more information than could be put out on the radio.

The dispatcher told me that they had another call at Penny's apartment. They said she'd called in on 911 and asked for the cops to "come quick, her apartment was covered in two inches of water."

The dispatcher said they confirmed over and over that she wanted us to come because her apartment had flooded. This made no sense. She was a frequent flyer, and they knew I knew her as well.

The dispatcher was sure that it was some type of code.

She said that she was afraid that Penny had really got into trouble this time and had to be pretending to call a plumber and complaining about the apartment being flooded because her old man was going to kill her; she was sure that Penny was really in trouble this time.

I agreed that that was the likely reason for the call and started to gear up for the battle about to occur.

The dispatcher said, "We have no back for you; it's too busy—but she's called twice. What do you think, Slick?"

I told her yes, I would go.

I'd fought her old man many times, and if it was too hairy, I could always back out and wait for a back. I'd be careful and keep them apprised of what was happening.

I showed up at the apartment and stood outside for a few minutes, listening. It was creepy silent. Not a sound from the volatile people inside.

I knocked and stepped back away from the door two or three steps.

I heard someone walk to the door, and a kindly female voice said, "Who is it?"

This was the voice she used when she wasn't an angry, psychotic drunk.

I said, "It's the police. Did you call?"

The door opened slowly. I'd already drawn my gun, expecting the worst, ready to shoot whoever came through the door at me; instead, Penny peeked out and smiled when saw me.

"Hi, Slick," she said.

I said, "Hi, Penny. Are you OK?"

She said, "Yes, Come in; I need your help."

Really on edge now, I slowly walked in, gun in both hands, expecting Penny's old man to attack me at any moment.

I said, "Where's your old man?"

She said, "Oh we broke up after that last fight, he left."

That was unbelievable to me.

As I continued to search for him, she said, "Really, he's gone!"

I looked at her and thought, *Oh my God, she's finally killed him.*

I searched the apartment over and over, looking for him dead or alive.

Finally, she sat down, angry. She said, "Why don't you believe me, Slick?"

I told her I'd dealt with them many times, and it had never been easy; this was by far the most reasonable she'd ever been—and she had called 911 about her apartment being flooded. I told her the dispatcher was sure she was in serious trouble this time.

Penny giggled, then said, "I'm sorry, but I had no choice. Come in here."

Still expecting trouble and expecting the worst, I followed (gun still at the ready; our battles had been that intense).

She took me into her bathroom and showed me that her toilet tank had broken and cracked and that water had flooded the bathroom, bedroom, and living room. That was her problem.

I looked around and saw nothing else wrong.

She said, "I didn't know what to do, so I called."

I had her step out of the room; I didn't trust her to be at my back while I was turning off the toilet.

I turned the valve at the base of the toilet off, then brought her back in and told her how to shut it off in the future.

She was so relieved, she grabbed me and gave me a big hug.

I was surprised, and I admit not really being sure what to think. She was so fast, I was sure I'd get stabbed or bitten or something; I wasn't expecting to be hugged.

I left the apartment and phoned dispatch, telling them it really was about the apartment flooding. I ended the account with Penny hugging me.

The dispatcher said, "You're shitting me?"

"Nope, not this time."

Another 911 call.

Dispatch said over the radio that some guy had called and that he sounded really high. They suspected that he was hallucinating because he was making no sense. He called 911 to report some problem with his furnace, saying that he could hear a bird inside it. They said he was very rude and that they were sure he was a tweeker.

I arrived at the house with another cop as back up.

We contacted the guy who called, and at the time he seemed OK; not high, not crazy. He asked us to come in, and we did go inside the home.

I asked him why he'd called.

He said, "Where are your tools?"

Not the usual response I'd get to that question, so I asked again, "Why did you call?"

He rolled his eyes and said, "Jesus Christ! I told them to tell you to bring tools!"

I decided to play along; I didn't know what his issues were, but he obviously had something going on.

I said, "Well, first, before I get the tools, I need to know the problem, sir."

He said, "Oh! OK, follow me."

He walked to the basement doorway and went down the stairs ahead of us.

We followed carefully, a little on edge.

When we got to the basement, he put one hand on his hip and pointed with the other at the old furnace in the basement.

I said, "So, what's wrong with it?"

He rolled his eyes again, sighed, and said, "Don't you people communicate with each other? No wonder crime is so out of hand in this city! Imbeciles!"

I said, "Sir, maybe you can explain the problem?"

He sighed again and said, "I have a bird in my furnace, officer, and I want you to get it out."

I said, "What?"

He said slowly, in a very condescending voice, "I said I have a goddamn bird in my furnace, and I want it out—now!"

I stepped closer to the furnace, and sure enough, I could hear a bird trapped in the flue, chirping and scratching. Apparently, it had somehow fallen down the chimney into the furnace.

I turned to my backup, smiled, and said, "There is a bird!"

My back up laughed and said, "Really?"

The guy was livid.

He yelled, "So what are you gonna do about it? Isn't this what you're supposed to do? I call you, and you come and fix the problem? Fix the problem, geniuses!"

I'd had enough of this arrogant prick's shit.

He wasn't crazy; he was simply an arrogant dickhead.

I said, "We'll fix nothing—and you better change your fuckin' tone real quick. You called 911 to report a bird in your furnace; that's abuse of the 911 system, asswipe. Keep it up with your attitude, and I'll take your ass to jail."

I continued, "We have our tools with us at all times: a gun, tazer, pepper spray, and ASP. We're not here to fix your goddamn furnace—we're here to save your ass from a burglar, murderer, the crazed tweeker, or the neighbor who's sick of your shitty attitude and wants to beat the fuck out of you! You call the HVAC repair guy for your furnace and the bird inside of it; you don't call us."

He suddenly had an epiphany—the five-watt bulb burning brightly inside of his head—and decided to walk us politely back to the door and wish us a good day.

TWENTY-TWO

FATE CAN BE AN EVIL BITCH

SEVERAL WEEKS HAD GONE BY, and the college ride along had never returned.

I was pretty sure I'd scared her off and that there was no way she'd come back. I'd forgotten all about the business suit and jacketed woman trying to fit in on my calls in the inner city while everyone stared at her.

One day I came out of briefing, and the dispatcher said I had a visitor at the front desk. I never had visitors; I frequently had complaints, but never a visitor.

I thought to myself, *What now?*

Maybe the wife was serving me divorce papers. We hadn't gotten along for years. Could I be that lucky?

Anyway, I went to the desk expecting the worst, and guess who showed up? The college ride-along.

She'd remembered that she couldn't come dressed as Executive Of The Year and had showed up in blue jeans and a sweatshirt, wearing a jacket and ball cap. The transformation was amazing.

She said, "Remember me?"

Stunned, I said, "Um, ya. So where you been?"

She'd been in a car crash and had totaled her car, and this was the first chance she had to finish the course and complete the ride-along to get credit for school.

She laughed and said, "Is this plain enough?"

I guess it was plain enough.

Now I realized why everyone was staring at her; it wasn't the business suit she'd worn before.

We started out as usual, only this time the tables were turned.

She got in the car and said, "So...no comments, no talking, don't touch the radio or the heater, and stay by you at all times, right?"

She was smiling this playful, mischievous smile.

I said, "Ya, right" thinking to myself, *Shit, I am in real trouble now; this woman was hot as hell and was not in the least bit intimidated.*

It was payback time for me being such a prick.

She hadn't left intimidated; she had left plotting and, scheming, ready to return and issue some payback.

We handled a couple of calls, and then went to get a drink. Instead this time she got out first and walked in ahead of me. I am sure she did it to make sure I watched her walk in.

I admit, the tactic worked. I was speechless. Wondering how the hell I had missed the fact that she was hot as hell.

I got a drink and waited while she took her time. The clerk was the same guy from before, and he whispered as I checked out, "What the hell is it with you and the supermodels?"

I said, "No shit! Can you believe that is the same girl from a few weeks ago?"

He said, "No shit? Really? Wow!"

"Ya," I replied, "It is gonna be a long night."

I was right—but not in the way I thought it would be.

We left and started to patrol the inner city.

Slowly, we started to talk about her car crash and what had been happening since we last met.

It was pretty uncomfortable being in the car with her. The tables had definitely turned on me, and I was hoping for calls to keep my mind occupied.

Every call that we went on, the people continued to stare and whisper to each other while they watched her.

Women would be instantly defensive and scowl at her, looking down their noses at her.

The men would be sidetracked and distracted and have a hard time paying attention while I questioned them, wanting to turn and see where she was or stare at her.

The transformation was amazing to me; how just one thing, a person's appearance, could totally change the dynamics of how difficult it was to handle a call effectively.

The reality was she was that strikingly beautiful. Finally, a call came in where even she couldn't distract the bystanders.

Car crashes are among my least favorite calls.

Cops are like hunters in my mind, and there are trackers and trappers. Trackers like to pursue the bad guy, learning the street, reading signs of the jungle that's the inner city, watching the gang signs, graffiti, learning the hangouts and back routes that drug dealers worked. It was a mental game of chess, and to me, much more of a challenge. I loved it.

Traffic cops are more like trappers. They set a trap and wait to see who falls into it. Anyone who speeds is caught; doesn't matter if it's grandpa and grandma on a drive—they speed, they get a ticket.

To a traffic cop, they're called "Violators"; they violated the law.

To me, that was mindless work. I couldn't stand it. I hated it and talked shit to traffic cops every chance I got.

We got a call of a traffic accident at 59th and Reynolds.

I groaned. First, I had to deal with the Playmate Of The Year riding with me all night; now I had a car crash that would take hours of paperwork and keep me from being available to handle the "real calls" that were so frequent in my area.

We headed towards 59th Street as the information on the crash continued to come in.

Rosa Sosa, Anita Delgado, and Tira Santillian were driving around the city, cruising the streets, talking to friends, and checking out guys as they drove the city streets.

The girls were seventeen, sixteen, and fifteen years old. They would usually have been drinking beer and looking for a party to go to, hoping to meet up with some hot guys from school. Tonight, however, was different.

The three girls were each a couple months pregnant, and instead of beer they were drinking chocolate milk.

They were sharing the plans they had for their children's future, talking about possible names if the child were a boy or a girl. They were each excited and happy and sharing their thoughts with each other about the future.

Lloyd Sears, Brent Rowe, and James Nye were out that night as well. They were at a party, drinking beers and hanging out, trying to pick up some women in one of the inner city apartment complexes.

A fight had broken out, and shots had been fired. They were SP-13 gang members, and another family from SP-13 had shown up at the party. The two families hated each other, and a battle broke out.

The three guys jumped into a car and thought they were being pursued by their rivals. Lloyd was driving and had no intention of being shot. He hit the gas and wouldn't let up.

He was crossing the city, trying to lose the pursing shooters. He felt that he had to make it more dangerous for the shooters to chase him so they'd stop shooting. He started to run stop signs, gaining speed as he crossed the city.

Rowe would tell me later that they were yelling at him to stop. The shooters had dropped off and they were safe, but Sears wouldn't let up. He continued crossing intersection after intersection, gaining speed as he went. No matter what Rowe and Nye said, he wouldn't let off the gas and wouldn't stop as they blasted through stop sign after stop sign.

He made it through five intersections untouched and had reached sixty miles per hour when they approached 59th and Reynolds.

Rosa, Anita, and Tira had just left a small convenience store.

They'd stopped to use the rest room, laughing about how much more they had to pee since they became pregnant. Then, all three of them got into the front seat of Rosa's car.

Rosa was driving, Anita was sitting in the middle, and Tira was on the far right nearest the door.

They decided to go west on 59th and hit the main drag. They were looking for some cute guys they saw earlier and wanted to flirt with them, see if they could get them to pull over and talk. They had six blocks to go to reach the main boulevard.

When they reached Reynolds, they were all laughing about a joke that Rosa had made about her boyfriend.

Suddenly, Tira saw a bright flash of light as they crossed Reynolds and tried to scream.

I arrived at the intersection a few moments after the call of a crash came in, and I wasn't prepared for what it would look like. I stopped, stunned for a moment, trying to figure it out.

Rosa's car had been T-boned, hit on the passenger side at sixty miles per hour as Lloyd entered the intersection; he'd ignored the stop sign and slammed into the car full of pregnant young girls.

Tira caught a brief glimpse of his headlights before he slammed into the car door inches away from her.

The momentum of the impact drove Rosa's car sideways across the intersection, off of the road, and across the front yard of the house on the opposite side of the street from where Lloyd had entered the intersection. The car slid sideways across the front yard until it hit a tree. All three girls were inside.

Lloyd's car continued to coast forward. After losing all of its momentum from slamming into the girls' car, it came to rest on the side of the road in front of the same house that Rosa's car had slid across. Both cars were destroyed.

Lloyd Sears and Nye were somehow uninjured in the impact, and each ran from the scene. Rowe said his legs felt funny, and he couldn't run. He later admitted he was too stunned to think clearly and couldn't have run if he tried.

When I arrived, Rosa was still behind the wheel, conscious and awake. Anita was unconscious, hanging backwards over the front seat. Her torso was in the back seat of the car and her legs were in the front seat. Her pelvis was shattered. Tira was dead, hanging out the shattered passenger window, basically half in the car and half out.

I checked her pulse; it was gone. I checked her eyes; her pupils were blown, and all brain activity was gone. She died from the impact, and her unborn child had died with her. The other two girls were still alive, and I advised medical of the situation, requesting they hurry.

Once the supervisors arrived, they gave the call to the traffic units and called in the traffic accident reconstruction specialists. They determined that the speed Lloyd was traveling was sixty mph. when he hit the three girls. There were no skids; he hadn't tried to stop at all.

The remaining two girls were carefully removed from the crash by paramedics. Tira was also removed and transported to the hospital so her family could identify her body. I was tasked with locating witnesses—and with this being the inner city, few people would cooperate.

My ride-along watched all this and actually became a huge help. She noticed Rowe struggling to stand. He was hiding in the crowd that had gathered, and she went to talk to him. He admitted to her that he'd been in the car.

She came to me and said, "That guy was in the car," pointing at Rowe.

I rolled my eyes; I didn't believe her.

Every ride-along that ever rode with me thought they were special and could see what we didn't. The last thing I needed was her photogenic ass feeling that she could make a difference or save the day.

She grabbed my arm and said, "Listen to me! He was in the car; he can barely stand up because he's hurt."

I looked at her and saw that she meant it. This was not some narcissistic need to be noticed; she really was trying to help.

I went over and spoke to Rowe, and he told me that he was in the car. He told me what happened then asked me to help him. He couldn't feel his legs; he could stand, but he had no feeling at all in his legs. I called medical to him immediately and got him transported to the hospital.

This was a fatal hit and run, and the ride-along had found the only one of the occupants of the car hidden in the crowd. After this call, I looked at my college ride-along in a new light, and I listened to her comments as we rode together.

I continued to investigate and helped the traffic guys do their thing. Detectives were also brought in on the case and started to look for Lloyd and Nye.

Lloyd was caught later that morning and gave a full written confession. He was convicted of automobile homicide and sentenced to prison.

Rowe would be a key witness as to what had happened inside the car before the accident. His spine was damaged, and he would have medical problems for the rest of his life.

Rosa and Anita both survived the crash; however, both of them lost their unborn children from the violence of the impact.

I went home that morning and was pretty shook up. I couldn't get the image of the Tira hanging out of the car out of my mind.

My wife at the time asked me what was wrong, and I told her the story, hopeful that maybe she'd be able to understand just once what I went through. She sighed and said, "That's so sad that those girls were pregnant and not married."

I looked at her in disbelief. I said, "What? What do you mean?"

She replied, "It's just sad that they had no morals and were pregnant and not married."

I wondered silently, *Who and what the fuck are you?*

I never told anyone, but I didn't sleep for three days after the crash; it really hit me hard. The girl hanging out of the car dead, all three girls' babies dead. None of them had done anything to deserve what happened to them.

This was another thing I hated about traffic: the victims were random. There was no logic to any of it. I could make no sense of it.

I did, however, listen to the hot college ride-along from that point on. She had earned my trust.

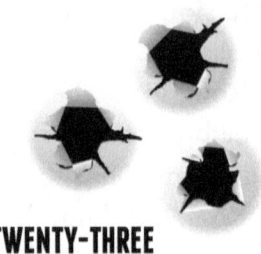

TWENTY-THREE
COPS ARE PARANOID FOR A REASON

PEOPLE ARE ALWAYS TALKING SHIT about how cops are paranoid.

They go to the mall and see bad guys everywhere. They go out for a drive and constantly worry about someone running the stop signs and hitting them. Don't even think about going out to eat in uniform unless you know the chef and the waiter. (Unless, of course, you're the Chief at one of the city's elite restaurants; no need to worry there, right?).

"Daywalkers" think that there's no way anything could happen. The rules are there to protect them, and of course everyone follows the rules…Ya, right.

Cops are funny about what they eat for a reason. The very nature of our job entitles us to information the rest of the world will never know – and sometimes it's stuff we *really* don't want to know.

There was this very popular restaurant on the east side of the city. It had a 50s décor and had food and soft drinks from the era. It did a lot of business. Older people in the city would fill the place, feeling it reminded them of a simpler, safer time.

The restaurant had music from the 50s, and the walls were plastered with posters from the 50s and pictures of movies and musicians from the era. Basically, it was a place to relive the memories of times gone by. The city's day people loved it.

One night, we got a call to the west side. It was called in as a domestic dispute. When we got the call, the woman who called was hysterical and in a rage. She was angry and sounded really upset. The patrol arrived and started to try and sort out what was going on. It was quite a mess.

The husband wouldn't talk to the cops, and there was no evidence that there had been a fight. The officers split the couple apart and tried to find out what had happened.

This was common procedure for most domestics. It allowed the couple to talk frankly about what the problem was and maybe open up a bit more than they would in the same room with each other.

The cop with the woman heard this story: they owned a large male German Shepherd, and it faithfully followed the husband wherever he went. It was a very loyal dog. It was the wife's dog, however, and this had irritated her immensely.

She did everything she could to try to win the dog's favor: bacon treats, long walks, and baby talk telling him what a great dog he was. Nothing worked.

As soon as the man walked in, the dog's ears would perk up, its tail would wag, and it would bark excitedly. As far as the dog was concerned, the woman had dropped off the face of the earth.

She was really mad explaining this to the officer, so mad she threw up a couple times, literally retching, and puking as she told the story.

The officer said that he thought she was crazy for being so angry about the dog liking her husband that it made her sick.

She continued. Tonight, she'd been at work at a local auto parts manufacturing company. Normally, she got off work at a specific hour. It was the same time every night; her schedule was written in stone. It never waivered. It never changed.

Tonight, however, the parts had been built, and the contract had been fulfilled ahead of schedule.

So, the manager had let the workers go early for the first time in years. Normally, they had to stay late to make the quota, but not tonight.

The wife was really excited to come home early.

Getting the unexpected time off made her really happy; she'd be able to come home and spend time with her husband. She emphasized this point to the cop, saying, "Imagine that I was excited to come home and see that motherfucker!"

The cop already knew what had happened. It happened a lot with our job.

One spouse or the other would get some unexpected time off and come home to find their better half locked in a passionate oral embrace with the neighbor's genitals—or even worse, the best friend of the unsuspecting spouse.

The rage and disgust suddenly made sense to the officer. That was what the cop thought as he listened to the story unfold.

He started to add his two cents about how he understood what she was feeling and asked if there was any way she could stay at a friend's house for the evening.

She was having none of this patronizing shit.

She pointed her finger at the cop and said, "Look, fucker, you have no idea what I feel! None! Shut the fuck up!"

The cop was new and didn't know yet never to assume anything on the street; never.

She chewed his ass for a while until he said, "OK, OK. Let me guess: you caught him with another woman, and you're pissed off. I'm sorry, lady, but it happens all the time."

The woman laughed and threw up her arms.

She said, "Really? You're telling me this happens all the time?"

He said, "Yes, spouses frequently come home unexpectedly and find their husband or wife having sex with another person."

It was heartbreaking, and he understood her pain, he said later as he told me this story.

She stared at him for a moment, then laughed hard and loud. A weird, angry, heartbroken laugh.

She shook her head violently and gagged again, coughing and spitting out bile.

She quietly said, "If only that was it."

She was silent for a moment, and the cop took that to mean that she'd caught her husband with another man.

It happened. Not as frequently, but it happened. He explained that he'd seen that as well.

He considered himself a veteran of the department now.

He'd been on the department five years and thought he'd seen it all. Well, he was almost right.

She looked at him with a dark, knowing look.

She was about to blow his mind, and she knew it.

She'd share her shock and disgust and put the young cop in his place.

She stood up and crossed her arms, gathering herself. He said she stared right into his eyes and started to tell him the rest of the story.

She had arrived home early and saw that her husband was home as well. He was a chef at the 50s-themed diner I told you about earlier.

They had both gotten off early that night, and neither knew the other was getting off outside their normal schedule. She was really excited that they both had time off together; unexpected time off.

She quietly sneaked into the house.

Dropping off her purse and keys quietly on the couch, she then slowly took off her clothes, leaving on her shoes and socks as she playfully stripped, quietly sneaking through the house, looking for her man.

When she stopped outside the bedroom, she'd dropped nearly all of her clothing. She was nervous with anticipation, hoping the expected encounter would be all that she'd built it up to be in her mind.

She said she dropped her panties at the bedroom door, then opened the door, expecting to surprise her husband; instead, she found this.

The husband had been working at the "diner" that evening, like she said. It was his normal shift. The restaurant had been slow that night for some reason. That was the nature of the fast food business. It's feast or famine. You're either so slow that you can't pay the light bill or so stacked up with customers waiting to get in that you can't possibly seat them all.

His manager had let him go early. The manager couldn't justify keeping two chefs in the kitchen with no customers, and it was his turn to be called off. He left the restaurant two full hours early. He arrived home to the excited, barking German shepherd—his best buddy! He let the dog out and started to read the paper.

A few minutes passed, and the dog was back at the door, scratching, wanting to be let in. He got up and let the dog in, then went back to take a shower. He was still kind of dirty from working over the grill at the diner and wanted to clean up.

Normally, this would lead up to a "Trojan" moment or maybe one of those funny lubricant commercials with rockets going off and the couple afterwards lying exhausted in bed; the showered husband and naked wife surprising each other, each coming home early and not telling the other.

Instead, the wife opened the door and found her freshly showered, soap-smelling husband lying on top of her German Shepherd.

He was sucking the dog's definitely erect penis and cupping its testicles while the dog was cooperatively staying very still.

They were all surprised by her sudden appearance in the room.

The cop told me he was sure he had heard her wrong.

But then he realized it all fit, her gagging and puking. The rage and disgust.

He said to me later, "What the fuck do you say to that? The woman caught her husband giving their dog a blowjob! How do you say you understand that?"

He said to make matters worse (in his mind) the wife was really amazingly attractive.

He said he thought to himself, *What the fuck, dude? You got a beautiful wife—and you wanna blow the German Shepherd?*

The wife glared at the cop and said, "What do you have to say to that, officer?! Still wanna tell me how you can understand my disgust? Well?"

She said, "Now, the dog makes perfect fucking sense as well! No fucking wonder the dog never liked me."

The cop said he was silent. He had no reply. He said he started to feel sick himself.

They arrested the husband for bestiality. He didn't deny the wife's claims and told the "veteran" cop he'd had a "problem" for years.

The beautiful wife started gagging again at this revelation and ran for the bathroom, dry heaving as the cops removed her husband from the house.

They put him into a patrol car to be booked into jail later.

So when you think of cops as paranoid and you're talking trash, wondering why they only go to certain restaurants, you may want to pay attention.

They may know who prepares the food.

TWENTY-FOUR
RECOGNIZING WHO IT IS MATTERS

ONE NIGHT, I HEARD A call go out in my area. I was busy writing reports, and the only reason I took notice was that the call came in as a loud party.

The complainant said that a large group of black men were playing music really loud and that they refused to turn the music off. The caller wanted the music turned down.

I heard the usual two units get dispatched then I heard Sergeant Peabody call out and say that he was also going to the call.

I knew this would end poorly if he pulled his usual shit. He wasn't known for diplomacy. The other two units assigned were new guys and would do whatever he said to do, even if it was obviously the wrong thing to do.

This was the new, up-and-coming cop's way of working: follow orders, no matter what.

The department had hired followers for years, trying to get rid of those that would think for themselves and not follow blindly.

I arrived to find the front porch of the house occupied by twelve guys listening to loud rap music. They refused to back down to three cops. I made it four.

I watched as Sergeant Peabody tried to bully his way onto the porch. He turned off the music, and then asked who rented the apartment. No one answered him, and as soon as he left the porch, the music went back up. Tempers were flaring.

This was gonna go to shit fast. It was no longer about music being too loud; it was now about respect and power. Who would be the first to blink?

Sergeant Peabody walked to each one of us and whispered that under no circumstances were we backing down; these motherfuckers would learn a lesson today to not disrespect the cops. I listened to him and nodded.

He had such a Black and White way of thinking. There were other alternatives, but he didn't see things that way. He was Black and White in everything he did, and in this case it was quite literally Black vs. White. It was also twelve against four.

I searched the group on the porch, looking for a leader among them.

Finally, I saw who the guy leading the defiant "stand against the man" was. It was a guy I had worked with and against many times on the street and in the Gang Task Force.

His street name was Ebony.

He was a major pain in the ass. He was the kind of guy who would always fight when he had a crowd around him. He never, ever fought one-on-one with anyone. He needed the crowd to feel safe and anonymous.

They had Ebony working them up, and we had Peabody. Two mental midgets not giving a shit about the outcome of the brawl that was definitely about to occur.

I thought about that for a minute and realized I needed to find a way to make the most out of Ebony's need to remain anonymous.

I stepped to the side quietly and switched frequencies on our radio. I had dispatch check Ebony by his real name on warrants. He had a minor warrant for a traffic infraction. I asked them to mark the inquiry into the warrant as 'Information Only Request' and went back to the group.

I called out to Ebony as he stood on the porch, quietly at first, then louder each time until he could no longer ignore me. I asked him to step away from his group and talk to me.

He said, "Fuck ya, motherfucker, I'll talk to you," as he hopped off the porch, jumping over the railing and strutting towards me in an attempt to prove that he wasn't afraid.

Several voices in his group said, "Kick his ass, man," "Don't take that cop's shit," and then, "We got them outnumbered!" "This shit is gonna be fun—kicking the popo's ass!"

We walked to the corner, away from anyone being able to hear what we said.

I said, "Hey, man, you see what's gonna happen here? This is gonna go to shit real quick."

He replied, "That's right, popo, it is! So you better take your white ass back to your car before it gets kicked!"

I laughed (getting pissed off) and said, "Look, man, I know you, and you know me. I was there the night you and Bobby kicked the shit out of Boo Rock. I know who you are, and if you don't know me, then maybe you need to shut the hell up and learn."

He replied, "So who the fuck am I, Mr. White cop?"

He glared at me, challenging me.

I told him his real name, and he stopped, stunned.

I continued, "I checked, and you have an outstanding warrant as well. No one here knows that except me."

He looked at me and quietly said, "I'm listening."

I said, "If this does go to shit, a lot of your homies are gonna get fucked up, no doubt a lot of my homies as well. You may have us outnumbered at the moment, but what you don't know is two K-9 units are on their way. The Land sharks are coming, so I'm giving you a chance to show real leadership."

He nodded and said, "Fo sho, Fo sho. Go on."

"The guy over there, the Sergeant, has already said that no way are we leaving or backing down. He wants to fight—and believe me, if he gets his chance, a lot of your homies will get seriously fucking hurt; that doesn't have to happen."

He was listening now, quietly watching the other cops as they watched us talk.

He said, "What do you suggest, man?"

I said, "Talk to your homies. Tell them I recognized the stripes, and out of respect to you we're letting you all leave. You have a warrant, and if this goes to shit, it'll all come back to you because I'm the only one here who knows the name of anyone in your group …do you get that? You're the only one here I know, you're in charge, and this will be on your head if it goes to shit."

He nodded and thought for a minute. He was no longer anonymous; there would be no hiding from this.

I could see I'd reached him. He agreed and made a big spectacle out of shaking my hand and thanking me.

He then strutted back to the porch and said, "Hey, fellahs, the man has shown me the respect I'm due. He recognized the stripes. Let's go; there's no need to make a stand here." (Whatever the fuck that meant, I don't know, and I don't care; it worked.)

No one wanted to fight, but no one wanted to appear to be afraid as well.

With Ebony willing to take the first step and announce that I'd recognized his "stripes," they could leave and save face with each other.

They did leave—and fast.

They really didn't want to fight, and neither did most of us—everyone, that is, except Sergeant Peabody. He was furious with me. He called me a fucking coward and stormed off.

Another night and another loud party.

We were called this time to a loud party in the 4200 block of Field. The landlord had rented the apartment to several known 18th street gang members, and they had invited the majority of the set to the apartment for a party.

I was called by one of the units there. They thought because I'd just left Gangs that I may have a rapport with the gang members and get them to shut down the party without a fight.

I tried to explain that 18th street hadn't been friendly with me and that West Side 18th street had actually had a hit out on me.

They laughed. "Ya, Ya, no one puts hits out on cops, Slick! You're so damn paranoid! You watch way too much TV. You're like 'Spooky Mulder' on the X files always seeing conspiracies!"

I sighed and said, "OK! If you say so."

I walked up to the door, knowing this wouldn't end well.

They'd already knocked once and asked the party to break up, and the person that they talked to agreed to break up the party and closed the door. Fifteen minutes later, nothing had happened.

I knocked, and the door opened. I recognized the guy who answered as Penguin from South Side 18th street. I told him the party was over; it was time to go.

He did the same thing as before, agreed to leave, and tried to close the door in my face.

I stuck my foot in the door so it wouldn't shut.

I said, "Look, motherfucker, we're trying to be nice—but if you push the issue, we'll break up the party by force. We'll put every fucking one of you in jail. You make the choice."

Penguin backed into the apartment and yelled out, "Pacman is here and wants to break up the party. He says we're all bitches and we will go without a fight!"

Shit...that wasn't what I had hoped for, but it was what I expected. I was never considered an ally to 18th street.

We ended up calling every available unit in the city to the party to make a statement to the gang.

When the cops show up and ask you politely to leave, take the easy way out and leave.

We took as many as we could to jail, and the others took off quickly; wisely escaping into the night.

There were some that fought us initially, but after the rest saw the outcome of those fights, they gave up. It all came down to respect.

Never try to close the door in the popo's face when you're getting a break.

TWENTY-FIVE
BRIGHT EYES

ONE NIGHT, I WAS SITTING on one of the main boulevards, talking with another cop.

It was snowing hard, and it was cold. We all got off the roads in weather like that, hoping not to have to drive too much.

As we talked, I noticed a woman walking down the road in nothing but a thin sleeping shirt and slippers. I said, "Hey, man, look at this: what's wrong with this picture?"

We watched while she walked down the sidewalk, aimlessly stopping and looking around, then walking again. She looked lost, and if she had been older I would have suspected that she was an escapee from a convalescent center, maybe someone who had Alzheimer's and thought they were on a beach somewhere in the Bahamas.

We crossed the street and stopped her, asking her name and what she was doing. She tried to give a response, but it made no sense.

We asked the same thing over and over and got gibberish as a response. We could tell that she thought that what she said made sense; watching her eyes and body language, it was obvious she knew we were there, but we couldn't make any sense of what she said.

We talked it over, and for her protection we decided to take her to the Emergency Room and see if we could commit her to the psych ward. We had no idea who she was or where she belonged.

While the other cop was taking her to the hospital, I tried to backtrack her footprints in the snow. It was snowing really hard, and I lost her tracks.

After five blocks, I knew about where she had been, but she'd wandered back and forth, walking in circles and sometimes doubling back. It was apparent she'd been out walking in the cold and snow for some time.

By the time I arrived at the Emergency Room about a half an hour later, the nurses had discovered her name; from that, they pulled up an address in their databases. They said she was diagnosed as a schizophrenic and that she had a daughter, a small infant.

We all looked at each other, worried about what that could mean. As lost as she was, and unaware of her surroundings, who knows where the baby was or in what condition?

I asked them for the last known address they had for her and cross-referenced it with the police department's database. We had two addresses that were different from their database.

I checked all three.

The first two were old addresses, and the people weren't happy to have been awakened at 3 a.m. looking for the ex-tenants. The third was a small garage in the rear of a house. The owners had renovated the garage and made it into a very small home.

I knocked on the door, and it swung open.

I was in central city, so I assumed nothing.

I pulled my gun out, ready to scrap with whatever came my way.

I called out, "Police! Is anyone here?"

I looked around the small house and immediately was creeped out.

The woman definitely lived here; the place was creepy as hell.

She had cut pictures out of every baby magazine that she could find, specifically the eyes of the infants. Then she plastered the infants' eyes all over the apartment.

Every square inch was a pair of baby eyes staring back at you. Every wall, every flat surface, every window covered with baby eyes glued to the surface. There were no pictures of complete babies; just the eyes. The shit creeped me out big time!

I was now even more apprehensive about the welfare of the child.

Searching the home, I found a crib and diapers, some baby clothes as well, but no baby.

I came into the kitchen and noticed that the oven was on and that there was smoke coming out of the oven.

I thought, *Oh shit! The crazy bitch has cooked her baby.*

I rushed to the oven and opened it.

There was a hunk of meat in the oven that was about the size of an infant. I could see what looked like legs and arms as well. I thought, *Fuck, I hate this job.*

Smoke came rolling out of the oven into the house, and the smoke alarms finally kicked in.

I looked for a potholder to try and get the pan with the smoking baby out of the oven.

Finally, I found one and removed the pan.

I was sick to my stomach with all the babies' eyes on the walls watching everything I did.

Trying to keep it together mentally, I waited for the smoke to clear and prepared to call for CSI.

Finally, I could see the baby, and the relief was incredible. What I thought was a baby baking in the oven was actually a large chicken.

I said a quiet, "Fuck me! This shit sucks ass!"

I threw the smoking chicken outside and cleared the smoke from the house.

I seriously thought that she had baked her child, and when I saw the shape of the chicken with four appendages, my mind filled in the rest.

I had to take a minute before I went back to the Emergency Room. This shit was traumatic; even though the child had not been baked, in my mind for a moment it had been.

I went back to the Emergency Room and told the other officer about the house, the baby eyes, and the oven.

We both laughed. It was all we could do.

By that time, we'd both seen a lot on the street; we knew anything was possible.

Still, we didn't know where the child was.

The Emergency Room had another point of contact that was in another state, and we called it.

The child was there. They had taken the child from the woman because she had gone off her medication and they didn't feel that the child would be safe with her. We all breathed a sigh of relief.

Several weeks afterwards, I'd have nightmares about the baby eyes and the burnt chicken in the oven. I'd wake up covered in sweat, breathing hard, thinking, *WOW! Man, that call really got to me.*

Sometimes, it wasn't the life-threatening calls that messed you up mentally.

Sometimes, it was simple shit like baby eyes quietly staring at you from all over the walls and ceiling and a burned chicken in the oven.

TWENTY-SIX
BRING YOUR MILKING BOOTS

EVERY ONCE IN A WHILE, I'd bump into one of the guys from my old department.

I left because I felt opportunities would be better in the city, and I felt like I'd never fit in there. The old department was rural law enforcement, and I had no feel for it at all.

I grew up in the city and had no idea what the difference was between a Western saddle and an English saddle. I didn't know the different breeds of cattle, chickens, or horses. I was lost in the world of rural law enforcement.

I could recognize the difference between a West Side 18th street gang member from a SP-13 gang member just from the way they dressed and how they carried themselves; still, I tried to understand the guys I worked with at that department and occasionally went to get a drink with them during slow times at work.

This incident would forever seal the fact that I didn't belong in that world.

There was a new convenience store on the border of the city and the county and both departments would mingle there during breaks.

I came in one night just to see who was there and what was new.

I saw two of the guys I used to work with when I walked in. They were sitting in a corner and called me over.

I bought a drink and headed over as they broke into a hearty laugh. I asked what was so funny. They wouldn't comment, instead asking what the latest was at the city.

We talked about the politics of the city police work, and the reality was that it was nothing compared to the politics in the sheriff's department.

We all knew that was a meat grinder that could destroy your career in a second.

Eventually, we ran out of things to talk about, and I said, "So what were you guys laughing about when I came up?"

They looked at each other quietly for a minute, and finally one of them started to talk.

He said, "You know how I own a dairy?"

I said I did.

He went on to tell me again how his family had owned the dairy for some time, and now he was running the family business.

He was about forty at the time and had recently been promoted to Sergeant.

He had been pretty successful since the new Sheriff had been elected and had risen through the ranks pretty quickly.

He said that he'd been forced to hire a lot of workers to keep up with the demands of the dairy and had resorted to hiring illegal aliens.

He said that he'd had a few problems with the workers and had to straighten one of them out.

He said, "I sort of wanted to make an example of him, ya know?"

I could see the gleam in his eyes, and I thought to myself, *That's what you get for asking, dumbass!*

He continued and told me that he and a couple of the large farm hands had discussed what to do to make an example of the outspoken illegal farm hand. They'd come up with a plan and waited for him to speak up before they implemented it.

They said that they didn't have to wait long. The worker started talking shit, and they grabbed him.

I thought they were gonna kick the shit out of him—but WOW, was I wrong.

He said that they brought him to a post and tied him to it, arms behind his back. They then brought up a young calf.

At this point, the other guy bursts out laughing; it was one of those good ol' boy laughs I never got used to.

The Sergeant said that he held the calf while the other two dropped his pants.

They were both laughing now.

He said he walked the calf up to the shit-talking guy's dick, and immediately the calf rammed the guy in the nuts. Then it started sucking on his dick.

Calves butt their heads into the cows' udders several times—hard—to get the milk to drop; this is normal behavior for a calf.

The calf kept butting the guy in the groin, then sucking on his dick.

They let the calf slam into the guy over and over for about ten minutes until he passed out from the pain.

This was the funny story they were telling each other when I walked in.

The Sergeant said that they never had any problem with any of the other workers after that and that the guy never came back to work after he left that day.

I looked at both of them and remembered that feeling I used to get when I worked with them, the feeling that the entire world had gone to shit.

The crime in the city, I understood; this good ol' boy shit was beyond me.

I got up and said, "Well, you two have fun sodomizing your cattle and chickens. I'm gonna go back to the streets; at least there I know no one would think of some fucked up shit like that!"

They didn't find the sodomizing comment funny at all; must have struck a nerve, I guess. Who knows? I don't wanna know.

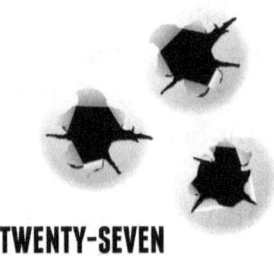

TWENTY-SEVEN
ALWAYS WEAR YOUR HELMET

SOMETIMES, YOU GO ON A call that's nothing close to what you think it'll be; nothing that you have any frame of reference for or would even know existed.

I had one of those calls one night.

I was dispatched to a home in central city. It was a large house and was home to a very large family. Grandparents, parents, an aunt and uncle, and kids all living in the same home. There was still plenty of room. The home was that big. Just one of the old mansions that had been built around the turn of the century by a wealthy railroad tycoon and was now in the worst part of town.

The call was supposed to be an unattended death, meaning someone had died and the family had called to request a mortician.

We always went to ensure that there was no foul play, nothing suspicious about the death.

I arrived at the same time as my back up, and we went to the door of the home. A middle-aged woman came to the door, crying, and asked us to come in. Everyone in the house was crying and upset. The mood was very sad.

There was also a weird undercurrent of relief. It wasn't the normal "unattended death" feeling from the family.

You always have to be paying attention to the things that are not being said in the communication when you're on a call. That's where the real details and information are.

I was already on alert. This wasn't the norm. There were tears, but the emotions were mixed…. grief and an overwhelming sense that this family was relieved that death had finally came.

We stopped for a moment and observed one family member after another showing the same conflicted emotions. I commented on this to the woman.

I said, "It appears that your family is in grief and relief at the same time," making a statement, not a question, waiting to see where the comment took her. She nodded in agreement and asked us to follow her to the basement of the home. We walked down a very old staircase to a renovated basement.

By this time, we had both unsnapped our holsters, and our hands were resting on the handgrips of the guns.

You never knew who you could trust or what you were being drawn into; this was really weird. So, you always assumed the worst and prepared.

We arrived at the basement, and nothing happened.

The woman began to explain to us that they had done all they could to protect the "girl."

They'd slept in shifts, each of the adult members taking turns at keeping watch. She said that they'd only let the "watch" slip for a moment. They thought she was safe, then realized no one was watching her.

I said, "So where is she?"

She opened a door to a room off a hallway, and there was a female lying naked, face up on the floor.

She had a large claw hammer on one hand, and her head was severely beaten. Her right eye was swollen shut, and the cheekbone on the opposite side of the swollen eye was caved in. She had several large dents in her skull.

The hammer was covered in blood, and hair and the blood still appeared to be moist. She appeared to be about twelve years old.

I looked around the room and saw blood splatters on the wall, typical of a homicide scene where a person had been beaten to death. There was a motorcycle helmet in the corner that was very pitted and damaged. It had blood on it as well. The whole scene was typical of a murder scene.

I looked at my back up, and we exchanged a look that communicated with eye contact only that this was not what it appeared to be. This couldn't have been an unattended death; it appeared to be a homicide.

I asked the woman how this had happened.

She said the girl was born "different" and that they'd tried to take care of her.

I asked the girl's age, and she said the girl was thirty-five. That wasn't possible; this girl looked twelve.

She said that the girl was born with a mental illness that caused her to try to harm herself. They had kept watch over her since the illness was discovered when she was very young. The woman said that the family kept her locked into the motorcycle helmet; she had to wear it night and day, or she'd slam her head into the wall or hit herself with a hard object like a hammer until she was stopped by someone else or knocked herself out. The girl had nearly killed herself many times.

The woman said the girl had been left alone for just a couple minutes today and had found a way of removing the helmet. She'd grabbed the hammer from the family's toolbox, which they kept in the basement and hidden in the room, closing the door. She then beat herself to death.

During this explanation, my back up had called for detectives and began to collect identification from all the people present.

We were pretty sure this was a homicide; not what the family was trying to portray. Most likely, the killer was still in the house, acting like they, too, were grieving.

I continued to interview the woman and looked for anything in her behavior that didn't fit, anything in her explanation that didn't make sense.

I had learned by this time that confrontation during an interview was pointless; instead, I let the people talk themselves into a hole while I documented the inconsistencies of their claims.

Although her claims were bizarre, everything fit: the physical evidence, the girl's injuries, the weird grief, and the relief emotions of the family. It all fit.

The detective who was assigned to the case arrived, and immediately the whole scene changed.

The other detectives on the department referred to him as Colonel Flagg, naming him after the paranoid character on the TV show M.A.S.H. The similarities were pretty accurate.

Flagg, the character on M.A.S.H., saw conspiracies everywhere; so did Detective Flagg, who loved to make a simple scene dramatic.

He had us detain the entire household, then called for the shift supervisor and Lieutenant. He criticized us for not calling him sooner. We had been in the house seven minutes when we called for him.

He came in, took one look at the scene, and loudly proclaimed, "This is a homicide. She's been dead a long time, and her skin is marbled." (Blood pools when a person dies, causing the skin to have a marbled appearance.)

He looked at the splatters on the walls and said, "That's high-velocity splatter. No way this girl could have created it. She's too short; a large male did this blood splatter!"

I'd been on cases with him before, and he was very theatrical and loved to be the center of attention.

He said out loud that the girl's physical appearance proved that the family had been starving her and that they had most likely killed her as well.

The family was shocked, and they were instantly outraged. Any cooperation we were going to get from them was instantly gone.

Anyway, in short order the theatrical Detective Flagg had turned the quiet scene into a circus, and we were banished to the perimeter.

After several hours, the body was removed and we were released to write our reports.

Occasionally, family members would be ushered out by patrol units and taken to the station for interviews.

A couple days later, it was determined that the girl had, in fact, killed herself. Her mental illness was well documented, as were her repeated self-inflicted injuries.

I went to Flagg's office to ask about the case.

His demeanor had changed; he was now confidently telling me how he'd disproved the homicide theory and that he'd known immediately when he arrived that it wasn't a murder.

I listened to him closely while he rationalized the day.

In his mind, the scene had changed. We had called him to report the homicide, but when he arrived he knew immediately that this wasn't a homicide.

He described the family's behavior, the girl's wounds, and the damaged helmet. He chastised me for not knowing better.

He looked down his nose at me, peering over the reading glasses he kept perched there, his lips pursed.

I said, "You know, there's just one thing I'm not clear on…"

He said, "What's that?" sure that he could clear up the discrepancy in my lack of understanding of the evidence.

I said, "At the scene, I clearly remember you making the comment that the blood splatters were caused by a large male. I know I was amazed that you knew the person who killed the girl was not only large, but was male as well, and you knew all that from just the splatters on the wall?! How did you know that?"

We stared at each other for a long time and said nothing. (Colonel Flagg could never be wrong on the show *M.A.S.H.*, and neither could Detective Flagg.)

His face was getting redder and redder, veins poking out on his forehead.

I admit, I was smiling a huge (fuck you) smile. Finally, I had the arrogant dickhead trapped in his own bullshit!

He blew up and threw me out of his office.

I've always had a way of making friends and smoothing out the ruffles in relationships.

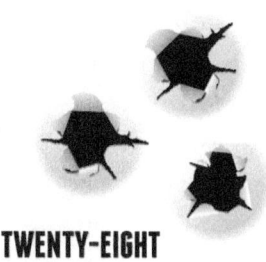

TWENTY-EIGHT
THE VOICES MADE ME DO IT

MARION COPE LIVED IN A rundown part of the city. It wasn't as bad a central city, but it was close.

The houses were all sixty years old or more, and they were built on the bed of an old river that had run through the middle of the city.

The river had changed course many years ago, and the land had been reclaimed and built up with houses, a community swimming pool, and an outdoor rodeo arena.

The area had been ravaged by gangs, and when meth hit the streets in the early 90s it was a knockout blow.

The area never recovered, the pool was closed, and the arena closed as well. Marion had been renting a house in the area.

He could afford the rent as long as he shared expenses with a roommate, so he had chosen to room with a friend he knew was in need of a place to stay.

His friend, Bill Williamson, had been kind of odd all through high school. They had stayed in touch through the years, and Marion never quite understood what bothered his friend. He knew that he had some kind of mental illness, but it seemed to be in check as long as he took his medication.

Marion didn't feel it was his place to ask about the illness. He believed that as long as he was fair to his friend, nothing bad would happen.

Bill Williamson never talked about the voices he heard. They would tell him things. Sometimes the voices were loud, sometimes a whisper. He would hear things, people walking past, voices, dogs barking. He would often turn to answer a question or reply to a comment and find there was no one there. The comments, questions, and whispers were all in his head. Usually, they were harmless comments; sometimes they weren't.

When he was on his medication, the voices became so quiet, oftentimes he'd barely realize they were there. Like a wisp of smoke appearing out of thin air across the room, he was never sure if they were really there or if they were his imagination.

One day, Williamson was walking back from the convenience store after buying some cigarettes. A neighbor had been dealing meth and offered Bill a small bit of the sandy, red-colored drug.

Mexican meth was red in color at the time. Each process of manufacturing meth creates a signature appearance. Sometimes it looks like little crystals of ice, sometimes yellow, sometimes red and brownish.

Bill was aware of meth and had never tried it. His doctors had given him medication that made the voices go away for the most part, but the medication made him feel fuzzy and he always felt like he was in a daze.

He asked the neighbor what the meth would do for him.

The dealer said the meth would make him as sharp as a razor and that things he had never understood before would become really clear.

Bill heard the magic words: "sharp as a razor."

That was what he wanted. To be clear, to think clearly, and to be able to function normally for once in his life.

He accepted the drug and went home to take it.

Bill was awake for three days straight the first time he took meth. He said he felt alive for the first time in his life. He had an amazing amount of energy, and his mind was racing, understanding things he'd never been able to before.

He felt he could fix anything. He took the television apart and was sure that he could find a way to make the phone work through the TV.

Finally, he came down and crashed.

Sleep came with a vengeance, and when he awoke he felt like shit. The dullness had returned.

He was exhausted. He had forgotten to take his medication during the three-day burst of energy the meth had given him, so he took a pill. The voices were loud now, telling him over and over that the pills he was taking were poisoned and that Marion had tried to poison him.

He ignored the voices, and after a couple days of pills, they subsided into the background of his mind, back into the fog.

A week or more went by, and Bill was out for a walk. The meth dealer saw him and stopped him and offered more meth, twice as much as he had the past time they had met.

He told Bill he could stay "up" as long as he took the drug, and he never had to come down as long as he kept taking it.

Bill liked how sharp he felt on the drug, so he accepted it and asked where he could get more when he ran out.

The dealer told him to come and see him; he'd make sure Bill was given as much meth as he could afford. He told Bill the meth was a gift, but now he'd have to buy it. Bill agreed.

He took the meth, and the high returned; not as intense this time, though, so he doubled the amount he took.

The voices returned and explained that Marion was a demon and that if he watched closely, he'd see signs of him being a demon.

Bill did watch, and on the fifth day without sleep he thought he saw for a brief moment something in Marion's eyes. A creature was behind the eyes themselves!

He jumped back, frightened.

The voices were right! Marion was a demon, and he'd been trying to poison Bill.

Bill left the house and walked for a while, unsure of what to do. He hadn't taken his medication for some time, and the meth had his tormented mind racing.

The voices were like a chorus; he couldn't shut them out.

They demanded that he kill Marion.

He had to save himself from the demon before the demon killed him. He made up his mind to do just that and went home.

He attacked Marion immediately after walking through the door.

Marion put up a good fight, but he didn't realize that Bill intended to kill him. Bill beat him senseless, then stabbed him, wounding him severely.

The voices weren't satisfied that the demon was dead.

Bill picked up Marion's head and looked into his eyes, looking for the demon hiding inside. He saw the demon hiding in fear, lurking behind Marion's eyes, flitting back and forth, trying to find a place to hide; trying to find a way out and kill Bill.

The voices told Bill he had to find a way to kill the demon. Only then would he be truly safe.

Bill went to the garage just outside the house and picked up a piece of rebar. He returned to the house and knelt over Marion, then stabbed Marion in the neck with the rebar.

Blood sprayed all over him as he pulled the rebar through the opposite side of the neck, then began to twist.

Bill twisted Marion's head completely off.

He then looked into the eyes of the detached head, trying to see the demon.

It was gone. He was safe.

He pulled Marion's body into his bedroom and hid it underneath the mattress.

Bill put Marion's head in a small garbage can in the kitchen.

Finally satisfied, he went back to trying to make the television work, adding wires and removing circuits.

His mind was racing, sure that he could repair it and make the phone and the TV work as one.

The fears of the demon in his dead friend were gone; the voices were quiet.

We got the call when friends of Marion's came over to the house, looking for him. They saw the blood sprayed all over the carpet and walls, and television parts and wires all over the house.

They began to search the house.

They went into Marion's room, smelling the unmistakable odor of a decomposing body, and saw the huge lump in the mattress.

Pulling up the mattress, they found Marion's decapitated body. They were horrified and called the police.

We found Bill in the garage, asleep. He was covered in Marion's blood, and when we asked him what had happened, he mumbled something about a demon and voices.

He was exhausted from the toll of the meth high.

It took the detectives quite a while to piece together what had happened in the house and why.

Bill had filled in the missing pieces of why he had twisted off the head of his friend after he was back on his medication and could think somewhat clearly again.

He claimed the voices had been silent ever since he'd killed the demon in Marion.

TWENTY-NINE

NEW AND IMPROVED ISN'T ALWAYS SUCH A GOOD THING

I HAD BEEN WORKING CENTRAL city for some time and started to notice an influx of heroin into the city.

I contacted a guy I knew in the strike force that dealt with narcotics and asked if they'd noticed it as well. He told me that there was no such resurgence of the drug in the city.

According to this expert, I must have been seeing a one-time event. Heroin was a thing of the past; meth was the drug of choice on the street, and no one would be interested in heroin as long as meth was around.

I told him that I had seen several cases and that it looked like heroin was back with a vengeance.

He laughed and said, "That's why you're on the street and I'm in here, on the Narcotics strike force. We're the experts, and you're the patrolman."

I was done trying to talk to this dickhead. I went back out on patrol.

Two days later, I got a call of an overdose. I went to the apartment and arrived well before medical. I went to the door and knocked, and a frantic man answered the door.

He said that his girlfriend had scored some "H" and that they were going to shoot up. He'd fallen asleep, and when he woke up she'd already shot up the drug and was lying on the bed. She'd stopped breathing. He was frantically trying to revive her.

I asked him how long she'd been asleep. He said for maybe an hour.

I looked at the woman's skin, and it had marbled. The blood pooled in a dead body and made the skin have a weird, marbled appearance. I could see she had been down for some time, the needle still stuck in her arm.

I looked at the frantic boyfriend, and I could see that he wasn't prepared to give up. There was no bringing her back, but he wouldn't accept that just yet.

I said, "OK, pull her off of the bed. We have to have a hard surface to start CPR."

He did pull her off the bed, and I said, "I'll do the chest compressions. You'll do the breathing."

I showed him what to do, and we started. He forced about four breaths into her lungs, and then she aspirated the contents of her stomach into his mouth.

This is the reality of CPR you never see on the TV: you get a mouthful of puke because some of the air always goes into the stomach and pushes the contents up the throat.

He wasn't deterred. He kept at it, trying to breathe life back into her and spitting out the puke as it blew back into his mouth.

Medical eventually arrived, and they could see she was dead; however, once CPR is started they have to continue. They could see this was pointless and asked me what was up.

I told them the boyfriend wasn't ready to give up. I'd started the CPR for his benefit. He needed to at least try to bring her back.

After a few minutes, they took him aside and explained that she was gone. He agreed. As awful as it sounds, he could taste the reality of her death. He was very upset but kept repeating, "At least I tried... at least I did everything I could...at least I tried."

The boyfriend had told me that they had scored some Mexican heroin and that it was supposed to be the best there was on the street. They were told it would be the best high from heroin they'd ever had.

I asked him what was supposed to be different about the heroin.

A paramedic on the scene spoke up. He said that they'd been on several heroin overdoses in the past two weeks. The heroin that had hit the streets was 99% pure. That was why people were dying.

In the past, heroin had hit the streets 60% or maybe 50% pure. The users then cut it down even more, making it safe to inject. The new batch was assumed to be as impure as the old stuff. It wasn't. So when the users cut it down and injected it, they were injecting a lethal dose. There would be no surviving this high.

We were cleaning up the scene afterward, and the paramedic had removed his surgical gloves, the same ones we all wore on scenes like this. He had picked up a flashlight that was on the nightstand and offered it to me. He said to me, "Here's your flashlight, officer."

I told him that it wasn't mine. I had my flashlight in my back pocket. I asked the Fire Battalion commander if it was theirs. He said no, that they all had their flashlights.

The boyfriend was watching this conversation, still kind of in shock from seeing his dead girlfriend.

He said, "I think it might be ours."

At the same time, the paramedic commented on the sticky stuff coating the outside of the long, black steel flashlight. He was throwing it up in the air and catching it.

The boyfriend shook his head and said quietly, "Umm...ya... you might wanna put it down."

The paramedic said, "Why?"

The boyfriend replied that the flashlight was the dead woman's dildo. He said that she had used it often and had been using it before they bought the heroin a couple hours before.

The look on the paramedic's face was priceless. He didn't catch the flashlight again and let it drop to the floor. He began trying to sanitize his hands.

The entire fire crew erupted in laughter and wouldn't give him anything to clean off his hands. He ended up going into the bathroom and frantically washing his hands. Even the dead woman's boyfriend laughed.

The heroin that had hit the streets had been found over and over to be too pure for its users. The suppliers were killing off their customers by offering the new and improved heroin. Word would be out soon to be careful of the new product. There would be several dead heroin users in the next few weeks before the word made it out to everyone.

I made sure to forward every case involving a heroin overdose that I was involved with to the Narcotics strike force, making sure the brilliant agent I'd talked to received each copy. So much for being in touch with the streets.

THIRTY
SOMETIMES THINGS GOT OUT OF HAND

COPS WERE CONSTANTLY PLAYING PRANKS on each other.

Jim Handy and Kevin Larson were competitors in the department. They'd been in patrol together on the same squad, working the same shifts. They each had a wicked sense of humor.

The two cops were every Sergeant's nightmare.

They were constantly pushing the limits of what they could get away with, breaking rules they could get away with breaking, and bending the ones they couldn't.

One of the long-standing rules was that we couldn't leave the city to eat lunch.

After several years of eating at the same restaurants, the temptation to eat at a new restaurant outside of the city was too great for the two officers. They started to sneak out of the city at lunch and eat at a newly opened restaurant.

After they'd been going there a while, Jim got up to use the restroom and left without paying for his food, leaving Kevin to pay for the bill.

Jim laughed about it the next day in briefing, telling everyone that he'd stuck Kevin with the bill. Of course, the cops ridiculed Kevin for being so dumb and falling for the prank.

Kevin was plotting his payback.

He pretended that he was OK with the prank and continued to go to the restaurant. Jim would go with him, but he knew payback was coming; he just didn't know when or where it would be coming from.

One night, Kevin finally set Jim up. He went to the vehicle fleet manager and was able to get a copy of the key to Jim's patrol car. He had to pay the guy extra to make the key and explain what he planned to do with it. He agreed to return the vehicle key when the prank was over.

They went to eat as usual, but what Jim didn't know was that Kevin had told the dispatchers to give him a fake call about ten minutes into the meal.

Kevin received the call and went out after paying for his meal. Jim was comfortable now, relaxed that at least today nothing would happen. Kevin left and picked up another cop. They drove back and took Jim's car from the parking lot of the restaurant. They drove it to the center of town and parked it in one of the busiest intersections.

The car was running, emergency lights, headlights, and warning flashers turned on, and the siren blaring. The doors were locked.

It took about two minutes for the Sergeant to find the vehicle and ask Jim over the radio why his car was parked in the intersection, lights and sirens blaring.

Jim ran out of the restaurant; his car was gone.

He had to explain why he was out of the city, and he had no explanation as to how his car had ended up in the city without him in it. Kevin was covered; he was on the fake call. Everyone heard it dispatched. But Jim knew what had happened. You'd think that they'd stop here...nope.

Kevin was married and had a really hot girlfriend on the side. He'd met at her at work, and he'd told her that he was single and that he could only see her occasionally because he had to work so much. He told her that he had to pay child support and picked up all the extra shifts that he could (he had no kids at the time), lying to cover his frequent absences when he was with his wife. The hot girlfriend believed him, and for a while he was able to cover his tracks with both women.

Jim thought this over and saw a way to one-up Kevin supremely.

Jim was talking one night about his new girlfriend. Jim was divorced and frequently dated different women. He was at Kevin's house and asked Kevin and his wife if they'd like to go out to eat with him and his new girlfriend. He said he felt that she really might be "the one," and he wanted them both to meet her. He raved on and on about her and convinced the couple to go out to eat with him and the new girlfriend.

Jim was sneaky as hell.

He'd talked to Kevin's secret woman on the side and told her about Kevin's wife. He agreed with her that Kevin was an asshole and a pig. He let her get herself really worked up and furious, adding in comments here and there about how Kevin had played her. He suggested that they play a prank on Kevin and pay him back in a way that he deserved. She agreed.

The night of the dinner date came, and Kevin and his wife arrived as they had planned. Jim made them wait, making sure they were seated and that Kevin had no escape. Then he walked in with Kevin's secret woman on the side.

He sat down and introduced Kevin's girlfriend to Kevin's wife, the two men eyeing each other, Jim smiling huge, Kevin seriously about to shit himself.

The two women talked about their men, and the hot girlfriend asked Kevin's wife how long they had been married. She explained that they'd been happily married for five years! They were thinking about having children but hadn't had any yet.

The girlfriend nodded; some day she wanted to have children, too, she just hadn't found the right man yet (glaring at Kevin).

Kevin's wife was unaware of the nonverbal communication going on and just kept chatting about their lives and how beautiful their wedding had been. The girlfriend decided to turn it up a notch or two.

She had arrived dressed to the max, and she'd turned on the heat, making Kevin squirm as much as possible. She started rubbing on Jim and kissing him, whispering how she couldn't wait to leave the restaurant and fuck his brains out; she whispered this just loud enough for Kevin and his wife to hear.

Kevin's wife was shocked. She was a churchgoing girl, prim and proper; the word 'fuck' had never left her mouth in public. She was disgusted and misinterpreted Kevin's obvious discomfort as the same disgust; it wasn't.

Kevin was forced to play the part, watching his best friend and his now ex-girlfriend rubbing and dry humping each other in the restaurant.

Eventually, they all left, Kevin and his wife in one car, and Jim and Kevin's now ex-girlfriend in the other. The hot girlfriend made sure that Kevin saw her rubbing Jim's dick with her hand in his pants pocket as they walked to the cars. Kevin was furious, but the night wasn't over yet.

A half an hour went by with Kevin listening to his prim and proper wife complaining about the slut that Jim was dating. She asked Kevin how Jim could possibly think that she was "the one?" Why couldn't Jim see what a slut she was? Kevin was silent.

Kevin and his wife arrived home, and the phone rang. Kevin raced to the phone, afraid to let his wife answer, afraid of what she might hear or be told. He said, "Hello?"

His girlfriend was on the other end, moaning and panting. She had called to let Kevin know that she was having sex with Jim and wanted him to hear it while it was happening. She and Jim passed the phone back and forth, commenting to Kevin about how great dinner was while they fucked and talked on the phone.

All Kevin could do was listen and fake the conversation, nodding and responding to their comments. He was afraid that if he hung up, they'd call back and his wife would answer; then who knows what she'd hear?

Jim won this battle big time. Kevin had nothing that could top this. When Jim shared this in briefing one night, we all laughed so hard, we could hardly breathe.

Kevin had finally been humbled, and no one could believe the perfection of the prank. It was a thing of beauty in the Cop world.

THIRTY-ONE
SENDING OUT POSITIVE ENERGY MAKES ALL THE DIFFERENCE

LISA JUDKINS AND HER BOYFRIEND, Travis Meeke, were both adventurers.

They had met in California and had decided to go on a road trip to see the world. They had read many stories about people in the late 1960s and early 1970s traveling the country and living out under the stars. The both longed for what they felt was a simpler time: the 60s and 70s. They were raised near Berkeley and had heard the stories about the era all their lives.

The second week of their amazing trip to see the real world under all the technology and falseness of the modern world had them landing in the rail yards that ran through our city.

Lisa was a beautiful girl and immediately attracted attention in the homeless shelters they frequented. Travis was very proud of the woman he was with and that she had chosen him to be her man.

They were total misfits in the world of the homeless. Young, beautiful Lisa, and smiling, shiny Travis. So in love, they were unaware of the company they were keeping. They actually believed the hippie bullshit they'd been told about the world at Berkeley.

Travis told me that he thought that if they sent out positive energy to the world, the world would return it. They were friendly to everyone they met.

They had taken up residence in an abandoned railroad caboose in the rail yards and had stayed there several days, keeping a regular schedule. Eating meals at the homeless shelter, meeting people, and talking to everyone in this totally naïve and unaware state of mind. Many people had noticed them.

The third night after they ate, they said goodbye to everyone at the soup kitchen. They were leaving in the morning for whatever the road and the railways would bring them. Smiles on their faces, they waved goodbye and headed back to the caboose.

They had no weapons, they hadn't locked the door to the caboose, and they had nothing but their positive energy to defend them from the real world.

About an hour after they went to sleep, the caboose door opened, and in stepped a man.

He had an aggressive attitude and beat the shit out of Travis, forcing him out of the caboose. He then pulled a knife and began to rape Lisa at knifepoint. She screamed over and over for Travis to help her.

Travis was her boyfriend, but he was no defender. He was gone, he left her and went for help—or at least that's what he said later. He eventually did get help, but it was much later.

Lisa was raped by the unknown assailant many times, both anally and vaginally. He beat her repeatedly while he raped her. When he'd finally finished beating and raping her, he held her down.

She later told me that he said he wanted her to remember this night for the rest of her perfect fucking life. He took the knife and cut deep cuts in her beautiful face. The rapist then left the caboose.

She screamed for Travis, but he was long gone.

We searched the rail yards and homeless shelters for anyone who might have heard or seen anything. No one knew a thing. Everyone knew the pretty young couple we were asking about. Everyone had seen them. The list of possible homeless men mentally ill enough to pull of the rape was huge.

To make matters worse, Lisa and Travis never saw the rapist's face. The caboose was pitch dark. They could barely see anything from the huge ballpark-style lighting that illuminated the rail yards.

Lisa and Travis flew home to their parents a few days later, their world tour cut short by reality.

The people at Berkeley were full of wonderful, amazing stories about traveling the world in the 60s and 70s. The problem was, the people who told those stories were the lucky ones who had survived.

The bodies that ended up buried in deserts and fields all over the country had no such stories to tell. They'd faced the same reality that Lisa and Travis had. Their positive energy hadn't protected them.

THIRTY-TWO
YOU REAP WHAT YOU SOW

ONE NIGHT, I WAS SENT to back up officer Divot on a fight at a hotel.

We arrived at the hotel, and Divot started doing what he called investigating. Basically, he belittled people until they either told him something or he got tired and just arrested them; this was his way of "investigating."

I arrived, and Divot asked me to keep one of the guys he had cuffed inside of my car while he interviewed the other.

I sat the guy inside of my car after Divot had searched him. He was handcuffed, and we sat there for some time, watching Divot talking shit to the other guy.

I started to talk to the suspect in my car. He said his name was Gary.

I asked Gary, "What happened here tonight? Why were the two men fighting?"

He wouldn't reply. He said they weren't fighting and he had no idea what I was talking about.

I told him, "Look, man, honesty goes a long ways with me. Tell me what happened, and maybe we can work shit out."

He was silent for a long time, then said, "Honestly?"

I replied, "Yes, honestly."

He said nothing for some time. I could tell he was really tired, exhausted more like it. Sweating profusely and tired.

It was cold outside, so his sweating told me he was most likely on something.

I just waited. Finally, the silence was too much, and he started to talk.

He said, "My name isn't Gary; it's Ronnie Bennett."

I nodded, remaining silent.

He said, "We, me and the other guy, were fighting over meth. I was gonna sell him some meth, and he tried to rip me off. I'm not gonna be ripped off by some fuckin' tweeker."

I said, "So do you know this other guy's name?"

He said no, that he just sold him "Ice," and that was it. They'd meet after the other guy called him, and he'd sell him some "Ice."

I said, "By 'Ice', you mean meth—the clear stuff?"

He said yes, that he wouldn't deal the dirty stuff that was on the street now. He had standards and wouldn't compromise by selling what he thought of as dirt.

This surprised me—a meth dealer with product standards—but I said nothing.

Divot had finished investigating and returned to my car. He asked me what I'd learned from my suspect.

I told him the guy's real name and that the fight had been over meth.

He said, "Is he carrying?"

I said, "You searched him; you tell me."

Divot blew up. Handling any call made him tense and edgy.

Personally, I think he was afraid that people would realize he had no idea what the fuck he was doing.

He was happiest polishing the brass, cleaning guns, and bragging about the latest SWAT call he'd been on. He did best in very structured environments. He fell apart in the chaos of the street. It was too chaotic and complex for his black-and-white thinking.

Anyway, Divot threw a few insults my way, then called my suspect a piece of shit, telling him that his meth problem would get him landed in jail tonight. He threatened Ronnie with being raped in the jail if he didn't start talking to me and stormed off.

I rolled up Ronnie's window and said, "Jesus, that guy's a dick."

Ronnie laughed; he agreed.

We were there a few more minutes, and finally I told Divot I'd take my guy to jail and get the paperwork started. He agreed, and I left the scene.

I arrived at the jail and asked Ronnie my standard question: "Are you carrying anything? Because once we're inside, if they find anything, you'll get charged; out here between me and you, it's another thing."

Ronnie looked at me, staring long and hard, then finally said, "He missed something when he searched me. I have some Ice on me now."

I said, "Where is it?"

He said, "It's in my shirt pocket."

I looked in his pocket, and there was a baggie sealed with about a gram of Ice in it. It was clear and looked just like small crystals of Ice.

I said, "Jesus! That's about the purest stuff I've ever seen."

He agreed.

I spoke to him for some time outside the jail about meth and the toll it was taking on his life. He was twenty-five years old and looked forty.

He was worn out. The life of dealing and using had beaten him down fast.

The more we talked, the more I could see he was hearing me. He started to cry, then really started sobbing.

I let him cry for some time until he gathered himself. He told me to keep the Ice, he wouldn't tell anyone.

I said, "What do you mean?"

He said he'd been stopped by cops several times and they'd taken his Ice for themselves.

I said, "Oh ya? Like who?"

He wouldn't tell me who, but his body language and eye contact had me wondering.

I told him I'd give him a break tonight. I'd throw the Ice away. I wanted no part of that shit.

I parked in front of a dumpster and made sure he watched me throw it away.

I took him into the jail and started the paperwork. When it came time for his charges, I only added what Divot had wanted him charged with: disorderly conduct.

He stared at me and said, "Why aren't you charging me with the drugs?"

I said, "I told you, honesty goes a long way with me. You were honest, so take this break and do something with it. Keep going the direction your headed, and you're gonna be dead before you're my age."

He stared at me in disbelief.

I told the correctional officers that Divot would be coming in for him and that these were the only charges he had.

Ronnie just stared at me quietly as they processed him. I told him to take care and left the jail, headed out to the next call.

Several months later, I was at the mall with my wife and our three little kids.

I didn't look the same out of uniform. I looked totally different; combing my hair different and wearing baggy clothes, people rarely recognized me.

I was walking along with my kids in front of me, their mother closer to them than I was.

I heard a voice say, "Officer Fortier?"

I turned, and there was Ronnie with two of his friends.

I checked my kids; they were still headed away from me. We were on the top floor of the mall. I started to slowly walk to the rail overlooking the bottom floor of the mall.

Ronnie reminded me of who he was while his friends walked on either side of me. Basically, I was surrounded.

No problem, as long as the kids kept going with their mom. They had no idea of this world; unfortunately, they were about to get a close up of what Dad did at work.

I walked to the rail so I had my back to something while Ronnie talked. I told him I remembered him, and he kept making small talk.

I didn't know what he wanted, but I'd made my plans already if he decided to fuck with me. I'd already checked, and none of them had weapons. No bulges in their clothing, nothing apparently hidden.

They were all about my size, so no one was a monster to fight. I sized them up, picking out which guy I'd go for first.

They were acting cocky, comfortable, self-assured, having me outnumbered three to one. That was a mistake.

Ronnie was about to go head first over the rail.

One guy had his hand in his pockets—he'd be next; he wasn't paying attention to me, and that would be his mistake.

The third guy was leaning over the rail, watching the girls below us. I figured he'd be the last I'd have to worry about; he might go over the rail as well.

Reality was, they were all tweekers.

I might end up hurt, but I'd fuck them up. I did this shit every night, outnumbered and overwhelmed.

While I was talking to Ronnie and planning his beat down, I heard my wife's voice say to my oldest son and daughter, "Go tell Daddy we're hungry and we want to eat."

A few moments later, I felt tiny hands wrapping around my legs, and I looked down to innocent little faces smiling at me.

"Daddy, we're hungry!" they said together.

I looked at Ronnie, and he smiled. "These are your kids?"

I told them to go now to their mother and pushed them off me.

Looking back now, I realize that my kids were never in any real danger. If Ronnie had wanted to jump me, he could have. He recognized me way before I saw him.

I started to casually close the distance between myself and Ronnie. I would have to hit first—and hit hard. No fucking way I'd let these guys touch my kids.

I started to close the distance, and he must have realized I was about to strike; he held up his hands and said, "Wooaah! Wait a minute, man—you misunderstand me!"

I stopped. Up on the balls of my feet, I was ready to fuck him and his homies up if they laid one finger on my kids.

Ronnie said, "Easy, man! Easy! I just wanted to thank you. I thought about what you said, about the meth and giving me a break. I had a lot of time to think in jail. I talked to several of the inmates in jail, and they knew you. They said you always treated them with respect, so I figured you were legit. I just wanted to say thanks, man. That's all."

He stared at me, smiling.

Still not convinced, I looked to make sure the kids were back with their mother. They were, but she still hadn't clued in to the body language.

Ronnie stuck out his hand and asked me to shake his.

He said, "Thanks!"

I shook his hand, waiting for the attack that never came, planning to break his arm first, then go to work on the other two.

Nothing happened; no attack.

He left the kids and me alone after thanking me over and over again for giving him a break.

Almost as an afterthought, he said, "You're good with me, man; your kids are safe! Have a good day, Slick."

I guess my state of mind must have at least been obvious to him.

It wasn't to my wife.

We sat down to eat, the adrenaline still flowing.

I wasn't hungry. She said, "So who were those nice boys you were talking to?"

I stared at her for a minute, dumbfounded, and said, "No one; just guys from work."

She said, "Well, they seemed nice."

I sat in disbelief, still trying to come back down from gearing up to fuck up Ronnie and his crew.

I never went to the mall again with my kids or their mother. She had no common sense for the world I worked in, and I couldn't jeopardize my kids by being there in a crowd of what she saw as "nice boys."

THIRTY-THREE
BE CAREFUL WHEN YOU POKE THE BEAR

ONE NIGHT, I WAS SENT to the Emergency Room to pick up a guy who had been arrested and had been injured in the arrest.

It happened often enough. People don't want to go to jail with a smile on their faces. Some fight back, literally, and in the battle for their freedom they get hurt. It doesn't have to be police brutality, although that definitely can happen when you have to fight night after night, call after call.

I arrived, expecting to find a guy that maybe had a cut or a scrape that would keep him from being booked into the jail.

I asked the nurses where the guy was that I'd been sent to pick up. They gave me an accusing look.

I was puzzled; usually, they were talking all kinds of shit, joking, talking trash to me, and making smart ass remarks.

They weren't friendly at all, not joking. They had a serious and critical attitude.

They said, "He's back there in Room 6. The doctor isn't done yet."

One of them said, "What the hell happened to him?"

I told them didn't know, that I was just sent to pick him up. I didn't know about anything that had happened.

They looked at me disapprovingly, then replied, "Uh huh, sure."

I thought to myself, *What the hell is wrong with them? Moody ass nurses!*

I lived with one; they were all crazy. I'd seen this disapproving look many times at home for no reason at all.

I shrugged my shoulders and went to the room, pulling back the curtain and being surprised at what I saw.

I found a guy about thirty-five being treated by a doctor and two nurses. He had a catheter in that was draining urine from his bladder. The urine wasn't the usual clear or yellow color; it was bright red with blood. The guy was crying and looked seriously hurt.

I watched for a minute and saw them checking his blood pressure and monitoring his heart rate. This couldn't be right; I must have entered the wrong room.

I pulled back the curtain and checked the room: yep, it was #6. I thought, *What the hell? This guy must be a DUI.*

He'd obviously been in a crash and had been seriously hurt. They'd patched him up enough to book him for the DUI, but I'd been sent to book him into jail for a burglary. This made no sense. They must have two people up here to go to jail, not just one.

I went back to the nurses' desk and told them I was here for someone else. This guy looked like he'd been in a car crash; I was here for the guy who had resisted arrest on the burglary.

They looked at me for a second, and no one said a thing. Then one of them stepped up and replied, "You don't know, do you?"

I said, "Know what?"

I didn't even hear anyone transported to the hospital. I was way too busy working the central city area to listen to the radio for every call that went on.

I said, "I was sent because I had a break in the calls, and you guys said he was ready."

This guy had obviously been in a car crash. He was pissing blood and still in shock. He was still shaking from the trauma.

The nurse who had spoken up motioned for me to follow her, and we walked back to Room #6.

She pulled back the curtain, and we went in. She handed me a large plastic bag and said, "These are his clothes. We double-bagged them. You'll wanna put them in your trunk because they're pretty rank."

I said, "OK"; that wasn't unusual.

DUIs frequently pissed their pants, and oftentimes they were so drunk they'd shit their pants.

Nothing yet to explain to me where the burglar was.

I set the bag down and said, "So where's my guy? This is a DUI, right?" The doctor stopped and stared at me.

He said "No, this is the guy your guys brought in to be treated."

I said, "What happened?" The doctor stared at me disapprovingly.

He said, "He'll be ready in a second, then you can take him. You'll have to leave the room while we clean him up and remove the catheter."

I was baffled.

The whole emergency room was acting weird, as if I'd just done something they really didn't like. I was in the ER every night and had never been treated like this before.

I stepped out of Room #6 and had had enough.

I said to the nearest nurse, "What the fuck is wrong with everyone tonight? Jesus Christ, you guys act like I'm your worst enemy."

She didn't reply.

I was fed up; I had to deal with this moody shit at home, and I had no patience for it at work.

I called the dispatcher on the phone and asked her who I was here to pick up, specifically the name of the person. I told her they were trying to get me to take a DUI to the jail, which I could do, but I wanted to make sure I took the right person.

She told me the suspect's name.

I looked on the board that the nurses wrote the patient's name and room number on to track the constant flow of emergencies through the Emergency Unit. The names matched. The doctor pulled back the curtain and said, "He's ready when you are."

The suspect stood up on shaky legs. I picked up his double bagged shit and piss-soaked clothing and took a hold of his arm.

I had to walk him out of the Emergency Room carefully. He was shaking severely and still lightly crying and gasping for air. He'd been really traumatized. He looked like shit.

I sat him in my car, hands cuffed in front; cuffing them in the back was out of the question. He was hammered. I put the bag of clothes in the trunk and got in my car.

I started it up, then said, "OK, man, what the fuck happened to you?"

He said, "One of you guys beat my ass 'til I shit myself and pissed blood—that's what fucking happened!"

I was thinking, *Ya, sure;* I'd witnessed many incidents of street justice, and none came close to this. He seriously looked like he'd been in a bad car wreck.

I said, "So what caused this to happen that you were beat so severely?"

He said, "Nothing. I was just walking down the street, and this cop pulled up and beat my ass."

No way that had happened.

I listened to him sob and whimper all the way to the jail. I took him in, and they already had the paperwork for him filled out.

I asked who the arresting officer was. They told me Riley Wilson.

I was shocked.

Riley worked my area and was notoriously lazy. That he had made an arrest at all was hard to believe, but that he did anything like this was nearly impossible to believe.

I said, "Can I see the paperwork?"

They showed it to me, and I saw that it was in fact Riley Wilson.

I said, "Jesus, he arrested someone?"

The booking officer laughed and said, "Yeah we had to show him how to fill out the paperwork; he said it was a new form and he wasn't familiar with it."

I laughed because they'd changed the form two years earlier; that was how often Riley went to the jail.

I constantly talked shit to Riley. We'd worked the same area for an entire year and he'd been a ghost in the area. I'd hear him on the radio, but he never showed up to any of my calls.

Riley was an ex-pro football player. He was huge, but in my mind he was a paper tiger.

He was insanely polite. I mean that literally. It drove me insane. He was like an English butler in the body of Junior Seau or Ray Lewis. A monster with disturbingly polite manners.

We were polar opposites. I was 5'11" and 190 lb, and I swore like a crazy man. Riley was HUGE and wouldn't swear, regardless of the situation. He also had the work ethic of a sloth.

He never moved fast anywhere. He drove me nuts. That he could have fired up and beat this guy 'til he shit himself and pissed blood was definitely physically possible, but not something I could begin to imagine.

I called Riley on the radio and asked him where he was; I had his paperwork from the jail, and his guy had been booked.

He politely answered that he was in the station and thanked me for completing his paperwork. (Totally unnecessary, but like I said, he was polite.)

I went to the station and met with Riley.

He was unusually quiet, and I could see that he was still shook up. I handed him the paperwork and asked what had happened on the call.

Forty-five minutes later, Riley finished his story; at the twenty-minute mark, I was regretting that I asked him.

His explanation was filled with polite discussion and sidebars that drove me fucking crazy.

Like I said, he was everything I couldn't stand and didn't want to be. With all of his polite bullshit, he could make a five-minute story drag out for hours. I'll spare you his account and cut to the chase.

Riley said that he and a female officer were sent to a burglary in progress. The female officer had arrived first. (When it came to responding to a call, he ALWAYS took his sweet ass time.)

When she arrived, she found a guy leaving a business with a portable welder. She stopped him, and instantly he became abusive. He repeatedly called her a "bitch" and a "fat cunt," and that's what Riley heard when he finally arrived and got out of his car.

Riley told me that he asked the man nicely to apologize to the female officer. He was polite and always told me and everyone else that we should all be gentlemen when speaking to ladies. ("Ladies" being *any* woman we encountered.)

The guy told him to fuck off.

Riley again asked the man to apologize to the young lady, saying he'd only ask him this one last time.

Riley said the guy went off on a verbal barrage that included accusing Riley of getting blow jobs from the ugly bitch cop and ended with him refusing to apologize to "the ugly cunt."

Riley put his head down and said nothing more for a few seconds. He sighed.

I asked him what happened then.

He said, "I lost my temper, Kiddo. I really lost my temper!"

I said, "And?"

Riley said he remembered picking the guy up by his shoulders and slamming him down on the ground—hard—three times. Then he blacked out.

I laughed hard at this.

Prim, Proper, and Polite—that was Riley.

Trying to imagine him picking this guy up and slamming him down on the ground for mere verbal abuse was too much.

I couldn't stop laughing.

Riley wasn't amused.

He apologized to me, politely saying that his mother had raised him as a gentleman. He was taught to be polite and courteous always, no matter what the circumstances.

He'd lost his temper at hearing the female officer referred to with such disgusting, foul language.

I couldn't stop laughing.

I patted the polite giant on the shoulder and said, "I'm glad to know something fires you up, Riley. I'll be sure never to call a woman a 'cunt' in your presence."

He winched at just hearing the word. I couldn't believe it.

I guess we all get fired up over something. I would be in a murderous rage at the drop of a hat over children being abused in any way.

For Riley, the breakdown of manners in the presence of a "lady" was his breaking point. He had no ability to rein his rage in when that happened.

From that point on, I kept my distance from Riley.

I was always foul-mouthed at work, and I didn't want to get a painful lesson in manners and respect from the monster English butler.

THIRTY-FOUR
COPS LIE

I WAS SITTING IN A parking lot one night, writing up a case report, parked backed up to the rear of the lot so that no one could walk up on me while I wrote.

I had a reserve officer with me, and I told him to keep a watch out while I wrote.

It was serious business; people sneaked up on cops all the time while they did reports, and ambushed them.

I was about halfway through the report when the dispatcher came over the radio, asking for anyone to clear from a call and respond to a fight in progress. It was two blocks away from where we were parked.

The caller said there had been a party at the address and that there were about seventy-five people present. There was fighting now, and people were leaving rapidly.

I looked at the reserve officer, and he looked at me. He smiled.

I said, "Ya, we're going. Tell them on the radio while I get this report put away."

We took off out of the parking lot, and just before we arrived at the scene the dispatcher came across the radio and said that they had reports that someone had been stabbed.

We arrived and pulled up across the street.

We got out, ready to scrap with whoever decided that they wanted to fight. Immediately, the crowd parted, and I saw a guy lying face up on the front lawn of the home.

A young woman ran up to me and said her boyfriend had been stabbed on the front porch, which had been the location of the party. She said he'd been stabbed in the back during a fight and had collapsed.

I saw that he was lying in the front yard now. There was one guy trying to do CPR on him while the crowd watched. Most were too drunk to understand what had happened or to help. I walked up and talked to the guy doing CPR.

He was doing it wrong.

He was very drunk and scared.

He was pushing on the chest in the wrong place and way too hard; he'd kill the guy if he didn't stop.

I told him to stop, and he refused.

I said, "You're doing it wrong. Stop, or I'll make you stop."

He ignored me.

I told the reserve officer to keep the crowd off me, then I grabbed the guy doing CPR by the shoulders. I pulled him back pretty hard and started to check the victim out. (The reserve would tell me later that I'd thrown the guy all the way across the yard; I guess I'd been rougher on him than I realized.)

The victim had a thready pulse, which came and went, and his pupils were blown completely. His heart was beating, but the blood wasn't making it to his brain, and he wasn't breathing.

I advised dispatch of his condition and started mouth to mouth.

Moments later, the paramedics arrived and took over. They grabbed him and rushed him to the hospital.

Later, after we'd finished at the scene, I went to the hospital to check on him.

They told me that the single knife wound had been perfectly placed and severed his aorta.

His heart had continued to beat and pumped the blood in his body into his abdomen and chest cavity. They'd done everything they could to save him. They even cracked his chest open to try manual heart massage and had discovered the severed aorta. He was only twenty years old.

At the scene, we contacted several witnesses and wrote down information on all the witnesses we could find.

We were able to locate names of the possible suspects right away and learned that the victim had started the fight.

He was a scrapper and had been looking for a particular guy he wanted to fight. When he confronted the guy he wanted to beat up on the front porch, they'd started to fight.

Another guy had come from behind and stabbed the victim in the back; one quick stab that just happened to be perfectly placed, severing the aorta.

It was an amazing stab wound that rarely occurred on the street.

We did our part, and detectives had the suspect arrested and in custody within hours. Months later, we went to court, and he was convicted.

The next night, I was back at work, sitting in the same lot, writing another case report.

Cops will try to tell you that this shit doesn't bother them. I tried to pretend that it didn't bother me. I didn't let it in until years later.

I ended up at a junkyard, looking for a car that had been seized in an arrest. An informant had called and said that the car was loaded up with cocaine.

I was sent to search the car with a drug dog and told to recover any drugs. The informant wasn't mine, and when I arrived with the dog we found no drugs at all. The dog didn't even act interested in the vehicle.

I went back to the office of the junkyard and told the secretary that we were done and had found nothing.

She said, "OK," then looked at me funny.

She said, "Are you Zach? Zach Fortier?"

I mumbled, "Shit, here we go."

I then said loudly, "Yes. Why do you ask?"

As I'd noticed she was wearing a wedding ring, I was sure she was gonna talk shit to me about arresting her or her husband. I wasn't about to take her shit.

She held up her hands and said, "Please relax. I'm not angry with you. You don't remember me; that's obvious—but I never had the chance to thank you."

I was kind of shocked; people rarely thanked us for anything.

In my work, the people that usually remembered your name hated you with a passion. It was a long-standing joke between cops that you hadn't done your job if someone on the call hadn't asked you for your name, how to spell it, and badge number.

Anyway, she started to recall the night of the stabbing.

She was the young woman who had come to me to tell me her boyfriend had been stabbed.

She went on and on about how she'd watched my face as I did the mouth to mouth on her boyfriend, wiping the blood off my face that came spraying out of his mouth as he exhaled, then kept going.

She told me she was there at the hospital when I came up to check on her boyfriend and found out he'd died; she'd watched my reaction.

She said she was there in court as I testified as to what had happened at the scene that night.

She told me that they had a daughter and that they'd planned on getting married.

I told her I didn't remember the event. I didn't want to discuss it with her now, but she wouldn't let it go.

She said, "I wanna thank you anyway. I told my daughter how you tried to save her daddy and that you did everything you could do."

I said, "Look, I don't remember this call; sorry. Are you sure you don't have me confused with someone else?"

She said, "No, absolutely not! I remember you. I'll always remember you. Thanks again, Officer."

I left, pulling out of the gravel parking lot fast.

I wasn't mentally prepared for this.

I drove around for a while, then I had to pull over. I started to cry.

Years later, there I was, pulled over and crying for this dead guy and his little girl growing up without her dad.

Cops will tell you this shit doesn't get to them. Cops lie.

THIRTY-FIVE
RAINBIRD'N

ONE SUMMER NIGHT, I WAS sent to a report of a large group of people gathered in the street.

The caller said that they were fighting and yelling at one another and we needed to get there fast. We got these kinds of calls all night long.

Sometimes you arrived to a quiet street, not a dog barking, not an angry voice or a door slamming, nothing.

It made you wonder: were you about to be shot at by a sniper? Had a crime just occurred where you'd just been the moment the call came in, and this was a diversion to get you to leave? You never had an explanation. There was rarely closure on a call; you just kept moving.

Anyway, I arrived, and so did my back up. Finally, I had a back up I could trust. He was a wiley veteran and had just come out of the Narcotics unit, Rinaldo Reyes. He wasn't an idiot like Divot or a traffic ticket-crazed stat whore like Skidmark. He was a balanced cop, smart and experienced. He'd worked informants successfully and solved many cases. I liked him being in my area; we worked well together.

We arrived and found the street full of people. Instead of the usual silent echoes of our footsteps, we found fifteen to twenty people in full all-out combat. We called for more units and waded into the melee.

We separated several combatants and sent them running off into the night. We didn't care why they were fighting; we just wanted the fight stopped before someone was seriously injured.

In no time at all, we were in the thick of the battle, throwing people off each other, yelling at others to back off, and then it all stopped.

We were surrounded, and the fighting stopped; now we were about to be attacked. The enemies now had a common enemy: US. Both sides started in on us. We went back-to-back and pulled out the pepper spray.

The spray was new at the time and hadn't earned the reputation (or respect) on the street it deserved. We were both on the SWAT team and had to be sprayed to carry the stuff.

It was liquid pain in my mind. I used it very sparingly because I knew the incredible agony it caused. We warned the mob to keep back or we'd spray them.

They kept advancing, mocking us, telling us we were gonna get our asses beat for interrupting the fight. One guy said we needed to be taught a lesson not to interfere in the affairs of the street.

He said confidently, "I hope you fuckers have medical insurance – you're gonna need it!"

Reyes yelled over his shoulder to me, "Are you ready?"

I said, "Ya! Let's spray these fuckers!"

The mob rushed us, and we went "Rainbird" on their asses. ("Rainbird" being a sprinkler used to irrigate large areas of land.) Anyone that came close got a face full of liquid agony. They quickly had a reality check and decided that the ass kicking we were about to receive was suddenly not worth it.

In less than thirty seconds, there was no one left in the street but Reyes and me. The mob was dispersed, running , stumbling, coughing—just trying to get away.

We laughed, turning to face each other, relieved. We laughed as someone can only laugh who's just narrowly avoided a life-and-death battle. We were outnumbered and had been surrounded, and any back up was minutes away, not moments. Without the pepper spray, we would have been in deep shit.

We laughed and high-fived, canceling our back up units and clearing the call.

No one had been seriously injured, and the calls were continuing to come in all over the city. We had other fires to put out, other battles to fight.

Another night, another call with Reyes and me again.

We were sent to a report of a suicidal man on the north end of the city.

We coordinated our arrival and arrived at the same time from opposite directions, driving in blacked out, all lights off. We used our emergency brakes to stop the patrol cars and not turn on the brake lights.

Silently, we got out and pushed the door to the cars shut slowly.

We listened; we could hear a family fight and walked to the sounds. The address was the one we were sent to for the suicidal man.

We knocked on the door and tried to talk the man out of the house. He came to the door but wouldn't exit the home; his wife and kids were inside.

He talked with us for about fifteen minutes, and we were getting nowhere with him.

He had a large knife and wouldn't put it down. He wasn't being aggressive to us or to his family, so we were at a standoff. We had nothing to gain by forcing the issue.

Finally, the guy was getting tired of us; he wanted to make a spectacle of his death. He wanted to make the whole family see him die, imagining, I guess, that they'd miss him—and in death, he'd finally feel he mattered.

He tried to close the door, and we rushed him.

He stood in front of his wife and children and raised the knife high in the air, readying himself to plunge it into his abdomen.

We entered the house as he raised the knife high, and I shoved him to the side, jumping back barely clear as he swung the knife wildly, narrowly missing me.

Reyes pulled his gun and was preparing to shoot the guy.

I know this is really stupid, but I had this thing where I never wanted to leave kids on the scene with a memory of us doing harm to their parents unless it was absolutely necessary.

I took a lot of shit for it, and I took a lot of risks as well.

I didn't want his children to see us kill their father or for them to watch him kill himself.

He'd swung at me wildly and missed.

I'd been in a few fights with guys with knives by this time, and I knew he was at his weakest point: the knife fully extended to his right side, the momentum of his swing stopped.

I stepped in quickly and pinned the knife against his side, both my hands on his hand, slamming him against the wall.

Reyes couldn't shoot him now, and I couldn't disengage him either. We were locked in a wrestling match over the knife.

The kids were screaming, and the scene was a mess.

Reyes yelled out, "Pepper spray!" and I turned my head away from the guy. Reyes sprayed his face, but still he didn't release the knife. He was screaming in pain, and I was coughing as well, but the fight wasn't over.

Reyes grabbed us and threw us both to the ground. He then pried the guy's hands free and cuffed him.

We took him out of the house and had paramedics respond to treat him for the pepper spray exposure.

We later put him into a nearby ambulance that had arrived at the scene.

Reyes looked at me, pissed off, and a bit alarmed.

He said, "What in the fuck were you thinking?"

I told him how I felt about fucking people up in front of their kids.

He just stared at me.

He then said, "Dude, that was a ballsy thing to do! You could have easily been stabbed or killed."

I didn't know if he was impressed or thought I was really stupid; either way, it was done, and the kids never saw us kill their father or watched him kill himself.

THIRTY-SIX
TOO CLOSE TO HOME

I GOT A CALL ONE night of a suspicious circumstance in an older rundown apartment house in the middle of my area.

The house had been owned by one of the many slumlords who owned property in the city and lived somewhere else so they didn't have to face the shitty housing they owned.

They had property managers rent the places out and collect the rent from whoever ended up there, and they then reaped the benefits, cash, tax deductions, etc., of being a slum lord.

The anonymous caller had made a very vague reference to something not being right in the rear apartment of the building and hung up. I got the call because it was my area, and we were unusually NOT busy that night.

Normally, a call like this would have sat for hours 'til we were absolutely not busy. For some reason that night, the powers that be gave us a break, and we were all trolling like street sharks: windows down, idling slowly back and forth in our areas, waiting for the chaos to break loose.

I was edgy because I arrived at work ready for a frantically busy night, and nothing had happened. The calm was eerie, and it made me nervous.

We all talked about it at break, wondering what the hell was going on. The normal rhythms of the street were off; nothing felt right. The city was quiet and calm. Most definitely not the norm.

I arrived at the address and quietly got out of the car.

I pressed the door closed on the patrol car until I heard it click softly, then slowly headed up the driveway to the rear apartment of the house.

It was pitch black, and the calm was creepy; not a sound. No dogs barking, no sirens from cops rolling from call to call, no gunshots…nothing.

I walked up the far side of the driveway, pressed against the next-door neighbor's house, taking three to four steps and stopping to listen. Nothing.

By this point in my career, I'd been ambushed several times. I never believed anything I was told about a call. I never took them at face value.

New cops will get pissed off at the dispatcher for not giving them every detail of the call, older cops know better than to listen to what the dispatcher tells them.

After I was reasonably sure no one was going to ambush me, I made my way to the door of the rear apartment. I listened outside the door for a few minutes to see if I could hear what was going on inside the apartment.

I could hear a soft banging inside, repeating randomly, and a baby screaming.

I was getting ready to knock on the door and noticed that there was no doorknob; just a rag plugged in the hole to keep the wind out and keep people from peering inside.

I slowly pushed the door open to the apartment and looked inside.

The apartment was actually a very unfinished back porch of the main house. It had a gas stove that had all the burners on, flames as high as they could be. I assumed they used the stove to heat the house.

There was a sink nearby that had water running heavily from a facet that was turned off. A bathroom built into what had been a closet with a toilet. There was also running water into an incredibly filthy tub.

There were three rooms total. The main living area, the "kitchen," and the "bathroom."

The banging noise I heard was an infant that was in the house…alone.

The infant was a little girl who had been left in the home. She was in a walker and was screaming, terrified and wearing only a diaper. She was the sole occupant of the apartment when I arrived.

I checked the place three times, looking for anyone. No one was there.

I couldn't believe that anyone would leave a young child alone in this place, open flames on the stove, running water in the sink.

The walls were roughed in, meaning they had no drywall or wallboard. Just 2x4s, exposed wiring to the lights, and an occasional plug. The ceiling was plywood, and a single wire hung down in the middle of each room: a light bulb hanging down from a utility outlet.

It was bare bones. More like what you'd see in an older rundown barn, not an apartment where a child would live—much less be left alone.

I called dispatch and asked when the call had come in. They replied that they'd held it an hour, nervous to send me on it if the city suddenly fell back into what we accepted as "normal." So I assumed the child had been left for an hour at least. Someone had come by and heard her inside crying and called.

I looked around and saw drug paraphernalia on the floors, a couple crack pipes and a syringe. I tried to calm the baby after I called for Child Welfare workers to come and take the child out of this shithole.

I waited an hour for them to show up. They finally did and weren't impressed with the home.

The child had finally calmed down a little bit. She was obviously very traumatized by being left alone for so long.

As we were getting ready to leave, the door burst open and a woman came running in.

I had my gun drawn immediately, expecting the attack to finally come. She was screaming at us, wanting to know "what the fuck are you doing in my apartment?"

She tried to take the baby from the Child Welfare worker, but I shoved her aside.

I asked her a few questions: was she the child's mother? Where had she been the past two and a half hours?

She spewed out "fuck you's" and "get the fuck out of my house!"

I don't remember what I did next.

My vision blurred, I had a wicked adrenaline dump, and then I started to hear and see again. The vision slowly came back into my eyes and sounds from the apartment started to come back; muffled, but I was aware of them.

I saw that I had the woman by the throat and the barrel of my gun under her chin.

I was talking to her and slowly started to be aware of what I was saying. I was telling her, "I should blow your fuckin' brains out right here, you glass dick-sucking bitch. I can smell the shit on you right now; you smell like piss. You've been getting high—you left your baby to get high! You don't deserve to have this baby, you piece of shit. I should do her a favor and put a bullet in your fuckin' head right now; she'd never remember you!"

She was quiet now, realizing perhaps that I wasn't the "Officer Friendly" she'd been told about in elementary school.

I was fucked up and damaged, and this call hit too close to home.

I held her there for a minute, her gagging from my grip on her throat. We exchanged a long, hard stare.

She started to cry and said, "I just want my baby."

I heard the baby cry, and then the caseworker said, "Jesus Christ!"

I gradually came back to earth and let her go.

The caseworker handed her the child.

I holstered my gun and gathered myself.

I started to write down her information and prepared to write the report.

The caseworker told me that they couldn't take the child from the home. I already knew this was going to be the case when the mother arrived.

The people who work these cases have very strict guidelines they have to follow. Common sense goes out the window, and children are seen as property of the parents.

If this were a disabled adult, the mother would have been arrested and the adult placed in a home; because it was a child, they released her to the mother.

These rules have since changed, but many children died because of the faulty "guidelines."

Before I left, I made sure the woman understood that I'd be watching her apartment. I'd be her worst fucking enemy. If anything happened to her daughter, she'd better pray I didn't get the call. Did she understand what I was saying?

She said yes, she understood, and nodded enthusiastically.

The caseworker stared at me, watching as I had the conversation.

I left the mother and the caseworker to work out their arrangements for their follow up and went to my car.

I hung around and waited for the caseworker to come out safely.

She came up to my car and said, "Are you OK?"

I said, "Ya, sure; another day in central city. How about you? Are you OK?"

She said, "Of course I am."

I said, "Ya well, hope we aren't back here in two weeks for another dead baby."

She said, "What do you mean, another dead baby?"

I told her I'd gone on the last three babies that had been killed in my area.

Kids die all the time in the central city; they get brutally shaken until their brains are so scrambled, they die from brain damage.

I'd been on one case a few weeks earlier where the child had been boiled to death in a pot of boiling water for peeing the bed.

My personal favorite (this really drove me into a rage): I told her I went to a class on child abuse and child homicide.

We were shown photos of a 2-year-old boy that had wet the bed. His loving parents had decided that he wasn't taking their discipline seriously enough. So the mother held him while the father (and I use those terms loosely) grabbed a Bic lighter and took hold of the boy's penis, stretching it away from his body.

The father lit the lighter and burned off the little boy's penis while his loving mother watched, restraining him and preventing his escape.

Was I OK? Fuck no, I wasn't OK.

I returned to the apartment the next week.

I meant to ensure that the child would survive this bitch who called herself its mother and not end up like the rest of the kids in these situations.

The apartment was vacant, emptied of all their stuff.

I asked all the neighbors where they'd gone. No one knew.

One guy finally admitted to me that he'd been the one that had called the week before. He said that the woman left in a hurry with the baby the morning after I came to the house.

He said she'd leave the child for hours at a time every night while she went out and got high, and he couldn't take it anymore. He was afraid that the child was going to get hurt or worse.

I asked him to let me know if he heard where the woman and her child ended up. I gave him my card and left.

I never heard from him, and I never saw the woman or the little girl again.

MORE TRUE CRIME STORIES FROM AWARD-WINNING AUTHOR ZACH FORTIER

AN IN-DEPTH LOOK AT THE DARK SIDE OF POLICE WORK

AVAILABLE IN PAPERBACK, EBOOK AND AUDIOBOOK

ABOUT THE AUTHOR
ZACH FORTIER

ZACH FORTIER WAS A POLICE officer for over 30 years specializing in K-9, SWAT, gang, domestic violence, and sex crimes as an investigator. He has written three books about police work. The first book, *CurbChek,* is a case-by-case account of the streets as he worked them from the start of his career. The second book, *Street Creds,* details the time he spent in a gang task force and the cases that occurred. The third book, *CurbChek Reload,* is by far the most gritty. The author is dangerously damaged, suffering from post-traumatic stress syndrome (PTSD) and the day-to-day violence of working the street. *Hero To Zero,* his fourth book, details the incredibly talented cops that he worked with but ended up going down in flames. Some ended up in prison and one on the FBI's ten most wanted list.

If you are looking for gritty, true crime stories, be sure to check out all of Zach Fortier's novels.

www.ingramcontent.com/pod-product-compliance
Lightning Source LLC
Chambersburg PA
CBHW020216170426

43201CB00007B/233